Trebisa's Dialogus inter Militem et Clericum
Sermon by FitzRalph
AND
þe Byggynnyng of þe World

EARLY ENGLISH TEXT SOCIETY

Original Series, No. 167

1925 (for 1924)

Dialogus inter Militem et Clericum
Richard FitzRalph's Sermon: 'Defensio Curatorum'
AND
Methodius: 'þe Bygynnyng of þe World and þe Ende of Worldes'

BY

JOHN TREVISA

VICAR OF BERKELEY

Now first edited from the MSS. Harl. 1900, St. John's College, Camb., H. 1, Add. 24194, Stowe 65, and Chetham's Library

WITH AN INTRODUCTION ON

THE DESCRIPTION OF THE MSS., TREVISA'S LIFE AND WORKS, AND A STUDY OF THE LANGUAGE

BY

AARON JENKINS PERRY, M.A.
ASSISTANT PROFESSOR OF ENGLISH
UNIVERSITY OF MANITOBA, WINNIPEG, CANADA

LONDON:
PUBLISHED FOR THE EARLY ENGLISH TEXT SOCIETY
BY HUMPHREY MILFORD, OXFORD UNIVERSITY PRESS,
AMEN HOUSE, E.C.
—
M DCCCC XXV

OXFORD

Great Clarendon Street, Oxford OX2 6DP
United Kingdom

Oxford University Press is a department of the University of Oxford.
It furthers the University's objective of excellence in research, scholarship,
and education by publishing worldwide. Oxford is a registered trade mark of
Oxford University Press in the UK and in certain other countries

© The Early English Text Society 1925

The moral rights of the authors have been asserted

Database right Oxford University Press (maker)

First Edition published in 1925

All rights reserved. No part of this publication may be reproduced,
stored in a retrieval system, or transmitted, in any form or by any means,
without the prior permission in writing of Oxford University Press,
or as expressly permitted by law, or under terms agreed with the appropriate
reprographics rights organization. Enquiries concerning reproduction
outside the scope of the above should be sent to the Rights Department,
Oxford University Press, at the address above

You must not circulate this book in any other form
and you must impose this same condition on any acquirer

Published in the United States of America by Oxford University Press
198 Madison Avenue, New York, NY 10016, United States of America

British Library Cataloguing in Publication Data
Data available

Library of Congress Cataloging in Publication Data
Data available

Original Series, 167

ISBN 978-0-85-991905-0

PREFACE

In this edition of John Trevisa's translations of (1) Occam's *Dialogus inter Militem et Clericum*, (2) Fitz-Ralph's Sermon, *Defensio Curatorum*, and (3) Methodius, *The Beginning and the End of the World*, all the known manuscripts containing them have been used, except the Burleigh House MS. The British Museum MS. Harleian 1900 contains the *three* works. This I have used as the basic text. The *Dialogue* and the *Sermon* are found in four others, viz.: (1) British Museum MS. Additional 24194, (2) Stowe 65, in the British Museum, (3) Cambridge University, St. John's College, H. 1, and (4) Chetham's Library MS., in Chetham's Library, Manchester. These are used in collating, and designated thus: Additional = A, Cambridge = C, Chetham's Library = Ch, and Stowe = S. In parallel columns with the Methodius tract is printed a somewhat different version in Northern English, found in the British Museum, MS. Additional 37049. In parallel columns with the *Dialogue* is printed Berthelet's edition (1530?).

In collating the MSS., only a few spelling variants have been noted. The introduction contains: (1) A description of the various English MSS. containing the texts, with a list of many of the Latin MSS. and printed editions; (2) an investigation into the life and works of John Trevisa; and (3) a study of the language of the MSS.

I wish to express my thanks especially to Professor James Finch Royster, Head of the Department of English, University of North Carolina, who first suggested this study to me, and who started me in the work; to Dr. John Matthews Manly, Head of the Department of English, University of Chicago, Professor Thos. Albert

Preface

Knott, formerly of the University of Chicago, now of the University of Iowa, and Professor Francis A. Blackburn, University of Chicago, who were my first teachers in Old and Middle English, and who gave me a love for the subject. Professors Manly and Knott were most kind and considerate in giving helpful suggestions, and in checking my material as the work proceeded.

During the summer of 1914, when I copied the MSS. in England, I received help and assistance from so many people that it would be quite impossible to speak of them all here. I wish, however, to mention the following: Mr. J. A. Herbert, Deputy-Keeper of MSS., and Supts. Flower and Wood of the MSS. Dept. of the British Museum; Mr. R. Farquharson Sharp, Supt. of the Reading Room, British Museum; Mr. C. Sayle and Mr. G. G. Butler, Librarians of University Library and Corpus Christi Library, Cambridge University; Mr. F. Madan, Librarian of Bodley, and Mr. W. A. Stevenson, Librarian of St. John's College, Oxford University; Mr. H. Crossley, Librarian of Chetham's Library, Manchester; the Librarian at Lambeth Palace; the Supt. and Assistants of the Record Office, London.

The following have my thanks, because of much information received through letters: Miss Alice D. Greenwood of Oxford—hints and suggestions most helpful; Mr. Thos. M. Rutter, Assist. Librarian of Edinburgh University; President H. N. MacCracken, Vassar College; the Librarian, University of Glasgow; Mr. Alfred de Burgh, Assistant Librarian, Trinity College, Dublin; Sir Leslie Faulkner, Burghley House, Stamford; Lady Tollemache, Helmingham Hall, Stowmarket; Mr. P. E. B. Porter, The Hermitage, Saltash, Cornwall; Lady Coryton, Pentillie Castle, St. Mellion, Cornwall; Henry Jenner, F.S.A., Hoyle, Cornwall; Rev. J. Harvey Bloom, Stratford-on-Avon; Dr. J. Hambley Rowe, Bradford; Rev. H. J. Wilkins, D.D., Vicar of Westbury-on-Trym; Mr. Charles Wordsworth, 8 Nicholas

Hospital, Salisbury. These and others gave me valuable bibliographical material and other information.

It is altogether impossible to express my appreciation and thanks for the kindly and courteous assistance of Mr. John Munro, former Secretary of the Early English Text Society. I am under a great debt to Mr. Munro for giving me the right start on my arrival in England.

I wish also to express my thanks to Sir Israel Gollancz, Hon. Director of the E.E.T.S., and to Miss Mabel Day, D.Lit., Assistant Director and Secretary of the E.E.T.S., who have shown consideration and kindness at every stage of the work.

A great debt of gratitude is due to Professor William H. Hulme, Western Reserve University, for valuable hints and suggestions, and for his kindness in loaning me his MS. copies of Trevisa's 'Nicodemus'.

It has been a real pleasure to work with Mr. Frederick Hall, Controller of the Oxford University Press, and his staff in the printing of this work.

And finally I appreciate the kindness of Dr. A. W. Crawford, Head of my own Department, who has shown consideration in so many ways.

I am above all indebted to my wife, who assisted me in copying the MSS., in reading the proof, and in checking my work.

A. J. P.

UNIVERSITY OF MANITOBA,
   WINNIPEG, CANADA.

March, 1925.

CONTENTS

	PAGE
BIBLIOGRAPHY	xi
INTRODUCTION	xv

PART I. MANUSCRIPTS AND PRINTED EDITIONS . . xv

A. English Manuscripts xv
    Harleian 1900 xv
    St. John's College, Cambridge H. 1 . . . xviii
    British Museum Additional 24194 . . . xix
    British Museum Stowe 65 xxii
    Chetham's Library xxiii
    British Museum Additional 37049 . . . xxiv
    Burleigh House xxv
    Relation of the Five Middle-English Manuscripts . xxviii

B. Latin Manuscripts xxxiv
    Dialogus inter Militem et Clericum . . . xxxv
    FitzRalph's Sermon, *Defensio Curatorum* . xxxvi
    Methodius, *The Beginning and the End of the World* xxxvii

C. The English Printed Edition of *The Dialogue* . xliii
    Relation of the Printed Edition to the English Manuscripts xlvii

D. Latin Printed Editions liii
    The Dialogue liii
    The Sermon liv
    Methodius liv

PART II. TREVISA'S LIFE AND WORKS . . . lv

A. Trevisa's Life lvi
    I. Place and Date of his Birth . . . lvi
    II. Life at Oxford lxi
    III. Life at Berkeley Castle lxv
        (a) Canon at Westbury Collegiate Church lxvii
        (b) Date of his Death lxxiv

Contents

		PAGE
B. Trevisa's Works		lxxv
I. *Translations*		lxxvii
(1) *The Polychronicon*		lxxvii
The Manuscripts		lxxvii
The Printed Editions (English)		lxxviii
Date of completion, 1357 or 1387		lxxxiv
(2) *De Proprietatibus Rerum*		lxxxvii
(3) *The Gospel of Nicodemus*		xci
(4) *De Re Militari* and *De Regimine Principum*		xciv
(5) *De Regimine Principum*		xcviii
(6) *Dialogus inter Militem et Clericum*		c
(7) FitzRalph's Sermon, *Defensio Curatorum*		ciii
Trevisa, the Translator		civ
(8) Methodius, *þe bygynnyng of þe world and þe Ende of Worldes*		cxi
Trevisa *not* the Translator		cxii
(9) Trevisa and the Bible—History of the Discussion		cxv
(10) Biblical Inscriptions on the Walls of Berkeley Castle Chapel		cxxiv
II. *Original Writings*		cxxvii
(1) *Dialogue between the Lord and Clerk on Translation*		cxxvii
(2) *Epistle to Lord Berkeley on Translation*		cxxvii
(3) Latin Pedigree Roll		cxxviii
(4) Poetry		cxxviii
PART III. LANGUAGE OF THE MANUSCRIPTS		cxxxiii
Introduction		cxxxiii
I. Vowels and Diphthongs		cxxxvi
A. Short Vowels		cxxxvi
B. Long Vowels		cxlii
C. The Short Diphthongs		cxlvi
D. The Long Diphthongs		cxlvii

		PAGE
	E. Short Vowels and Spirants	cxlviii
	F. Long Vowels and Spirants	cxlix
	G. Diphthongs and Spirants	cxlix
	H. Vowels and Diphthongs + *w*	cxlix
II.	Consonants	cxlix
III.	Loan Words	cl
	French	cl
	Old Norse	cl
IV.	Inflections	cli
	Nouns	cli
	Adjectives	clii
	Adverbs and Prepositions	clii
	Pronouns	cliii
	Verbs	cliii
V.	Remarks on the Manuscripts	clv

TEXTS.

Part	I.	*Dialogus inter Militem et Clericum*	1
„	II.	FitzRalph's Sermon, *Defensio Curatorum*	39
„	III.	Methodius, þe Bygynnyng of þe World and þe Ende of Worldes	94

GLOSSARY 113

BIBLIOGRAPHY

PARTS I AND II: INTRODUCTION

Ames, Joseph : *Typographical Antiquities.* London, 1749.
Atkyns, Sir Robert : *History of Gloucestershire.* London, 1807.
Babington, C., and Lumby, J. R. : Higden's *Polychronicon* (Rolls Series). 9 vols., London, 1865.
Bale, John : *Scriptorum Illustrium Majoris Bryt. Catalogus.* Bâle, 1559.
Blades, W. : *Life and Typography of Caxton.* 2 vols., London, 1861-3.
Boase, Rev. C. W. : *Registrum Collegii Exoniensis* (Ox. Hist. Soc.). Oxford, 1894.
——, Geo. Clement : *Collectanea Cornubiensis.* Truro, 1890.
Borlase, Wm. Copland : MS. Collections at Castle Horneck, 1720-72. (*Quarterly Review*, vol. 139, Oct. 1875.)
Brayley, E. A., and Britton, J. : *Beauties of England and Wales.* London, 1818.
Caley, John : *Catalogue of Lansdowne Manuscripts.*
Carew, Richard : *Survey of Cornwall.* London, 1602, 1769, 1811.
Carte, Thos. : *Catalogue des Rôles, Gascons, Normans et François,* 1753.
Clark, G. T. : Description of Berkeley Castle. (*Trans. of Bristol and Gloucester Arch. Soc.,* 1876.)
Cooke, Jas. Herbert : A Sketch of the History of Berkeley, its Castle, Church, and the Berkeley Family, 1875. (*Trans. of Bristol and Gloucester Arch. Soc.,* 1876.)
——: Account of the Inscriptions in Berkeley Castle Chapel. (*Trans. of Bristol and Gloucester Arch. Soc.,* 1876.)
——: Trevisa's Translation of the Bible. (*Notes and Queries,* vol. x, 1878.)
Cornish Notes and Queries : Trevisa and the Bible, by Amherst, 1906.
Courtney, W. P. : *Parliamentary History of Cornwall,* 1867-72.
Cowie, Rev. Morgan : *A Descriptive Cat. of MSS. and Scarce Books in the Library of St. John's Coll., Camb.* 2 pts., 1843.
Coxe, H. O. : *Cat. Cod. MSS. qui in Coll. Aulisque Oxon. adservantur.* 2 vols., 1852.
Daniell and Collins : *History of Cornwall.* Truro, 1894.
Demans, Rev. R. : *Wm. Tyndale: A Biography.* London, 1871. (Religious Tract Society.)
Dibdin, T. F. : *Ames's Typographical Antiquities.* 4 vols., 1810-19.
Douce, Francis : *Illustrations of Shakespeare and of Ancient Manners.* 2 vols., London, 1807.
Dugdale, Wm. : *The Baronage of England.* 3 vols., 1675-6.
——: *Monasticon Anglicorum,* 1846.
Eadie, John : *The English Bible.* 2 vols., London, 1876.
Forshall, J., and Madden, Sir F. : *The Holy Bible, made from the Latin Vulgate, by John Wycliffe and his Followers.* 4 vols., 1850.
Foxe, John : *The Acts and Monuments,* ed. Rev. Geo. Townsend and S. R. Cattley. 8 vols., 1841.

Bibliography

Fry, Edward A. : *A Collection of Inquisitiones Post Mortem for Cornwall and Devon* (Devon and Cornwall Record Soc.), 1906.
——— : *Cal. of Wills and Administration relating to the Counties of Devon and Cornwall,* 1908.
Fuller, Thomas : *Church History of Britain,* ed. Rev. J. S. Brewer. 6 vols., Oxford, 1845.
——— : *Histories of Worthies of England,* ed. P. A. Nuttall. 3 vols., London, 1840.
Gilbert, C. S. : *A Hist. Survey of the County of Cornwall.* 2 vols., Plymouth, 1817-20.
———, Davies : *The Parochial History of Cornwall.* 4 vols., London, 1838.
Greenwood, Alice D. : The Beginnings of English Prose (*Camb. Hist. of English Literature,* vol. ii, chap. iii), 1908.
Gutch, J. : Anthony Wood's *Antiquities and Annals,* Oxford, 1792.
Hals, Wm. : *Complete History of Cornwall,* Part II, pp. 1-169. Pr. Truro, 1750.
Herbert, W. : Ames's *Typographical Antiquities.* 3 vols., London, 1785-90.
Hingeston-Randolph, F. C. : *The Episcopal Registers of the Diocese of Exeter,* 1901.
Historical MSS. Commission Report. London, 1870-87.
Hitchens, Fortescue, and Drew, S. : *The History of Cornwall.* 2 vols., Helston, 1824.
Hoare, Sir R. C. : *History of Modern Wiltshire.* 14 pts., London, 1822-44.
Horne, Rev. T. Hartwell : *Cat. of Queens' College Library, Camb.* 2 vols., London, 1827.
——— : *Manual of Biblical Bibliography,* 1839.
Huddersford, Wm. : *Catalogus Lib. Manuscriptorum Antonie a Wood,* 1761 and 1824.
Hulme, Wm. H. : *The Middle English Harrowing of Hell and Gospel of Nicodemus* (E.E.T.S., Extra Series, 100). London, 1907.
James, M. R. : *A Descriptive Catalogue of MSS. in Library of St. John's College, Cambridge.* Camb., 1913. (See also James's Catalogues of other Colleges at Cambridge.)
Jeayes, I. H. : *Descriptive Catalogue of the Charters and Muniments in the Possession of the Rt. Hon. Lord FitzHardinge at Berkeley Castle,* 1892.
Jenner, Henry : Cornwall a Celtic Nation. *Celtic Review,* 1904.
Kingsford, C. L. : Life of Trevisa. *Dictionary of National Biography,* vol. lvii.
Körting, G. : *Grundriss der Geschichte der englischen Literatur,* 1905.
Lewis, John : *The New Testament of John Wiclif.* London, 1731.
——— : *A Complete Hist. of the Several Translations of the Holy Bible and New Testament into English.* London, 1818.
Lyte, H. C. Maxwell : *A History of the University of Oxford.* London, 1836.
MacCracken, H. N. : Vegetius in English (*Kittredge Anniversary Papers*). N.Y., 1913.
MacLean, Sir John : *The Parochial and Family History of the Deanery of Trigg Minor in Cornwall.* 3 vols., 1873.
——— : *The Lives of the Berkeleys* (the Berkeley MSS.), by John Smyth of Nibley. 3 vols., 1883.
Macray, Rev. Wm. D. : *Catalogue Cod. MSS. Digby.* Oxford, 1883.
——— : *Manual of British Historian to 1600.* London, 1845.
Madan, Falconer : *A Summary Catalogue of Western MSS. in the Bodleian Library.* Oxford, 1895.

Nicholls, J. F., and Taylor, John : *Bristol Past and Present.* 2 vols., Bristol, 1881.
Nordeen, John : *A Typographical Hist. Des. of Cornwall.* London, 1728.
Polsue, Jos. : *Parochial Hist. of Cornwall*, 1807–72.
Petrie, Henrie : *Monumenta Historica Britannica.* Vol. i, 1848.
Pitseus, Joannes : *Relationum Historicarum de Rebus Anglicis,* or *De Illustribus Angliae Scriptoribus.* Paris, 1619.
Pollard, A. W. : *Introd. to Fifteenth Century Prose and Verse.* London, 1903. (An English Garner.)
Polwhele, Rev. R. : *History of Cornwall.* London, 1803.
Rogers, John J. : Notice of John de Trevisa ; a Cornish Mediaeval Author (1342–1412). (*Journal of the Royal Institution of Cornwall,* April, 1870.)
—— : John de Trevisa (1342–1412). (*Journal of the Royal Institution of Cornwall,* April, 1874.)
Saturday Review, April 5, 1879 : Westbury Monastery.
Smith, Thomas : *Catalogue of Cottonian Manuscripts.* London, 1696.
Statutes of the University of Oxford, 1853.
Tanner, Thomas : *Notitia Monastica.* London, 1748.
—— : *Bibl. Britannico-Hibernica.* London, 1748.
Taylor, Rev. C. S. : The Church and Monastery of Westbury-on-Trym (*Proceedings of Clifton Antiquarian Club*), 1897.
Thompson, Wm. : *An Open College Best for All,* 1870.
Townley, Rev. Jas. : *Illustrations of Biblical Literature.* 3 vols., London, 1821.
Trevelyan, Geo. M. : *England in the Age of Wycliffe.* New York, 1904.
Ussher, J. : *Historica Dogmatica.* London, 1690.
Vivian, Lieut.-Col. J. L. : *The Visitations of Cornwall.* 16 pts., London and Exeter, 1887.
—— : *The Marriage Licenses of the Diocese of Exeter,* 1887.
Wanley, Humphrey : *Catalogus Libr. Manuscriptorum Bibl. Harleianae* (1708). Ed. Rev. Thos. Hartwell Horne. 4 vols. (Pr. 1808–12.)
Wilkins, Rev. H. J. : *Some Chapters on the Ecclesiastical History of Westbury-on-Trym.* Bristol, 1909.
—— : *Was John Wycliffe a Negligent Pluralist?* Also *John De Trevisa, His Life and Work.* Longmans, Green & Co., London, 1915.
Williams, R. : *Lexicon Cornu-Britannicum.* London, 1865.
Wood, Anthony : *The History and Antiquities of the Univ. of Oxford.* 2 vols., Oxford, 1792–6.
Young, Julian, and Aitken, P. H. : *A Catalogue of MSS. in the Library of the Hunterian Museum in Univ. of Glasgow.* Glasgow, 1908.

PART III : INTRODUCTION, LANGUAGE

Baldwin, C. S : *The Inflections and Syntax of the Morte d'Arthur of Sir Thomas Malory.* Boston, 1894.
Björkman, Erik : *Scandinavian Loan-Words in Middle English.* Halle, 1900, 1902. (Bd. 7 und 11, Morsbach : *Studien zur Eng. Phil.*)
Blume, Rudolf : *Ueber den Ursprung und die Entwickelung des Gerundiums im Englischen.* Bremen, 1880.
Böener, O : *Die Sprache Robert Mannings of Brunne,* 1904. (Bd. 12, Morsbach : *Studien zur Eng. Phil.*)

Bibliography

Bosworth and Toller: *An Anglo-Saxon Dictionary.* Oxford, 1882-98.
Bradley-Stratmann: *Middle English Dictionary.* Oxford, 1891.
Ten Brink, B.: *Chaucer's Sprache und Verskunst.* Leipzig, 1884.
Bülbring, Karl D.: *Geschichte der Ablaute der Starken Zeitwörter innerhalb des Südenglischen.* Strassburg, 1889.
——: *Altenglisches Elementarbuch.* Heidelberg, 1902.
Cook-Sievers: *An Old English Grammar.* New York, 1903.
Dibelius, W.: *John Capgrave und die englische Schriftsprache. Anglia*, 23, 24.
Einenkel, Eugen: *Streifzüge durch die mittelenglische Syntax unter Berücksichtigung der Spr.*
Emerson, F. O.: *A Middle English Reader.* New York, 1905, rev. ed. 1921.
Frieshammer, Johann: *Die sprachliche Form der Chaucerschen Prosa.* Halle, 1910. (Bd. 42, Morsbach: *Studien zur eng. Phil.*)
Horn, W.; *Historische neuenglische Grammatik.* I. Laut. Strassburg, 1908.
Jespersen, Otto: *A Modern English Grammar.* 2 vols., Heidelberg, 1909 and 1914.
Kaluza, M.: *Historische Gram. der engl. Sprache.* Berlin, 1906-7.
Kellner, Leon: *Caxton's Syntax and Style (Trans. Phil. Soc.*, 1890); also in Introd. to *Caxton's Blanchardyn and Eglantine.* E.E.T.S., Extra Series, No. 58.
——: *Historical Outlines of English Syntax.* London, 1892.
Lekebusch, J.: *Die Londoner Urkundensprache von 1430-1500.* Halle, 1900. (Bd. 23, Morsbach: *Studien zur eng. Phil.*)
Mätzner, Edward: *Altenglische Sprachproben.* Berlin, 1867.
——: *Englische Grammatik.* 3 Bd., Berlin, 1880-5.
Mayhew, A. L.: Some Words from Trevisa (*Notes and Queries,* July, 1880).
Morsbach, Lorenz: *Ueber den Ursprung der neuenglischen Schriftsprache.* Heilbronn, 1888.
——: *Mittelenglische Grammatik.* Halle, 1896.
Murray and Bradley: *New English Dictionary.* Oxford, 1888- .
Neumann, Georg: *Die Orthographie der Paston Letters von 1422-1461.* Marburg, 1903.
Pabst, Felix: *Die Sprache der mittelenglischen Reimchronik des Robert von Gloucester.* Berlin, 1889.
Pfeffer, Bernhard: *Die Sprache des 'Polychronicons' John Trevisa's in der Hs. Cotton Tiberius D. VII.* Düren, 1912.
Reul, Paul de: *The Language of Caxton's Reynard the Fox, a Study in Historical Syntax.* London, 1901.
Royster, Jas. Finch: *A Middle English Treatise on the Ten Commandments.* (Vols. vi, viii, Studies in Philology, Univ. of North Carolina.)
Schmidt, Fredrik: *Studies in the Language of Pecock.* Upsala, 1900.
Schwan-Behrens: *Gram. des Altfranzösischen.* Leipzig, 1907.
Skeat, Rev. W. W.: *Etymological Dictionary.* Oxford, 1888.
Sweet, Henry: *A New English Grammar.* Oxford, 1892-8.
Zickner, Bruno: *Syntax und Stil in Reginald Pecock's 'Repressor'.* Berlin, 1900.

INTRODUCTION

PART I

MANUSCRIPTS AND PRINTED EDITIONS

THE MANUSCRIPTS

A. ENGLISH MANUSCRIPTS

MS. Harleian 1900.[1]

THIS MS. is described in *Catalogus Librorum Manuscriptorum, Bibl. Harl.*, vol. ii, pp. 318-20 (1808). The writer names the different works in the MS., giving a description and digest of each. He seems not to have known that the *Dialogus inter Militem et Clericum* was a translation of a Latin work, as his opening sentence shows:

'A parchment book in fol. bought and given by my noble Lord Harley: wherein are contained more of the Translations & Compositions of John de Trevisa, Vicar of Berkeley & Chaplain to Thomas Baron of Berkeley, than I have seen in any other book. They are:
1. Dyalogus inter Militem & Clericum: i. e. between the above mentioned Lord & himself: in English.'

---

[1] Babington and Lumby made some use of this MS. in their edition of Trevisa's translation of Higden's *Polychronicon* for the Rolls Series (1865-86), 9 vols. They begin to use it occasionally for collation in vol. ii, along with the MS. Cotton Lib. D. VII, designating them as β and γ respectively. Mr. Babington, in vol. i, in enumerating the works of Trevisa, mentions the Harl. MS. as containing our three works: the *Dialogue, Sermon*, and *Methodius* tract. He thinks that it belongs to the beginning of the fifteenth century.

In the appendix to vol. vii of the above work (pp. 501-38), we find a selection from Harl. 1900 printed, beginning at fol. 248 a (three lines from bottom), consisting of chapters 15-26. This is printed in full, and Cot. MS. is collated with it, because they differ widely from the version contained in the MS. used, viz. St. John's College MS. H. 1. This

The MS. is a folio volume, containing 310 folios, 310 b only half written. Size $13\frac{7}{10} \times 9\frac{1}{2}$, printed portion 10×7 in. The initial letters of the chapters are three or four lines deep in red and blue. It is written in a large plain hand, with many abbreviations. Mr. J. A. Herbert, of the British Museum, dates it at the beginning of the fifteenth century.

Contents:

1. *Dialogus inter Militem et Clericum.*

    ff. 1–5. Single columns, 40 lines to a page, except last page $35\frac{3}{4}$. Each line averages about 15 or 16 words. Written in a large careless hand, with many abbreviations. Some of first pages are greatly worn, or much faded. They give evidence of much examination. The first line, consisting of the title, is in Latin. There are catchwords on every page.

2. *Sermo Domini Archiepiscopi Armacani.*

    ff. 6–21 a. Single column. 6 a = 38 lines, others 40, except 21 a = 37 lines and three words. Title at first in Latin. At end Latin 'Explicit'. Catchwords. Written in same hand as above, and as free from mistakes. Scarcely any marginal notes. The beginning of many sentences indicated by red and blue sign ⁋'. The same sign is used in the three extracts.

3. *Methodius*, 'þe begynnyng of þe world and þe Ende of Worldes.'

    ff. 21 b–23 b. Double columns, 49 lines, six or seven words to a line. Chapters or sections begin with large letters, either all red, or with blue groundwork and red border. Written in the same hand as the two former, but

is the only part of the Harl. MS. that has thus far been printed.

Miss Alice Greenwood, in her article on 'The Beginnings of English Prose', in the *Cambridge History of English Literature* (vol. ii, pp. 503–4) speaks of Harl. 1900 containing the three works of this edition. She gives it as dated 1448. Dibdin describes it in his *Typ. Antiq.* 1810 (Dibdin, Ames's *Typographical Antiquities*, vol. i, p. 140); it is also described by Townsley in 1821 (*Illustrations of Bibl. Lit.*, vol. ii, p. 49). It is mentioned by Körting in his *Grundriss* (p. 141), but only with reference to the *Polychronicon*; by Morris and Skeat (Part 2, pp. 235 ff. and 339) in their *Specimens*, where they take a few readings from it, in the selection from the *Polychronicon* from MS. Cot. Lib. D. VII; Professor Emerson (*Middle English Reader*, pp. 220–5 and p. 311) mentions it as containing *Polychronicon*.

much smaller. The same abbreviations are used, and as many of the words were proper names difficulty was experienced in reading them. There is no title at the beginning. It closes with 'liber Metodij epi*scopi*'.

4. *Index to Polychronicon.*

ff. 24–41. This is in two columns, and is written in the same hand as above. In ff. 24 and 25 there is a hole 1½ × 2 in. The same blemish is found in ff. 29 and 30. Otherwise this portion is very clean. f. 41 b is blank except part of col. 1. Each new section begins with a large illuminated letter, usually with blue ground-work and red outline, or vice versa. On f. 41 b in right column, near the top, in a later hand is written: 'This indenture made The eight Day off Nouember The Yere off oure lord Mccccxlviii betwyxt William Goodman.'

Across both columns near bottom of f. 41 b are the following words in another hand: 'This indenture made the eight day of nouembre the yere of oure lord Mccccxlviii betwyxt william goodmann of chestre citie gentilmann and'[1]

5. *Dialogue between Dominus and Clericus.*

ff. 42–3 b (6 lines). Single column, 40 lines.

6. *Trevisa's letter to Thomas Lord Berkeley,* 43 b (lines 7–32).

7. *Polychronicon.*

ff. 44–310 b (20½ lines). Single column, 40 lines to a page, written in same hand as previous. A few marginal notes, most of these in the same hand as MS.

(a) Prefaces ff. 44–6 b (⅔ page).
(b) Book I. ,, 47–91 a (½ page).
    II. ,, 91 a–121 b (⅓ page).
    III. ,, 121 b–164 a (½ page).
    IV. ,, 164 a–196.
    V. ,, 196–234 a (whole page but four lines).
    VI. ,, 234 a–264 a ,, ,, ,,
    VII. ,, 264 a–310 b (½ page).

It closes thus: 'God be þonked of alle his dedes þis *trans*lacioun is ended in a þursday þe XVIII day of Aueryl þe ȝere of oure lord a þousand þre hundrid foure score & seuene, þe tenþe ȝere of Kyng Richard þe secunde after þe conquest of England, þe ȝere of my lordes age sire Thomas Lord of berkeleye þat made me make þis *tran*slacioun fyue & þritty.'

---
[1] Four words are erased.

On the leaf before folio 1 the following are found in different hands:

'Sent in by my Lord Harley 12 July 1714.'
'This MS. is become doubly valuable since the loss of Cott. Lib. D. VII. It is much more ample than the printed copy of Trevisa's *Higden*, in which Caxton has greatly changed the language, and omitted many passages. F. D.'

In pencil is written:
'Other copies, equally fine with this, are in the Bodleian Library, and in Tennison's Library. T. M.'

St. John's College, Camb. MS. H. 1.[1]

This MS. does not contain the *Methodius* tract. Babington and Lumby used it as the basis of their edition of Trevisa's *Polychronicon*. A partial description is found in Vol. I, lv and lvi. Full descriptions are given by James and Cowie.

The following is a part of James's description:[2]

'Vellum, $15\frac{5}{8} \times 12$, ff. $206+2$, double columns of 44 lines. cent. XIV late, after 1387.'

'Very well written and with good ornaments. On fly-leaf: "Elegantissimum hunc librum manuscriptum Bibliothecae Coll. S. Joh. Evang. donavit Mr. Baile de Newington in agro Middlesexiae A. D. 1674."'[3]

Contents: 1. 'Dialogus inter clericum et militem', translated by Trevisa from the Latin of Ockham. f. 1.

A fine border of English ornament, gold, blue, and pink. Initial D green ground with gold flourishing. On L. the Knight in pink gown, gold chain, and loose blue cap: on R.

---

[1] Mr. Babington (Rolls Series of *Polychronicon*, vol. i, p. lviii) thinks this and Add. 24194 are only a few years later than Trevisa's translation of *Polychronicon*. Mr. C. W. P. Orton, of St. John's College Library, Camb., in a letter July 9, 1915, points out to me that the dress of the Knight in the first miniature is of about 1399. Miss Greenwood speaks of this MS. as used by Babington and Lumby in their Trevisa, and as containing the *Dialogue* and *Sermon*. Körting speaks of it only in connexion with *Polychronicon*. Morris and Skeat give a few readings in their selection. Emerson speaks of this MS. being printed by Caxton in 1482. Mätzner (*Altenglische Sprachproben*, vol. i, pt. 2, pp. 341-73) and Dr. Manly (*English Prose*, 1137-1890, 1909, pp. 11-12) take their selections from this MS.

[2] *Descriptive Catalogue of MSS. in the Library of St. John's College, Camb.*, p. 235.

[3] Fol. 1 b. This is the only mark on a blank folio.

the clerk in blue gown with tippet, lined with white fur, black skull-cap, holding book.

Ends f. 5 : and nouȝt man for þe holy day.

Expl. Dialogus inter clericum et militem.

2. Inc. sermo domini Archiepiscopi Armachani (translated by Trevisa). f. 5.

Demeþ nouȝt bi þe face but riȝtful dome ȝe deme. Joh. 8⁰ c⁰ holy fader in þe byginnynge of my sermon.

There are some marginalia in a hand of the fifteenth century, also in English, traversing the preacher's statements.

Ends f. 18 b : but riȝtful dome ȝe deme. Qui cum patre, etc.

   3. Table in Latin to the *Polychronicon*. f. 19.
   4. Table in English to the same. f. 26 b.
   5. The *Polychronicon* of Ranulph Higden in the English version of Trevisa. f. 34.

Ending : 280 a : 'to conferme þe pees and couenantes in eyþer side. God be þonked of al his nedes þis translacioun is I-ended in a þorsday þe eyȝtēþe day of Aueryle, þe ȝere of oure lord a þowsand þre hundred foure score and seuene, þe tenþe ȝere of kyng Richard þe secunde after þe conquest of Engelond, þe ȝere of my lordes age sire Thomas of Berkeley þat made me make þis translacioun fyue and thrytty. Deo gracias.'

Cowie[1] says of the *Dialogue* 'that it appears to be different from that in the printed edition'. He also has this note on the sermon :

'This is mentioned by Dibdin among the translations of John de Trevisa, "a translation of the Latin sermon of Radulf or Fitz-Rauf, Archbishop of Armagh, No. 3, 1357." Among the Harl. MSS. 1900. It is against the Mendicant Friars.

vide Dibdin, *Typ. Antiq.*, vol. i, p. 141.'

Br. Mus. MS. Additional 24194.[2]

This MS. was used in preparing the Rolls Series of Trevisa's *Polychronicon*. It is designated as δ in the collation notes. Mr. Babington uses it to correct the errors and supply the defects of Cambridge MS. H. 1.[3] It was formerly in the

---

[1] *Des. Cat. of MSS. and Scarce Books in St. John's College, Camb.*, pp. 75, 76.

[2] Descriptions are found in (*a*) Trevisa's translation of *Polychronicon*, ed. Babington and Lumby, in Rolls Series, vol, i, pp. lvi, lvii. (*b*) *Cat. of Add. to MSS. in Br. Mus.*, *1854-1875*, vol. ii, p. 19. (*c*) Paleographical Soc. ii. 171.

[3] Rolls Series, vol. i, p. lvi.

possession of Thomas Tenison, Archbishop of Canterbury (d. 1715); and was bought by the British Museum July 1, 1861.[1] It is vellum, consisting of 263 leaves, measuring $16\frac{1}{2} \times 11\frac{1}{2}$ in., in double columns of 47 lines. It is usually assigned to the beginning of the fifteenth century. Mr. Babington thinks this and Camb. MS. are only a few years later than the date of Trevisa's translation (1387). To Mr. Bond this MS. seems slightly the older.[2] It is written in a clear hand, and beautifully ornamented with an illuminated border at the beginning of each book, and with initials in gold and colours.

The MS. appears to have been written for Richard de Beauchamp, Earl of Warwick, whose arms are introduced into two of the ornamented borders, viz. pp. 1 and 33. Sir Frederic Madden says: 'The Earl of Warwick, for whom this MS. was executed, is Richard Beauchamp, who died in 1439, and who married Margaret, sole daughter and heiress of Thomas, Lord Berkeley,[3] for whom the translation was made by Trevisa.'[4]

Mr. Babington, in a note, vol. i, p. lviii, of *Polychronicon*, gives evidence as to this marriage as taken from MS. Life of the Berkeleys by Smyth. The contract of the marriage was entered into in September, 17 Richard II. The date of the marriage is not given, but it is stated that the marriage was intended to be solemnized 'as soon as conveniently may be', and that the bride was then under the age of 'seven yeares'. Her death took place on the 28th September, 1 Henry VI.

The description of contents as given in *Catalogue to Additions* is:

24194. English Translations of John of Trevisa, Vicar of

---

[1] On fol. 1 a is written: 'Purchased at the sale of Archbishop Tenison's Manuscripts, 1st July, 1861.' It was listed in his library as MS. No. 1.

[2] Rolls Series, p. lviii. Mr. R. Flower, Superintendent in the MS. Department of the British Museum, writing to me June 21, 1915, thinks it earlier than 1439, for it contains the arms of Richard Beauchamp, Earl of Warwick, who died in that year. Supt. Wood of the British Museum is also of the same opinion.

[3] The writer in *Cat. of Add. to MSS. in Br. Mus.*, vol. ii, p. 19, has Thos. 10th Lord Berkeley. The writer in Pal. Soc. ii. 171 designates him as 5th Lord Berkeley.

[4] *Polychron:con*, vol. i, p, lvii. Same written on fol. i a unsigned.

Introduction

Berkeley, Gloucester, and Chaplain to Thos. 10th Lord of Berkeley, viz. :

1. 'Dialogus inter militem et clericum' on spiritual and temporal power (see the Latin tract in Royal 6 E. III, f. 130), f. 4.
2. 'Sermo domini archiepiscopi Armacani' (Richard Fitz-Ralph, Archbishop of Armagh) preached at Avignon in 1350,[1] against the begging friars. f. 8.
3. The *Polychronicon* of Ralph Higden, preceded by an index and three prefaces. A whole quire containing Bk. III, c. xli, to Bk. IV, c. iv, is wanting after f. 139 ; and Bk. I, c. cci–iv, and part of chapter xiv to xxv of Bk. VI (f. 214) have been omitted. f. 21.

The initials E.W. are on a fly-leaf at the beginning; and at the end in green paint, R. P. At the end of the index, f. 35 b, occurs 'William Bradwell, Anno Domini, 1610'. At the end of the volume are found the following: 'John Knighton', f. 262 ; 'William Knighton', f. 262 b ; 'Edward Coulson', f. 263 b ; and on the last leaf, 'Emanuel, Anno Domini. 1570.'[2]

Trevisa's ending is as follows : ' Þis translacion is yended in a þorsday þe ey3teþe day of Aueryl, þe 3ere of oure lord a þowsand þre hondred foure score and seuene, þe tenþe 3ere of Kyng Richard þe secounde after þe conquest of England, þe 3ere of my lordes age sire Thomas Lorde of Berkeley þat made me þis translacioun fyue and þirtty.'

In answer to the query in regard to this MS. which appeared in *Notes and Queries*, 2nd Series, vol. v, p. 110, ' Is it known where this MS. is now preserved? If lost, as I fear, are there any known transcripts of it, and where?' the following answer signed by Bibliothecar Chetham appeared in *Notes and Queries*, 2nd Series, vol. v, No. 112, February 26, 1858, pp. 159–60 :

'I was informed by the Rev. Philip Hale, ex-librarian of Abp. Tenison's Library, not many months since, that the

---

[1] Mr. Bond, who compiled the *Catalogue* in 1877, has wrong date. See discussion of place and date, p. ciii.

[2] Miss Greenwood speaks of this MS. as used by Babington and Lumby in their edition of Trevisa, and as containing the *Dialogue* and *Sermon*. Körting and Emerson speak of it only in connexion with *Polychronicon*.

collection remains intact in the building formerly used as the reading room, 42 Castle Street, Leicester Square. Of the translation by John de Trevisa of the Latin sermon of Radulph, or Fitz-Rauf, Archbishop of Armagh, Nov. 8th, 1357, there are, I believe, several copies in various collections. Among the Harl. MSS. 1900; in the library of St. John's College, Cambridge (see Transactions of the Cambridge Antiquarian Society: A Descriptive Catalogue of the Manuscripts and Scarce Books in the Library of St. John's College, Cambridge, by the Rev. Morgan Cowie, Cambridge, 1843, 4to, p. 77); in the Chetham library, Manchester. This copy contains thirteen leaves, beginning " Demeþ noght by preface bote ryȝtful dom ye deme, Joh. viii. 5".

This learned tract against Mendicant Friars, which has escaped Bale and Pits, is noticed in Dibdin's *Typ. Antiq.*, vol. i, p. 141.'[1]

Br. Mus. MS. Stowe 65.

This MS. is not mentioned in the Rolls Series of Trevisa's *Polychronicon*; nor is it mentioned by Miss Greenwood, Körting, Morris and Skeat, or Emerson. It is fully described in the *Catalogue of Stowe MSS. in the British Museum*, vol. i, p. 42, 1895. It is a well-written manuscript. I have used it in my edition, designating it in the notes as S. It differs somewhat from the three previous MSS., and resembles the Chetham MS.

It is written on vellum, consisting of 222 folios. It is early fifteenth century, and written in double columns of 49 lines. The initials of the chapters are in red and blue. The several books begin with illuminated borders. On the last page is an acquittance to Edw. Clere (of Blickling, Sheriff of Norfolk in 1567) for rent of a tenement in 'Saynt Edmondes in Norwiche, in old tyme Sir Nicholas Goldwell', November 24, 1559.

The text of the *Polychronicon* differs from the MSS. used in the Rolls Series. The writer in the *Catalogue* lists a number of passages, which are supplied in a 'modern imitative hand', chiefly from Caxton's edition, including the false date 1357 (for 1387) at the end. The *Polychronicon* covers ff. 1–202. This is followed by:

(a) 'Dialogus inter clericum et militem'; a Dialogue on the spiritual and temporal power, beginning, 'Ich wondere, sore

[1] This was reprinted in *Bibl. Chet.*, vol. iv (1862), p. 433.

Introduction   xxiii

noble Kni3t', translated from the Latin of Wm. Occam. ff. 202–5 b.

(b) Sermo dni. Archiepiscopi Armacani (Richard Fitz-Ralph) factus Auinione 8º die mensis Nouembris, anno dni. 1358º; a sermon against the Mendicant orders, on John vii, 24, 'Demeþ no3t by þe face.' ff. 205 b–217.

(c) 'Dialogus inter dominum et clericum': a dialogue in English on translation as an introduction to the *Polychronicon*, beginning: 'Seþþe þat Babel was buld.' ff. 217–18.

(d) Letter of Trevisa, on his translation of Higden, to his patron, Thomas Berkeley, 5th Baron Berkeley (ob. 1417), beginning, 'Thomas lord of Berkeleye, I John Trevisa, etc.' f. 218.

(e) Alphabetical table of contents of the *Polychronicon*, f. 218. The Latin index found in other MSS. is wanting here.

On a half-leaf between ff. 201 and 202, in a different hand, we find this closing: 'Thankynges and praysynges be to Almyghty God of all his dedes. This translation is ended on a Thursday the eyghtenth daye of Apryll. The yere of oure lorde a thousande thre hundred fyfty seuen. The one & thyrty yere of Kynge Edwarde the thyrde after the conqueste of Engelonde. The yere of my lordes aege Syre Thomas lorde of Barkley, that made me make this translacyon fyue & thyrty.'

Chetham's Library MS.

This manuscript is not mentioned by Babington and Lumby, nor by Miss Greenwood, Körting, Emerson, or Morris and Skeat. Boase and Courtney refer to it in their *Bibl. Cornubiensis*, vol. ii, p. 797 (1878). It is described in *Bibliotheca Chethamensis*, vol. iv, p. 433 (1862), as No. 11379.

The MS. is a folio, vellum, single column, 37 lines on a page. Size, $13\frac{4}{5} \times 10\frac{1}{2}$ inches; reading material, $9\frac{1}{5} \times 7\frac{3}{10}$. It is beautifully written, with illuminated capitals frequently interspersed.

Contents:
(1) ff. 1 a–5 b (ll. 30½): Dialogus inter clericum et militem.
(2) ff. 5 b (l. 31 title)–18 b (37 lines): Sermo dni. Archiepi. Armacani.
(3) ff. 19 a–34 b (½ col.): Index to *Polychronicon* in two cols.

xxiv   *Introduction*

(4) ff. 35 a-36 b (½ page): Prefaces, about ⅝ of first preface wanting, f. 37 a blank.
(5) ff. 37 b-60 a (25 lines: First book of *Poly.* 60 caps. (caps. 19-31 omitted, also 33-43). Trevisa's notes occur cap. 10 near end, 13, 31 near end, 46, 58, and 53.
(6) ff. 60 a-74 b: Second book of *Poly.* 74 b ends cap. 17 abruptly; 75 à begins Bk. III, cap. 27. Notes by Trevisa caps. 1, 2, 4, 6, 10, 11.
(7) ff. 75 a-86 b: Third Book of *Poly.* caps. 27-35. Notes by Trevisa caps. 32, 33, 34, 35.
(8) ff. 87 a-108 b: Fourth Book of *Poly.* beg. at cap. 2. Notes by Trevisa cap. 2.
(9) ff. 109 a-125 b: Fifth Book of *Poly.*
(10) ff. 126 a-140 b: Sixth Book of *Poly.*
(11) ff. 141 a-178 b: Seventh Book of *Poly.*[1]

It will thus be seen that parts of the *Polychronicon* are wanting in this MS.

On folio 2 a is written:

'Polycronicon
wrytten in Latine by Ran. Higden Monk of St. Werburg's in Chester
translated into English
by
John de Trevisa.'

The first five leaves of the MS. contain 'Dialogus inter Militem et Clericum'. The next thirteen leaves contain a Discourse of the Archbishop of Armagh, entitled 'Incipit Sermo Dni. Archiepi. Armacani: Demeth nogt by Preface bote rygtful Dom ye deme. John 8, 5'.

Fol. 1 has been much damaged. The right side of fol. (a) is almost impossible to read. The lower right-hand corners of the first eight or nine folios are badly wrinkled and marred.

Br. Mus. MS. Additional 37049.

This is a copy of the *Methodius* tract on the 'Beginning and Ending of the World', in a Northern dialect. I have printed it in parallel columns with the same tract from MS. Harl. 1900.

---

[1] It closes Book VII near the beginning of chap. 44 with these words: 'her many men conspired for to help at his deliverance, but he died about the feast of . . .' (see *Polychronicon*, Rolls Series, vol. viii, p. 325).

Introduction

In the *Catalogue of Additions*[1] it is numbered 37049, headed: 'The Desert of Religion & other poems and religious pieces, etc., mostly illustrated in Northern English.' The collection consists of 71 articles, ours being No. 4, and running from folio 11 to 16 b (20 lines). It is said to be a translation from the Latin version (Royal MS. 8 F. VIII, f. 170, and elsewhere) of the *Revelationes* of the pseudo-Methodius.

The MS. consists of ff. 1 + 96, single columns, $10\frac{3}{4} \times 8$ in. paper, except 1 and 2. First half of the fifteenth century. About one-third of each page is covered with crude coloured drawings, illustrating the text. The rest of the space is taken up with from 24 to 26 lines of writing, carelessly written and hard to decipher. Many of the pages are mutilated at bottom, especially articles 70 and 71.

Fol. 11 a has three drawings: (1) The Lord to Adam and Eve, (2) The Serpent beguiling Eve, (3) The Angel with the Sword, and 25 lines of writing.

Fol. 11 b has two pictures: (1) The Flood, (2) The Ark, and 26 lines.

On f. 12 a we find pictures of Noah and the Altar, and the Tower of Babel, with 26 lines of writing. On every page we find one or two pictures, covering about the same space. There is writing explaining each of these drawings, sometimes written over the top, often through the picture, sometimes at the right or left.

Burleigh House MS.

This is a valuable MS., as it contains the three works in the present edition. It is especially important, as it is the only MS. of the five used, besides the Harleian, that contains the *Methodius* tract in Southern English. Thus it is greatly to be regretted that it could not be found for use in this edition.[2]

---

[1] *Cat. of Add. to MSS. in the Br. Mus.* (1900-1905), pp. 324-32.

[2] A serious effort was made by myself, assisted by Mr. J. Munro, then Assistant-Secretary of the E.E.T.S., to obtain a copy of this MS. The Marquis of Exeter, through his Secretary, Sir Leslie Falkiner, Bart., was most kind in searching his library, but after several efforts, in a letter under date of July 19, 1914, he writes ' that there was no

A full and complete description of the MS. is given by Alfred J. Horwood, in the *Sixth Report of the Royal Commission of Historical Manuscripts, 1877*. In Part I, p. xi, he says:

'The Marquis of Exeter's library contains a fine copy, on vellum, of Trevisa's translation into English of Higden's Polychronicon; and in the same volume are translations by Trevisa of other works, including Archbishop Turpin's romance chronicle of Charlemagne and his Peers at Roncevalles. This volume was probably the property of William Cecil, Lord Burghley, for his hand writing is seen on the margin of one of the leaves.'

In the appendix (p. 234) to the same report, just before the description, Mr. Horwood says:

'The MSS. of the Most Honourable, the Marquis of Exeter, at Burghley House, Stamford. One of the MSS. at Burghley house bears marks of having been consulted by Lord Treas. Burghley; it is a very fine copy of Trevisa's translation into English of Higden's Polychronicon, accompanied by Trevisa's translation of other works, and by a translation into English of Archbishop Turpin's legendary chronicle of Charlemagne and his peers.'

Miss Greenwood speaks of it as containing the *Dialogue between Dominus and Clericus*, the *Epistle to Lord Berkeley*, the *Methodius* tract, the *Sermon*, and *Dialogus inter Militem et Clericum*. She makes a mistake, however, in placing the last three with Bartholomaeus at Burleigh House. According to Mr. Horwood's report this MS. contains the *Polychronicon*, together with those just mentioned. It seems, therefore, to have the same contents as MS. Harl. 1900.

The following is part of the description as given in Mr. Horwood's report:

'Large folio, vellum C 1420 (and later) in two columns.
I. Dialogus inter militem et clericum. Clericus. Y wonder trace of the MS. anywhere, neither in the Library Catalogue or elsewhere, and that there seems to be no trace of it as far back as 1845.' Miss Alice Greenwood, who refers to the MS. in her article in *Camb. Hist. of Eng. Lit.*, writes me July 29, 1914, ' that she did not verify it as being at Burleigh House, at the time of her writing in 1908. The correspondence with librarians was done by officials of the Cambridge University Press.' It was not used by Babington and Lumby in their Rolls Series edition.

sir noble Kny3t þat in fiue daies tymes be changid, ri3t is y-buried, lawes.biþ ouertorned and statutes biþ y-trode under feet. Ends on folio 5 b. (This is a translation into English of Ockham's tract under the same title. An English translation was printed by Berthelet (temp. Hen. VIII.)

II. Folio 5 b. Incipit sermo domini archiepiscopi Armacani. Begins: Demiþ nought ye face, but ri3tful dome ye deme. John 8º, 1º. Holy fadyr, in the begynynge of my sermon I make a protestation. Ends (20 b): as I prayed in þe first þat I touched, demith nou3t bi þe face, etc. (This is a translation of the 'Defensio curatorum contra eos qui se privilegiatos dicunt', composed by Richard Fitz-Ralph, Archbishop of Armagh, in 1357. The Latin version, with Roger Conway's counterblast, was printed by John Trechsel in 1496.)

III. The book of Methodie the bishop of the church of Paterene and martir of (sic) Crist, which he charged to translate of hebrue and greek speche in to Latyn, þat is of ye beginyng of ye worlde wich ye noble man Seint Jerom in his workes praysed. Begins: For whi hit is to wite. Ends in the first column of 23 b.

IV. Trevisa's translation of Higden's *Polychronicon*. First comes a table (in 16 leaves) to the Chronicle. Next is the dialogue between a Clerk and a Lord (i. e. Trevisa and Lord Berkeley) beginning: Siþþe þat Babel was y-buld men spekiþ diuerse tonges. (This is printed at the beginning of Caxton's edition.) Then comes Trevisa's epistle to Lord Berkeley, beginning: Welþe and worship to my worthy and worshipful Lord, Sir Thomas lord of Berkley, I John Treuysa etc.

The text of the *Polychronicon* begins: 'after solempne and wise writers of art'. Ends: 'and soon þer after were messengers sent to Auenion to the Pope to conferme ye pees and the couenants in eiþer side. God be thanked of all his dedis þis translacion is ended on a þursday ye 18th day of Aueril, ye yere of our Lord 1347' (adding that Sir Thomas Lord of Berkeley was then aged 35).[1]

The last date in the text is 1347, and very little space is occupied with the events between the date of the last sentence which refers to the confirmation of the Treaty of Bretigny made in 1360.'

The report closes with Horwood's acknowledgements to the Marquis of Exeter for the hospitality at Burleigh House.

---

[1] Compare this date with other endings, and discussion of closing date, pp. lxxvii ff.

Relation of the Five Middle-English Manuscripts.

Orthographically the MSS. group themselves thus: (1) H, (2) A C, (3) S Ch, as is shown by the following forms:

	H	A C	S	Ch
Dial.				
2/12	haueþ	haþ		habbeþ
6/26	dide	dede		dude
7/3	sey3	seigh		sy3
14/16	sey	seie		sygge
16/13	dewe (*vb.* do)	þow	þew	þuwe
18/1	seyn	seieþ	seggeþ	syggeþ
21/6	due (*adj.*)	dewe		þew
25/13	biggeþ	beggeþ		buggeþ
26/8	myrþe	merþe		murþe
Sermon.				
38/9	her	hire		here
50/20	dar	durre	þere	þurre
51/8	here (*adverb*)	hire	huyre	heyre
52/5	sueþ	seweþ	seweþ	syweþ
52/7	ony	any		eny
54/2	ferþe	fourþe	ferþe	veurþe
57/9	hereþ	hireþ		huyreþ
60/11	fleece	flees		vluys
62/2	due	dewe		þewe
73/11	gossippes	gossibbes		godsybbes
78/20	dide	dede		dude
79/21	þou3	þei		þey3
80/6	,,	,,		,,
80/12	,,	,,		,,

In many cases H resembles A C, thus making two groups in spelling.

Dial.	H	A C	S	Ch
3/12		he		a
6/4		from	fro	vram
6/17		3ede	3uede	3ude
7/7		þei	hey	hy
10/12	(many times)	haueþ		habbeþ
16/6		rule		reule
21/7		lese		leuse
21/7		fee		feo
22/13		here		huyre
27/5		siluer		seluer
32/9		chirche		cherche
32/14		dewe (due)		þewe

Introduction

Sermon.	H A C	S	Ch
48/4	herde		y-hurd
51/1	dewe (due)		þewe
52/13	leseþ		lueseþ
56/12	þider		þuder
56/22	þei		þay
58/26	lese		luese (leuse Ch)
67/22	nynþe		nyþe
74/30	þilke		þulke
76/14	þese		þues
88/8	stalworþe		stalword
88/30	wrouȝt		wroȝte
93/3	feiþ		fey
93/3	truþe	trewþe	treuthe
93/8	seuenthe		seueþe.

In a few cases H S Ch agree: H S Ch write 'axeþ', A C 'askeþ', H S Ch 'turne', A C 'torne'.

S and Ch almost invariably have 'a', where the other MSS. have 'þei'. They also write 'a' for 'he'. In the 3rd pers. pron., when S and Ch do not write 'a' for 'þei', S has 'hey', Ch 'hy'. In *Sermon* 47/2 the following occurs:

H	S	Ch	A	C
þei	a	a	þei	he
þei	hey	þei	þei	hy

This irregularity, however, is not usual. Rarely does A use 'a' for 'þei'.

The following readings group the manuscripts thus:
Dial.

	H S Ch	A C
6/14	cupes	cupes ful
20/5	forfadres	forme fadres
24/7	myldliche	mekeliche
35/5	wityng	writinge

Sermon.

42/29	þerby	þei be
43/17	þat	þat þat
56/8	come	þere come
62/10	reulere	reguler
71/10	but a nouys	hote noon
71/28	folly (fully, volly)	cristene
82/13	half (hal Ch)	al
85/13	lowe (Lat. *humilis*)	lewede (also S)
87/8	strenger (L. *fortiora*)	certeyn
89/23	a	on

Group A C

Although S is nearer the original Latin, as will be shown later, I shall first discuss the group A C. The scribe of C is most careless. His mistakes are (1) omissions of lines, usually one or two, but in *Sermon*, p. 48, ll. 29-35, eight lines, and p. 61, ll. 22-7, six lines; (2) words different from the other MSS.; (3) an occasional repetition of a line or part of a line; (4) wrong translations.

(1) The omissions:

These are very numerous, and mostly visual errors. The eye has in nearly every case dropped from one word to a like word in a lower line. These errors appear very frequently, not only in the *Dialogue* and *Sermon*, but also in *Polychronicon*. A close examination shows that in the great majority of omissions the words which caused the omission are directly under each other in A. This points to A as the direct origin of C. There are facts, however, as will appear later, that make this impossible.

Some of the C omissions are:

Dial.
- 9/6   temporalte—temporalte, one line.
- 11/8 deme—deme, one line.
- 11/9 vn rightful—vn rightful, mid. of lines 1 and 3 in A.
- 25/5 pees—pees.
- 28/8 places—places (in same place in A).
- 28/10 eȝechias—eȝechias (under each other in A).
- 32/10 seruise—seruise ('seruise', lines 1 and 4, in A exactly under).

Sermon.
- 45/14 dedes—dedes (in A 'dedes' first word in 1 and 4).
- 48/29 parische—parische (in A 'parische' middle of lines 1 and 9).
- 49/23 heste—heste (in A 'heste' middle of lines 1 and 4).
- 52/20 persone—persone (in A 'persone' exactly under 1 and 5).
- 61/22 heeste—heeste (in A 'heeste' middle of lines 1 and 7).

Then certain passages are omitted by A and C, which would seem as though C were direct from A. These are, however, not numerous. *Dial.* 9/3 Kyngdom—Kyngdom, *Dial.* 31/4 'for þe & for me', instead of 'for me & for þe' in other MSS.;

Sermon 62/5 'þe same' in A C, but not in Latin or other MSS.

(2) C's words different from other MSS. in the *Dialogue*: 9/13 'alwey', Lat. and MSS. = 'awey', 10/12 'whan', MSS. = 'whom', 14/1 'causes' for 'cases', 23/7 'begile not'. This is correct form in Lat. and Pr., other MSS. omit 'not'.

Instances in the *Sermon* are:

H S Ch A	C
39/17 þere nyne	þer ynne (wrong)
45/5 such (Lat. *tales*)	seche (*verb*)
60/20 wiþ hem (Lat. *secum*)	awey
60/30 þei	þat
62/12 do	vse
63/18 by	but
68/18 kepe	keke
72/7 fre	þe
72/9 be dewe	be dede
76/19 þefþe	þe fecte
77/7 euel getyng	mater
79/14 worschip	pouert
80/24 þreuyng	reprefynge
87/18 ,,	prechynge
88/12 catel	trauaille
88/29 folewe	knowe
89/18 slowe (Lat. *pigrum*)	soule

Some of the differences are evidently scribal errors, but they point to an independent source for C.

(3) Repetitions in C :

Sermon 41/20 after 'þee', repeated 'þat þow sixte wiþ þyn ey3e'. The eye of the writer glanced above and brought the line down.

Sermon 53/31 after 'pryuyleges' 'schulde voide many damage'. This is repeated from above. 54/17 after 'hym', written, 'in token of his lordschippe'. In this passage the eye dropped two lines, and thus the phrase was repeated.

Further proof that C did not copy from A is found in the fact that a few passages and words are omitted in A, but occur in C.

Sermon 63/19 about two lines. Also 74/13, 84/1, 87/20. Further, referring to Ch *Polychronicon*, several chapters are absent from A (see description of Additional 24194, p. xxi). Thus it would seem that A and C are independent copies of some original.

GROUP H S Ch

In this group S Ch fall together, not only in orthography but by certain readings:

Dial.	H	S Ch	Sermon	H	S Ch
2/12	þei	hey or hy	41/20	wiþ ynne þee	wiþ þyn ey3e
2/12	haueþ	habbeþ	43/8	his	þis (Lat. *hoc*)
5/9	feiþ	fey			
6/1	herde	y-hurd	17/23	þese	in þis
6/22	þanne	þo	50/20	dar	þurre (þere Ch)
10/7	bade	heet	57/12	mawme-trie	mametrie
			60/11	fleece	vluys
16/13	dewe (*vb.*)	þewe (þuwe)	63/11	seeþ (Lat. *viderit*)	seweþ (suweþ Ch)
			63/12	lecherie	spusebreche
19/10	stireþ	stureþ	73/11	gossippes	godsybbes
21/6	due (*adj.*)	þew	79/8	þis	þese
			84/27	bade	hete
25/7	comyneþ	comuneþ (comneþ Ch)	87/8	til (Lat. *donec*)	forto
			90/25	þat	þan (Lat. *quam*)
			91/27	kitt	kutte

S is a comparatively late MS., perhaps twenty or thirty years later than H. Many passages are omitted in the *Polychronicon*. These are filled in by a later hand. Therefore H could not be derived from S. Ch omits fols. 6 a–8 a (pp. 39–47) of the *Sermon*. Ch cannot then be the source of H.

As has been shown, H is related to A C in orthography. On the other hand, it is related to S Ch by certain readings. And yet H has a few distinct readings which seem to point to an independent manuscript as its source. Examples: *Dial.* 10/7 H 'bade', all other MSS. read 'heet'; *Dial.* 29/5 H 'a3ensaye', others 'wiþseie'.

Sermon 41/20 H 'wiþ ynne þee'. A C S Ch read this correctly 'wiþ þyn ey3e'. 42/29 'þer by' H S, Lat. 'ac þer hoc', A C is wrong having 'þei be'. 46/7 and 8 H has misinterpreted, left out 'þat', and begun a new sentence with '3if þei', A C and S have corrected this. 46/29 Lat. 'imponendam', H 'enioye', A C S 'enioyne'. This looks like a mere scribal error on the part of H. 59/1 Lat. 'aliud', H 'more', other MSS. 'anoþer'; 63/11 Lat. 'viderit', H 'seeþ', other MSS. 'seweþ'; 79/8 Lat. 'iste', A 'þis', other MSS. 'þese'; 87/8 Lat. 'donec', H 'til', other MSS. 'forto'; 88/23 Lat. 'verbo nostro', H 'lord', MSS. 'word'; 90/25 Lat. 'quam', H 'þat', MSS. correct 'þan'.

H is probably the oldest of the five manuscripts. The scribe has been careless in a few places. None of the omissions is very significant. They are *Dial.* 8/6, 11/6, 34/1 ; *Sermon* 41/32, 60/10, 63/31, 90/4. The passages omitted thus in H are found in the other MSS. Inasmuch as S has these omitted passages, H cannot be the source of S. Furthermore S is quite independent of H, because it contains many passages, identical with the original Latin, which are not met with in H, or any of the other MSS. This places S nearer the original MS., and in it we have the purest form of the *Dialogue* and the *Sermon.* And yet it is a late MS., and has many long passages omitted in the *Polychronicon,* which are supplied by a later hand.

In the *Dialogue* the following passages occur only in S, which agree with the Latin, and the printed edition :

5/4 'not' in 'may not be wiþseid'; 8/3 a passage after 'temperalte'; 35/8 a passage after 'nede'; 25/12 S wrongly writes 'sueþ', when all the other MSS. Lat. and Pr. write 'seeþ'.

Examples in *Sermon*:
39/19 S 'to þis holy court', Lat. 'sanctus', other MSS. omit 'holy'.
41/32 S has 'place', omitted in others, Lat. 'locus',
55/10 After 'falliþ to' a passage in S and Lat. not found in other MSS.
57/14 ' to þe riȝtful manes offiȝs it longeþ '. 'it longeþ ', Lat. 'pertinet', only in S.
57/32 After 'schryue' a passage in Lat. and S.
59/1 'þe lore of', only in S, Lat. 'doctrinae'.
63/3 S 'symonye', other MSS 'money', Lat. 'pecunia'.
64/1 after 'gospel', two lines found in S, but om. in other MSS.
65/24 S 'noon', other MSS. newe, Lat. 'cum sit nulla'.

68/10 S 'þei were noȝt', other MSS. 'þei were', Lat. 'non fuerant'.
73/17 S only correct 'þat y wolde noȝt þenke of a mayde', Lat. 'ne cogitarem de virgine'.
79/19 S 'ynow for me', others 'ynow', Lat. 'mihi sufficiant'.

That S is not the original of the other four manuscripts is shown from a number of omissions, which are found in the MSS., and in the original Latin:

Dial.:
12/12 after 'demynge'.

Sermon:
51/11 'ech ȝere' for 'al þe ȝere', Lat. 'per totum annum'.
57/26 om. of 'þe beste' in 'þe beste beestes', Lat. 'pinguiora'.

The above evidence seems to point to a group S Ch, standing nearest to the original. They are probably from the same copy. H is from a different MS., and further from the original than the S Ch group. The MSS. A C form a third group further removed from the original copy than the other two groups.

B. LATIN MANUSCRIPTS

John Trevisa was a noted translator of the fourteenth century. His literary work is an effort to render into simple English some of the outstanding scientific, historical, and religious material of his time. In his epistle to Lord Thomas of Berkeley on the translation of the *Polychronicon*, he says:

'For travell will I not spare comfort I have in medefull makeing and plesinge to God, and in knowing that I wote that it is your will: for to make this translation clere and plaine, to be known and understandyn. In some place I shall set word for word and actiffe for actiffe and passife for passife arowe right as it standeth without changinge the ordre of words. But in some places I must change the order of words and set actiffe for passife and aȝen word. And in some places I must set a reason for a word, and tell what it meaneth; But for all such changing the meaning shall stand and not be changed.'[1]

The material that he used was ready at hand, found in many

---

[1] Taken from *Epistle* as printed by Smyth, *Lives of the Berkeleys*, vol. i, p. 343.

Introduction

Latin MSS. The chief of these MSS. are here listed, most of which were examined and compared with the English.

Dialogus inter Militem et Clericum.

(1) **Br. Museum MS. Cotton Nero D. VIII.**[1]
Codex Membrane, in folio, contains 347 ff., double columns, 41 lines. No. 10, 'Disputatio inter clericum et militem super potestate commissa praelatis, ecclesiasticis, atque principibus terrarum.' ff. 183 a (col. 1) ½–196 a (col. 2) 14 lines. Written in a large hand, with no ornamentation.

(2) **Br. Mus. MS. Reg. 6 E. III.**[2]
Vellum, 16 × 11 in. 56 articles, ff. 292. The *Dial.* is article No. 41, ff. 130–2 b (col. 2). 56 lines in a column, written very plainly. No ornamentation or colouring.

(3) **St. John's College, Camb., No. 160 (F. 23).**[3]
Vellum, 9⅜ × 6½ in. ff. 187. Mostly 29 lines to a page. Cent. XV. An ugly hand. Contents, i. Will Occham. Disputatio inter clericum et militem, ff. 1 b–6 a.

(4) **St. John's College, Camb., No 115 (E. 12).**[4]
Vellum, 8 × 4⅝ in. ff. 160 + 2. 37, 35 &c. lines to a page. Cent. XIV and XV. Well written, but filled with contractions. Contents, No. 4 (Ockam). Disputatio inter clericum et militem, etc. ff. 87 b–95 a.

(5) **Corpus Christi College, Camb., No. 156 (p. 21).**[5]
Paper and vellum, 11⅘ × 8⅕ in. ff. 74 + 13 + 115 + 99 + 21. Cent. XV and XVI. Several vols. in various hands. Contents, iii, 22. ff. 110–15. Disputatio inter clericum etc.

(6) **Br. Mus. MS. Additional 33243.**[6]
Liber dyalogorum (Willelmi) Okam. Vellum, ff. 283. Single col. 45 lines. 11½ × 8 in. Index at first: Dialogues between Magister and Discipulis, entitled 'Dialogi Okami de

---

[1] *Catalogue of MSS. in Cottonian Library*, 1802, p. 238.

[2] Casley, David, *Catalogue of MSS. in King's Library*, 1734, pp. 114 and 115.

[3] M. R. James, *A Descriptive Catalogue of MSS. in Library of St. John's College, Camb.*, 1913, p. 191.

[4] James's *Catalogue*, p. 149.

[5] M. R. James, *Cat. of MSS. in Corpus Christi College, Camb.*, vol. ii, 1912, p. 351.

[6] *Cat. of Additions to MSS. in Br. Mus. from 1882–1887.*

Jurisdictione et potestate Ecclezie.' Our dialogue not found in this list.

FitzRalph's Sermon, Defensio Curatorum.

(1) **MS. at Peterhouse Library, Camb. (No. 223.)**[1]
Vellum, $11 \times 7\frac{1}{2}$ in. ff. 286. 45 lines to a page. 15th cent. Contents (2): Propositio Ricardi Ardmachani Archiep.—facta in consistorio coram D. papa et cardinalibus, etc., 8 Nov. 1357. Begins: 'Nolite iudicare secundum faciem.' ff. 43 b (l. 6)–55 a (l. 5).

(2) **MS. at Sidney Sussex College Library (64 Δ 4. 2).**[2]
Paper, $11\frac{1}{8} \times 7\frac{7}{8}$ in. ff. 132. 49 and 32 lines to a page. 15th cent. Not so well written as No. 1, but in a larger hand Contents (13): Proposicio d. Armachani facta in consistorio—apud Auinonem, 8 Nov. 1357. ff. 72–87 a.

(3) **Bodley MS. No. 144, A. 5.**
Parchment, $10\frac{7}{8} \times 8\frac{3}{4}$ in. iv + 280 leaves. Several hands of 15th cent. Begins f. 255, one line from bottom. In this MS. there are no less than 88 sermons[3] delivered in various parts of England, Ireland, Scotland, and Avignon. It ends f. 271, line 23. Down to f. 266, line $13\frac{1}{2}$, written in a rather small, but plain hand. Balance in a larger hand. Much easier MS. to read than either Bodley 158 or 865.

(4) **Bodley MS. No. 158, B. 3.**
Parchment, $10\frac{7}{8} \times 7\frac{1}{4}$ in. 1 + 224 leaves. Four separate MSS. written early in 15th cent. Contents: No. 9. Richardi Ar—. Propositio coram Papa ad Avineone*m* 8 Novembris 1357, super materia Mendicitatis ac Privilegiorum contra Frates. ff. 153 a–165 a (35 lines).

(5) **Bodley MS. 865.**
$10\frac{7}{8} \times 7\frac{3}{8}$ in. ii + 115 leaves. In Latin and Old English. Three MSS. written in 11th to 15th centuries. The sermon consists of ff. 26 b–55 a (20, 1), 29 and 30 lines to

---

[1] M. R. James, *A Descriptive Catalogue of MSS. in Peterhouse Library*, Camb., 1899, p. 276.

[2] M. R. James, *Descriptive Catalogue of MSS. in Sidney Sussex Coll.* Lib., Camb., 1895, p. 46.

[3] R. L. Poole, *Dict. of Nat. Biog.*, vol. xix, p. 195. (MS. 144 contains 88 sermons in full or in reports.)

a page. 'Proposicio—facta in consistorio coram . . . Nov. 8th, 1357, the treatise usually known as the Defensorium Curatorum, often printed.'

(6) **Corpus Christi MS. Oxford, No. CLXXXII.**[1]
13 × 9½ in., 2 cols., 51 lines. Cod. Memb., fol. ff. 82. Date beg. of 13th and 15th centuries. Art. 3: Ricardi filii Radulphi, Archiep. Cantaur. sermo habitus Avinoniae VIII die mensis Novemb. A. D. 1357. Inc. istud: 'Nolite judicare secundum faciem,' etc. contra fratres. fols. 53 a (col. 1)–66 b (col. 2) 22 lines.

(7) **Magdalen College MS. Oxford, No. XXXVIII.**[2]
8⅓ × 7 in. 2 cols., 53 lines. Cod. Memb. small fol. ff. 70. Cent. XV beg. No. 19: Ricardi Radulphi Armachani, propositio facta—die mensis Novemb., Anno Domini MCCCLVII. ff. 53 b (col. 1) line 27–68 a.

(8) **Reg. MS. Oxford, No. CCCLXXX.**[3]
Chartaceus, in 4to, ff. 74. Time 17th cent. Six articles. No. 4: Ex Ricardi, Archiep. Armachani, Defensione curatorum. ff. 34–9.[4]

Methodius, The Beginning and the End of the World.

I. THE BRITISH MUSEUM MSS.

(1) **Royal MS. 8 F. VIII.**[5]
10¾ × 7 in. ff. 176. Contains seven articles. No. 7, Methodii Eubulii, Tyri Episcopi, Revelationes, ff. 170 a (col. 1)–172 a (col. 2). This is supposed to be the Latin MS. from which the Northern English MS. Addit. 37049 is taken. From beginning of fol. 170 a (col. 2)–fol. 172 a (col. 2) half of column corresponds very closely with the English versions. The article then continues to 176 a (col. 1) one-third of column, where it stops abruptly. The latter part has to do with Antichrist, and is found in the medieval printed books of the *Revelationes*, and also in

---

[1] H. O. Coxe, *Catalogus Codicum MSS. qui in Collegiis Aulisque Oxon. adservantur*, Pars ii, 1852, p. 72.

[2] H. O. Coxe, *Cat. Cod. MSS. Coll. Magdalenae*, p. 22.

[3] H. O. Coxe, *Cat. Cod. MSS. Coll. Reginensis*, p. 88.

[4] This is evidently an extract only. I failed to examine this MS.

[5] D. Casley, *Cat. of MSS. in King's Library*, 1734, p. 159.

the Greek and Latin version of *Revelationes* as printed by Grynaeus, in *Monumenta Orthodoxographa*, Greek, pp. 93-9, Latin, pp. 100-13.

(2) **MS. Additional 34018.**[1]
Vellum, $9\frac{1}{4} \times 6$ in. ff. 99. 13th cent. Written very fine in double cols. 58 lines. Very many abbreviations. Our article No. 5 of the seven, headed 'S. Methodii Episcopi Patarensis liber de principio saeculi'. 946-96.

(3) **Arundel MS. 326.**[2]
Vellum. $6\frac{3}{4} \times 4\frac{1}{2}$ in. Single columns. 34-38 lines to a page. Early 14th cent. Small quarto, ff. 60. Meth. *Revelationes*, ff. 57-60 b (23 lines.)

(4) **Sloane MS. 289.**[3]
$7\frac{1}{2} \times 5\frac{1}{2}$ in. Single columns, 32 lines. Contains ten articles, Methodius being No. 9. Fols. 94-102. New numbering, ff. 85-88 a (21). The text is practically the same as the three first mentioned.

II. UNIVERSITY OF CAMBRIDGE LIBRARIES.

(a) Camb. Univ. Lib.

(1) **No. 869 (Dd. XV. 15).**[4]
$4\frac{3}{4} \times 3\frac{1}{4}$ in. Single columns, 23 lines. 15th cent., 24 mo. 218 leaves. Written very small with many contractions. Meth. 'The beg. & End. of time', No. 2, ff. 153-61.

(2) **No. 1164 (Ff. I. 31).**[5]
13th cent. 181 leaves. Meth. 1 a-6 b. A parchment book in folio. Very plainly written.

(3) **No. 1514 (Gg. IV. 15).**[6]
Parchment, 11×7 in. 12th cent. Folio, ff. 111. 'Liber Methodii Martiris et Episcopi Ecclesie Paterensis, etc.,' article No. 2, ff. 108-11.

---

[1] *Cat. of Additions to British Museum for 1888-1893*, pp. 163-4.

[2] H. L. D. Ward, *Cat. of Romances in Dept. of MSS. Br. Mus.*, i (1883), p. 246; H. Suchier, *Denkmäler Prov. Lit.* (1883), p. 166.

[3] H. L. D. Ward, *Cat. of Romances*, vol. i, p. 250; H. Suchier, *Denkmäler Prov. Lit.* (1883), p. 166.

[4] *Cat. of MSS. in Camb. Univ. Library*, vol. i, p. 541.

[5] Ibid., vol. ii, p. 332.

[6] Ibid., vol. iii, p. 160.

Introduction xxxix

(4) **No. 1524 (Gg. IV. 25).**[1]
$10\frac{1}{2} \times 8$ in. Single column, 34 lines. Quarto, on paper (excepting 13–17, which are on parchment). Written in various hands. 15th cent. No. 7, 'Liber Methodi Martiris', ff. 58–61 a. Many proper names underlined in red. Well written and easy to read. This and Ff. I. 31 are the two best copies in the Library.

(5) **No 2019 (Kk. IV. 4).**[2]
$14\frac{4}{5} \times 11$ in. A tall thin quarto on paper (excepting f. 64 and the fly-leaves, which are on parchment). ff. 76, double columns of 53 lines. 15th cent. No. 14, ff. 75 a–76 b, 'Liber Metodii Martiri de Primo Miliario Secule'. Begins in the usual way: 'Sciendum nobis namque est fratres,' etc. In a note is added: 'This is Methodius Patarorum Episcopus, who flourished in 290. See Oudin, i. 299. This tract does not appear in the collection of his works.'

These five MSS. resemble each other very closely, and also the English version in Harl. 1900.

(b) **St. John's College Library, Cambridge.**[3]

(1) **No. 184 (G. 16).**
Vellum, $8\frac{5}{8} \times 6\frac{1}{4}$ in. ff. 322 + 5, double cols. of 41 lines. 14th cent. Contents, No. 10: Inc. liber Methodii ep. de Principio Seculi, etc. ff. 304–6 a, five lines from end. Contents, No. 11 : De Antichristo, ff. 305 b–308. A note states this was printed in *Orthodoxographia*, etc., Sackur (*Sibyllinische Texte*, Halle, 1898). This copy is the same as English in MS. Harl. 1900.

(c) **Peterhouse Library, Camb.**[4]

(1) **No. 45 (O. 4. 6).**
Vellum, $15\frac{3}{4} \times 10\frac{5}{8}$ in. ff. 391, double columns of 60 lines.

---

[1] *Cat. of MSS.*, vol. iii, p. 69.
[2] Ibid., vol. iii, p. 641.
[3] M. R. James, *A Descriptive Cat. of MSS. in St. John's Coll.*, Camb. Univ. Press, 1913, p. 217.
[4] M. R. James, *A Descriptive Cat. of MSS. in Peterhouse Lib.*, Camb. Univ. Press, 1899, p. 66.

xl   *Introduction*

Early 13th cent. Contents, No. 2 : 'In nomine Christi inc. liber Metodii', f. 383 a (col. 2)–383 b (col. 2). Very closely written, with pale ink, hard to read.

(*d*) **Trinity College, Camb.**

(1) **No. 943 (R. 15, 21, 165).**[1]
Vellum, 10 × 7 in. ff. 6 + 31 + 82, double columns of 41 lines. 15th cent. (1408). c. 98 is from the pseudo-Methodius 'de initio et fine seculi'; c. 99, On the Ages of the World.

(2) **No. 1122 (O. 2. 18).**[2]
Vellum, $8\frac{5}{8} \times 5\frac{3}{4}$ in. ff. 186, 44 lines to a page. 14th and 15th cent. Contents, on f. 4 (13) b, on the fly-leaves, is the end of the prophecy of Methodius (XV), No. 22, in a later hand. The beginning of the Methodius prophecy of which the end is on the fly-leaves, ff. 151 b–153: De creacione celi et terre et de primo miliario breviter ostendit.   Sciendum namque est nobis.

(3) **No. 1228 (O. 3. 51).**[3]
This is in Greek, paper, $9\frac{3}{8} \times 5\frac{3}{4}$ in. ff. 16 + 266 + 69. 15th and 16th cent. Contents, No. 10, ff. 28–42.

(*e*) **Corpus Christi College, Camb.**[4]

(1) **No. 59 (D. 11).**
(2) **No. 66 (D. 12),** ff. 235 b–238. Cent. XII & XIII, art. 26.
(3) **No. 275 (A. 4),** ff. 18–22. Cent. XV & XIII, art. 6.
(4) **No. 288 (O. 11),** ff. 98 b–101 b. Cent. XIV, art. 6.
(5) **No. 404 (G. 5),** ff. 4–7. Cent. XIV, art. 2.

A note by James tells us that these were printed in *Orthodoxographa*, and by Sackur in *Sibyllinische Text*, Halle, 1898.

---

[1] M. R. James, *Cat. of Western MSS. in Trin. Coll.*, Camb. Univ. Press, 1900–1904. 4 vols. Vol. ii, p. 358.
[2] James, vol. iii, p. 106.
[3] James, vol. iii, p. 236.
[4] M. R. James, *Cat. of MSS. in Corpus Christi Coll., Camb.*, 2 vols., 1907–1908.

III. OXFORD UNIVERSITY LIBRARIES.

(a) St. John's College.[1]

(1) No. CXXVIII.

$9 \times 5\frac{1}{2}$ in. Single columns, 31 lines. Cod. Memb. Small folio, ff. 237. 11th cent. beg. Ten articles. Ours is No. 9, occupying ff. 217 b–223. Incip. 'Sciendum namque est nobis', etc. An excellent copy, although belonging to 11th cent.

(2) No. CXXXV.

Cod. Memb. 4to, ff. 57. 15th cent. Ours is the second of two articles in the MS. S. Methodii, episcopi Paterensis, et Martyris, ' de initio seculi et fine, de creatione caeli et terrae '. fol. 48 b.

(3) No. CLXXXII.

$7\frac{3}{10} \times 5$ in. Single columns, 20 lines. Memb. 4to, ff. 148. 15th cent. Ten articles. Ours is No. 9, ff. 126 b (line 6)– 136 a (line 13). This copy contains more than the others. A different copy with added material.

(b) Corpus Christi College.[2]

No. CCCXXX.

$8\frac{3}{10} \times 6\frac{1}{2}$ in., 2 columns, 27 lines. Cod. Chart. and Memb. ff. 163. 17th and 15th cents. Art. 3, Liber Methodii, ff. 159 a (col. 1, line 22)–163 b (col. 1, line 15). Written large and very readable. In a note ' cf. opera in Bibl., ed. Galland, tom. iii, p. 798 '.

(c) Trinity College.[3]

No. III.

$6\frac{7}{10} \times 4\frac{7}{10}$ in. Single columns, 25 lines. Cod. Memb. Small 4to. ff. 305. 15th cent. Contains four articles. No. 2, Methodii, etc., ff. 246 b–53 a ($11\frac{1}{2}$ lines). Few contractions, beautifully written.

---

[1] H. O. Coxe, *Cat. Codicum MSS. qui in Coll. Aulisque Oxon. adservantur*, 1852. 2 pars. (1) p. 39 ; (2) p. 41 ; (3) p. 61.

[2] H. O. Coxe, *Catalogue, etc.*, p. 174.

[3] H. O. Coxe, *Catalogue*, p. 1.

(d) **Lincoln College.**[1]

No. E. XXVIII.

$8 \times 4\frac{1}{2}$ in. Double cols., very narrow, 24 lines. Cod. Memb. in small 4to. ff. 108. 15th cent. Contains fourteen articles. No. 6, Methodii Patarensis libellus, etc., ff. 43 b (col. 2, line 14)-51 b (col. 2, line 7). A very readable MS.

(e) **Magdalen College.**[2]

No. LIII.

$9\frac{4}{5} \times 6$ in. 48 lines on a page. Cod. Memb. 4to. ff. 165. 12th, 13th, and 14th cents. Contains thirty-one articles. No. 15, Liber Methodii, episcopi Patarensis, etc., pp. 207-11 ($28\frac{1}{2}$ lines).

(f) **Merton College.**[3]

No. XIII.

Cod. Memb. Folio. ff. 239, double cols. 14th and 15th cents. Contains fifty-seven articles. Art. 13, Liber et historia 'Metodii', episcopi, etc., ff. 53 b (col. 1, last three lines)-55 a (col. 1, line 26).

(g) **University College.**[4]

No. E. XCIX.

$8\frac{1}{2} \times 6$ in. Single col., 34 lines. Cod. Chart. 4to. ff. 170. 15th cent. Contains nine articles. No. 5, Methodii, episcopi Patarensis, etc., pp. 238 b (line 3)-250 b (line 15).

(h) **Bodleian Library.**

The following are excellent copies. I give them as they appear in the 1697 Catalogue of MSS.

(1) **MS. 722, Art. 3.** Now numbered **Laud Gr. 27.**

This is one of the best Greek MSS. Size, $8\frac{1}{2} \times 6$ in. fols. 8-23.

---

[1] H. O. Coxe. *Catalogue*, p. 27. (Now deposited in Bodley.)
[2] H. O. Coxe, *Catalogue*, p. 32.
[3] H. O. Coxe, *Catalogue*, p. 8.
[4] H. O. Coxe, *Catalogue*, p. 30. (Now in Bodley.)

(2) MS. 1021 in Cat. of 1697. Now **Laud Misc. 270**, Art. No. 2.

(3) MS. 2016 in Cat. of 1697. Now Bodl. 163. Described in 1912 Cat., p. 164. Lat. parchment, two MSS. written late in 11th and 12th cents.

(4) MS. 2746 in Cat. of 1697, p. 147. Now Bodl. 867. New Cat., p. 525. Lat. parchment, early 15th cent., in several hands. Begins f. 299 a at line 13, ends f. 301 at 34th line. On examination this was found to be identical with Harl. 1900.

(5) MS. 3650 in Cat. of 1697, p. 175. Now **62 Musaeo** (unprinted New Cat.), f. 135 b (col. 1, 2 lines)–f. 137 b. Like Engl. Harl. 1900. Not finished.

(6) MS. 10394 (New Catalogue). Now **MS. Sancroft 93.** Late MS., first half of 17th cent. Written in Gk. and Lat., on paper. 108 b–111 a, Methodii. Patarensis Revelationes, a brief extract.

(7) MS. 14732 (New Catalogue, p. 338). Now **MS. Rawlinson Poet. 241.** In Fr. and Lat. on parchment, written second part of 13th cent. in England. No. 6, pp. 189–195 a, 'In Nomine Christi incipit liber Metodii... id est De Principio seculi.' This is fully described by E. Stengel in the *Zeitschrift für französische Sprache und Litteratur*, Bd. xiv, p. 128 (1892).

C. THE ENGLISH PRINTED EDITION OF THE DIALOGUE.

The *Dialogue* was printed in English in the sixteenth century. This sixteenth-century text is printed in parallel columns in this edition. C. L. Kingsford, in his article on Trevisa in the *Dictionary of National Biography*, writes: 'Dr. Babington ascribes to Trevisa the translation of the "Dialogue inter Militem et Clericum de potestate ecclesiastica et civile" (a Latin tract inaccurately attributed to William Ockham), which was published at London in 1540.'[1] R. L. Poole, in his article on Ockham, says: 'Ockham's political writings have all been

[1] *Dictionary of National Biography*, vol. lvii, p. 213.

enumerated in his biography. To them is usually added a
" Disputatio inter militem et clericum" on the civil and ecclesiastical powers (printed by Goldast i. 13 ff.), which was translated into English in the sixteenth century, and twice published
by Berthelet (2nd ed., 1540), but Dr. Riezler has shown
(pp. 144-8) that it is not by Ockham, but probably by Pierre
du Bois.'[1]

In the British Museum Catalogue under 'Clericus' appears:
'A Dialogue betwene a Knyght and a Clerke, concerning the
power spiritual and temporal (A translation of the "Dialogus
inter clericum et militem" of Gulielmus de Occam). T.
Berthelet; London (1533).' Catalogue number C. 12. c. 24.

This book contains 26 folios. Size, $5 \times 3\frac{1}{4}$ in.; print,
$4 \times 2\frac{1}{3}$ in., 25 lines to a page. The *Dialogue* begins in fol. 2 a.
On fol. 1 a we find: 'A Dialogue betwene a Knight and a clerke
concernynge the power spiritual and temporall.' There are
catchwords on each page, thirty unprinted leaves at the end.

A second copy is found in Cambridge University Library,
catalogued under the number Syn. 8. 54. 52[3]; without title
and date. In the Catalogue the date is given (about 1540),
printed by T. Berthelet. On the blank folio is written in ink:
'A Dialogue between Miles & Clericus touching the Popes
power in temporalls.' In pencil is written:

'By W. of Ockham
Herbert Ames
p. 460.'

This is the same edition as that in the British Museum, but
is bound up in a book with other articles. On a leaf at the
beginning of this book is written 'Pasguyle The Playne,
Anno MDXL'. Below in the lower margin of ornaments is the
date '1534'. The contents are given on the first page over
the signature of Robb. Gghibbon 1683. They are:

(1) Pasguyle the Playne, by Thos. Eliot, Knight to the
Gentle Reder. Printed by Berthelet, 1540.
(2) Confession of the Church of Scotland. Printed at London
by Rowland Hall, 1561.

---

[1] *Dictionary of National Biography*, vol. xli, p. 362; S. Riezler, *Die literarischen Widersacher der Päpste zur Zeit Ludwig des Baiers*, Leipzig, 1874.

(3) Clericus. No author, no date. Printed by Berthelet.
(4) A short description of Antichrist. No author, no date.
(5) A wonderful prophecie for MDXXXI.
(6) A Treatise against Magical Sermons, by Francis Gore.
(7) Epistle of Henry VIII.

In St. John's College, Cambridge (A. 3. 15²) is another copy, printed by Berthelet. No author, no date. In the Catalogue the date is given (1555?). It is the second article in a book containing seven other articles. Another copy is to be found in the same library indexed (EE. 13. 30¹¹), giving no author or date. The Catalogue gives the date 1540. It is bound up with a number of other 'tracts', to which there is no index.

Reference is made to this book in Ames's *Typographical Antiquities*:[1] 'A Dialogue between a Knyght & a Clerke, concerning the power spiritual & temporal, 26 leaves, written ²(in Latin)² by W. Ockham, 1305. ³See the *British Librarian*, p. 5.³

On a blank leaf just before p. 171, where the list of books printed by Berthelet begins, the following is written:

'1540—A Dialogue betwene a knight and a clerk, concerning the power spiritual & temporal By Wm. of Occham, a great philosopher. In English and Latin. See the Br. Librarian, p. 5, where mention is made of its being printed this year; and as T. Berthelet printed the former edition without date, I presume he might print this also. p. W. H.
W. H. = Wm. Herbert.'

This is Herbert's note, as he came into possession of Ames's material, and worked on it years before he brought out his edition of the *Antiquities* in three volumes, 1785, 1786, and 1790.

In vol. i, p. 437, he has a reference similar to his note in Ames's original, as printed above; 'Pr. by Thomas Berthelet, A dialogue betwene a knyght and a clerke, concerning the power spiritual & temporal, by Wm. Occam, the great philosopher, in English & Latin, also without date'; and in the next line below is written '1540, octavo'. In a foot-note, 'See

---

[1] Joseph Ames, *Typographical Antiquities*, London, 1749, p. 176.

[2-2] Written in ink above the line.
[3-3] Written in margin in ink.

the *British Librarian*, p. 5, note, & Fox's *Martyrs*, vol. i, p. 510, Ed. 1641.'

Thos. F. Dibdin, in his edition of the *Antiquities* in 4 vols., 1810-19, reproduces the previous references of Herbert in vol. iii, p. 311, under No. 1230. Also in vol. iii, p. 345, he has the following notice. I give it because of his note :

'Pr. by Thos. Berthelet. No. 1322 : Dialogue. Duodecimo.

A Dialogue between a Knyght and a Clerke concernynge the power spiritual and temporal. In a neat architective compartment as to Fitzherbert's Surveying, 1555. The whole on 26 leaves.

Imprinted in Fleetstrete in the house of... nere to the condite at the sygne of Lucrece, Cum Privilegio. See it in 1540. In Herbert's Coll.

Note. My copy has in MS. "written by Wm. Ockam in the year MCCCV. Prohibetur, saith Pits, p. 458. Extat Latin in Goldast's *Monarchia*, vol. i, p. 358, No. 40, Herbert."'

The *Dialogue* is also referred to in Andrew Maunsell's *Catalogue of English Printed Books*, London, 1595, p. 112, thus: 'Against the Pope's Supremacy A Dialogue between a Knight and a Clerke, concerning the power Spirituall and Temporall. Printed by Thos. Berthelet.'

In the *British Librarian* (Lond. 1738, pp. 5-10) William Oldys gives a fairly full outline of this work. It is prefaced by the following notice :

' A Dialogue betwene a Knyght and a Clerke concernynge the power Spiritual and Temporall. Imprinted at London in Flete Strete, in the House of Tho. Berthelet, near the condite at the sign of Lucrece : cum Privilegio ; without date or name of the author. 52 pages. 8vo.'

Then follows the object of the dialogue :

'This notable little tract was written to silence the clergy, and answer their unreasonable expectations, and the Pope might exercise a Jurisdiction over the Temporalties of Princes, and the church be exempted from contributing of its riches in time of need, either for the Relief of the poor or the security of the Nation where they abide ; as may appear by the following abstract thereof.'

Here follows a digest of over 1,500 words.

Introduction

In the note, p. 5 of this article, referred to by Herbert and Dibdin, the writer speaks of the author and date: 'And tho the Author's name was not yet published to it, it is well known to have been written by that famous clerk and schoolman William of Occham. It was written by our author so early as the year 1305, if the MS. Note on the copy before me is right.' He also mentions another edition of it in 1540, 'wherein it is said to be written by William of Occham, the great philosopher in English and Latin (Extat Lat. in Goldast's *Monarchia* T. Ed.).' Reference is also made in this note to Foxe's *Book of Martyrs*, ed. 1576, fol. 376, where he speaks of Gulielmus Occham 'as a worthy Divine and a right sincere Judgment, as the times would then either give or suffer'. Also in fol. 393 Foxe mentions the Dialogue as of Occham's writing, 'tho' it appeared without the name of the author'.

Relation of the Printed Edition to the English Manuscripts.

A careful comparison of the original Latin and the Trevisa MSS. with the printed edition leads conclusively to the following results:

A. That the printed edition is Trevisa's translation.
B. (1) That this edition has been revised by its editor from one of the Trevisa MSS. in our possession, with the help of the Latin original, *or*
   (2) That it is a copy of an original Trevisa MS. which is not now in existence.

A. *A Trevisa Translation.*

That the printed edition is a translation of Trevisa is evident from the following:

(*a*) There are many passages, sometimes two or three sentences, in the Pr. edition, exactly identical with the MSS. Very often these are very free translations of the Latin. Only a few examples are here given. The reader may test this for himself by comparing the Tr. MSS. with the Pr. in the text:

(1) 1. First Speech of Clericus.
(2) 2/12. Speech of Miles beg. 'what þei ordeyneþ' etc.— closing with 'vppon þe Kyngdom of England'.

(3) 4/10. A trewe cristen man. Lat. Christianus.
(4) 4/4–7. Beg. but ȝif hit may be schewide ... spiritualte.
(5) 6/2. twey diuerse tymes of crist. Lat. duo tempora in Christo.
(6) 10/2. Sentence beg. 'And ȝif ȝe wolleþ ȝett stryue etc.' l. 5, ȝoure strif schal not turne ȝow to worship atte laste. Lat. forsan ista pertinacia non erit in fine vobis gratiosa.
(7) 11/1. Tr. þanne it is soþe. Pr. for it is sothe. Lat. tenendum est igitur.
(8) 11/14. Lat. ergo etiam ratione peccati papa de sanguine iudicare. Tr. = Pr. þerfore bycause of synne þat siche men doþ þe pope schal deme and be domesman? In cause of felony & of mannes deþ.
(9) 16/10. Lat. quam homo mortalis. Tr. = Pr. in þat þat he was man y-schape for to dye.
(10) 17/10. Lat. utique operatiis & stipendiariis. Tr. = Pr. to werk men, to hyred men, to oxen & nouȝt to kynges.
(11) 22/10. Lat. regis religio. Tr. = Pr. þe good entent of þe kyng.
(12) 23/16. Lat. quod de bonis Ecclesiae secum tollunt. Tr. = Pr. takiþ to hem of holy chirche (Pr. churches) goodes & catel.
(13) 25/9. Lat. cogeremini omnibus seruire. Tr. = Pr. compelle ȝou to be þralles.
(14) 26/8. Lat. comedere splendide, iucunde bibere. Tr. = Pr. etc. & drynke wiþ grete solace & myrþe.
(15) 33/2. Lat. super orbem terrarum. Tr. = Pr. þe Emperour of his empire & þe kyng of his kyngdom.

(*b*) Certain Latin words are translated by two, sometimes three words. The words in Pr. are usually the same as in Tr. This coupling of words is one of Trevisa's characteristics:

(1) 4/5. Lat. quia non constat eum super temporalibus vestris dominium accepisse. Tr. = Pr. ffor ȝe knoweþ nouȝt þat he haþ lordschipe, power & auctorite vppon ȝoure temporalte (Pr. temporalties).
(2) 5/14. Lat. de vestris temporalibus statuere posse. Tr. = Pr. may ordeyne & make statutes of ȝoure temporalte.
(3) 6/3. Lat. alterum potestatis. Tr. = Pr. and anoþer of his power & mageste.
(4) 8/9. Lat. non ad temporale seu dominium assumptum. Tr. = Pr. & nouȝt in temporal lordschipe of casteles & of londes.
(5) 10/13. Lat. tollere principatus & regna. Tr. = Pr. þat he may take of princes & of kynges principates & kyngdoms.

Introduction

xlix

(6) 11/8. Lat. cognoscet de justo & iniusto. Tr. = Pr. schal knowe & deme of riȝtful & vnriȝtful.
(7) 11/10. Lat. debeat iudicare. Tr. = Pr. þe pope schal deme & rule.
(8) 12/12. Lat. in iudicio temporalium. Tr. = Pr. in knowleche & demynge of temporalte.
(9) 13/3. Lat. lacerata est lex. Tr. = Pr. þe lawe is y-tore and to-rent.
(10) 13/12. Lat. vestra cognitio. Tr. = Pr. ȝoure knowleche & ȝoure dome.
(11) 13/13. Lat. accedere debet. Tr. = Pr. schal refreyne & chastee.
(12) 14/7. Lat. per sententiam iuris. Tr. = Pr. by sentence & dome of lawe.
(13) 14/8. Lat. aut euidentiam sceleris. Tr. = Pr. oþer by open euydence & knowleche of þe trespass.
(14) 14/15. Lat. cognoscere de causa matrimonii. Tr. = Pr. to know & to deme in cause of matrimonye & of wedlock.
(15) 15/12. Lat. & saepe firmari possit regalibus instrumentis. Tr. = Pr. & schal be preued oþer dispreued by preues oþer dispreues of þe kynges lawe.
(16) 15/14. Lat. in cognitione. Tr. = Pr. in dome & in knowleche.
(17) 16/1. Lat. de haereditate iudicare. Tr. = Pr. to deme & dele heritage.
(18) 16/6. Lat. debet regere. Tr. = Pr. schal gouerne & rule.
(19) 23/13. Lat. vestram violentiam. Tr. = Pr. ȝoure violence & ȝoure wrong.
(20) 24/10. Lat. & bonorum vestrorum. Tr. = Pr. & of ȝoure owne godes and catel.
(21) 24/14. Lat. non perstrepite. Tr. = Pr. y pray ȝou leteþ be ȝoure noyse & ȝoure grucchyng.
(22) 26/2. Lat. sic estis nunc in vestris profectibus querulosi. Tr. = Pr. & so now ȝe playneþ & grucchiþ in ȝoure owne profit.
(23) 28/9, 29/5. Lat. materiali. Tr. = Pr. of lyme & of stoones.
(24) 28/14. Lat. salus. Tr. = Pr. helpe & sauacioun.
(25) 33/14. Lat. principum. Tr. of princes & of kynges. Pr. = kinges & princes.

(c) A number of short passages found in Tr. and Pr. which do not appear in the Latin original:

(1) 4/12. Whole sentence quoted beg.: 'axe of me' given in Tr. & Pr., but only the first part is given in Latin, viz. postula a me & dabo tibi gentes.

d

(2) 8/3, wolde have made hym kyng.
(3) 10/4, after his resurrectioun.
(4) 12/13, in what þat longeþ to temporalte.
(5) 13/15, whanne he seiþ euereche soule, hit semeþ þat noon is out take (Pr. = excepted).
(6) 14/17, for þe knyttinge of þe dede.
(7) 17/13, and of þe spiritualte.
(8) 20/11, beg. 'for þe whiche'. Tr. & Pr. nearly the same.
(9) 20/15, while ȝe recchiþ. 21/4, holy entent. 24/1, grete sclandre. 21/6, god almyȝty.

(d) A few phrases are found in Tr. and Pr., but are different in Latin:

(1) 3/1. Lat. super regnum Franciae. Tr. = Pr. vppon þe Kyngdom of Engelond.
(2) 15/1. Lat. ego vado Paduæ. Tr. = Pr. lo ich go into ȝoure cuntraye.
(3) 15/7. Lat. ducatum Burgundiae. Tr. = Pr. a ducherye.

(e) Passages not found in all the Tr. MSS., but where the Pr. agrees with the Latin:

(1) 5/4. Lat. quia Christianus sum & esse volo. Pr. = S. for he may not be wiþ-seide in no maner wise. (The other Tr. MSS. omit 'not' in 'may not'.)
(2) 8/6. Lat. quod procul a vobis sit. Pr. but god forbydde that they shulde so now (om. in H, but with slight variation found in the other Tr. MSS.).
(3) 11/6, after 'Miles'. Lat. hoc absit, nam qui hoc nega-uerit, poenitentiam & confessionem abnegabit. Pr. = other Tr. MSS. except H, but god hit forbydde for who þat denyeþ þat denyeþ.
(4) 23/7. Lat. ne animas mortuorum salutemque viuorum defrauderis. Pr. that ye begyle not and deceyue the quycke and the deed. (C only Tr. MS. similar to Pr.)—þat ȝe bigile not þe quyk and þe dede. (Other Tr. MSS. omit 'not' after 'bigile'.)
(5) 34/1, after 'nede', passage om. in H, but found in other Tr. MSS. and agrees with Lat. & Pr. Lat. nam & irridet scripturam vestram praescriptionem, cum a Salomone vsque ad Ioas & a Ioas vsque ad Ezechielem non legitur esse factum quod tamen Ezechiel perfecit (for English of Pr. & MSS. see text, p. 34).
(6) 35/1, after 'comynte', S similar to Pr. & Lat. Not in other Tr. MSS.
(7) 35/8, after 'nede', S similar to Pr. & Lat. Not in other Tr. MSS.

Introduction li

B (1). *An Editor's Revision.*

That the printed edition is a revision of one of the Trevisa MSS. with the help of the Latin original is evident from the following:

(a) Certain passages are found in Lat. & Pr., but not in the Tr. MSS.:

(1) 2/2. Lat. si nostra bono non damus. Pr. if we gyue not oure goodes. Tr. ȝif we ȝeueþ nouȝt.
(2) 2/8. Lat. iniurias innumeras. Pr. innumerable wrongs. Tr. wrong.
(3) 3/5, after 'auctorite'. Pr. beg. 'wherefor it is a thynge in vayne' etc. to end of sentence.
(4) 3/10, after 'whanne he haþ y-write'. Lat. sic totum erit vestrum. Pr. and so all thyng shall be yours.
(5) 5/1, after 'wordes'. Lat. nec nos ea scripsimus, sed ea misit Dominus & spiritus sanctus dictauit. Pr. nor we wrote them not, but god sente them, and the holy gooste spake them.
(6) 7/12, after 'erþe'. Lat. quia illa nobis necessaria sunt. Pr. for these thynges are necessary for us.
(7) 8/6, after 'kyngdom of heuene'. Lat. constat. Pr. also it is euydent & playne.
(8) 9/12, after 'first state'. Lat. sic patuit. Pr. it is playne.
(9) 10/16, one sentence after '& he dide so to ȝow'. Lat. = Pr.
(10) 11/12, after 'is riȝt nouȝt'. Lat. = Pr.
(11) 11/14, after 'vnriȝtful'. Lat. & peccatum etiam. Pr. and also synne.
(12) 15/2, after 'is eyr þerof'. Lat. videtis quod ratione matrimonii. Pr. ye see that by reason of matrimonye.
(13) 15/13, after 'kynges lawe'. Lat. = Pr. sentence beg. and for so moch.
(14) 18/12, after 'primat'. Lat. = Pr. for as the power — confounded.
(15) 21/11, after 'plesyng'. Lat. coram Domino. Pr. to oure lorde.
(16) 22/9, after 'goddes hous'. Lat. = Pr. and þey gaue hit — goddes hous.
(17) 36/1, after 'goddes lawe'. Pr. beg. Cleri. The emperours 35/27 ... be subiecte to the realme 36/26. The Pr. is a literal trans. of Latin.

(b) Passages in which Pr. is more literal than Tr.:
(1) 1, first speech of Miles. Tr. translates briefly, but Pr. is full and very close to Latin.

d 2

(2) 6/2. Tr. oon of his manhed. Pr. one of his humilitate. Lat. alterum humilitatis.
(3) 9/5. Tr. & serue mete bordes & gouerne temperalte. Pr. & serue meate, bourdes, that is to saye, to dispose temporall thyngs. Lat. ministrare mensae : id est temporalibus dispensandis.
(4) 11/12. Tr. þis argument is riʒt nouʒt. Pr. this is a forked argument. Lat. argumentum istud cornutum est.
(5) 13/5. Tr. riʒt wisnesse. Pr. ryghtful dome and iustyce. Lat. iustitiam & iudicium.
(6) 13/15. Tr. to þe over power. Pr. to the hyghe powers. Lat. potestatibus sublimioribus.
(7) 18/11. Tr. þe kynges prest. Pr. my priest. Lat. meus sacerdos.
(8) 19/10. Tr. ʒe stireþ me & wakiþ me as hit were of my sleep. Pr. ye awake the slepynge dogge. Lat. vos exercitatis canem dormientem.
(9) 22/8. Tr. & helde out & tolde þe money. Pr. and poured oute and tolde the money. Lat. effundebantque & numerabant pecuniam.
(10) 23/10. Tr. in chiuelrie. Pr. on your busy and unruly souldiers, and on shippes and ingins of warre. Lat. sed militares tumultus & bellicosas classes.
(11) 27/13. Tr. þat he hymsilf had do þere. Tr. that he hymselfe had there stycked up. Lat. quas ipse affixerat.
(12) 31/6. Tr. tribute. Pr. the tribute or dragme. Lat. census siue didrachma.

There are other passages, longer than these listed, where Pr. gives a literal translation, while Tr. is frequently incorrect, and very free.

(c) In the printed text the Biblical allusions are filled in and completed. Very often Trevisa differs from the Latin in the number of the chapter. Again, he is careless about giving the chapter number. These faults are remedied in the printed text. In nearly every case the printed agrees with the Latin. In one instance 21/10, Pr. = Lat. 2 Paral. 14 cap., which is corrected by Tr. to 2 Paral. 24º. 9/1. Lat. & Tr. give reference Luce. Pr. corrects this to Jo. 18 and Matt. 20. These, however, are exceptions. Usually Pr. has corrected Tr. to agree with the Latin. (The complete corrections will be found in the notes.)

(d) The printed edition omits Trevisa's note, pp. 6–7, on the nature of Christ's power and majesty.

(e) The printed edition gives a completed and finished ending to the *Dialogue*.

B (2). *The Dialogue as printed is from a copy of an original Trevisa MS.*

All the evidence given above under B (1) *a, b, c,* and *e* would also go to show that the editor or printer of the printed edition had a manuscript copy of the *Dialogue* much closer to Trevisa's original translation than our five MSS. If this be so our MSS. must be later mutilated copies. Why did the scribe in the MS. from which the printed copy is taken leave out the Trevisa note? The absence of this note seems to point to an editor's revision.

D. LATIN PRINTED EDITIONS.

The Dialogue.

1. 1470? Cologne. Printed by U. Zell. 4to. Without title-page, pagination, or catchwords; 16 leaves, 26 lines to a page. This edition contains a brief compendium concerning the nature of Antichrist.
2. 1475. Cologne, a second edition. 4to.
3. 1480? Vienna. Pr. by Johannes Salidi. 4to. 17 printed leaves, without title-page, pagination, or catchwords. 26 lines.
4. 1485? Ulm. 4to. 14 pages. Has section on Antichrist.
5. 1490? Augsburg. Pr. by J. Froschauer. 4to. 12 leaves with no pagination. Contains account of Antichrist.
6. 1490? Colonie. Pr. by Henricum Quentell. Account of Antichrist at end. Two copies in British Museum.
7. 1491. Deventer. Pr. by R. Paffroet. 4to. 9 leaves, 37 or 38 lines. No pagination or catchwords. Contains account of Antichrist.
8. 1495? Colonie. Pr. by Henricum Quentell. 4to.
9. 1531? Londini. Pr. by Thome Bertheleti. Disputatio inter Clericum et Militem ... sub forma Dialogi (Gulielmus de Occam).

10. 1609. Argentorati. Pr. by S. Schardius in *Syntagna Tractatum de Imperiali Jurisdictione.* 172 i. 1.
11. 1612–14. Hanover. 3 vols. Melchior Goldast, *Monarchia S. Romani Imperii.* (*Dialogue*, vol. i, pp. 13–18.)

The Sermon.

1. 1475? Louvain. 34 leaves, 30 lines to a page. No title-page, pagination, or catchwords.
2. 1480? Louvain. 26 leaves, 33 lines to a page.
3. 1485. Rouen. 50 leaves, 23 lines, without pagination. (Two copies in Br. Mus.)
4. 1495. Paris. Pr. by Ant. Caillant. 47 pages, 34 lines to a page. (Camb. Univ. Lib.)
5. 1496. Lyons. Pr. by J. Trechsel. 28 leaves, in double cols. 55 lines, no pagination. (Two copies in Br. Mus.)
6. 1496. Lugduno. Pr. by Marco Alexandro Beneventano. (Bodl. Library.)
7. 1500? Paris. Pr. by A. Cayllant. 27 leaves, 34 lines to a page. No pagination.
8. 1535. Coloniae. By O. Gratius. 1690, London, ed. Edward Brown. 2 Tom. *Fasciculus rerum expetendarum et fugiendarum.* (*Sermon* in vol. ii, pp. 466–86.)
9. 1612–14. Hanover. 3 vols. Melchior Goldast, *Monarchia S. Romani Imperii.* (*Sermon*, vol. ii, pp. 1392–1410.)
10. 1625. Paris. Pr. by Joan Libert. (Two copies in Bodl. Library; one, 136 pages, bound up with a number of other articles in Latin and Greek; the other bound alone, same number of pages, same date and printer.)
11. 1633. Paris. Pr. by Petrum Billaine. 8vo. (Two copies in Br. Mus.)

Methodius.

1. 1470? *Revelationes.* Pr. by Bonaventure. 4to.
2. 1490? Memmingen. By Albert Kunne. Edition of *Revelationes.*
3. 1496. Augsburg. Pr. by Johannes Froschauer. 4to. (Three copies in Br. Mus. A few MS. notes.)
4. 1498. Basilee. Pr. by M. Furter. 4to. Ed. by S. Brant. 68 pages, without pagination.

5. 1504. Basilee. Pr. by M. Furter (also in 1514 and 1515). Ed. with a preface by S. Brant. 4to. (All copies in Br. Mus.)
6. 1555. Basileae. Pr. by Johann Heroldt, *Orthodoxographa Theologia Sacro Sanctae ac Syncerioris Fidei Doctores numero LXXVII*.
7. 1569. Basileae. J. J. Grynaeus, *Monumenta S. Patrum Orthodoxographa*, etc. (*Revelationes* in Greek, vol. i, pp. 93–100. Latin, pp. 100–13.) 3 vols.
8. 1618–22. Coloniae Agrippinae. Ed. Margarinus de la Bigne; *Magna Bibliotheca Veterum Patrum, et Antiquorum Scriptorum Ecclesiasticorum*. 15 tom.
9. 1654. Paris. Ed. by M. de la Bigne, *Magna Bibliotheca*, etc. 17 tom.
10. 1677. Lugduni. Genuae. Ed. M. de la Bigne, *Magna Bibliotheca*, etc. 28 tom. (*Revelationes*, tom. 3, pp. 727–34.)

PART II

TREVISA'S LIFE AND WORKS.

It shall be my aim in these notes to put into condensed form some of the things written about Trevisa, the present known facts in regard to his life and work, and one or two discoveries that have been made during the course of this investigation. I regret that I have not been able to get at all the possible sources, that I was not able to go to Cornwall to examine the muniments at Castle Horneck, Pentillie Castle, and Mount Edgcumbe.[1] The Charters and Muniments of Berkeley Castle,[2] where Trevisa spent most of his life, were not examined.

---

[1] In a letter dated June 3, 1915, Mr. P. E. B. Porter, The Hermitage, Saltash, Cornwall, wrote me that in a recent interview Lord Mount Edgcumbe told him that the Edgcumbe MSS. had recently been noted and classified. There was no reference to Trevisa.

[2] The MSS. at Berkeley were catalogued by Mr. J. H. Jeayes in 1892. Lord Fitzhardinge's secretary, May 31, 1915, wrote me that this catalogue is complete.

I was greatly aided in this search by the suggestions of noted Cornish antiquarians. They all think that careful search will reveal new information in regard to Trevisa's life.

The known facts about Trevisa are that he belonged to a Cornish family, he was a student at Oxford, was Vicar of Berkeley, and while there translated certain works from Latin into English.

A. Trevisa's Life.

The notes on Trevisa's life group themselves around:
(1) The place and date of his birth.
(2) Oxford days.
(3) His life at Berkeley.

I. *Place and Date of his Birth.*

No records thus far have come to hand giving us the exact place and date of his birth. Most of his biographies mention Crocadon or Caradok, Cornwall, as his birthplace. Later writers give the date of his birth as well. These dates run from 1322 to 1342.

Bale[1] and Pits[2] mention Cornwall only, while Tanner,[3] Fuller,[4] Carew,[5] Townley,[6] and Sir John MacLean[7] speak of his birthplace as Caradok or Crocadon, without giving the date.

Gilbert[8] says: 'In 13— was born at Crocadon, in the parish of St. Mellion, near Saltash, John Trevisa, who was educated

---

[1] John Bale, *Scriptorum Illustrium Majoris Brit. Cat.*, Bâle, 1559, p. 518 (genere ac pàtria Cornubiensis).

[2] Joannis Pitsei, *De Illustribus Angliae Scriptoribus*, Paris, 1619, No. 724 (Patria Cornubiensis).

[3] Thomas Tanner, *Bibl. Britannico-Hibernico*, London, 1748, p. 720 (Patria Cornubiensis apud Caradok natus).

[4] Thomas Fuller, *Worthies of England*, 2 vols., 1622, ed. 1811, vol. i, p. 217 (born at Caradok in Cornwall); id., *The Church History of Britain*, London, 1655, Bk. IV, p. 151 (born at Crocadon in Cornwall).

[5] Richard Carew, *Survey of Cornwall*, ed. 1602, 1769, 1811 . . . p. 269 (Crocadon is the mansion of Charles Trevisa, Esq., descended from John Trevisa, born in this place, as I am informed, bred at Oxford).

[6] Rev. Jas. Townley, *Illustrations of Bibl. Lit.*, 1821, vol. ii, pp. 49-55 (born at Caradoc in Co. of Cornwall).

[7] Sir John MacLean, *The Lives of the Berkeleys* (The Berkeley MSS.), by John Smyth of Nibley, 3 vols., 1883, vol. i, p. 343.

[8] C. S. Gilbert, *Historical Survey of the Co. of Cornwall*, 2 vols., 1817, p. 128, vol. i.

Introduction

at Oxford &c.' Rogers[1] quotes Carew: 'John de Trevisa was born according to our county historian, Carew, at Crocadon, near Saltash (Carew's *Cornwall*, ed. 1811, p. 269) &c. in the year 1342.' Boase and Courtney:[2] 'Born at Crocadon in St. Mellion 1326.' Cooke[3] places his birth at Crocadon, in the parish of St. Mellion, near Saltash about 1322. C. W. Boase gives the date 1342.[4] Hals[5] says he was born in Gloucestershire, giving Baker as his authority.

Crocadon was situated in the parish of St. Mellion in Hundred of East. An adjoining parish was St. Enedor, in Hundred of Pyder, in which was situated Trevisa, or Tre-wisa.[6] Carew[7] speaks of Crocadon as a district near Halton and Cultayle (Calstock), describing it thus: 'Upon the top of a creek herby lyeth Crocadon, the mansion of M. Trevisa, a Gent. deriving himself from the ancient and wel deserving chronicler of that name: he beareth G., a garbe, O.' Hals in his note gives us the meaning of the word, which agrees with Carew: 'Croca-don, or Croucadon, Cruco-don, words signifying bank, hillock or tumulus, hill or town, a place noticeable for banners.'

There is evidence that this Crocadon, near Saltash, was the family seat of the Trevisas, at least through the sixteenth and seventeenth centuries, and up to the beginning of the eighteenth, but this evidence does not go back far enough for our present study.

The earliest marriage in the Trevisa family recorded by Vivian was in 1596, December 1, between John Trevisa of St. Mellion and Margaret Courtney of Lazacke.[8] Many marriages

[1] John J. Rogers, *Journal of the Royal Institution of Cornwall*, No. XI, April 1870, pp. 147 ff.
[2] G. C. Boase and W. P. Courtney, *Bibl. Cornubiensis*, 3 vols., 1874–82, vol. ii, p. 795.
[3] Jas. Herbert Cooke, *Trans. of Bristol and Gloucester Arch. Soc.*, 1876, vol. i, p. 138.
[4] Rev. C. W. Boase, *Registrum Collegii Exoniensis* (Ox. Hist. Soc.), Clarendon Press, 1894, p. 11.
[5] Wm. Hals, *Parochial Hist. of Cornwall*, 4 vols. 1867–72 (ed. Jos. Polsue), vol. i, p. 339; vol. iii, p. 309.
[6] Hals, *Parochial Hist. of Cornwall*, vol. i, p. 339; vol. iii, p. 305; Daniels and Collins, *History of Cornwall*, p. 419; John Norden, *A Typographical Hist. Des. of Cornwall*, London, 1728, p. 92.
[7] Carew, *Survey of Cornwall*, ed. 1602, p. 114.
[8] Col. J. L. Vivian, *The Marriage Licences of the Diocese of Exeter*, 1887, p. 12.

Introduction

of the Trevisas of St. Erth and St. Mellion are recorded in the seventeenth century.

We get no help concerning John Trevisa and his ancestry from the parish registers of Cornwall, as the earliest begins in 1539.

The best evidence we have that Trevisas lived at Crocadon, at or near the time of our Trevisa's birth, is given by Vivian in his *Visitations of Cornwall*.[1] The earliest date he gives in his genealogical table is 1598. This is, however, the death of a Trevisa of the third generation in his list. The first of this table is here given:

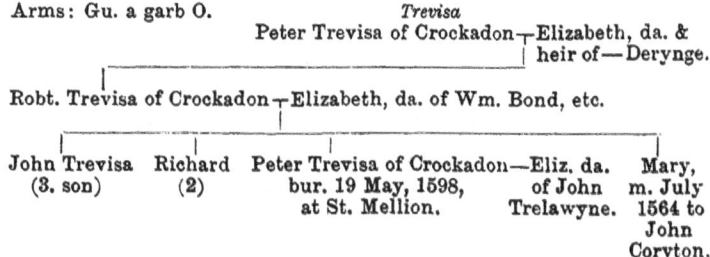

Arms: Gu. a garb O.   *Trevisa*
                Peter Trevisa of Crockadon—Elizabeth, da. & heir of—Derynge.

Robt. Trevisa of Crockadon—Elizabeth, da. of Wm. Bond, etc.

John Trevisa (3. son) | Richard (2) | Peter Trevisa of Crockadon—Eliz. da. of John Trelawyne. bur. 19 May, 1598, at St. Mellion. | Mary, m. July 1564 to John Coryton.

The pedigree continues (pp. 509–10) to 1703, to Wm. Trevisa, posthumous son of Wm. Trevisa of Crocadon and Mary Dorothy, da. ———. He was buried March 19, 1703–4, at St. Mellion. He took his seat in Parliament for Callington in 1679.[2] Mr. Cooke[3] thinks the family became extinct with the death of this William in 1703. The estate was sold about 1690 to Sir Wm. Coryton, the ancestor of the present owner, Col. Coryton of Pentillie Castle. Crocadon was the seat of the Corytons until they removed to Pentillie in Pellaton, 1812.[4]

By Vivian's tables we learn that the Trevisas married into many of the noted families of that part of Cornwall, e. g. (1) Courtenay of Landrake, p. 117; (2) Coryton of West Newton (see above table), p. 101; (3) Buller of Shillingham

---

[1] Col. J. L. Vivian, *The Visitations of Cornwall* (comprising the Heralds Visitations of 1530, 1573, 1620), London and Exeter, 1877, pp. 506–10.

[2] W. P. Courtney, *Parl. Hist. of Cornwall*, 1889, p. 273.

[3] J. H. Cooke, *Trans. of Bristol and Gloucester Arch. Soc.*, 1876, vol. i, pp. 138 ff.

[4] Joseph Polsue, *Parochial Hist. of Cornwall*, 4 vols., 1867–72, vol. iii, p. 309.

(Trevisa of Trevisa), p. 56 ; (4) Battersby of Battersby Hall, in Com. York, p. 21.

Gilbert[1] says : 'The Arms of Trevisa, Gules, a Garbe, Or.[2] appear among the quarterings of several of the principal families of Cornwall, and that few have a fairer claim with respect to antiquity.' They are found in the quarterings of such families as Vyvyan, Trelowarren and Buller.[3] The Vivian family coat of arms is as follows : ' Arms :—Arg. on the waves of the sea, Az. a lion rampant, Gu. quartering ; 2 Ferrers, 3 Arundel, 4 Glyn, 5 Thretherffe, 6 St. Aubyn, 7 Chalons, 8 Charlton, 9 Leigh, 10 Courtney and Redvers quarterly, 11 Trevisa. Crest : a horse, passant, . . .'[4]

Many of the Trevisas held seats in Parliament during these centuries. Polsue points out that Ralph de Trevysa was M.P. for Liskeard in 1357 ; for Lostwithiel 1360-2 ; and Ralph and Richard Trevisa were M.P.s for Launceston in 1371.[5] In Cal. of Close Rolls, 45 Edw. III, m. 33 d, Mar. 29, and m. 29 d, Apr. 27, Ralph Trevysa is one of the burgesses for Donhevedburgh, although in index given under Launceston. We thus see that the Trevisa family was of some importance in the fourteenth century in the county of Cornwall.

The only reference to the Trevisas in the Calendar of Wills and Administrations relating to the counties of Devon and Cornwall (1540-1798)[6] is to Wm. Trefusis, St. Earth in 1594. This is a very common name, in this part of Cornwall, during the fifteenth century. In ancient deeds, numbered A 10401, 14 Henry IV ;[7] A 9948, 4 Henry V ;[8] and A 11429, 18 Richard II,[9] Henry Trefusa appears as a witness. In an Ancient Deed marked A 13009, 13 Henry VI,[10] John Trefusis appears as a witness to a feoffment.

---

[1] Gilbert's *Survey of England*, vol. ii, p. 309.

[2] Rogers (see p. lvii) points out that this coat of arms is confirmed by a MS. note-book of the Heralds' Visitation of Cornwall in Camden's time in possession of Wm. Borlasse, of Castle Horneck.

[3] Gilbert's *Survey*, vol. i, p. 159.

[4] Pedigree of Family of Vivian of Cornwall, reprinted from *Visitations*, by Lieut.-Col. J. L. Vivian.

[5] Polsue, *Hist. of Cornwall*, vol. iii, p. 309 ; Gilbert, vol. ii, p. 309.

[6] Edward Alex. Fry, *Cal. of Wills and Administrations of Devon and Cornwall*, 1908, p. 183.

[7] *A Description of Ancient Deeds in Public Record Office*, London, 5 vols., 1902, vol. iv, p. 550.

[8] Ibid., p. 482.

[9] Ibid., vol. v, p. 143.

[10] Ibid., vol. v, p. 426.

Ancient Deeds, A 10385,[1] Feoffment of John Trevisa and Amisia his wife to Henry Trewysa and Martin Pendre of all lands, &c., in the towns of Lannargh Mor, &c., 10 Aug., 22 Edward IV. Also in Ancient Deeds, A 9454,[2] a general release by John Carewe, clerk, and Richard Lannargh Vian to John Trevisa, Christopher Barlowe, &c., 16 Oct., 2 Henry VII. In A 10293,[3] bond by Wm. Luddi to John Trevisa, Elizabeth Lannargh and Marina Lannargh in 20l. at Easter, 13 Feb., 1 Richard III. Also a deed dated 1390, by which Henry de Trefussa grants to John Myn of Helstonburgh, in tail, a messuage and an acre of land in Helston (Anc. Deeds, A 10341).[4]

We thus see that the Trevisas resided at Crocadon at least in the sixteenth and seventeenth centuries, that this was an important family in the adjacent sections during the fourteenth and fifteenth centuries; but it is not evident that they resided at Crocadon at the time of John Trevisa's birth. The evidence seems to be that the family did not settle there until the middle of the fifteenth century. According to Feudal Aid 1428 the landholder in demesne of Croketon, in that year, was Richard Geade. He receives a feudal aid of 11s. 11d. for land held in Croketon, in Hundredum De Est.[5] Feudal aid was granted to the previous owner Johanne (de Ferrariis) in 1346.[6]

The name *Trevisa*.

Cooke, in his article on Trevisa and the Chapel at Berkeley Castle, was the first of the modern writers to call attention to the name. 'There is no authority,' he says, 'for the *de* often prefixed, the name being one of the old Cornish, "Tre, Pol, and Pen" names.'[7]

There was a place, Trevisa, or Tre-wisa in S. Enedor, and Hals thinks the family name came from this.[8] The same opinion is held by Henry Jenner, F.S.A., Hon. Secretary of the Royal Institute of Cornwall. He says: 'The family name

---

[1] *A Description of Ancient Deeds in Public Record Office*, London, vol. iv, p. 548.
[2] Ibid., vol. iv, p. 425.
[3] Ibid., vol. iv, p. 532.
[4] Ibid., vol. iv. p. 548.
[5] *Feudal Aids* (1284–1431), vol. i, p. 234.
[6] Ibid., vol. i, p. 212.
[7] Jas. Herbert Cooke, *Trans. of Bristol and Gloucester Arch. Soc.*, 1876, vol. i, p. 138.
[8] Hals, *Parochial Hist. of Cornwall*, vol. iii, p. 305.

Introduction

evidently comes from a place called Trevisa, which is *Trev-isa*, the lower town. When it occurs it is contrasted with Trewhella, which is *Tre whella*, the upper or higher town. There is a Trevisa in St. Enedor, and close by a Trewhella. But the more usual contracted names with the same meaning are Trewartha and Trewallas.¹ In his article in the *Celtic Review*, he speaks of these differentiating epithets, *wartha* and *wallas*, for upper and lower, *gwida* and *dew*, for white and black, *mear* and *bean* for great and little.²

II. *Life at Oxford.*

When we come to consider his student days at Oxford, we are on surer ground. There are at least a few definite records as to his career. This period of his life is not mentioned by either Bale or Pits. Tanner speaks of it thus: 'Trevisa (Johannes) Collegi Exon. dein reginalis Oxon. socius.'³

According to Boase, he entered Exeter College, Lent 1362, remaining there until the winter of 1365. A Fellow of Queen's 1369-74, he was expelled in 1379, but as late as 1396 was paying xiii *s.* iiii *d.* for a chamber at Queen's.⁴ He was a student at Exeter in 1362, for in one of the Computi of the then Rector of Exeter College, Robert de Clist or Clyst, mention is made of John Trevysa.⁵ Among the Rector's accounts is that for the 'allowances dietis of John Trevyse, who came into commons on Sunday in the same week'.⁵ Lent 1362, 'pro dietis Johannis Trevyse qui venit ad comunas die dominica, viii *d.*'⁵ In the

---

¹ In a letter dated August 4, 1914.

² Henry Jenner, 'Cornwall a Celtic Nation', in *Celtic Review*, 1904, vol. i, pp. 234-45. The Rev. R. Polwhele, in *Hist. of Cornwall*, 1803, has the note: ' *Trev*, a house, ' *Trevissan*, the lower town.' In the *Cornish Drama*, 2 vols., trans. and ed. by Edwin Norris, Oxford, 1859, vol. ii, p. 427, under the word Trevedic (*trefedig*, inhabited, *trefedigion*, dwellers, from *tref*, a hamlet, W. *treb*, anc. Ir.); *treabh*, f. Gaelic, pron. *trev*. In *Parliamentary Hist. of Cornwall*, by W. P. Courtney, 1889, we find several Cornish names in 'Tre', Trelawny, Tremayne, Treffry, Trenwith, Trewinnard, still surviving in Cornwall.

³ Thos. Tanner, *Bibl. Brit.-Hib.*, 1748, p. 720.

⁴ C. W. Boase, *Register of Exeter College*, 1894, p. 11.

⁵ *Historical Manuscripts Commission*, Report II (Exeter College, 1870, pp. 128, 129); also Boase, *Register of Exeter College*, Introd., li. Noticed by John J. Rogers of Penrose, *Journal of Royal Institution of Cornwall* (*Trans.*), vol. iii, April 1874, p. 262.

computi of the Rector Robert de Clist for the year 1364, in his rendering of accounts, we find: 'xii *d.* pro condutione duorum equorum quando Rector et Johannes Trevyse fuerunt apud West Wyttenham ad componendum cum firmariis pro horreo faciendo. Autumn 1364 (pensiones sociorum) vii *s.* v *d.* ob. q. Johanni Trevisa.'

We have no record of when he left Exeter and became a Fellow at Queen's. As noticed above, Boase says, 'he was a Fellow at Queen's from 1369-74, was expelled in 1379, &c.' Among the Computi of 1371-2 of Queen's, in a list of payments to the Fellows, we find that 'Trevisa (who had now removed to this College from Exeter College) received half a mark and one penny'.[1] Also in the same year under the expenses of the chapel is the following entry: 'The expenses of Middelworth and Trevisa, in showing the muniments of the Church of Newbold (Newbold Pacey, Co. Warwick) at Strettone, and their charges on the road 36 *d.*).'[1] In the Computus of Robert Blakedone for 1372-3 the name of John Trevisa appears as a Fellow.

In 1379 he, with the Provost and other Fellows, was expelled from Queen's. There seems to have been serious trouble at Oxford about the beginning of Richard I's reign. Anthony Wood, referring to the year 1379, speaks of certain controversies, and says:

'For so great was the enormity between the Provost and Fellows of the same three years since, whether upon account of heresy or elevation of a Provost, I know not, that they not only brought a scandal but a visitation on the College. Alexander Nevile, Arch. of York, receiving divers appeals and complaints from them, sent his Com. to visit the College.'[2]

Evidence of this trouble is found in Close Rolls, 50 Edw. III, m. 9:

'The Provost and Scholars of the College called La Quenehalle, Oxford, of which the Arch. of York is visitor, are commanded to observe all ordinances and statutes of the College, and to be obedient to the Arch., and to the Commissaries whom he

---

[1] *Historical MSS. Commission*, Report II (Queen's College, Oxford), 1870, p. 140; Rogers. *J. of R. I. C.*, vol. iv, April 1870, p. 262.

[2] J. Gutch, edition of Anthony Wood's *Antiquities and Annals*, 1792, vol. i, Bk. I, p. 495.

Introduction lxiii

sends to correct defects and disputes which have arisen in the College, 18 Nov.'¹

There appear expulsions before that of Trevisa and his associates, for in a Close Roll, 1 Richard II, January 10, Fellows were excluded from the College because of disputes between the Provost and the Scholars, concerning statutes of the College: 'and these statutes having been ratified and confirmed by the King, he commands Thomas de Karlell, Provost of the College, and the Scholars to re-elect the excluded Fellows, if there be evidence of humility and amendment in them'.² (1378, Jan. 10.)

The next mention of trouble at Queen's in the Rolls is that in Patent, 1 Richard II, pt. v, m. 26 (April 6), where a commission is given to Thomas de la Mare, Knight, Edmund de Stonore and Reginald de Sheffeld and those deputed by them, to command Richard de Thorpe, clerk, William Frank, and William Middleworth, clerk, to restore to Master Thomas de Carlol, Provost of the College called 'Quenehalle', Oxford, the college seal, writings, muniments, keys, books and goods, failing to do which they are to be arrested and brought before the Council at Westminster for punishment.³

On June 26, 1379 (Close Rolls, 3 Rich. II, m. 41), the Chancellor and Rectors of the University of Oxford were commanded to inquire by a jury, in whose hands now are the charters, books, jewels, and other muniments, goods, and chattels of the College called The Quenhalle, which were taken away by certain of the scholars now removed.⁴ Trevisa's name does not appear in the order.

On May 1, 1380 (Patent Rolls, 3 Rich. II, pt. ii, m. 30), a pardon of outlawry was granted to Master William Middleworth, for not appearing to render chattels to Master Thomas Karlell, Provost of the College called 'le Quenhall'.⁵

---

¹ *Calendar of Close Rolls*, 1374–7, p. 400. Mentioned in *Statutes of Oxford Colleges*, 3 vols., 1853, vol. iii, App., p. 32.

² *Calendar of Close Rolls*, Rich. II, 1377–81, p. 42; also *Statutes of Oxford Colleges*, vol. iii, App., p. 33.

³ *Calendar of Patent Rolls*, Rich. II, 1377–81, p. 204; also *Statutes of Oxford Colleges*, vol. iii, App., p. 33.

⁴ *Calendar of Close Rolls*, Rich. II, 1377–81, p. 258; *Statutes of Oxford Colleges*, vol. iii, App., p. 34.

⁵ *Calendar of Patent Rolls*, Rich. II, 1377–81, p. 432.

Anthony Wood[1] states that in 1379 Mr. Henry Whytefield, the Provost, Mr. Will Fraunke, Mr. Robert Lydeford, and Mr. John Trevisa, Fellows, were expelled by the second visitation of the Archbishop of York (no reference to this in Patent or Close Rolls), and that they took with them divers charters, books, jewels, money, and goods belonging to the College. Wood makes the order as in Close Rolls, 3 Rich. II, m. 41 (see above), refer to these thefts by the Fellows first mentioned. His statement is not in agreement with the Rolls, nor is there any mention of the expulsion of Trevisa before October 20, 1379 (Patent Rolls, 3 Rich. II, pt. i, m. 20 d), when a 'Commission of oyer and terminer' is granted

'to the chancellor of the University of Oxford for the time being, Master John de Bloxham, Master Thomas Walleworth, Master John de Calton, and Master Robert Dix after enquiry at Oxford into the complaint of Master Thomas de Karlell, Provost of 'Quenehalle', and the scholars of that college, that Master Henry Whitfield, late provost, and Master William Fraunk, Master Robert Lydeford, and Master John Trevisa, late scholars and fellows thereof, who have been excluded therefrom for their unworthiness (*exigentibus demeritis*), refuse to account for certain moneys of the college that came to their hands as well before the cession of the said Henry and the exclusion of the other three as after, and have taken away charters, books, jewels and muniments, besides goods belonging to the college.'[2]

Also Feb. 7, 1380 (Patent Rolls, 3 Rich. II, pt. ii, m. 12 d) a commission of oyer and terminer

'to Master William Berton, Chancellor of the University of Oxford, Master John Shirburn, Master Thomas Swyndon and Master Robert Bix, on complaint of Master Thomas Karlell, the provost, and the scholars of the college " Le Quenehall ", Oxford, that Master Henry Whitfield, the late provost, Master William Fraunk, Master Robert Lideford and Master John Trevisa, late scholars and fellows of the college, now excluded therefrom, refuse to account for money which came to their hands, as well before the resignation of the said Henry and the exclusion of the said William, Robt. and John, as afterwards, and also took away charters, books, jewels and other muniments belonging to the college and pledged the same. The commis-

---

[1] *Antiquities and Annals*, vol. i, Bk. I, p. 495.

[2] *Calendar of Patent Rolls*, Rich. II, 1377–81, p. 420.

Introduction

sioners are to proceed by sworn examination of both parties and other scholars of the University and to compel restitution.'[1]

These charters of the University were found and voluntarily restored by Mr. Whytefield to Mr. Thomas Karliel, Provost of the College.[2]

Trevisa's career at Oxford did not end in 1379, for, according to Thomson, he was mentioned as a Fellow in a Computus of 1385, along with William Trevillis, another Cornish man. Also in 1386-7 he paid the College four marks for four years' room rent, 'and six and eight pence for expenses of some proceedings against him ; whilst on the back of the roll where these entries occur is a memorandum half illegible, that seems to say he did not pay the sum, ' *de obligatione* '.[3] Later than this we find him at Oxford. In the Computi for 19 Richard II (1395-6) he is entered as paying 14*s*. 4*d*. yearly for a chamber rented at Queen's, although no longer a Fellow. In the Roll for 22-3 Rich. II, 1398-9, he is entered as still paying, and it is further stated that this is only part of the amount which he formerly paid.[4]

III. *Life at Berkeley Castle.*

Bale, Pits, and Tanner all tell us that he was Vicar of Berkeley (Vicarius de Berkeley). Rogers says: 'He was appointed domestic chaplain at Berkeley Castle by Thomas Lord Berkeley, who subsequently presented him to the Vicarage of Berkeley, where he is believed to have died A.D. 1412, at the ripe age of 70.'[5] Boase and Courtney say that he was 'Vicar of Berkeley, Gloucestershire, Chaplain to Thomas, Maurice, and Thomas, eighth, ninth, and tenth Lords of Berkeley, 1350-1412 ; that he resided generally in Gloucestershire, travelled in Germany and Savoy, died at Berkeley 1412, and was buried in the Chancel of the church '.[6]

Trevisa was at Berkeley when he finished his *Polychronicon*

---

[1] *Calendar of Patent Rolls*, Rich. II, 1377-81, p. 470.

[2] Gutch, ed. of Wood's *Antiquities and Annals*, vol. i, Bk. I, p. 496.

[3] William Thomson, *An Open College Best for All*, 1854.

[4] *Hist. MSS. Com.*, Report II, 1870, p. 141.

[5] J. J. Rogers, *J. of R. I. C.*, No. 11, April 1870, p. 147.

[6] Boase and Courtney, *Bibl. Cornub.*, vol. ii, p. 798.

in 1387,[1] and when he finished his *Bartholomaeus* in 1398.[1] His death took place there in 1402.[2] We have no evidence as to when he was appointed Vicar of Berkeley. If the Berkeley MS., *Lives of the Berkeleys*, is correct, he was there as early as 1357, and had completed his most important translation at this early date.[3] The only information of his life at Berkeley, beside the above date, is to be found in the *Lives of the Berkeleys* (from the Berkeley MSS.) from 1066-1618, by John Smyth of Nibley, edited by Sir John MacLean, 3 vols., 1883. A very careful examination of recent date of the Bishops' Registers (unprinted) of the diocese of Worcester, 1350-1420, gives us no information concerning Trevisa except the date of his death.

Trevisa was Vicar at Berkeley under three of the Lords, viz. Thomas III, eighth lord, born 1293, ruled 1326-61; Maurice IV, his son, 1361-8; and Thomas IV (grandson of Thomas III), born 1353, held sway 1368-1417.[4] The first entry concerning Trevisa in Smyth's *Lives of the Berkeleys* is in the life of Thomas III, and reads thus:

'And pardon mee, oh my God, in my overflowing affection to this Lord Thomas, if I break out in prayer before thee, to remember the dust of this thy honorable servant, resting in Berkeley Church, in the travells and pious ways wherein hee walked, and forget not (lord) thy doctrine taught him by thy learned servant his Chaplen, John Trevisa, vicar of the same church, whose bones rest there alsoe.'[5]

A few pages later, we find that he was at Berkeley a short time before 1361. 'In the later days of this lord Thomas flourished John Trevisa, a gen^t. of an antient family bearing gules, a garbe *or*, born at Crocadon in Cornwall, a secular preist and vicar of Berkeley; who translated the Bible, etc.'[6]

---

[1] See closing words of these works, pp. lxxxiv and lxxxviii.

[2] See p. lxxv for Register's entry.

[3] See p. lxxxiv for discussion of dates 1357 and 1387. Smyth has him Vicar of Berkeley in 1351 *Lives of Berkeleys*, vol. i, p. 19). Rev. J. H. Bloom, Vicar of Whitchurch, Stratford-on-Avon, who examined the Bishops' Registers of Worcester for me, writes Feb. 12, 1915, that, in 1360, 'one Master David was Vicar of Berkeley'. Bishops' Reg. Bryan 1. 108 d.

[4] Sir John MacLean, *Lives of the Berkeleys*, by John Smyth, 3 vols., 1883, vol. i, pp. 279-361; G. F. Clark, 'Berkeley Castle', in *Bristol and Gloucester Trans.*, 1876, p. 115.

[5] MacLean, ibid., vol. i, p. 338.

[6] Ibid., p. 343.

He speaks of him dedicating the Bible and *Polychronicon* to this lord, and *Bartholomaeus* and other treatises to this lord's son and grandson.

(a) *Canon at Westbury Collegiate Church.*

Boase says he was 'canon of Westbury, near Bristol'.[1] Boase and Courtney that he was 'Canon of Collegiate Church of Westbury on Severn or Gloucestershire (or, according to another account, of Westbury in Wiltshire)'.[2] Cooke states: 'Wickliff was appointed in 1374 to the crown living of Lutterworth; he also held the prebend of Aust in the Collegiate Church of Westbury-on-Trym in Gloucester, of which church Trevisa was likewise a Canon.'[3] Miss Greenwood: 'He also, like Wyclif, held a non-resident canonry of the Collegiate Church of Westbury-on-Trym.'[4] H. J. Wilkins: 'In 1387 John Trevisa, who was one of the fathers of English prose, became a canon, and held it till he died in 1412.'[5] C. L. Kingsford, in the *Dictionary of National Biography*, writes: 'He was also a canon of Westbury-on-Severn.'[6] Tanner, quoting Dugdale: 'Canonicus ecclesiae collegiate de Westbury in comit Wilts sive Gloucest.'[7] Dugdale: 'A cannon of the Collegiate Church of Westbury in Com. Wilts,' and gives the important reference Rot. Franc., 14 R. 2, M. 10.[8] Babington says: 'Canon of the Collegiate Church of Westbury on Severn in Gloucestershire, or, according to Dugdale, *Baronage*, vol. ii, p. 360, of Westbury in Wiltshire.'[9]

These writers have noticed three different Westburys:

1. Westbury, Comit. Wilts., in the diocese of Salisbury.
2. Westbury-on-Severn, now having a population of 2,000, post town Newnham, in the Archdeaconry of Hereford, in the diocese of Gloucester, and formerly with the church in the patronage of Vicar's Choral of Hereford.

---

[1] Boase, op. cit., p. 11.
[2] Op. cit., p. 798.
[3] Op. cit., p. 138.
[4] Miss Alice Greenwood, *Camb. Hist. of Eng. Lit.*, vol. ii, pp. 80–100.
[5] Rev. H. J. Wilkins, *Some Chapters in the Eccl. Hist. of Westbury-on-Trym*, Bristol, 1909, p. 96.
[6] C. L. Kingsford, article on Trevisa, vol. lvii.
[7] Op. cit., p. 720.
[8] Wm. Dugdale, *The Baronage of England*, 1675-6, 3 vols., vol. i, p. 360. Rot. Franc., 14 R. etc. is now catalogued at Record Office as Treaty Roll, No. 75 (see next page).
[9] Higden's *Polychronicon* (Rolls Series), vol. i, p. liv (note).

3. Westbury-on-Trym (or Trim), with a population of 10,000, near Bristol, in the Archdeaconry of Gloucester, now of the diocese of Bristol and formerly of Gloucester, and before the sixteenth century in the diocese of Worcester.

Trevisa was canon of a collegiate church at Westbury in 1390–1. The Treaty Rolls, 14 Rich. II, m. 10 (now catalogued in the Record Office as Treaty Roll No. 75) referred to by Dugdale, has this entry:

'Magister Johannes Trevysa vicarius ecclesie de Berkele et canonicus ecclesie collegiate de Westbury (qui de licencia Regis ad partes transmarinas profecturus est habet literas Regis de generali attornatu) sub nominibus Magistri Roberti de Hodersale clerici et Magistri Williami de Faryngton, clerici. Teste Rege apud Westmonasterium quinto de Novembris.

'Robertus de Faryngton, clericus, recepit attornatum usque redditum predicti Johannis in Anglia.'

It is not clear why Dugdale, from this evidence, makes Trevisa 'a cannon of the Collegiate Church of Westbury in Com. Wilts.' Nor is it clear why Tanner, quoting from Dugdale, makes him 'canonicus ecclesiae collegiate de Westbury in Comit. Wilts sive Glocest.' No evidence has thus far come to hand showing at which Westbury he was canon. The Treaty Roll states that he was 'canon of the collegiate church at Westbury'. The Episcopal Bishops' Registers of Worcester (1350–1420), recently examined, make no mention of his canonry, in either Westbury-on-Severn or Westbury-on-Trym.

Which of these Westburys had a Collegiate Church in the last part of the fourteenth century? As will be seen from the following, Westbury-on-Trym seems to have been the Collegiate Church. There is no evidence whatever in favour of the Wiltshire Westbury, or the Westbury-on-Severn.

Westbury, Wilts., was never a Collegiate Church. At an early date the Westbury Rectory was assigned to the Precentorship of Sarum, and was exempt from supervision of an Archdeacon. A copy of the original endowment of the vicarage of Westbury is in the Bishop's Palace at Salisbury,

Introduction lxix

A.D. 1377, 1 Rich. II.¹ Phillips, in his *Institutions of Wiltshire*, A.D. 1297–1810, has but one reference to Westbury, in a foot-note as to a Vicar there at the Restoration. Hoare² mentions only two appointments of clergy there in our period, viz.:

1342. Rector, Richard de Anesy, Vicar, Nic. Fitzwaren.
1377. Rector, Robt. de Walton, Vicar, W. Nisbe.

No mention is made of Westbury, in Wiltshire, having a Collegiate Church in either the Patent or Close Rolls, nor in the Papal Letters or Papal Petitions of our period, where so often we find references to the Collegiate Church of Westbury. Where Westbury in Wiltshire is mentioned in these registers it is in connexion with land or property.³

Again, there appears to be no evidence that Westbury-on-Severn had a Collegiate Church. References in the Patent and Close Rolls are always to a transfer of land or a reference to property of some nature. In Patent Rolls, 11 Rich. II, pt. i, m. 28, July 12, 1387, Thos. Bellying, Vicar of Westbury (on Severn), Co. Glouc., holds certain lands.⁴ In Patent Rolls, 11 Rich. II, pt. ii, m. 7, June 12, 1388, a certain transfer of lands in the parish of Westbury (on Severn, Co. Glouc.⁵). Also Pat. Rolls, 18 Rich. II, pt. ii, m. 10, June 4, 1395, the church of Wesebury (on Severn, Co. Glouc.) is spoken of in connexion with a land transaction.⁶ In Patent Rolls, 19 Rich. II, m. 36, Nov. 28, 1395, six acres of land in Wesebury and the advowson of Wesebury, not held in chief, were granted to the Warden of the College of Vicars and the vicars in the choir of the Cathedral Church of Hereford, in aid of their support, and in augmentation of divine service there, &c.⁷

This Westbury is spoken of as being by Newenham, in connexion with a charter of John Billyng, giving with

---

¹ Sir L. C. Hoare's *History of Modern Wiltshire*, vol. iii, p. 19.
² Ibid., vol. ii.
³ Pat. Rolls, 2 Rich. II, pt. ii, m. 26; Pat. Rolls, 3 Rich. II, pt. i, m. 45; Pat. Rolls, 12 Rich. II, m. 27 (1385–9, p. 6); Pat. Rolls, 17 Rich. II, pt. ii, m. 8 (1391–6, p. 417); Pat. Rolls, 20 Rich. II, pt. iii, m. 21 (1391–6, p. 126); *Papal Letters*, vol. i, 1209.
⁴ *Cal. of Patent Rolls*, Rich. II, 1385–9, p. 341.
⁵ Ibid., p. 454.
⁶ *Cal. of Patent Rolls*, 1391–6, p. 574.
⁷ Ibid., p. 661.

warranty an acre of land to the Bishop of Hereford (Close Rolls, 43 Edward III, m. 21d, June 5, 1369).[1]

Among the Papal Petitions, 1343, 1 Clement VI, we find that Richard Talbot, Baron, had founded an Augustinian priory in his lordship of Flanesford, in the diocese of Hereford, with a church and divers offices for a prior and several canons, with sanction of the Bishop and Chapter; that the Prior and convent of Flannesford may be more independent, they pray that the parish church of Westbury (district not specified), value not exceeding £20, and served by a vicar, may be granted to their uses; possession of the same being taken on death of present rector, the diocesan's permission not being requested (Avignon, 4 Kal. May, 1343).[2] The 'Church of Westbury by Gloucester on Severn' was appropriated as per this request, by command of the Pope, at Avignon, 8 Id. Aug. 1347 [3] (6 Innocent VI). The few other references to this Westbury, in the Patent and Close Rolls, or in the Papal Registers, are to lands, property, &c. No reference anywhere is there to a Collegiate Church.

The facts in regard to Westbury-on-Trym are as follows: As early as 883 King Oswald placed monks there.[4] As early as 1257 there seem to have been prebends there, for in 3 Alexander IV, 1257, 6 Kal. July, a mandate was issued to induct Master Gregory of Naples into possession of the prebend in the church of Wisbere, in the diocese of Worcester.[5] In 1288 [6] Godfrey Gifford made his first effort to join the churches of his manors to the prebends of Westbury. This was opposed by a Papal Bull in 1288.[6] The Bishop received the royal assent and in 1290 [6] installed three persons as prebends. Dugdale gives the date 1288 as the founding of the College for a dean and canons by Godfrey Gifford, Bishop of Worcester, dedicated to the Holy Trinity.[7] It seems that in 1095 Sampson, Bishop of Worcester, placed canons there in place of the Benedictine

---

[1] *Cal. of Close Rolls*, 1369–74, p. 89.
[2] *Cal. of Papal Petitions*, vol. ii, p. 16.
[3] Ibid., vol. xxix, p. 336.
[4] *Annales Monastici*, vol. iv, p. 369.
[5] *Cal. of Papal Letters*, vol. xxv, p. 346.
[6] *Annales Monastici*, vol. iv, pp. 496, 498, 500, 502, 504.
[7] *Monasticon*, 1846, vol. vi (Tom. VIII), p. 1439.

Introduction

monks, placed there by Bishop Oswald in 928.[1] It appears that there were five canonries, with prebends, at the time of the Taxation of Pope Nicholas in 1291. The College was more fully endowed by J. Carpenter in 1464, who sometimes styled himself Bishop of Westbury. He died and was buried at Westbury in 1476.[2] Tanner gives in an appendix to *Notitia Monastica* a list of deans but not of canons. This College of the Holy Trinity, founded in 1288, with a Dean and five Canons, in the patronage of the Popes of Worcester, is said by Tanner to have been at Westbury on Trim, or Trymme, in the County of Gloucester.[3] In *Beauties of England and Wales* we have the following:

'Westbury-on-Trim is a small neat village, chiefly consisting of respectable residences belonging to the merchants and traders of Bristol. Here was a College for a Dean and five Canons, generally said to have been founded by Bishop Carpenter, but more truly by the famous, though eccentric, William Cungrys of Bristol, who became the first Dean. The building was entire till the time of Charles I, when Prince Rupert ordered it to be destroyed, lest it should afford shelter to the Parliament's troops in annoyance to the garrison of Bristol; the remains are now incorporated in a genteel mansion, the property of John Hobhouse, Esq.'[4]

The Collegiate Church of Westbury mentioned in *Valor Ecclesiasticus* is Westbury-on-Trym. It speaks of it at that date (1334–5) as being a well-endowed College in diocese Gloster, but Antea Wigorn.[5]

I close this discussion by giving a number of references in the Patent Rolls, and also in the Papal Letters and Petitions, all referring to the Collegiate Church of Westbury-on-Trym, in regard to its canons or prebends.

Calendar: Patent Rolls:
    23 Edward III, m. 29, Sept. 28, 1349 (1348–50, p. 29).
    24 ,, pt. i, m. 36, Jan. 30, 1350 (1348–50, p. 466).
    49 ,, pt. ii, m. 11.

---

[1] Rev. C. S. Taylor, 'The Church Monastery of Westbury-on-Trym', 1897 (*Proceedings of Clifton Antiquarian Club*, 1897-9, pp. 20–42).

[2] Leland's *Itinerary*, 1910, vol. v, p. 227.

[3] *Notitia Monastica*, 1744, p. 142.

[4] E. W. Brayley and J. Britton, *Beauties of England and Wales*, vol. v, p. 729.

[5] *Valor Ecclesiasticus*, 1524–5, vol. ii, pp. 432–5, 474.

lxxii   Introduction

    7 Richard II, pt. ii, m. 6, May 31, 1384 (1381-5, p. 408).
   10   ,,   pt. i, m. 35, Aug. 1, 1386 (1385-9, p. 200).
   11   ,,   pt. i, m. 14, Sept. 28, 1387 (1385-9, p. 361).
   12   ,,   pt. ii, m. 20, Feb. 26, 1389 (1385-9, p. 18).
   12   ,,   pt. i, m. 35, July 6, 1388 (1385-9, p. 542).
   13   ,,   pt. i, m. 27, July 8, 1389 (1389-92, p. 88).
   14   ,,   pt. i, m. 22, Sept. 16, 1390 (1388-92, p. 308).
   14   ,,   pt. ii, m. 41, Jan. 12, 1391 (1388-92, p. 363).
   15   ,,   pt. i, m. 25, Sept. 14, 1391 (1388-92, p. 476).
   18   ,,   pt. i, m. 10, Sept. 27, 1394 (1391-6, p. 503).
   18   ,,   pt. ii, m. 19, Apr. 6, 1395 (1391-6, p. 559).
   18   ,,   pt. ii, m. 18 d, Apr. 28, 1395 (1391-6, p. 590).
   18   ,,   pt. ii, m. 5, June 10, 1395 (1391-6, p. 581).
   3 Henry IV, pt. ii, m. 2, Sept. 17, 1402 (1401-5, p. 121).
    4   ,,   pt. i, m. 27, Oct. 14, 1402 (1401-5, p. 157).
    5   ,,   pt. i, m. 32, Feb. 18, 1403 (1401-5, p. 305).

There may be other references that I have missed, but this will suffice. The Collegiate Church of Westbury-on-Trym, Co. Gloucester, diocese of Worcester, was an important church during the last half of the fourteenth century, having a dean, canons, and prebends in its jurisdiction. The Papal Petitions of this period often mention it. A few of these will be noted:

1 Clement VI, 1342, *Cal. of Papal Registers—Petitions*, 1342-1419, vol. i, p. 4.
1   ,,   1342, Ibid., vol. i, p. 10.
4   ,,   16 Aug. 1345, Ibid., vol. ix, p. 79.
7   ,,   1349, Ibid., vol. xvii, p. 148.
8   ,,   6 id. Oct. 1349, Ibid., vol. xix, p. 177.
9   ,,   non. June, 1350, Ibid., vol. xx, p. 199.
9   ,,   id. Aug. 1350, Ibid., vol. xx, pp. 202-3.
2 Innocent VI, 1354, Ibid., vol. xxv, pp. 263-4.
2   ,,   3 id. Dec. 1354, Ibid., vol. xxv, p. 268.
2   ,,   9 Kal. Feb. 1355, Ibid., vol. xxvi, p. 279.
5   ,,   6 Kal. May, 1357, Ibid., vol. xxvii, pp. 294-5.
1 Urban V, 5 Kal. Mar., 1363, Ibid., vol. xxxvi, p. 407.
10 Clement VII, 12 Kal. Apr. 1389, Ibid., vol. lxix, p. 571.

These all refer to canonries and prebendaries of the Collegiate Church of Westbury-on-Trym. The nature of the entries can easily be found by referring to the *Calendar of Papal Registers—Petitions* for 1342-1419, contained in one volume; Index, p. 750.

Many references may be found to this college and church in Papal Letters (*Cal. of Papal Letters*, 9 vols.).

Introduction lxxiii

In vol. i, p. 603, Boniface VIII, in his first year (non. Aug. 1303), grants dispensation to Peter de Laicestria to hold canonries and prebends of Lichfield, Westbiri (Gloc.), and Warwick.

Vol. ii (1305–42) mentions it a number of times, but the compilers of the index simply speak of it as Westbury (Co. Gloucester). The references have to do with the appointments of the Canons and Prebends, and no mention is made of a Collegiate Church. This doubtless, however, is the same church, Westbury-on-Trym. Some of these are:

3 Clement V, 5 Kal. Aug., 1308, vol. ii (LV), p. 42. Grant of Canonry of Westbury in dio. of Worcester to Wm. de Melton.
4 ,, 12 Kal. June, 1309, vol. ii (LVI), p. 53. Grant of Canonry and Preb. of Westbury to Wm. de Briston.
9 ,, 8 id. June, 1314, vol. ii (LXI), p. 121.
1 John XXII, 5 id. Apr., 1317, vol. ii (LXV), p. 148.
3 ,, 6 Kal. May, 1319, vol. ii (LXIX), p. 185.
14 ,, 4 id. Mar., 1330, vol. ii (XCV), p. 316.
15 ,, 18 Kal. Feb., 1331, vol. ii (XCVII), p. 332.
18 ,, 3 id. Mar., 1334, vol. ii (CVI), p. 399.
In 13 John XXII, 11 Kal. Nov., 1329, vol. ii (LXXXIX), p. 285, the only mention of a Collegiate Church at Westbury occurs.

In the second volume of *Papal Letters* (1342–62) Westbury-on-Trym is mentioned often, and so indicated in the index.

In vol. iv (1362–1404) we find the entry concerning Wiclif. This is in 3 Greg. XI, 7 Kal. Jan., 1373 (p. 193). Provision to John Wiclif, Canon of Lincoln, Master of Theology, granted to him, who holds also the church of Lugdgersale in the diocese of Lincoln, to retain even after getting possession of a canonry and prebend, under a provision lately made to him by the Pope of a canonry of Lincoln reservation of a prebend—his canonry and prebend of (Aust in) Westbury, in the diocese of Worcester, &c.

In vol. vii, p. 322 (1417–31), during the rule of Martin V, 1422, a grant to John Powle, Dean of Holy Trinity, Westbury, in the diocese of Worcester. As late as 1438–9 mention is made of the Dean of Holy Trinity, Westburi, in diocese of Worcester (vol. ix, 1431–47), p. 59.

lxxiv   *Introduction*

(*b*) *Date of his Death.*

Trevisa was at Berkeley during the last days of the third Thomas, 8th Lord of Berkeley, who died in 1361.[1] The 9th Lord, Maurice IV, died in 1368. The greater part of Trevisa's life as Vicar of Berkeley was spent in the service of the 10th Lord of Berkeley, Thomas V, born 1353, died 1417. To this lord he dedicated his translation of the *Polychronicon*, in 1387, in the following words: 'This translacioun is y-ended in a Thursday ey3tēþe day of Aueryl, the 3ere of our Lord a þowsand þre hundred foure score and seuene: þe tenþe 3ere of Kyng Richard þe secounde after þe conquest of Engelonde: þe 3ere of my lordes age Sire Thomas lorde of Berkeley, þat made me make þis translacioun, fyue and þritty.'[2] Also his translation of Bartholomaeus, *De Proprietatibus Rebus*, in 1398, in the following words: 'Endless grace, blisse and thankinge to our lord God Alweldinge, these translations ended at Berkeley the sixth day of February the year of our lord 1398, the year of King Richard the second after the conquest of England the 22nd. The year of my lords age Sir Thomas lord of Berkeley that made me make this translation, the 47th.'[3]

MacLean gives the date of Trevisa's death as 1412, basing his statement on Register Wigorn.: 'This Trevisa dyed the 13th year of King Henry the fourth, when John Bone John succeeded in that vicarage, whom this lord made one of his Executors, and proved a false priest to the heir male of his said lord as after I shall touch.'[4]

Henry Wharton, the seventeenth-century antiquarian and collector, gives the same date. His note preserved for us in Codices Whartoniani is a part of the MS. Lambeth 585, p. 637, in Lambeth Palace. The reference is as follows: 'Trevisa obit. 13 H. 4. et successorem habuit in Vicaria Johan. Bone-John. Ex. Regro. Wigorn.' Following this record, Tanner, Townley, Babington, Rogers, Boase and Courtney, Cooke, Jeayes, Boase, and Kingsford

---

[1] MacLean, op. cit., vol. i, p. 343. But see reference to Bloom's search (above, p. lxvi).

[2] This is taken from Add. 24194.

[3] This is quoted from MacLean, op. cit., vol. ii, p. 22.

[4] MacLean, op. cit., vol. ii, p. 22.

Introduction lxxv

all place his death in 1412. Fuller has 'about 1400'. Gilbert either 1399 or 1410. Atkyns[1] gives his death in 1409. The date of his death has been settled by the discovery of the entry, dealing with the appointment of his successor to the Berkeley Vicarage. The entry is found under the date, 1402, in vol. xvii, memb. 14 d, in the unprinted Bishops' Register of the diocese of Worcester,[2] during the bishopric of R. Clifford, 1401-7. These registers are preserved in Worcester Cathedral. The entry is as follows:

'1402 Berkelegh Vicaria—Vicesimo primo die dicte mensis Maii dictus Vicarius in spiritualibus apud London ad vicariam ecclesie parochialis de Berkelegh Wygornensis diocesie per mortem magistri Johannis Trevisa ultimum vicarium ejusdem vacantum; dominum Johannem Bonjon Presbyterum ad presentationem Religiosorum virorum Abbatis et Conventus Monasterii Sancti Augustini juxta Bristoll admisit ad vicarium perpetuum de corporaliter inibi residendo iuxta formam constitutionem dominorum Othonis et Ottoboni quondam sedis apostolici in Anglia legatorum in hac parte editarum iuratum instituit canonicum in eadem cum suis iuribus et pertinentiis universis. Quibus die et loco dictus dominus Iohannes iuravit obedien*ti*am domino et habuit litteras institutionis ac mandatum ad inducendum directe Archidiaconus Gloucestrensis ut est moris.' *Reg. Clifford,* 14 d.

B. TREVISA'S WORKS.

Lists of Trevisa's works are given by Bale, Pits, Tanner, Babington, Rogers, and Miss Greenwood.

Bale gives the following:

1.	Utrumque Testamentum.	Lib. 2.
2.	Bartholomaeum de Proprietatibus.	Lib. 19.
3.	Ranulphi Polychronicon.	Lib. 7.
4.	De sua translatione dialogum.	Lib. 1.
5.	Continuationes Polychronici.	Lib. 1.
6.	Gesta regis Arthuri.	Lib. 1.
7.	Britanniae descriptionem.	Lib. 1.
8.	Hyberniae descriptionem.	Lib. 1.
9.	De Memorabilibus eorum temporum	Lib. 1.

et alia plura fecit et transtulit.

[1] Atkyns, *History of Gloucestershire.*
[2] These registers, from 1350–1420, were examined for me by the Rev. J. Harvey Bloom, Whitchurch, Stratford-on-Avon. The above entry was communicated to me in a letter under date of 12 Feb., 1915. No other reference to Trevisa appears in the Registers.

Pits gives the same list:
1. Sacra Biblia, Libros duos.
2. Ranulphi Polychronicon, Libros septem.
3. Dialogus translatione. librum unum.
4. Polychronici continuationes.—librum unum.
5. Bartholomaeus de proprietatibus rerum—libros, novem decem.
6. De memorabilibus temporum.   Librum unum.
7. Gesta Regis Arthuri.   ,,   ,,
8. Descriptionem Britanniae.   ,,   ,,
9. Descriptionem Hiberniae   ,,   ,,
   et alia nonnulla.

In addition to the above Tanner mentions the following:
1. De calore thermarum Bathoniensium.
2. Genealogia Davidis regis Scotiae.[1]
3. Richardi Armachani defensorium curatorum.[2]
4. Vegetii de re militari.
5. Aegidii Romani de regimine principum.

Babington, in the Introduction (pp. liii ff.) to his edition of *Polychronicon* in the Rolls Series, mentions the works of Trevisa, taking them from Tanner's bibliography and Dibdin's *Typographical Antiquities*. He includes in his list, in addition to those mentioned by Bale and Tanner, two new works, both mentioned by Dibdin, viz. (1) *Dialogus inter Militem et Clericum*, Trevisa's translation from the Latin of Wm. Occam, and (2) Methodius's tract, *On the Beginning and End of the World*. Dibdin in mentioning these works is describing the Harleian MS. 1900. In describing the *Dialogue* he makes the same mistake as does the compiler of the Catalogue of Harleian MSS., viz. that the dialogue between the soldier and the clergyman was between Lord Berkeley and the author Trevisa.

Rogers, in his article in the *Journal of the Royal Institution of Cornwall*, 1870, includes all the above in his list. He lists the following as: I. Original writings: (1) *De Calore Thermarum Bathoniensum*, (2) *De utilitate translationum, dialogus inter patronum et clericum*, (3) *Gesta Regis Arthuri*, (4) *Britanniae descriptio*, (5) *Hiberniae descriptio*, (6) *De Memorabilibus temporum,*

---

[1] Tanner says: 'Haec MS. citatus ab Usser.' *Dogmatica Historica*, p. 123.

[2] Tanner refers to this: 'In eodem libro (*Dog. Hist.*, p. 430), Whartonus adnotat Iohannem Trevisam transtulisse in linguam Anglicanam....'

Introduction lxxvii

(7) *Genealogia Davidis Regis Scotiae*. II. Translations into English: (1) *Polychronicon*, (2) Bartholomaeus, *De Proprietatibus rerum*, (3) Ricardi Armachani, *defensorium curatorum*, (4) Vegetii, *de re Militari*, (5) Aegidii Romani, *de regimine Principum*, (6) Gulielmi Occam, *Dialogus inter Militem et Clericum*, (7) Methodius, *On the beginning and end of the world*.

In an article in the same *Journal*, on Trevisa, in 1874, Rogers mentions as a translation the 'Nicodemus treatise on the passion of Christ'.

Miss Greenwood is more cautious in listing Trevisa material. She omits all the original works listed by Rogers, and questions *de re Militari* and *de Regimine Principum*.

I. TRANSLATIONS

(1) The Polychronicon.

The Manuscripts.

This was a most popular medieval history written in Latin by Ranulf Higden, a monk of St. Werburgh's, Chester, about 1350. 'The Latin MSS.', says Mr. Babington,[1] 'are prodigiously numerous, and amount in all, I believe, to a number considerably greater than one hundred.' Mr. Macray (p. 39), in *Manual of British Historians*, mentions upwards of seventy, and says, 'There are MSS. in nearly all the libraries in England'. Trevisa translated the *Polychronicon* in the fourteenth century. This translation is preserved in the following MSS.: Cotton Tiberius D. VII; Harleian 1900; Brit. Mus. Additional 24194; St. John's College, Cambridge, H. 1; Burleigh House; Chetham's College Library, Manchester; Stowe 65 in British Museum.[2] In addition, two others have been mentioned: (1) that in the Hunterian Museum, University of Glasgow, mentioned briefly in the third report of the Historical MSS. Commission, 1872, p. 424, by John Stuart on 'MSS. in Glasgow University'. The brief notice there is: 'Higden's Polychronicon by Trevisa. Folio. vellum.' It is noticed by Mr. Lumby, vol. v, p. xliv, of the Rolls Series. For a full description see Catalogue of MSS. in the Hunterian Collection, University of Glasgow, by Young and Aitkin, 1908, No. 83, p. 88. It is

[1] Op. cit., vol. i, p. xlii. [2] Described pp. xv ff.

fifteenth century, written on paper 11-3/8 × 8-5/8, ff. 148, originally 166. Contents given as Trevisa's Chronicle. On Verso II, 1, in Dr. Wm. Hunter's hand: 'Fructus Temporum or Croniclis of Englonde; which were afterward printed by Caxton.' (2) Another MS. attributed to Trevisa is in Trinity College, Dublin.[1] The brief notice in Historical MSS. Commission Report, No. IV, p. 598, is 'History of Britain by Trevisa, 4to vellum. Imperfect.' In the Catalogue the description is brief. It is numbered 506, E. 54, fol. parchment, 8-8/10 × 6-9/10, writing 6-4/10 × 4-5/10, 15 cent., 94 leaves, defective, begins in Chap. 17, ends Chap. 127, under 4th year of Henry IV. In answer to an inquiry, Mr. Alfred de Burgh, Assistant Librarian, wrote me under date of Jan. 1, 1915, that the Librarian, Dr. J. Gilbart Smyly, had examined the MS. afresh, and found that it did not correspond with Trevisa's version. Dr. Smyly also compared the MS. with other chronicles, and found the closest resemblance in an anonymous Chronicle from a Lambeth MS. edited by James Gairdner in *Three Fifteenth-Century Chronicles*, Camden Society, 1880. There was much similarity in the names of persons, and sometimes a close correspondence of phrases, but the Dublin MS. was, on the whole, considerably fuller. In a letter dated Jan. 5, 1915, Mr. de Burgh has this further bit of information: 'The Chronicle covers the same ground at about the same length, with omissions and additions, as *The Brut or The Chronicle of England*, ed. by F. W. D. Brie (E. E. T. S., 1906, 1908, pts. 1, 2). The proper names in the mythical period are not in the same form.' Brie used Dublin MSS. 490, 500, 501, but Mr. de Burgh is not sure whether he was familiar with 506.

The Printed Editions (English).

I. *1482, printed by Wm. Caxton.*

Caxton finished his *Polychronicon* July 2, 1482. He altered Trevisa's English, as will be seen from his proheme. He prefaced it by Trevisa's dialogue between himself and his patron, by his epistle to Lord Berkeley, and a table of contents

[1] Noted by Boase and Courtney, *Bibl. Cornub.*, vol. ii, pp. 798 ff.

covering 17 leaves. A part of Caxton's proheme is here given:[1]

'And that other book is named Polychronycon in whiche book ben comprised briefly many wonderful historyees. Fyrst the descripcion of the vniuersal world as well in lengthe as in brede with the diuisions of countrees royaumes and empyres the noble cytees hye mountaynes famous ryuers merueylles & wondres, & also the historical Actes & Wonderful dedes syth the fyrst makyng of heuen & erth vnto the begynnyng of the regne of Kyng edward the fourth, & vnto the yere of our lord MCCCCLX. As by thayde of almyghty god shal folowe al a longe after the composynge & gaderynge of dan Ranulph Monke of Chestre fyrste auctour of this book, and afterward englisshed by one Treuisa vycarye of barkley which atte request of one Sir thomas lord barkley translated this sayd book the byble & bartylmew de proprietatibus rerum out of latyn into englyssh. And now at this tyme symply emprynted & sette in forme by me William Caxton and a lytel embelysshed fro tholde makyng, and also haue added suche storyes as I coude fro thende that the said Ranulph fynysshed his book which was the yere of our lord MCCCLVII vnto the yere of the same MCCCCLX, whiche ben an hundred & thre yere whiche werke I haue finysshed vnder the noble protection of my most drad natural and souerayne lord and moost cristen Kynge Kyng Edward the fourth humbly besechyng his moost nobile grace to pardone me yf ony thynge be sayd therynne of Ignoraunce or other wyse than it ought to be....'

The Latin *Polychronicon* as well as Trevisa's translation contain seven books, carrying the events down to 1357. From the above it will be seen that Caxton, in an eighth book, carried on the history to 1460. At the end of 'Liber Septimus' Caxton has the following colophon:[2]

'God be thanked of al his dedes. This translacion is ended on a thursdaye the eyghtenthe daye of Apryll the yere of our lord a thousand thre honderd and LVII, the XXXI yere of kyng Edward the thyrd after the Conquest of England, the yere of my lordes age Syr thomas lord of berkley that made me make this translacion fyue and thyrtty.'

At the end of 'Liber Septimus' Caxton places his epilogue.

---

[1] W. Blades, *Life and Typography of Caxton*, 2 vols., 1861-3, vol. i, p. 194. Also Rolls Series, vol. viii, p. 352; Ames, *Typ. Antiq.*, ed. Dibdin, vol. i, p. 143.

[2] Blades, *Life of Caxton*, vol. i,

Then he writes 'Liber Ultimus', carrying the history from 1357 to 1460. His epilogue or apology is as follows:[1]

'Thus endeth the book named Proloconycon made & compiled by Ranulph monk of chestre whiche ordeyned it in latyn & atte request of the ryght worshipful lord Thomas lord of berkeley it was translated in to englisshe by one Treuisa thenne vycarye of the Paryssh of barkley: and for as moche as syth the accomplysshemente of this sayd booke made by the sayd Ranulph ended the yere of oure lord MCCCLVII many thynges haue fallen whiche ben requysyte to be added to this werke by cause mennes wyttes in this tyme ben oblyuyous and lyghtly forgeten many thyngys dygne to be putte in memorye and also there can not be founden in these dayes but fewe that wryte in theyr regystres suche thynges as dayly happen and falle: therfore I, William Caxton, a simple persone haue endeuoyred me to wryte fyrst ouer all the sayd book of proloconycon and som what haue chaunged the rude and old englyssh that is to wete certayn wordes which in these dayes be neither vsyd ne vnderstanden & furthermore haue put it in emprynte to thende that it maye be had & the maters therin comprised to be knowen for the boke is general touchyng shortly many notable maters & also am auysed to make another booke after this sayd werke whiche shal be sett here after the same And shal haue his chapytres & his table a parte For I dar not presume to sette my booke ne ioyne hit to his for dyuerse causes one is for as moche as I haue not ne can gete no bokes of auctoryte treatyng of suche cronykes except a lytel boke named fasciculus temporum and another callyde Aureus de Vniuerso in whiche bookes I fynde ryght lytel mater syth the sayde tyme § And another cause is for as moche as my rude sympleness and ignorant makyng ought not to be compared set ne ioyned to his boke Thenne I shal by the grace of god set my werke after a parte for to accomplysshe the yeres syth that he fynysshed his book vnto the yere of our lord MCCCClx and the fyrst yere of the Regne of Kyng edward the fourthe whiche amounte to an honderd and thre yere.'

II. 1495. *Printed by Wynkyn de Worde.*

The following notice appears in Dibdin,[2] as No. 90: 'Polycronycon: ended the thyrtenth daye of Apryll, the tenth yere of the regne of kynge Harry the seuenth, And of the

---

[1] See Blades, vol. i, p. 194; pp. 147, 148. Dibdin's Ames, *Typ. Antiq.*, vol. i,   [2] Ibid., vol. ii, p. 49.

Introduction   lxxxi

Incarnacyon of our Lord MCCCCLXXXXV. Enprynted by Wynkyn Theworde, at Westmestre, Folio.' Boase and Courtney¹ give this notice :—' Polycronycon. (Made and compyled by Ranulph, Monke of Chestre ... in Latyn and ... translated into Englysshe by (J.) Trevisa.) In seuen books, "the rude and olde englissh somewhat chaunged," by W. Caxton and an eighth book containing a continuation from 1357 to 1460 added by him. Edited by Wynkyn The worde 1495, fol.'

de Worde used Caxton's edition,² and even his proheme, except he substitutes his own name for that of the modernizer, and instead of mentioning the continuation of the history to 1460, de Worde promises to continue it to ' Henry ye Seuenth ye yere of his regne & vnto the yere of our lord MCCCCLXXXV, which ben an C & XXXVIII yere, which werke (says he) I haue fynyshed vnder the noble protecyon of my moost drad naturall and souerayne lorde & most crysten Kynge, Kynge Henry the seuenth.' The work, however, was not continued any further by W. de Worde. He closes with Caxton's colophon and conclusion as given above.

III. 1527. *Printed by Peter Treveris.*

This is a reimpression of de Worde's edition. Dibdin³ gives a full description of it under No. 751, and says, ' the title-page is perhaps the most magnificent title-page of which the early annals of English printing can boast'. The following imprint is found on a separate leaf at the end : ' Imprented in Southwerke by me Peter Treveris at ye expences of John Reynes boke seller at the sygne of Saynt George in Poules Chyrchyarde, the yere of our lorde god MCCCCC and XXVII, the XVI daye of Maye.' The following notice is given by Boase and Courtney :—' Polycronycon (translated intoo Englyshe by (J.) Trevisa). (In seven books, "the rude and olde Englysshe somewhat chaunged," and an eighth book containing a continuation from 1357 to 1460 added by Wm. Caxton.) Peter Treveris, Imprinted in Southwerk, fol.'⁴

---

[1] Op. cit., vol. ii, p. 798.
[2] Ames, vol. j, p. 138.
[3] Op. cit., vol. iii, p. 40. It is also described in *Brit. Bibl.*, vol. iii, p. 349.
[4] Op. cit., vol. ii, p. 798.

f

lxxxii *Introduction*

IV. *The Rolls Series*, 1865–86. 9 vols.

Vols. i and ii and introduction by Churchill Babington; vols. iii–ix by J. R. Lumby. The editors print the MS. in St. John's College, Camb. H. 1, and collate with it Caxton's edition and MS. Add. 24194. Beginning with vol. ii, they make some use in collation of MSS. Harl. 1900 and Cotton Tib. D. vii.[1] As noted above, p. xv, a selection from Harl. 1900 is printed in Appendix, vol. vii. Babington and Lumby, in addition to the Latin text, print a fifteenth-century MS., viz. Harl. 2261. It is different from the translation of Trevisa, and continues the history to 1401.[2]

Extracts from the *Polychronicon* have been printed and may be found as follows:

1. *Specimens of Early English*: Morris and Skeat, Part II, 1889, pp. 235–47.

   (A) Description of Britain. Lib. I, cap. 41 and 42, vol. ii, pp. 13–31 of Rolls Series.
   (B) De Incolarum Linguis. Lib. I, cap. 59, vol. ii, pp. 157–63 of Rolls Series.
   (C) The Norman Invasion. Lib. VI, cap. 29, vol. vii, pp. 233–45 of Rolls Series.

These extracts are taken from MS. Cotton Tiberius D. vii, leaf 38, back. The Editors omit the name Trevisa, usually found before his additions. See notes, however, p. 344.

2. *A Middle English Reader*: O. F. Emerson, 1905, rev. ed., 1921, pp. 220–5.

   (A) The Inhabitants of Britain. Bk. I, chap. 58, vol. ii, pp. 143–57 of Rolls Series.
   (B) The Languages of the Inhabitants. Bk. I, chap. 59, vol. ii, pp. 157–63 of Rolls Series.

This is taken from MS. Cotton Tiberius D. vii. The editor omits the name Trevisa, but indicates the omission in a foot-note.

---

[1] Miss Greenwood (*Camb. Hist. of English Lit.*, vol. ii, p. 444) states that the MS. at Burleigh House was used. I have not been able to ascertain that this is correct. There is no mention of the Burleigh House MS. by Babington and Lumby.

[2] *Cat. of Harl. MSS.*, vol. ii, p. 596.

Introduction lxxxiii

3. *Altenglische Sprachproben*: Eduard Mätzner, 1867, vol. i, pt. 2, pp. 341–73.
> De Graecia et eius prouinciis. Lib. I, cap. 22, vol. i, pp. 175–99 of Rolls Series.
> De Italia. Lib. I, cap. 23, vol. i, pp. 199–207 of Rolls Series.
> De Urbe Romana. Lib. I, cap. 24, vol. i, pp. 207–39 of Rolls Series.
> De quibusdam Romanorum. Lib. I, cap. 25, vol. i, pp. 239–53 of Rolls Series.
> From St. John's College, Camb. MS. H. 1.

4. *Die Sprache des 'Polychronicons' John Trevisa's*: Bernhard Pfeffer, 1912, pp. 99–144.
> Lib. VI, cap. 29 (near end)—Lib. VII, cap. 12 (part)—vol. vii, pp. 245–421 of Rolls Series.
> From MS. Cotton Tiberius D. vii, ff. 246–60 b.

5. Part of fol. 94 b, Harl. MS. 1900, printed by Blades,[1] showing contrast with Caxton's text.

6. *Altenglisches Lesebuch*: R. P. Wülker, vol. ii, pp. 205–8.
> De Incolarum Linguis, MS. Harleian 1900. Reprinted from Rolls Series, ii. 157.
> (Of Allemeyne or Germany, from the later translation of Higden, MS. Harleian 2261, Wülker ii, pp. 209–10. Reprinted from Rolls Series, i. 255 ff.)

7. *English Prose* (1137–1890): Dr. John M. Manly, 1909, pp. 11–12.
> De incolarum linguis. Book I, chap. 59, vol. ii, pp. 157–63 of Rolls Series.

This is printed from St. John's College, Camb. MS. H. 1, and the name Trevisa indicating his additions is not omitted, as in Emerson, and Morris and Skeat.

8. Fly-leaf, vol. ii, Rolls *Polychronicon*, a facsimile of a page from B.M. Add. 24194, containing one of Trevisa's notes, and his conception of Noah's ark. The same passage is found in St. John's Coll. Camb. MS. H. 1, in the text, p. 229, l. 17, a wylde beste—p. 235, l. 9, clere i-now there it was. Higden, Lib. II, cap. 5.

---

[1] Wm. Blades, *Biog. and Typ. of Wm. Caxton*, 1897, p. 258.

lxxxiv   *Introduction*

Date of completion, 1357 *or* 1387.

Each of the four MSS. examined gives the date on which Trevisa finished his translation, April 18, 1387.[1] The Cotton MS. agrees:[2] 'Thys translacyon ys yended in a thorsday the eyȝetūthe day of Aueryl & the ȝer of vr lord a thousand thre hondred vour score & seuene the tnethe ȝere of Kyng Rychard the second.'

On the other hand, evidence for 1357 comes first from Smyth's *Lives of the Berkeleys*:[3] 'God be thanked for all his deeds. This translation is ended on thursday the 18th of Aprill 1357, the 31st year of King Edward the third, the year of my lords age, Sr. Thomas lord Berkeley that made mee make this translation, the 65th.' Caxton gives the same year, but changes the age of Lord Berkeley from 65 to 35. The following is the conclusion of Trevisa's translation of Bartholomeus *de proprietatibus Rerum* as given by Smyth:[4] 'Endles grace, blisse and thankinge to our lord God alweldinge these translations ended at Berkeley the sixth day of February the year of our lord 1398, the year of King Richard the second after the conquest of England, the 22nd. The year of my lords age Sr. Thomas lord of Berkeley that made me make this translation the 47th.'

According to Smyth, as has been shown before, Trevisa was at Berkeley during the rule of three of the lords, viz. Thomas, 8th lord, Maurice, 9th lord, and Thomas, 10th lord. Thomas, 8th lord, was born in 1293,[5] and thus was 65 at the time of the completion of the *Polychronicon* in 1357, as stated in Smyth. Thomas, 10th lord, was born in 1352,[6] and thus was 47 years of age at the finishing of Barth. *de Prop. Rerum* in 1398, as stated by Smyth, and as given in the MSS. Smyth is thus consistent in his dates. He claims also that Trevisa was at Berkeley some time during the rule of Lord Thomas 8th,

---

[1] Harleian 1900; St. John's College H. 1; Stowe 65; Burleigh House MS.; Chetham's, incomplete.

[2] Herbert's Ames's *Typ. Antiq.*, vol. i, p. 140.

[3] Smyth's *Lives of the Berkeleys*, ed.

MacLean, vol. i, p. 343.

[4] MacLean's ed., vol. ii, p. 22.

[5] Smyth's *Lives*, and *Berkeley Castle*, by G. T. Clark (*Bristol and Gloucester Trans.* 1876), p. 115.

[6] Smyth's *Lives of the Berkeleys*, vol. ii, p. 2.

who died in 1361 (see above). We know that Trevisa had not received his appointment as Vicar in 1360. Ames,[1] in discussing this matter, uses the entry from Caxton, making the age of Sir Thomas 35. He then continues:

'The year 1357, indeed, is the last date expressly mentioned in this Polycronycon, but the history is continued for some years after, viz. to the peace between England and France; but without any date. It is evident the dates there given are not concordant, for the 18th of April 1357, was not on Thursday, but Tuesday; also, the year of Lord Berkeley's age does not agree with that given in the colophon to Bartholomeus de Proprietatibus Rerum, printed by W. de Worde, in which we are informed that it was translated by Trevisa, and finished 26 Feb. 1398, the year of Lord Berkleys Age XLVII. So that the true reading, or time when Trevisa finished the translation of the Polychronycon will be according to the Cottonian MS.' (quoted p. lxxxiv).

Babington[2] agrees with Ames, and, like Ames, refers to Caxton's entry. He says, 'Caxton (fol. 389 b) falsely makes Trevisa's translation end in 1357.' After giving the entry he proceeds:

'The true date is 1387, and Caxton's error has been corrected in the Harleian MSS. Catalogue (n. 1900) and in the general introduction to the Monumenta Historica Britannica, p. 4. The last date mentioned in Trevisa's text is 1357; hence, perhaps, Caxton's mistake; but the chronicle is continued to the year 1360.'

Cooke, on the other hand, thinks the 1357 date the correct one. In a note to an article, ' on the Ancient Inscriptions in the chapel at Berkeley Castle, with some account of John Trevisa,'[3] he says: 'Prof. Babington, on the authority of a MS. in the Bodleian Library,[4] makes this date 1387. It is probable, however, that this is a clerical error, or perhaps a later copy in which the scribe has altered the date to correspond with Thomas IV, 10th Lord Berkeley, grandson of Thomas III. Smyth, quoting perhaps from Trevisa's original MS., thus fixes

[1] Herbert's ed. of Ames's *Typ. Antiq.*, vol. i, p. 140.
[2] Rolls Series of *Polychronicon*, vol. i, lxii.
[3] *Transactions of Bristol and Gloucester Arch. Society*, 1876, vol. i, p. 138.
[4] Harleian MS. 1900, in British Museum.

the date' (see ending as given by Smyth above, p. lxxxiv). Cooke bases his claim solely on Smyth's entry, on the ground that perhaps he possessed the original Trevisa. This work should be correct. The lives have been supposed to be written by John Smyth of Nibley, based on the Berkeley MSS. 1066–1618. And yet he places the death of Trevisa ten years later than it actually happened, even basing his statement on the Worcester Episcopal Register.[1] If Smyth's work is a fabrication he has made his dates coincide.

We readily agree with Ames and Babington that Caxton changed the date from 1387 to 1357, to make it agree with the last date in the work. This is his 'embellishing' carried to the extreme. He doubtless did this, as he gives the age of Lord Berkeley 35, as in the MSS., not 65, as in Smyth.

One other bit of evidence is forthcoming, which proves beyond a doubt the authenticity of the date 1387. This comes from Trevisa himself, and is to be found in one of his additions, or explanatory notes, or interpolations, of which there are numbers in the *Polychronicon*, and which occasionally are to be found in some of his other translations. The passage is in *Polychronicon*, Book I, chapter 59,[2] dealing with the language of the people of England. Part of Trevisa's note reads thus (taken from St. John's Coll. MS. H. 1):

'Þis manere was moche i-vsed to for firste deth and is siþþe sumdel i-chaunged; for John Cornwaile a master of Grammer. chaunged þe lore in gramer scole and construccioun of Frensche in to Englische; and Richard Pencriche lerned þe manere techynge of hym and of oþere men of Penrich; so þat now, þe ȝere of oure Lorde a þowsand þre hundred and foure score and fyue, and of þe secounde Kyng Richard after þe conquest nyne, in alle þe gramere scoles of Engelond, children leueþ Frensche and construeþ and lerneþ an Englische, and haueþ þerby auauntage in oon side and disauauntage in anoþer side', &c.

[1] See discussion of his death, p. lxxiv.
[2] Rolls Series of *Polychronicon*, vol. ii, p. 161. Same passage in Emerson, p. 224; Morris and Skeat, Part II, p. 241; Manly's *Prose*, p. 12. See also article by W. H. Stevenson, 'The Introduction of English as the vehicle of Instruction in English Schools', in *An English Miscellany*, p. 421. He also quotes the passage. Dr. Hickes quotes it in 'Praefatio' to his *Thesaurus*, vol. i, p. xvii.

Thus, in 1385, Trevisa was still writing the first book of the *Polychronicon*. Tanner[1] refers to this as follows :
'Versionem ad finem perduxit, uti ex nota calci annexa patet, A. MCCCLXXXVII (rectius iuxta Cod. Cotton MCCCLXXXV) die Aprilis, [uti MS. nota ad finem MS. Cotton. In MS. Tenisoniano nota Trevisae, in lib. i, cap. 59. De desuetudine linguae Gallicae, vocat annum praesentem MCCCLXV, (ut male habet codex impressus) 9 Rich. II, qui est A. MCCCLXXXV].'

Ames,[2] in closing his discussion of this date, says: 'That Trevisa was living and wrote 9 Rich. 2, see Poly. Lib. 1, cap. LIX.'

(2) De Proprietatibus Rerum.

This is 'the Great Cyclopaedia of the Middle Ages', the noted work of Bartholomew Anglicus, or Bartholomew de Glanville (1230-50).[3] The date is uncertain. It was known in Italy in 1283, known and prized in Paris 1297 and 1329. It was known in England in 1296, as is proved by a MS. at Oxford (Ashmole 1512) which was copied in November of that year. The facts are arranged in nineteen books, with a religious and moral object. It was first printed at Basle about 1470, and went through fourteen or more editions before 1500; it was translated into French 1372, and was translated into English from the Latin in 1398 by John Trevisa, for Lord Thomas, 10th Lord of Berkeley.[4] This translation is preserved in the following MSS. :

(a) Helmingham Hall, Stowmarket, Suffolk. This was examined in 1874 by Arthur J. Horwood for the Royal Commission on Historical MSS.[5] His description is brief: 'Trevisa's translation into English of Bartholomew de Glanville's work, " De proprietatibus rerum ", a superb MS. in folio, with illuminated letters and marginal ornaments : parchment, 14th century. It commences with 24 lines of verse, not in the printed edition.'[6]

[1] Op. cit., p. 721.
[2] Herbert's ed., vol. i, p. 40.
[3] For life see *Dict. of Nat. Biog.*, vol. xxi, p. 409.
[4] See ending, p. lxxxviii.

[5] Hist. MSS. Com. Report I, App., pp. 60-1.
[6] In a letter dated July 1, 1914, Lady Tollemache of Helmingham Hall, was kind enough to invite me

lxxxviii   *Introduction*

Rogers,[1] in his article on Trevisa, tells us that Mr. Tollemache exhibited this beautiful medieval Encyclopaedia at the annual meeting of the Archaeological Institute, at Bury St. Edmunds, July 1869.

(b) Harleian MS. 614.[2] The notice in the *Catalogue* is very brief and incomplete. The writer finishes his description when he describes Harl. 4789. The description under 614 is: 'A parchment book in folio, fairly written, containing an English translation of Bartholomaeus de Proprietatibus rerum, made at Berkeley, at the influence of Thomas Lord Berkeley, about A. D. 1398, perhaps by John Trevisa. At the end of the contents of the chapters, which are written at the beginning of the Book, is a short song, or copy of the verses made by the Trans.'

(c) Harleian MS. 4789.[3] An imperfect copy ending in the 46th chapter of the nineteenth book. The complete copy has 146 chapters. The compiler here tells us that No. 614 is complete, and gives its ending because of the importance of the dates, as follows :

' Eendeless grete bliss & thankynge to our Lord God alweeldynge ; these translacyons eendid at Berkeley the sixte day of Feuer, the ȝheer of our Lorde a thousynde three hundrid fourscore & XVIII ; the ȝheer of Kyng Rychard the secunde after the conquest of Yngeland, the 22 ȝheer. And of my lordis age, Sire Thomas lord of Berkeley, that made me make this translacyon XLVII.'

(d) Additional 27944.[4] Folio, vellum. Beg. XV. Verses at first beginning :

> Troys was maad al of reed.
> In þe bigynnynge of my book
> That is clepid god me spede
> In þe firste lessoun þat I took.

---

to go to Stowmarket and examine the MSS. This was found impossible. In answer to a recent letter, her secretary, Miss E. Lynd, writes that the MSS. have been removed to a place of safety because of the war.

[1] *Journ. of R. Inst. of Corn.*, No. XI, Apr. 1870.
[2] *Cat. of Harl. MSS.*, vol. i, p. 390.
[3] Ibid., vol. iii, p. 205.
[4] *Cat. of Additions to Brit. Mus.*, *1854-1875*, vol. ii, p. 382.

Introduction

I give the ending to show the difference in spelling between the MSS. :

'Endeles grace blisse and þonkynge to oure lord god all weldynge. Þise translasiouns I-endede at Berkeleye the sixte day of ffeuerer. The ȝere of oure lorde a thousande þre hundrid foure score and eiytetene : The yeere of Kyng Richarde the secounde after the conqueste of Engelonde two and twenty. The ȝeere of my lordes age Sire Thomas lord of Berkeley that made me make this translacioun seuene and fourty.'

Then follows a list of authors quoted in the work.[1]

Rogers, referring to this work, says that Watt in his *Bibl. Brit.* gives no less than nine editions of the book, inclusive of the translation into English by Thomas Berthelet, the edition of Wynkyn de Worde 1498, in double columns, in nineteen books, and the reprinted edition by Batman 1585. In regard to the latter edition this reference is found : 'Batman uppon Bartholome, his Booke, De Prop. Rerum, newly corrected, enlarged, and amended, with such additions as are requisite unto every severall book. London 1582. Fol.'

The three editions are described by Tanner, and by Boase and Courtney.[2] Tanner : 'Wynkyn de Worde, circa MCCCCXCIV : Tho. Berthelet, Lond. MDXXXV ; Et tandem correct. et auctius a Steph. Batman, Lond. MDLXXXII.' Boase and Courtney give two editions by Worde : (1) 'Bartholomeus De Proprietatibus rerum. Translated into English by John Trevisa (woodcuts), Westminster, by Wynkyn de Worde (1494) fol.' (2) 'Bartholomew de proprietatibus rerum (Translated into English by John Trevisa), 2 parts, Black Letters (Wynkyn de Worde ; Westminster, 1495 ?), 4º.' It is deposited in the Grenville Library, British Museum. In the Prohemium is the following : 'And John Tate the younger mote he broke which late hath in Englonde doo make this paper thynne That now in our Englyssh this boke is prynted Inne.' Concerning No. 2, a note states that this copy was bequeathed to the British Museum by Sir Joseph Banks, and that it is

---

[1] I was unable to find a record of any MS. at Burleigh House, as Miss Greenwood suggests (*Camb. Hist. of Eng. Lit.*, vol. ii, p. 444.
[2] *Bibl. Cornub.*, vol. ii, p. 798.

amongst the early printed books exhibited in a case in the King's Library. The next Englishman to print this work was Berthelet. Boase and Courtney have the following : 'Anno MDXXXV. Bartholomeus de proprietatibus rerum. Londini in aedibus Thomae Bertholeti regii impressoris cum privilegio a rege Hn. VIII (1535), fol.' In a note the ordinary ending is given, but this curious statement is added : 'A MS. in Berkeley castle says the translation was finished 18 April 1357, the 31st Edw. III, and in the 65th year of the age of Syre Thomas, lord Berkeley.'[1] The entry in regard to Batman reads thus : 'Batman vppon Bartholome his booke De Proprietatibus rerum, newly corrected, enlarged and amended with such additions as are requisite vnto euery seuerall booke taken foorth of the most approued authors, the like here to fore not translated in English. Profitable for all estates as well for the benefite of the mind as the bodie, 1582. Lond. imprinted by Thomas East, dwelling by Paules Wharfe, fol.'[2] Dr. Furnivall, in his edition of Thomas Vicary's *Anatomie of the Bodie of Man* (E.E.T.S., Extra Series, liii, 1888), quotes fifteen or more lines from Berthelet's 1535 ed., Bk. V, of *de Prop. Rerum*. He begins his note: ' Hear Bartholomeus de Glanvilla (*de Proprietatibus Rerum*, in John Trevisa's English) on Members simple.'

A new edition by Dr. R. von Fleischhacker is promised by the E.E.T.S. in the Extra Series.

A facsimile page of Wynkyn de Worde's edition, parts of caps. 67 and 68 of Book XVIII, is to be found in vol. i, p. 202, of Garnett and Gosse's *Illustrated History of English Literature*.

Various sections from this work have been collected and edited under the title *Medieval Lore from Bartholomaeus Anglicus*, by Robert Steele, 1893 and 1900. Mr. Steele lists ninety-four sources of the book, and also lists the various editions with dates as follows : Latin, twenty-one editions from 1480-1609 ; Dutch, two editions, 1479 and 1485 ; French, twenty-one

---

[1] This is evidently a mistake. Boase and Courtney must refer to the ending of the *Polychronicon* as given in the Berkeley MSS. (Smyth's *Lives of the Berkeleys*).

[2] Copies of Berthelet and Batman are in the British Museum and Bodleian ; in British Mus. numbered 456 a. 1 and 456 b. 15 ; in Bodleian, Douce B, subt. 292, and Douce B, subt. 28.

Introduction xci

editions, from 1482–1556; Spanish, two editions, 1494 and 1529; English, by John of Trevisa in 1397, three editions: (1) no date, at Westminster, printed by W. de Worde; (2) 1535, at London, printed by Berthelet; (3) 1582, at London, printed by East. (Steele's 1907 edition is in the King's Classics Series.)

(3) **The Gospel of Nicodemus.**

This translation of Nicodemus, *de Passione Christi*, was not known to Pits, Bale, or Tanner. It is not given in Dibdin's list. Blades first mentions it in vol. ii of his *Life of Wm. Caxton*, published 1861.[1] He also refers to the MS. usually listed Add. 16165. Rogers missed it in his otherwise complete list in 1870, but in his article of 1874 refers to it thus: 'A work of Trevisa's, previously unnoticed, viz. "Nichodemus' treatise on the passion of Christ", which is to be found in the British Museum Shirley's MSS. Additional 16156,[2] mentioned by Mr. J. Rawson Lumby at p. xxviii of his Introduction to vol. iii of the Master of Rolls Edition of Higden.' This notice by Lumby was in 1871. Boase and Courtney[3] refer to it in the words of the *Catalogue of Additions to MSS. in the British Museum*:[4] 'The translacon of Nichodeme (i.e. Nichodemi pseud.-Evangelium de passione et resurrectione Jesu Christi) out of latyn into englisshe laboured by Maystre Johan Trevysa, doctour in theologye, at the instaunce of Thomas, some tyme lord of Berkley, fol. 94 b.' They (B. and C.) also give the wrong number 16156. A study of the MSS. has been made by Prof. W. H. Hulme, Western Reserve University, in his edition of the poetical Gospel of Nicodemus for E.E.T.S., Extra Series C, 1907, pp. xxxii ff. He lists nine prose MSS. of the Gospel in Middle English, and thinks that others may be found. The MSS. as listed are: (1) Magdalen College, Cambridge, Pepys 2498 (pp. 459–63); (2) Brit. Mus., Egerton

---

[1] Op. cit. He noticed that Dibdin in *Typ. Ant.*, vol. i, p. 140, did not list it.
[2] Mistake of 16156 for 16165. He copied from Lumby, who has the same mistake.
[3] *Bibl. Cornub.*
[4] *Cat. of MSS. of Additions, 1846–1847*, p. 155. For another description of this MS. see Miss Hammond's article, 'The Departing of Chaucer', *Mod. Phil.*, vol. i, pp. 331–6.

2658 (ff. 15 b–18); (3) Stonyhurst College, B. xliii (ff. 83–96); (4) Salisbury Cathedral Library, 39 (ff. 129 b–147); (5) Brit. Mus. Additional 16165 (ff. 94 b–114 b); (6) Oxford, Bodleian 207 (ff. 120 b–124); (7) Brit. Mus. Harley 149 (ff. 255–76); (8) Worcester Cathedral Library, No. 172 (ff. 4–16); (9) Cambridge Univ. Library, mm. 1, 29 (ff. 8–16). The MSS. group themselves thus: (a) Egerton, Stonyhurst, Bodley; (b) Salisbury, Additional; (c) Pepys 2498; (d) Harley 149; (e) Worcester Cathedral; (f) Cambridge Univ. Library.

The Trevisa MSS. are the Salisbury and Additional, fully described by Prof. Hulme, pp. xl–xlvi.[1] The Additional MS. 16165 is a quarto containing 258 leaves, all of which, excepting the first three and the last one, are paper. The vellum leaves are a little smaller than the others, measuring 11×8 inches; the paper ones measure $11\frac{1}{2} \times 8\frac{1}{2}$ inches. It belongs to about 1450, and is written in the hand of John Shirley. Over the top of 94 b and 95 a the following is written, in the same hand as the MS., ' Þe passyoun of oure Lord ihesu translated by mayster John Treuysa '; over 95 b and 96 a is written, 'The passyoun of Jhu Cryst by Nichodemus'; over the other pages merely ' The Passyoun of Nichodemus'. Shirley ascribes this work to Trevisa, for near the beginning, f. 94 b, he writes: 'Maistre Johan Treuysa haþe here in mynde þat some tyme þe Greekes maden Ioustes and tournamentes ', &c. In the Salisbury MS. we have: ' Here haue muynde, þat sumtyme þe Greces made Iustes and tornementes and oþer Pleyes of Maysterye etc.' Trevisa has only one of his comments in this work, found in both the Additional and Salisbury at the same place. In Additional it is found on fol. 112, where he gives a definition of ' Alleluya '. Beg. at fol. 112, a few sentences including Trevisa's addition:

'And our lord put forthe (f. 112) his honde and made þe signe of þe croys, ouer Adam, and alle þe holy seyntes, and helde Adam by þe right hande and went vp out of helle, and alle þe holy seyntes folowed oure lord þanne Dauid cryed strongelich, and seyde singe þe to oure lorde nowe a nuwe

---

[1] I examined only Add. 16165. Prof. Hulme, some years ago, transcribed the nine MSS. as well as de Worde's edition. He has been most kind in loaning me three of these transcriptions, viz. Additional, Salisbury, and Harl. 149, for the purposes of my study.

Introduction   xciii

songe for he haþe edoone merueylles and wonders, he haþe esaued his right-syde and his holy arme, oure lorde haþe emade his sauacou*n* eknowe in þe sight of nacou*n*s he haþe shewed his rightwysnesse and seyde, þis is ioye and blisse to alle his holy seyntes amen, Alleluya. *Trevysa*,[1] Alleluya is to meene preyse ye and heryeþe god alle at oones, and also lorde saue þowe me. And hit haþe menynges also as dyuers Auctours tellen þanne hit foloweþe in þe booke, here affter. Abacus seyde. . . .'

The same passage from Salisbury, f. 144 a (near end):

'*And* oure lord pute forþ ys hond *and* made þe syngne of þe croys ouer adam *and* alle þe holy seynt*us and* huld adam by þe ryȝt hond and wente vp oute of helle *and* alle þe holy seynt*us* folwede oure lord þanne David c*r*ide stronglych *and* seyde syng ȝe to oure lord a newe song for he haþ ydo m*er*ueylus *and* wondrus he haþ ysewed hys ryȝt seyde *and* hys holy Arm oure lord haþ ymad ys sauacou*n* yknowe in (f. 144 b) seyȝt of nacou*n*s he haþ yschewed hys ryȝtwysnesse *and* al þe multytude of seynt*us* answerede *and* seyde þys ys Ioye *and* blysse to all hys holy seynt*us* amen alleluia *teruisa*[2] amen ys to mene so mot hyt be alleluia hys to mene p*r*ayse ȝe *and* heryuþ god alle aton*us and* also lord saue þou me : *and* hyt haþ oþer menyn*gus* also as dyuerse aucter*us* telluþ þanne hyt folueþ in þe bok her aft*ur* þe prophet Abacus c*r*ide *and* seyde. . . .'

In none of the other seven MSS. do we find this addition. In Harl. 149 is the reading: 'thys ys the glorye to alle Sayntes Amen, All*elu*ia, Than cryed Abacuch the prophete and seyde, etc.'

Hulme prints (p. xlv) a part of f. 94 b of Add. 16165. He also mentions the early Black Letter edition of the English Gospel of Nicodemus (p. lvii). He mentions the 1507 edition by Julyan Notary, London ; Wynkyn de Worde, 1509 ; John Skat, London, 1529. The de Worde version is the most magnificent. Prof. Hulme, who looked into the matter, says :[3] ' Now, a casual comparison of the prologue, and the beginning and conclusion of the text with those of the Trevisa version (MS. Add. 16165), shows that no other connexion can possibly exist between the two versions than that of being different translations of one and the same story.' Prof. Hulme thinks

---

[1] Beg. 'Trevysa', ends 'here affter'—is Trevisa's addition.
[2] Beg. ' teruisa', ends ' her aftur '
—is Trevisa's addition.
[3] Op. cit., p. lviii.

the original of de Worde's text is to be found among the numerous Latin MSS. of the Evang. Nicod., preserved in English libraries.[1]

(4) De Re Militari and De Regimine Principum.

Trevisa's translation of the two works we are now to consider have been questioned. They are not spoken of by Pits or Bale. Tanner is the first writer to mention them. He seems sure that Trevisa translated them. Note his reasons: 'In Cod. Bodl. Digby 233, est translatio Vegetii *de re militari.* Pr. "In olde tyme it was the manere." Haec verisimiliter Trevisae debetur, quia facta erat ad mandatum dom. Tho. Berkley: A MCCCCVIII in vigilia Omnium Sanctorum finita. In eodem codice simili manu habetur translatio, cum eleganti pictura monachi regi librum dantes, Aegidii Romani *de regimine principum.* Pr. "To hys special, etc. politik sentence that is."' Dibdin merely notices them in his list. The Rev. Jas. Townley in 1821 lists them.[2] Babington,[3] after mentioning the MS. Digby 233 at Bodleian, and saying that the work was composed at the request of Lord Berkeley and finished in 1408, concludes: 'This is reasonably presumed to be executed by Trevisa, as well as a translation of Aegidius Romanus' *De Regimine Principum,* contained in the same volume.'[4] Rogers lists them as Trevisa's without doubt or comment. Cooke, in his Trevisa article in 1876 for the *Transactions* of the Bristol and Gloucestershire Archaeological Society, regards it as Trevisa's last work, finished in 1408, four years before his death at the age of 90. He says: 'The translation of Vegetius has been attributed to Hoccleve, from a copy of it in the Bodleian Library being bound up with Hoccleve's *De Regimine Principis.* The characteristic dedication, however, at its conclusion, sufficiently proves its true authorship.' Cooke gives the dedication thus: 'To us alle God graunt grace of our offen-

---

[1] Op. cit., lix. I glanced into a great number of these Latin MSS. in the Brit. Mus., Bodl., and Univ. of Camb. Libraries.

[2] *Illustrations of Biblical Lit.*, vol. ii, pp. 49-55.

[3] C. L. Kingsford, *Dict. of Nat. Biog.*, vol. lvii, p. 212, refers to these works in about the same manner as Babington.

[4] Rolls Series of Higden's *Polychronicon*, vol. i, p. lv.

dynge, space to our amendynge, and his face to be seen at our endyng. Amen.'[1]

Boase and Courtney [2] refer to both of them as MS. Bodl. Lib. Digby 233, and in a note says: ' *De re Militari* was composed at Lord Berkeley's request and finished in 1408. It is sometimes said to have been done by Trevisa, but from the account in H. O. Coxe's *Catalogus Codicum MSS. qui in Collegiis Aulisque Oxon. adservantur* (1852), ii. 19, of another copy at Magdalen College, Oxford, the translation would seem to have been executed by Clifton.' Coxe, in describing the Magdalen MS. 30, has it, ' e Latino in Anglicum Sermonem, versi per Clifton quendam, iussu Thomae domini Berkeley '.[3] He also gives the prologue and ending. The name Clif or Cleftoun was first given by Francis Douce.[4] He was followed by Caley in describing one of the Vegetius MSS., viz. B.M. Lansdowne 285. Macray is of the same opinion.[5] F. Madan, the late Librarian of Bodley, in his examination of the manuscripts, suggests Bannerton.[6] The most recent and perhaps most valuable note on the authorship of this work is by Prof. H. N. MacCracken, in an article entitled *Vegetius in English*, written for the Kittredge Anniversary Papers, published 1913.[7] Prof. MacCracken gives the various guesses to date, has some remarks about the meaning of the word Trevisa, and lists, with important notes, the nine known English MSS. Very significant is his discussion of the Trevisa authorship from internal evidence (p. 393). His notes comparing Vegetius with *Polychronicon*, although brief, are important. As he says: ' So closely does the Vegetius conform in style, dialect, and vocabulary to the acknowledged work of John Trevisa, that it is hard to believe any other had a hand in it.'[8] Prof. MacCracken continues: 'The mystery under present knowledge, seems insoluble, and may

---

[1] Compare this with dedication as taken from the MS., below, p. xcvi.

[2] *Bibl. Cornub.*, vol. ii, p. 798.

[3] *Cat. Cod. MSS. qui in Coll. Aulisque Oxon. adservantur*, by H. O. Coxe, 1852, vol. ii, p. 19.

[4] Caley's *Cat. of Lansdowne MSS.*

[5] Rev. Wm. Dunn Macray, *Cat. Cod. MSS. Digby*, 1883, p. 243.

[6] *Summary Catalogue of Western MSS.*, iv. 582.

[7] See *Papers*, pp. 389-403.

[8] After a study of months in the Trevisa material, and an examination of much of the Digby MS. 233, the present writer is of the same opinion.

be no clearer when a full comparison of the Vegetius with Trevisa's known work is made, for the writer believes it will only confirm the claim of identity here advanced.' So much for the various opinions as to authorship.

Tanner, who led the way in the Trevisa theory, based his claim on the Digby colophon, which runs thus:

'Here endeth þe book þat clerkes clepun in latyne Vigesius de re militari þe book of Vigesii of dedus of kny3thod þe whiche book was translated & turned fro latyn in to englesh at þe ordinaunce & byddynge of þe worthi & worschepful lord sire Thomas of Berkeley to gret disport & dalyaunce of lordes & alle worthy werryours þat ben apassed by wey of age al labour & trauaillyng & to grete informacion & lernyng of 3onge lordes & kny3ttes þat ben lusty & loueþ to here & see & to vse dedus of armes & chiualrye. Þe turnynge of þis book into englisch was wreton & endud in vigile of al halwes þe 3eer of oure lord, a þousand foure hundred & ei3te þe X^e 3eer of Kynge henry þe forþe. To him & to vs alle god graunt grace of oure offendynde space to oure amendynge & his face to seen at oure endyng. Amen. This is his name þat turned þis book fro latyn into Englische

Worschepful ⊏⊐ toun.'[1]

The same colophon is found in MS. Magd. Coll. Oxf. 30,[2] but with 'worschepful' omitted, and cryptogram written thus: ⊨ ton. The other changes are in spelling: clepeth for clepun, dedes for dedus, ended for endud, se for seen, vIII.te for ei3te, tenthe for X^c, herry for henry, and usually i for y in many words. fols. 1–115, 15th cent., vellum, folio.

In MS. Bodley Douce 291, fols. 4–120, the colophon is the same but cryptogram thus: ▆▆ ton. This MS. vellum, folio, mid-15th cent.

Bodl. Laud, Misc. 416, fols. 182–226, omits cryptogram, but contains colophon on date and patron. Modern.

---

[1] Colophon as copied from MS. Digby 233, f. 227, at Bodleian. MacCracken prints it, op. cit., p. 389. Vegetius follows *De Regimine Principum*, which runs for fols. 1–183, mid-15th cent.

[2] Printed by Coxe in *Cat. Cod. MSS. qui in Coll. Aulisque Oxon. adservantur*, Part II, p. 30.

Introduction   xcvii

B.M. Royal 18 A. xii, fols. 1-123. Author's name omitted. Modernized.

B.M. Lansdowne 285, fols. 82-136. Colophon on date and patron, but not on author.[1]

From this closing in Digby, which Tanner knew, he concludes, and with good ground, that Trevisa was the translator. For had not the Vicar of Berkeley concluded two famous translations, viz. *Polychronicon* 1387, and *De Prop. Rerum* 1398, in the same fashion, and at the bidding of the same Lord Berkeley, Thomas X ? And, moreover, Tanner had evidence when he wrote that Trevisa was living and Vicar of Berkeley in 1408, and that he continued as such until his death, 1412. He gives as his authority Wharton's copy, purporting to be from the Worcester Registers, which copy is now deposited in Lambeth Palace Library.[2] The recent discovery of his death in 1402, instead of 1408, would seem to destroy utterly the Trevisa theory. There is but one saving clause, viz. that a late scribe might have written 1408, as a wrong date. This seems scarcely possible.

The counts against Trevisa as the translator are:

1. The newly found date of his death, 1402, instead of the heretofore accepted date, 1412. The colophon says the Vegetius was written and ended in 1408.

2. Trevisa in no other translation gives his signature in this form.

3. A careful reading of the Digby MS. 233, Vegetius, revealed none of the well-known Trevisa annotations or notes. These occur at every turn in the *Polychronicon*. There are over one hundred of them, covering some six hundred lines. Except in a few cases they are signed at the beginning 'Trevisa'. We find these notes also in *De Prop. Rerum*. Once he has a noted

---

[1] The other MSS. as noted by MacCracken are: (1) B.M. Add. 14408, fols. 49-66, no preface, and ends i. 28. Late 15th cent. 'Translated into Eng. by John Walton?' (*Cat. of Add. MSS. 1841-5*, p. 64). In same MS. *De Regimine Principis* or *Secretum Secretorum* in English verse.

(2) B.M. Sloane 2027, fols. 1-36. Ends iii. 24. Late 15th cent. (3) Petworth 6 (Duke of Northumberland) omits colophon. (Hist. MSS. Com., 6th Report, 289, Ap.)

[2] Wharton's MS. L, p. 637, ex. Reg. Wigorn., in Bibl. Lambeth.

annotation in the *Gospel of Nicodemus*, twice in *De Regimine Principum*, and even in his short translation of *Dialogus inter Militem et Clericum* he has a most interesting note. We might look for Trevisa notes in Vegetius, had he been the translator. The work is fairly long, covering fols. 183-227. There is excellent material for explanation and comment. A close comparison with the Latin original may reveal notes unsigned; such occur occasionally in the *Polychronicon*.[1]

(5) De Regimine Principum.

This prose work of the Rule of Princes is found in one MS., viz. Bodleian Digby 233, covering fols. 1-182 b (2). It is followed by Vegetius. Both are written in the same hand.

We have already, in connexion with Vegetius, noticed the comments in regard to this work. Cooke and others in the seventies regarded it as Hoccleve's; Boase and Courtney only remark, 'This translation is supposed to have been executed by Trevisa.' MacCracken regards it as Trevisa's. In naming MSS. of Vegetius under Digby he says: 'Follows translation by same author of *De Regimine Principum*.' Miss Greenwood mentions it in the Trevisa list, but questions it, as well as Vegetius.

We have no evidence of Trevisa's handiwork from the ending. There can be no controversy in that regard. It ends with no reference to patron, date, or author. It reads thus:

f. 182 b (2) 'þanne ȝif kynges & princes hauen riȝtful werre & bataille & ȝif here enemys disturbe wrongfulliche þe pees .& þe comyn profit it is not in conuenyent to teche hem al maner fiȝtynge of bataille & al maner doynge by þe whiche þei mow ouercome here enemyes. And al suche doynge þei scholde ordeyne for þe comyn profit & for pees of citeseyns. ffor ȝif þei desiren þe comyn profit & pees of þe citeseyns þei schulle haue þat perpetual pees in þe whiche is cheef quiete & reste. Þe whiche pees god grauntep & byhateþ to his owne trewe seruantes þat is Iblessed for eueremore. Amen.'

---

[1] An edition of Vegetius and further investigation may help to settle the matter. The E.E.T.S. announces an edition in Original Series, *Trevisa's englisht Vegetius on the Art of War*, from MS. 30 Magd. Coll. Oxon., by Mr. L. C. Wharton, Superintendent in British Museum.

Introduction

We find, however, evidence of Trevisa from two interesting annotations or additions.[1] These are typical Trevisa notes, and should be compared with those from the *Polychronicon* and the *Dialogue*. The first is found in fol. 143 b (2), Chap. xvi. Just before the entry Aegidius is speaking of the four powers that 'Scholde be knowe in rewelyng of a citee: þe prince, þe consaile, þe ȝeedhalle, & þe puple'. The work of the prince has been discussed, then he comes to speak of the consaile. He proceeds to enumerate six things:

'Þat falleþ not vnder consaille; first al þyng þat is in mutable & may not chaunge is out of oure consaile, for we taken consaille for to be reweled in oure dedes & nedes, & for to voide euel & for to haue good þan þynges þat may not be voided & þynges þat may not be changed falleþ not vnder counsaille. Þerfore iii ethicorum, it is Iseid þat of euere lastynge þynges & of þynges þat may not chaunge no man axeþ consaille for no man axeþ consaille of þe dyameter þat may not be Imeete by þe costa neþer oþer thinges þat may not change. f. 143 b (2) *Treuisa*, for þe menynge herof it is to wetynge þat in quadrate liche long & brood ben foure lynes liche longe & þe foure sides þerof & eche of thilke foure side lyned is Icleped costa, and a lyne Idrawe in lengþe fro þe oo cornere of þe quadrate to anoþer corner in þe oþer side is Icleped dyameter & þat diameter is lenger þan costa & it may not be knowe in nombrane in what proporcioun þe dyameter is longere þan costa.[2]

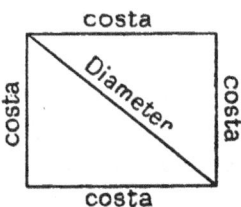

Þe seconde also of þynges þat meuen alwey in on manere wise is no consaille Itake for þynges þat meueþ alwey in on manere wise mot nedes meue in þat wise for of þynges þat ben necessarie & nedeful is no consail etc. etc.'

[1] These were found on a hasty survey of the entire MS. A careful reading and comparison with a Latin MS. may reveal others. Sometimes, in the *Polychronicon* notes, a scribe has failed to insert the word 'Trevisa', thus indicating the note. Hence a comparison with the original Latin is necessary.

[2] Trevisa's note ends with the diagram.

c   *Introduction*

The second addition or note is Chap. xvii, folio 144 b (1):

'ffor as it is Iseide iii⁰ ethicorum þere eche consail be a questioun, ȝut not eche questioun is a counsaile. ffor ȝif consaille is Itake onliche of thinges þat stonde in oure dedes consaille is a questioun not of alle thinges but onliche of doynge & dedes of mankynde. Of speculatif thinges & of kynde of thinges & of euere lastynge thinges may be manye questions but suche questions ben not Icleped consailes. *Treuysa*, cours of sterres & planettes & of oþere things of kynde þat may not chaunge ben Icleped speculabilia, doynge & dedes of mankynde ben Icleped agibilia.'[1]

From Tanner, who writes of this work, 'In eodem codice (Digby 233) simili manu (as Vegetius) habetur translatio. . . . Forte Trevisa eius auctor', to MacCracken, all writers except Cooke (who speaks of Hoccleve) and Miss Greenwood (who questions it) have assigned it to Trevisa without hesitation or doubt. The reason is not evident. Is it because the work is bound up in the same MS. as Vegetius? The above Trevisa notes, the only sound evidence of authorship so far adduced, have never been noted before. Perhaps Trevisa's authorship may be more firmly established when a close study of the style, structure, &c., is made, and the work is compared with Trevisa's known works, *Polychronicon*, *De Proprietatibus Rerum*, and *Nicodemus*.

A further word must be said in regard to the three works in this edition.

(6) Dialogus inter Militem et Clericum.

This work is not mentioned by Pits, Bale,[2] or Tanner. It was first assigned to Trevisa by Humphrey Wanley, 1708, in his description of Harleian MS. 1900. He gives no reason for making Trevisa the author. He even makes him not a translator of a Latin dialogue, but an original author, for he begins thus: 'Dyalogus inter Militem & Clericum': i.e. between the above-

---

[1] There is no indication of the closing of these additions in the MS. I referred to Latin MS. in each case.

[2] Bale's *Scriptores*, fol. 199, ed. 1548: 'Interim in monachos utcunque mordax erat, eorum & fastum & luxum multifariam taxans.

Legimus Christum (inquit) pro uerbi sui ministerio, presbyteros instituisse, sed monachos aut mendicantes fratres fecisse non inuenimus, & cetera cum similibus sententiis.'

Introduction

mentioned lord and himself (in his title he has referred to Trevisa as Chaplain to Thomas Baron of Berkeley). Wanley knew nothing of Occam's dialogue, and regarded Trevisa as the Clericus, for, after giving the opening words of the *Dialogue*, he refers to Trevisa and his work thus: 'And the main Drift thereof seemeth to be to impugne the Papal power in Temporal matters; for, as may be gathered from John Bale, he was no great friend to the Regular Clergie of those times; and might possibly differ in Opinion from them, touching more matters, than their Pride, Luxury & Hypocrisie.'

Dibdin, in 1810,[1] in describing Harl. 1900 and Trevisa's works, knew nothing of the original, for he makes the same mistake as Wanley: 'A Dialogue between a soldier and a clergyman (viz. Lord Berkeley and the Author Trevisa)'. He then quotes the beginning and the ending.[2] The Rev. Jas. Townley,[3] in 1821, makes the same mistake as Wanley and Dibdin. From the nature of his list of Trevisa's works he copied directly from Dibdin. Dibdin knew of the printed edition (Berthelet) of the *Dialogue* (he had both Ames and Herbert) and Occam; he knew that the Latin was extant in Goldast's *Monarchia*, and he must have been acquainted with Oldys' *The British Librarian*, published 1738.[4] How then did he make the mistake of making Trevisa, the clergyman in this dialogue? Did he merely follow Wanley? He evidently did not know that Trevisa was the translator of the Latin Dialogue. Trevisa's name is not mentioned by Ames, Herbert, or Oldys.

Prof. Babington, 1865, was the first to connect Occam and Trevisa. He also tells us that Occam's original *De Potestate Ecclesiastica et Saeculari* is published in Goldast's *Monarchia S. Romani Imperi*, vol. i, pp. 13–18.[5] Rogers and Cooke both list it as a translation of William of Occam's dialogue. Boase

---

[1] Op cit., vol. i, p. 140.
[2] Dibdin evidently knew the last part of the *Dialogue*. The last two sentences are not given by Wanley. In the last sentence he had trouble with the phrase 'panes proposicionis'. He writes it 'thaves' (shewbread). He also has two other glosses in his quotation, viz. lewd (ignorant) and nought (not). He has modernized the spelling.
[3] Op. cit., vol. ii, p. 49.
[4] See p. xlvi.
[5] Rolls Series of *Polychronicon*, vol. i, p. liv.

and Courtney are the first and only (except *Dict. of Nat. Biog.*) authority to make Berthelet's copy Trevisa's translation. The entry is: ' M. Guilhelmi de Ockam, Angli, doctoris Parisiensis ex ordine minorvm Disputatio svper potestate praelatis ecclesiae ... sub forma "Dialogi inter clericum & militem". In Melchior Goldastus' Monarchia S. Romani Imperii (1611), i. 13-18.' Then follows a note: 'The above is a copy of that which J. Trevisa translated into English with the following title: "A dialogue betwene a knyght and a clerke concerning the power spiritual and temporall." (Imprinted at London in Flete-strete in the house of Thomas Berthelet nere to the cundite at the sygne of Lucrece) n. d. (1555).' Boase and Courtney then mention the MSS. in which it is found, viz. St. John's Coll. Camb. H. 1, Harl. 1900, and B.M. Add. 24194.

Kingsford is not so sure of the Trevisa authorship as he is of the other works. He names FitzRalph's *Sermon* and the *Methodius* tract as Nos. 3 and 4 of the seven works listed, making no comment, but puts the *Dialogue* among the doubtful works, with the remark that Dr. Babington ascribes the translation to Trevisa. He says it was printed at London 1540, thus ascribing to Trevisa the translation of Berthelet's edition. Kingsford agrees with Poole that Occam is not the author of the *Dialogue*.[1] Miss Greenwood regards the *Dialogue* as Trevisa's translation, referring to it in her list as 'Translation from pseudo-Ockham on temporal power of the church'.

No reason has been given from Wanley downwards for assigning the *Dialogue* to Trevisa. That it is his translation is established by one of his annotations, if on no other grounds. This annotation is found, near the beginning of fol. 16, headed by his name (see p. 6). The clerk and the knight are discussing the time of Christ's *manhed*, and the time of his power and *maieste*. Here we have Trevisa's definition of these phases of Christ's life. The addition takes up the greater part of fol. 16, ending at 'ffor the Kny3t spekiþ in þis manere', p. 7, l. 8.

---

[1] See articles in *Dict. of Nat. Biog.* under Ockham and Trevisa; also above, pp. xliii ff.

(7) FitzRalph's Sermon 'Defensio Curatorum'.

The translation of this sermon by Trevisa is not mentioned by Pits, Bale, or Tanner. It is first mentioned by Wanley in his examination of Harl. MS. 1900. He tells us the purpose of the sermon, also the date and place, by quoting the title of the Latin original as published in Brown's *Fasciculus Rerum expetendarum & fugiendarum*, App., p. 466: 'Defensorium Curatorum contra eos qui privilegiatos se dicunt: Propositio Richardi (Filius Radulfi, sive Fitz-Rauf) Archiepiscopi Armachani Primatis Hiberniae, facta in Consistorio coram Domino Papa, & Dominis Cardinalibus ac Praelatis, ad utilitatem Cleri & populi Christiani, super materia Mendicitatis & Privilegiorum, contra Fratres de Ordinibus mendicantium quibuscunque: apud Avinionem octava die Mensio Novembris, A. D. 1357.' After quoting the passage fol. 11 b,[1] in regard to the number of students at Oxford (see text, p. 58, l. 26) he mentions two other sources of the Latin text, viz. Lambeth MSS. and Appendix to Usher's *Hist. Dogm.*[2] Dibdin gives the same quotation as Wanley down to 'haþ' (text, p. 59, l. 10). He has no reference to the originals, but only 'A translation of a Latin sermon of Radulf or Fitz Rauf, Archibishop of Armagh, Nov. 8th, 1357, against Mendicant Friars'. Babington has it preached at Oxford, 1357, against the mendicant friars.[3] Rogers, 1870, follows Babington; Cooke, 1876, fails to list it. Boase and Courtney give Nov. 8, 1357, at Oxford. They also name the MSS. containing it: Harl. 1900; St. John's Coll. Camb. H. 1; B.M. Addit. 24194; they also mention the Latin in Brown's *Fasciculus, etc.* Miss Greenwood fails to give place or date, simply: 'Sermon by Richard Fitz Ralph, abp. Armagh, addressed to the pope, against the mendicant friars.' Not one of these writers hesitates in ascribing this to Trevisa,[4] and yet

---

[1] The passage quoted beginning 'So þat'.

[2] Wanley does not mention the original Latin MSS. of the sermon.

[3] Not preached at Oxford. See Poole, *Dict. of Nat. Biog.*, vol. xix, p. 196. Why does Babington make this mistake, and why is he followed by Rogers and Boase and Courtney? As we have seen, the original was known by Wanley. He gives Avignon.

[4] None of them give any reason for ascribing to Trevisa.

there is no evidence of authorship in the MS. itself. Trevisa has failed to find anything worthy of his annotations. Of course it is bound up in five manuscripts, with two of Trevisa's works, viz. the *Dialogue* and *Polychronicon*. Does this prove anything?

TREVISA THE TRANSLATOR.

My conclusion that Trevisa translated the sermon is based upon (A) his method of translation, and (B) his arrangement of words in the sentence.

A. *Method of Translation.*

As a translator Trevisa had regard always to exact accuracy. He wished to be understood—this resulted in wordiness. In his original works, 'Dialogue between a Lord and a Clerk upon Translation', 'The Epistle of Sir John Trevisa upon the translation of *Polychronicon* into our English tongue', and 'Notes to the *Polychronicon*', he is extremely verbose. But he is even more so in his translations.

This verbosity displays itself chiefly in two ways: (1) The use of doublets, translating one Latin word by two or more words. (2) Expansion of the Latin phrase, often adding words and phrases not found in the original.

1. *The use of Doublets.*

The most notable characteristic of Trevisa's style is the doubling of words. This is a constant practice, as well in his original works as in his translations.

Original Works:
Dialogue between a Lord and a Clerk.
  (1) but God of his mercy and grace.
  (2) of their goodness and courtesy.
  (3) to make translation trusty and true.
Trevisa's note in *Dialogue between a Soldier and the Clerk*,
    text, p. 6.
  (1) of his myȝt, power & maieste.
  (2) & hadde þe see & wynde & weder & fendes.
  (3) over alle þe deueles & fendes.
  (4) also his lore was in myȝt & power.

Translations:

Out of many examples listed I give only a few.

1. *The Polychronicon.*
   (1) Vol. i, p. 359. L. deformes = wonderfoule & yuel i-schape.
   (2) Vol. i, p. 359. L. in nundinis = chepinge and in feires.
   (3) ,, p. 361. L. novis prodigiis = newe meruailles & wondres.
   (4) Vol. iii, p. 241. L. fortunam = þe fortune & happe.
   (5) ,, ,, L. straverat = i-heled & i-sprad.
   (6) ,, iv, p. 9. L. eius ditioni = to his lordschipe and mageste.
   (7) Vol. iv, p. 19. L. dolose = by fraude & by gyle.
   (8) ,, p. 21. L. propter pium cultum = for his riȝtful byleue and worschippinge of God.

2. *The Dialogue between the Soldier and the Clerk.*
   (1) 2/10. L. statuta = statutes & ordinances.
   (2) 4/6. L. dominium = lordschipe, power, & auctorite.
   (3) 6/5. L. potestas = power & mageste.
   (4) 13/4. L. lacerata lex = þe lawe is y-tore and to-rent.
   (5) 15/10. L. cognitionum = of doome & knowleche of dower.
   (6) 23/13. L. vestram violentiam = ȝoure violence & ȝoure wrong.
   (7) 24/11. L. tollitis = ȝe to-tereþ & to-heleþ & takiþ awey.

3. *The Gospel of Nicodemus.*
   Þat þowe have and comande, þat he come and stande, gret reverence & worship, destroye and vndo, lowted & bowed, bowed and bended, nys neyþer truwe ne soþe, and tellen þe sooþe and þe trouþe, hade pitie & mercye, we wit ner avyse hem, ye witteþe & knoweþe.

4. *De Regimine Principum.*
   Dignytees & hye astates, by heritage & by successioun, his children & successours, resoun & lawe, gret & perfite loue, to kepe & saue, precepte and commandement, syngel power and myȝt, schal be wise & konnynge to gouerne & to rule, to declare & determine.

5. *The Sermon.*

(1) 43/2. L. ex quo est acceptior Deo = & more alowed & leef to god.
(2) 45/9. L. involuti = beþ wrapped & snarled.
(3) 46/4. L. involuti = beþ y-wralled & y-snarled.
(4) 48/30. L. hoc implicat contradictionem = hit closeþ contradiccion & wiþ saiyng.
(5) 50/33. L. suo proprio sacerdote = to her prest & her ordinarie.
(6) 63/32. L. inobedientes = vnobedient & vnbuxom.
(7) 72/16. L. quod commodum temporale = þat worldliche profit & wynnyng.
(8) 75/30. L. habenti corporalem defectum = a wemme & defaute in his body.
(9) 76/19. L. sicut in furto = as in þefþe & stalþe.
(10) 92/12. L. de victu & vestitu = of mete & drynke & cloþ.

II. *Expansions and Additions.*

1. *The Polychronicon.*

Vol. i, 137 ff. Lat. in prima namque expeditione Aciana, post Vesorem regem Ægypti fugatum, in redeundo circa Asiam pacandam quindecim annis vivi immorati, querelis uxorem tantam moram non ferentium revocantur=in þe firste iourney in Asia after þat þey hadde i-dreue and i-chased and i-pursewed Vasore þe kyng of Egipt into þe tornynge aȝe, þey abede fiftene ȝere for to make pees in Asia. But wyfes made grete pleyntes and sorwes þat hire housbondes were so longe from home, and so þe men were of-sent and torned home to dwelle wiþ hir wifes.

Vol. i, p. 361. Lat. ut aliquam aquam transeunt, in propriam naturam redeunt = but anon as þere swyne passeþ any water þey torneþ aȝen into his own kynde, where it be straw, hey, gras, oþer torues.

Vol. iii, pp. 239 and 241. Lat. reliquam partem de nocte soporatam dispersit=and fil vppon the oþer deel anyȝt whanne þey were a-slepe, and slowȝ of hem, and chased hem, and brake and to schad hem everich oon from oþer.

Introduction

Vol. iv, p. 11. Lat. cuius veneni tanta vis fuit = þe strengþe and þe malice of þis venym was so grim and so grisliche.

Vol. iv, p. 25. Lat. qui respondit ei amphibolice = and Appolyn answered hym amphabolice, þat is, that he 3af hym an answere of double understondynge.

2. *The Dialogue.*

(1) 4/10. Lat. Christianus = a trewe Cristen man.

(2) 6/3. Lat. humilitates vsque suam passionem = þe tyme of his manhed was from þat he toke flesch & blode anon to his passion.

(3) 11/15. Lat. ergo etiam ratione peccati debet papa de sanguine iudicare sed plumbeum est argumentum id = þerfore bycause of synne þat siche men doþ, þe pope schal deme & be domesman? In cause of felony & of mannes deþ, þe argument is nou3t.

(4) 15/12. Lat. & saepe firmari possit regalibus instrumentis = & schal be preued oþer dispreued by preues oþer dispreues of þe kynges lawe.

(5) 17/10. Lat. vtique operatiis & stipendiariis = to workmen, to hyred men, to oxen & nou3t to kynges.

(6) 23/3. Lat. & quicquid superest = and al þat is ouer þat nediþ to mete & drynke & helyng.

(7) 24/14. Lat. non perstrepite = y pray 3ou leteþ be 3oure noyse & 3oure grucchyng.

(8) 25/12. Lat. videtis ergo, cum pauca regi traditis, quomodo salutem vestram redimatis, quando omnia bona vestra deperdenda saluat = þanne 3e seeþ þat whanne 3e 3eueþ a lytel what to þe kyng 3e biggeþ 3oure owne sauacioun & saueþ 3oure owne goodes & catel þat schulde be distried wiþ 3oure owne nei3bores & wiþ men of straunge londes, nere þe kynges help & his socoure.

(9) 26/15. Lat. sed non quiescitis = & 3e resteþ nou3t but grucchiþ alwey.

(10) 32/8. Lat. reddite omnibus debita, cui tributum, tributum, cui vectigal vectigal = 3eldeþ & payeþ to alle men what is dewe to hem to whom tribute is dewe payeþ tribute. And to whom oþer rente and seruise is dewe payeþ hem oþer rent & seruise.

(11) 36/12. Lat. posse addere, posse minuere quae libet temperare = & þat he may putt to pryuyleges & lawes & wiþdrawe & chaunge & redresse euereche þat erreþ.

(12) 37/11. Lat. panes propositionis = loues þat were cleped panes proposicionis.

3. *Sermon.*

(1) 45/2. Lat. incendiarios = incendiaries þat settiþ houses afyre.

(2) 49/4. Lat. suo sacerdoti sive ordinario = to his owne prest þat is his curator & his ordinarie.

(3) 50/4. Lat. confitens = he þat is y-schryve to freres.

(4) 52/11. Lat. scilicet obedientiae quoad legem confessionis, & etiam quoad legem personae = for he is obedient in þat he schryueþ hym & also in þat he schryueþ hym to his ordynarie, þat is his curatour.

(5) 55/33. Lat. fratribus confitentur = & children beþ y-schryve to freres.

(6) 56/21. Lat. quale est furtum huiusmodi = siche þefþe and trespace is siche stilyng.

(7) 56/32. Lat. pro aliquo malo vitando = for-to avoyde & ascape harme what harm hit euere were.

(8) 60/11. Lat. per hoc clerum & populum importune velut effrontes ubi libet overantes = and bynymeþ þerby þe fleece of þe peple & of þe clergie & chargiþ hem in euerech place.

(9) 62/19. Lat. quod habere jus praedicandi fidelibus = having riȝt to preche and to cristen men.

(10) 72/7. Lat. recipiendi ad sepulturam = to fonge dede bodyes to sepulture.

(11) 73/28. Lat. in paupertate & humilitate = in þe heiȝeste pouert and mekenesse.

(12) 81/18. Lat. nec fingere quis potest quod praemissum praeceptum est ceremoniale = & no man may feyne þat the forseide heeste is cerymonial, to be vsed among þe Jewes aloone.

(13) 82/12. Lat. & aperto ore eius invenies staterem = & open his mouþe & þou schalt fynde a stater a þinge þat weyeþ half an vnce.

(14) 83/23. Lat. condemnat eos qui quaestum aestimant

pietatem = dampneþ her trowyng & her opinioun þat trowiþ þat beggerie & gaderyng is holy myldnesse.
(15) 86/11. Lat. quorum neutrum providus homo affirmabit = but no wise man wole saye þat þe holy gost had forȝete his office noþer þat þe apostles hadde sich enuye.
(16) 87/3. Lat. quod a vulgo vocatus non solum filius fabri, sed faber = ffor he was nouȝt y-cleped oonlich a carpenters sone, but also he was openlich y-cleped a carpenter.

B. *Arrangement of Words.*

I. *Position of the Subject.*
Very rarely does the subject follow the verb in Trevisa. In the first three hundred pages of vol. v of the *Polychronicon* the following cases occur : p. 5 & þere came a wydewe wepynge ; p. 19 but speke wolde he nevere ; p. 115 þat tyme come up Arrian his heresie.
The Dialogue: 13/12 þanne bigynneþ ȝoure knowleche & ȝoure dome ; 20/4 ȝaf nouȝt oure forfadres.
The Sermon: 45/4 of þe whiche vnneþe comeþ to me & to my penitaunseres fourty aȝere ; 47/27 most be ordeyned his propre medicyn ; 86/3 may nouȝt be y-founde oon notable worde.

II. *Position of Object.*
Exceptions to the regular order are :
Polychronicon, vol. v, pp. 1-300 : p. 31 cruel lawes he tempered ; p. 91 myȝte tho non answere gete ; p. 129 olde chirches he mendede, and new chirches he bulde.
Dialogue: 21/2 masses ȝe siggiþ nouȝt noþer syngiþ in chirche.
Sermon: 46/2 & so of þe grettest wynnyng, no teþing paie ; 48/3 þei myȝt noon siche bildyngis make ; 84/3 bot God hit forbede ; 89/16 his resouns ich ouerpasse at þis tyme.

III. *Position of the Adjective.*
In the case of a single adjective, it almost invariably precedes the noun. In the case of two adjectives, Trevisa does not

adhere to the old rule, one before the noun and one after. The following examples illustrate his usage:

1. *The Dialogue between the Lord and the Clerk*: the great & high tower; great & noble information; to make translation trusty & true.

2. *Epistle on Translation*: my worthy and worshipful Lord; a bettere English translation & more profitable.

3. *Polychronicon*: vol. v, p. 47 a wel trewe iuge and stedefast; vol. v, p. 199 with grete batailles and stronge; vol. v, p. 203 & hadde weder hard and stormes; vol. ii, p. 227 wiþ smale twigges and wiþ red; vol. ii, p. 231 couenable and clene mete; vol. ii, p. 303 of oon colour whyte oþer blak.

4. *De Rerum Proprietatibus*: the noble and expert doctrine; of wise and well-learned; ye witty and eloquent readers; diuers and contrary shapes; many riuers and great; a strong land and a sturdy; white bears most great and right fierce; vseth vile meat and little.

5. *Rule of Princes*: youre chaste & worthi childhode; eny singuler profite; by liknes rude & bystrous; vnder hiʒ & derk materes.

6. *Nicodemus*: chese ye many men and stronge; chose twelve þe strengest men and most mighty; a wonder dredful sweven and a grisly; many gloryous myracles; eight and thritty wynter; clene lynen cloþe.

7. *Dialogue between the Soldier and the Clerk*: 1/4 sotil & derk speche; 6/26 & many oþer grete dedes; 20/9 in pore men & nedy; 20/12 grete lordschipes & huge; 30/4 to holy vse & mylde; 31/12 to comyn & greuouse charges; 35/3 by witnesse cleer & trewe.

8. *Sermon*: 39/15 seuen sermons oþer eiʒte; 43/22 þat were damage & desauauntage greuous & huge; 49/16 hereþ oon masse oþir many; 55/34 wiþ smale ʒiftes and gileful; 59/9 is a noble librarie and a grete; 63/2 of þe laste riʒtful dome; 91/9 in þe mouþe of a wise man & redy.

IV. *Position of the Adverb.*

The adverb is almost always placed after the verb. Very often the object separates it from the verb.

1. *Polychronicon*: vol. v, p. 2 dede noþing wrongfulliche;

p. 17 brouȝte hym by myȝte prieueliche ; p. 27 þat recceþ neuere ; p. 91 offrede sacrifise besiliche ; p. 207 he ȝaf neuere bataille.

2. *Dialogue*: 8/2 lo þou herest openlich ; 11/12 þis argument is riȝt nouȝt ; 24/5 þat recchelesliche suffreþ ȝou so frowardliche wirche ; 37/4 suffre ȝe hit pacientliche ; 37/6 no man kike vnriȝtfullich.

3. *Sermon* : 39/23 never beggide wilfulliche ; 40/1 never tauȝt wilfulliche to begge ; 40/3 no man may redilich & holiliche beggyng vppon hym take euermore to holde ; 40/21 y pray ȝowre holynesse mekelich & deuoutliche ; 42/16 þat freres counseileþ so men ; 44/24 ffer þei payeþ neuere teþinge ; 61/35 schulde coueite his catel wrongfulliche ; 64/23 schal examyne hem bisiliche of þe riȝt feiþ ; 64/32 þei doþ neuerþelas vnobedientliche ; 65/8 by þe which þei beþ so made riche ; 67/11 ich hote alle freres heiȝliche by obedience ; 79/5 he takeþ þat office wilfullich ; 82/32 ſanne Crist dide so neuer.

(8) Methodius ' þe bygynnyng of þe world and þe Ende of Worldes '.

This is not mentioned by Pits, Bale, or Tanner, unless it is the one listed *De Memorabilibus temporum*. The Harleian Catalogue recognizes it among Trevisa's works; and quotes the title (p. xvi above). The Catalogue has this remark on the original : ' Learned men generally deem it supposititious ; it being idle enough, and making mention of the great Conquests & Cruelties of the Sarazens, who brake not forth from Arabia until many Centuries after the decease of Methodius Patarensis.' Dibdin notices it, as part of Harl. 1900. Townley has the same notice as Dibdin. Rogers : ' A spurious production "On the beginning and end of the world ", ascribed to Methodius.' Cooke does not mention it. Boase and Courtney : 'Erroneously ascribed to Methodius, Patriarch of Constantinople, who died 14 June, 846.' Miss Greenwood : 'Translation of a tract by pseudo-Methodius.'

The authorities quoted assign this to Trevisa without giving any reason. It is bound up with Trevisa material in but two MSS., viz. Harl. 1900 and Burleigh House.

TREVISA NOT THE TRANSLATOR.

My conclusion that Trevisa did not translate this work is based upon his method of translation, and his arrangement of words in the sentence.

A. *Method of Translation.*

We have in English not a full and complete translation of Methodius's *Revelationes*. The Latin work consists of about 7,000 words; the English translation has been shortened to about 3,500. A great number of lines and passages, however, have been translated literally. There is a complete absence of the Trevisa habit of using doublets. The tendency is to shorten the Latin expression. Very rarely does the translator make explanations. The following illustrations will show the method employed:

96/6 þere were men wickid doeris & fynderis of worst crafte of þe sones of Caym. Lat. surrexerunt viri malae artis inventores, iniqui, & omni nequitia plani, ex filiis Cain.

99/2 afterward þe sones of Iaphet senten to Iointum men and gaftis men of heliynge & buylderis. Lat. miserunt viros potentes filiis Iaphet, nimis sapientes & artifices in arte tectoria constructores.

100/5 Cusdro herynge, lete hem aloon til þat þei passide þe flood of Tigre. Lat. audiens autem de eis Cosdrum, subrisit & dimisit eos vsque transierunt flumen Tygrim.

102/3 & þe ȝok of hem schal be heuy vppon þe nolles of folkes. Lat. & in duplum erit iugum illorum, super colla vniuersarum gentium.

104/15 and þei schule go togidre seruauntis & olde men riche men & pore wiþ affliccioun & weelynge schule seye: 'Blessed be þei þat wente before vs of þis liȝt.' Lat. & gradiuntur in ea senes & seniores, inopes & diuites, esurientes, sitientes, compedibus vincti, & manicis ligati, & beatificant eos qui iam mortui sunt.

105/15 her horsis þei schule tyȝe to þe sepulcris of seyntis, as to rackis. Lat. et iumenta sua ad sepulchra sanctarum alligabunt, tanquam ad praesepia.

106/6 þus soþly þei pursuede þe prophetis þat weren before

Introduction cxiii

vs, but whiche dwelleþ stille vnto þe ende, he schal be saf. Lat. sic enim persecuti sunt prophetae qui fuerunt ante vos: qui autem sustinuerit in finem hic saluus erit.

108/5 as þei were in þe dayes of Noe etynge and drinkinge, gladinge & weddinge. Lat. sicut enim in diebus Noë erant homines manducantes & bibentes, & nubentes, & nuptias contrahentes.

108/12 and þei schule hyde hem silf in hilles and in spelunkis. Lat. abscondent se in montibus, & speluncis & in monumentis.

108/15 siche perfere schul ete þe flescheͥ of men & serpentis & iumentis. Lat. comedent carnes hominum, & bibent sanguinem bestiarum sicut aquam, & comedent immunda, serpentes, scorpiones.

B. Arrangement of Words.

1. *Position of the Subject.*

In many cases the subject is compound, and the parts are separated by the verb. This peculiarity never occurs in Trevisa. Examples are:

94/12 þei beþ cast out virgyns of paradise.

95/11 fornicaciouns beþ ouermyche enlargide vppon erþe & vnclennessis of þe sones of Caym.

95/17 and Caym dwellide & his kynrede.

97/12 Noe bigan to buylde agein newe possessioun, & his sones in þe erþe.

98/18 þei made to hem a kyng þe sones of Cham.

104/4 & alle þingis schulen be vnder þe ȝok of hem & in þe tribute of hem & alle ournamntis of riche men.

108/11 & þei schule bigynne to wexe pale for drede, alle men þat dwellen vppon erþe.

2. *Position of the Object.*

Four examples of object preceding the verb: 98/10 al astronomye & sterres of heuene he fonde; 102/15 fiȝteris wiþ armes þei gaten; 105/15 her horsis þei schule tyȝe; 108/16 wymmen wiþ lytel children þei schul ete.

3. *Position of the Adjective.*

The translator is most sparing in his use of adjectives. A

h

single adjective before the noun is the rule. Contrary to Trevisa's custom, very few predicative adjectives occur. The only deviation is to be found in the following:

95/1 þei gendride Caym the first geten; 95/7 a man geaunt & grete; 96/9 þe sones of Lameth þe blynde.

4. Position of Adverbs.

Very few adverbs are used. The translator appears to have difficulty in placing them, especially the adverbial phrases.

95/13 in þe IX^c ȝere soþly & XXX Adam is deed, & is buried in Ebron, in þe first þousand of þe world.

100/16 wente oute firste of wildernesse to stryue in batail.

'Soþly' is used very often, in time phrases, as, 'Soþly in þe sixe hundred ȝere etc.', which is but rarely used by Trevisa. ('It is soþe' is occasionally used in Trevisa.) The adverb in 'liche' does not occur. This is used by Trevisa, not only as an adverb, but also as an adjective.

5. Other Peculiarities.

(a) forto used but once: 103/6 wiþ þat þat is most foule forto saye. In Trevisa, used very often, in the following senses: *Poly.* v. 207 forto = Lat. donec. *Dial.* 7/12 but for to folowe hym = Lat. ut, in order that; also *Dial.* 7/14 &.forto preue þis.

(b) tofore = before, is very common in Trevisa, but is never found in Methodius.

(c) The Genitive in his, -es, -is is very frequent in Trevisa, but found only once in Methodius, e. g. 110/2 a man of mannes seed of þe kynred of Dan. In all other cases the genitive is formed with 'of'.

(d) The indefinite 'me' occurs again and again in Trevisa.[1] This does not occur in Methodius.

(e) *Impersonal verb.* The only example of the impersonal use in Methodius is 96/18 it forþinkiþ me þat y made man. The impersonal construction is very common in Trevisa. *Dialogue*: 3/9 him nediþ nouȝt but write; 10/14 & ȝeue where hym likeþ;

---

[1] Malory uses 'men' (Baldwin, p 20), so also does Caxton (Keelner, xlvi).

14/12 hit nediþ nouȝt but close þe ȝates; 28/9 þanne me schal nouȝt spare; 33/10 ffor hem nediþ. *Sermon*: 40/29 me is leuer suffre; 41/3 as me semeþ; 58/24 for hem is leuer make hem erþe tilyers; 78/19 hereby as him semeþ.

(*f*) *Vocabulary*. Trevisa's familiar words do not occur in the tract. Among these may be listed: bynyme, vnneþe, eueriche, wiþsigge, outtake (except).

(*g*) And finally, the loose sentence, as displayed here, is not Trevisa's. One example will suffice. 96/5 in þe CCC & XL^c ȝere of þe lif of Iareth in þe secunde þousand of þe world, þere were men wicked doeris & fynderis of worst crafte of þe sones of Caym, & of al vnclennesse, & filþe, þat is Obal & Tubal, þat is to wite þe sones of Lameth þe blynde, which was þe first blynde man þat slow Caym.

(9) Trevisa and the Bible—History of the Discussion.

That Trevisa translated the Bible was first mentioned by Caxton in the proheme to his edition of the *Polychronicon* (1482), where he states that: 'Treuisa vycarye of barkley which atte request of one Sir thomas lord barkley translated this sayd book [*Polychronicon*] the byble & bartylmew de proprietatibus rerum out of latyn into englyssh.' Bale[1] (1495–1563) follows Caxton: 'In Anglicum idioma, ad petitionem praedicti sui domine de Barkeley, transtulit Bibliorum opus.' Smyth[2] in translating *Balaeus de Scriptor Angl. Centur.* 7, No. 18: 'Into the English tongue hee likewise at the request of said lord Berkeley translated the whole bible, as well the old as New Testament.' Pits (1560–1616) simply says: 'Sacra Biblia libros duos.' Bishop Ussher[3] (1581–1656) seems to follow Bale. Carew[4] (1602) writes, referring to Trevisa:

'At whose request [Thomas Lord Berkeley] he translated the Bible into the English tongue; though the same was done by John Wickliffe fifty years before, but not with that perfection of language, that Trevisa did it, altho Trevisa's translation

---

[1] *Script. Illustr.*, ed. 1559, p. 518.
[2] *Op. cit.*, vol. i, p. 343.
[3] *Hist. Dogmatica*, p. 157 (Ussher quotes Bale and refers to him).
[4] *Op. cit.*, ed. 1811, p. 269.

cxvi   *Introduction*

is altogether as far short of Tyndall's in Henry VIII days, by reason the English tongue was still improving to a higher pitch, for they all agreed in the original sense and meaning of the text.'

In 1611 the translators of King James's Version of the Bible seemed to have believed it. The preface says: 'Much about that time, even in our King Richard's the Seconds dayes, John Trevisa translated them into English.'

Cooke says:

'Fuller writes as if he had seen the translation itself and compared it with Wyckliff's. In his *Church History of Britain* (1655), in an entry under the year 1395,[1] 19 Rich. II, on the death of Trevisa, he says: " But his masterpiece was the translating of the Old and New Testaments, justifying his act herein by the example of Bede, who turned the Gospel of St. John in English. I know not which more to admire, his ability that he could, his courage that he durst, or his industry that he did perform so difficult and dangerous a task, having no other commission than the command of his patron, Thomas Lord Berkeley. It may seem a miracle that the bishops being thus busy in persecuting God's servants, and Trevysa so obnoxious to their fury for this translation, that he lived and died without any molestation. Yet was he a known enemy to monkery, witness that (among many others) of his speeches, that he had read, Christ had sent apostles and priests into the world, but never any monks or begging friars. But whether it was out of reverence to his own aged gravity, or respect to his patron's greatness, he died full of honor, quiet, and age, little less than ninety years old."'

In his *Worthies of England*[2] (first ed., 1662) Fuller, in writing of the Worthies of Cornwall, gives almost the entire space of Trevisa to this translation of the Bible :

'A daring work for a private person in that age, without particular command from Pope or public council. Some much admire he would enter on this work, so lately performed (about

---

[1] Fuller, *Ch. Hist. of Britain*, in ed. of 1655, given in pars. 43, 44, 45, under date 23 Rich. II, 1397. In Brewer's ed. 1845, put under year 1395, 19 Rich. II, vol. ii, p. 380. In Nichols's ed. 1868 same date as 1845 ed. (3 vols.), vol. i, Bk. IV, pp. 543-4.

[2] 1662 ed. (in 4 parts), Part I, p. 214; 1811 ed., John Nichols (2 vols.), vol. i, p. 217; 1840 ed., P. A. Nuttall (3 vols.), vol. i, pp. 316, 317.

fifty years before) by John Wickliffe. What was this, but, *actum agere*, to do what was done before ? Besides, Wickliffe and Trevisa agreeing so well in their judgments, it was much he would make a re-translation. Such consider not, that in that age it was almost the same pains for a scholar to translate as transcribe the Bible. Secondly, the time between Wickliffe and Trevisa was the crisis of the English tongue, which began to be improved in fifty, more than in three hundred years formerly. Many coarse words (to say no worse) used before are refined by Trevisa, whose translation is as much better than Wickliffe's, as worse than Tyndal's. Thus, though the fountain of the original hath always clearness alike therein, channels of translation will partake of more or less purity, according to the translators age, industry, and ability.'

Wharton (1664-95) follows Ussher in ascribing the translation to Trevisa. He even ascribes the revised version of Wycliffe to Trevisa. John Lewis (1675-1747) in his work on Wycliffe's translation [1] in 1731, writes of Wharton's opinion thus:

'I am assured by a learned friend that the late Mr. Humfrey Wanley [2] (1672-1726), who had taken a great deal of pains in this matter and been very curious in his searching told him, that Mr. Wharton in ascribing the translation commonly called Wicliff's to Trevisa was misled by John Bagford [2] (1650-1716), and that Trevisa translated no more of the Bible than certain sentences painted upon the walls of the Chapel in Berkeley Castle.'

Mr. Wanley, who examined the Trevisa MS. (now Harl. 1900) some time between 1708 and 1726, expresses his doubt of the Trevisa translation thus :

'As to the Bible's being wholly translated by our author Trevisa : I perceive it mentioned by Caxton : from him by Bale and Pits, who give the beginning of the Preface thereunto : from Bale, Primate Usher takes the notion ; and at length Mr. Wharton (App. ad Cav. Hist. Litt., p. 49) [3] believes it may still be extant ; it relating not to the book [*Polychronicon*] in hand. I shall say no more but this ; I shall be very glad to see one of them.'

Lewis thinks that Bale was misled by mistaking the dedica-

[1] *The New Testament Translation of John Wicliff*, 1731, p. 13. Also in Lewis, *A Complete Hist. of Translations of Bible and New Testament*, ed. 1818, p. 50.

[2] See *Dict. Nat. Biog.*

[3] *Cat. Lib. MSS. Bibl. Harl.*, vol. ii, p. 320.

tion, 'I Johan Trevisa your preeste & bedemen obedyant and buxom to werke your wylle', to Trevisa's Epistle to Lord Berkeley on translation of the *Polychronicon*, for a dedication to a translation of the Bible. As noticed above, Bale and Pits and Tanner (below) all have this translation beginning: 'Ego Iohannes Trevisa, Sacerdos.' Mr. Lewis proceeds: 'So far as I can find, no body ever yet saw an English Bible with a preface on it beginning in this manner.' He takes exception to Wanley's statement that Trevisa translated only certain verses painted on the chapel of Berkeley Castle, and gives a number of verses taken from Trevisa's translation of Barthol. *De Prop. Rerum*, given to him by Dr. Daniel Waterland (1683-1740). The verses[1] are Matt. xii. 45, 46, Matt. xviii. 32, Matt. xix. 13, 16, Matt. xxv. 18, Matt. xxvii. 19.

Tanner (1674-1735) thought that Trevisa translated the Bible: 'Jussu nobilis viri Thomae Dom. Berkeley patroni sui benignissimi transtulit in sermonum Anglicum Utrumque Testamentum, lib. II. "Ego Iohannes Trevisa, Sacerdos."[2] Huius translatione meminit G. Caxtonus in Praefat. ed. tr. Polychronici.'

In the beginning of the nineteenth century Dibdin made an investigation. While delivering a course of lectures on Ancient English Literature at the Royal Institution, he became interested in Trevisa and his Bible. He wrote to his friend, the Rev. J. Hughes, who was resident in the Berkeley family, for information. Part of the letter referring to the Bible is as follows:[3]

'Berkeley Castle,
'Nov. 7th, 1805.

'I take the earliest opportunity of answering yours, having been here but a few days. I have made every inquiry and search respecting the information you want, and am sorry to say it is not in my power to remove the uncertainty you labour under respecting Trevisa's translation of the Bible, notwithstanding, I have the strongest reason to suppose, from circumstances I have met with, that such a translation was made, and

---

[1] See below, p. cxxvi.
[2] These words by Bale and Pits are the opening words of Trevisa's epistle to Berkeley on translation of *Polychronicon*.
[3] This letter is quoted in full by Dibdin, Ames's *Typ. Antiq.*, vol. i, pp. 141 ff. Parts are quoted and discussed by Cooke and Rogers, who take the opposite view (see below,

was even made in the English language, and that it existed in this family so late as the time of James 2nd. The book, translated by Trevisa, was given, as a very precious gift by the lord of Berkeley to the prince (I suppose) of Wales, and the prince's letter thanking the Lord of B. for his gift, I have read: he does not say positively that it was the Bible, but as he hopes (as far as I recollect) to be able to make good use of so valuable a gift, there is reason to suspect that he meant the Bible. The letter is still extant among the archives of the Castle. Lord Berkeley (of whom I have made inquiries in order to ascertain what you wanted if possible) has informed me that the book, given by his ancestors is at present, as he has reason to believe, in the Vatican at Rome. When he was there, several persons had mentioned their seeing such a book written by Trevisa, but he had not an opportunity to go and examine it himself, therefore cannot ascertain that it was the Bible. . . . I suspect all his translations, both from French and Latin were into English; but suspicions won't do for you. I wish it were in my power to give you more certain information.

'Yours very sincerely
'JNO. HUGHES.'

Dibdin thinks the opinion started 'from a loose assertion of Caxton in the proheme of *Polychronicon*' (above, p. lxxix). Bale and Pits got their view from this. Then Dibdin adds: 'But upon what authority our printer asserted it, or, if he saw such a translation, why he did not think it at least as deserving of publication as the *Polychronicon*, are questions which may be thought to press hard upon the probability of its existence.'

Townley, writing a few years later, 1821, is not so positive as Dibdin. He goes over much the same ground, quoting him and Wharton, and in addition has this to say in defence of Caxton:

'In reply also to what has been urged against Caxton's assertion of a translation having been made by Trevisa, it is sufficient to remark, that the danger attending the printing of an English Bible in Caxton's time was such, that it would have required the utmost religious intrepidity to have attempted it; and that it is therefore highly probable, that whatever preference our printer might have for the Scriptures, he would not place his life in jeopardy for its publication.'

To show the dangers of printers of this time he gives Sir Thomas More's defence for the printers (*Dyalogus*, fol. 49, col. 1, ed. 1529):

'That on account of the penalties ordered by Arch. Arundel's Constitution, though the old translations that were before Wycliff's days remayned lawful and were in some folkys handys had and red, yet he thought no prynter would lightly be so hote to put any byble in prent at hys owne charge, whereof the loss should lie wholly on his own necke, and then hange upon a doubtfull tryall whyther the fyrst copy of his translacyon was made before Wycliffs days or synnes. For yff yt were made synnys, yt must be approved before the pryntyng. But such an approbation was not then to be had.'

In 1839 the Rev. Thomas Hartwell Horne, who devoted most of his life to Biblical research, and who was on the staff of the British Museum, writes thus:[1]

'As no part of this work appears ever to have been published, the translation ascribed to him is supposed to have been confined to a few texts, which are scattered in some parts of his works (several copies of which are known to exist in MS.) or which were painted on the walls of his Patron's Chapel, at Berkeley Castle.'

Forshall and Madden (1850) in the Preface to their Wycliffe Bible,[2] in trying to establish the position of the two versions in respect to time, and that John Purvey was the author of the General Prologue, and also of the second version[3] have this reference:

'Henry Wharton in his Auctarium to the Archbishop's work, which it should be observed, was posthumous and unfinished, truly determined the respective characters and dates of the two versions: rightly giving the earlier to Wycliffe, and the later to the author of the General Prologue, whom, however, he erroneously conjectured to be John Trevisa [Auctarium Historiae Dogmaticae J. Usserii, p. 424 seqq., Auth. Harmer's (Hen. Wharton's) Specimens of Errors on History of Reformation, Lond. 1693, p. 16].'

Babington[4] (1865): 'Of his other translations, that of the Bible, said by Caxton, Bale, and others, to have been made by Trevisa, and possibly still extant at Rome, is the most important on all accounts. It is not, however, certain, though by no

---

[1] *Manual of Biblical Bibliography*, 1839, p. 66. Noticed by Rogers.

[2] *The Holy Bible, made from Latin Vulgate by John Wycliffe and his Followers*, 4 vols., vol. i, p. xxi.

[3] See Pollard's view, p. 84.

[4] Higden's *Polychronicon*, Rolls Series, vol. i, lv. (Babington refers to Mr. Hughes's letter.)

means improbable, that Trevisa ever translated the Scriptures at all.' Rogers tells us that William Watt (ob. 1869), head of the printed book department in the British Museum, 'was not aware of any part of the reputed translation having ever been printed, nor did he know of the existence of the MS.' Mr. Rogers's paper on Trevisa appeared in 1870. He was so much interested in the translation that he made some effort to obtain the MS., supposed to be at the Vatican. He concludes the account of his research, not without hope: 'I regret to say that the search has not been attended with success, owing to the very imperfect way in which its contents are catalogued. I can only express a hope that if at a future time a catalogue should be completed some Cornishman may remember that this "last stone" has still "to be turned".'

Cooke, the strongest exponent of the Trevisa translation, wrote two articles, appearing in 1876[1] and 1878,[1] in which, after mentioning the authorities in favour of Trevisa, he attacks Dibdin and Hughes. Dibdin questions Caxton's statement, because he does not give his authority. Cooke defends Caxton thus:

'The truth or falsehood of Caxton's statement, made so soon after Trevisa's time (70 years after his death) would, however, be well known to many persons, and it was not necessary at that period to bring forward proofs or anticipate objections. Had it been false, the Berkeley's, all of whom were good Catholics, would have been only too anxious to clear their Chaplain and themselves from the suspicion of heresy which the charge at that time involved, by denying it. So far from being contradicted, however, Caxton is repeated by every writer of eminence down to the beginning of the present century. Caxton most probably had not access to Trevisa's translation of the Bible, but if he had, he is not likely to have undertaken a publication which would have immediately embroiled him with the authorities. The translation had brought nothing but persecution, toil and trouble to Wyckliff, and its publication soon afterwards cost Tyndale a life of exile and a death at the stake.'

He goes on to say that because Trevisa's patrons were faithful and devoted sons of holy Church, that they would

[1] Account of the Inscription in Berkeley Castle (*Trans. of Bristol and Gloucester Arch. Soc.*, 1876) and Trevisa's Translation of The Bible (*Notes and Queries*, vol. x, 1878).

not identify themselves with the reforming party by allowing Trevisa's translation to be copied and circulated, and hence it would probably remain confined to the family and household at the castle, for whose use it was made.

In his 1876 article Cooke speaks of a copy or draft of a letter, in the Evidence Room at Berkeley Castle, written by George, the first Earl of Berkeley, addressed to James Duke of York, afterward King James II, in which the Earl begs the Duke's acceptance of 'an ancient collection in Manuscript of some part of the Bible', which he says has been carefully preserved near four hundred years. The name of 'Trevyse' occurs in the letter, though not as the name of the author of the MS., of the real nature of which Lord Berkeley was evidently entirely ignorant. In his 1878 article he tells us that 'this draft or copy is folded up in a sheet of paper, on which is an endorsement by the late W. F. Shrapnell, F.S.A. (who had charge of the Evidence Room down to 1817), to the effect that it refers to Trevisa's translation of the Bible, "since in the catalogue of books in the Vatican of Rome"'. He concludes his 1876 article by asserting that 'there is in the catalogue of the Vatican Library a manuscript of Trevisa's, and if this is not the missing translation of the Bible, it will probably be found at Frascati, as the collection of James II descended to Cardinal York, by whom they are bequeathed to the monastery there.' In 1878 [1] he says that inquiries have been made at the Vatican by the Rev. Joseph Stevenson, of the Public Record Office, and by Bishop Clifford, but without effect, and also that he has information that there is no such MS. at Frascati, and that numbers of old MSS. have been sold of late years to English and other collectors. He concludes: 'Will any collector into whose hands Trevisa's MS. may have fallen inform us of the fact, and thus set this most interesting controversy at rest?'

The latest to enter the discussion is Alfred W. Pollard, the famous English scholar. His statement is brief, and direct, and on the side of Trevisa. In his Introduction (1903) to the English Garner Collection of *Fifteenth Century Prose and Verse*, as a preface to his two selections, viz. (a) Chapter XV of the Prologue

---

[1] *Notes and Queries* (5th S., vol. x, 5 Oct., 1878, pp. 261-2).

to the Second Wycliffite Version on Translating of the Bible, and (b) John Trevisa's Dialogue between a Lord and a Clerk upon Translation, he thinks there is not sufficiently strong evidence, as produced by Forshall and Madden, to prove that John Purvey was the author of the General Prologue and of the second version of the Wyclif Bible. Pollard shows how Caxton first introduced Trevisa's name, as the translator of the Bible; then how Daniel Waterland (1683–1740) 'guessed' and 'pitched' upon Purvey as the author of the second version, partly because he was a noted Lollard, and also because he owned a Bible in Trinity College, Dublin. 'The text', says Pollard, 'is the first version, not the second. Inasmuch also as the manuscript was not completed till 1427, or later, its bearing on the question of authorship of a translation, which had then been in circulation for some thirty years, does not appear to be very great.' He then proceeds to Forshall and Madden: 'Lightly arrived at as it was, Waterland's "guess" was adopted by Forshall and Madden in their fine edition of the two versions published in 1850, and as buttressed up by them with what seems to me a weak additional argument, has ever since been repeated as an established fact.' He sums up Forshall and Madden's arguments thus:

(1) The author of the Prologue is the author of the translation of the Bible;

(2) The Prologue has verbal resemblances to the treatise designated *Ecclesiae Regimen*;

(3) The *Ecclesiae Regimen* resembles Purvey's confession at his recantation in 1400;

Therefore the translator of the Bible is the author of the *Ecclesiae Regimen*, and the author of this is Purvey.

Pollard's conclusion is:

'I must repeat the chain seems to me lamentably weak, and that the resemblances which may be found between Section XV of the Prologue and Trevisa's Dialogue and Letter to Lord Berkeley are stronger, because not arising out of quite such common topics. That they are only to a slight extent verbal resemblances is no drawback. We do not expect a man to repeat his own words exactly. What is interesting is to find two translators both interested in their own methods, and these methods similar.'

Then again:

'At any rate, William Caxton seems a better authority than an eighteenth-century divine as to the authorship of a translation made only a few years before he was born. We know that Trevisa was what we may call a professional translator, well equipped for his task; and we find him in the preface to the *Polychronicon* discussing the translation of the Bible in a strikingly similar spirit to that in which it is discussed in the Prologue to one of the translations which have come down to us. It is to be hoped that the subject may receive further investigation, and that without the importance of theological bias.'

(10) Biblical Inscriptions on the Walls of Berkeley Castle Chapel.

The best account of these is that of Cooke in 'On the Ancient Inscriptions in the Chapel at Berkeley Castle, with some account of Trevisa'. He also gives specimens of the tracings as they then (1876) existed. These writings have usually been attributed to Trevisa, because in his Dialogue between the Lord and the Clerk, he puts the following words in the mouth of the Lord: 'Also thou wotest where the Apocalips is wryten in the walls and roof of a chappel both in Latyn and in ffrensche.' Fuller[1] has the following reference:

' which Lord (as the said Trevisa observeth) had the Apocalyps in Latin and French, (then understood by the better sort as well as English) written on the roof and walls of his chapel at Berkeley; and which not long since (viz. Anno 1622) so remained as not much defaced. Whereby we may observe, that midnight being past, some early risers even then began to strike fire and enlighten themselves from the Scriptures.'

Smyth[2] writes:

'In urging whereof (i.e. translations) hee bringeth in this lord Thomas instancing his own Chapple in Berkeley Castle wherein the Apocalips is written on the walls and roofe in latin and french: which in this year, 1622, lo yet remaineth, somewhat, but not much defaced.'

---

[1] Op. cit. Also noted by the Rev. R. Demaus, *William Tyndale*, 1871, pp. 11, 12; also by Eadie, *The English Bible*, vol. i, pp. 24–5.
[2] Op. cit., vol. i, p. 343.

Introduction

Hughes's letter of 1805, given by Dibdin,[1] mentions this:

'The only vestige of Trevisa remaining here now, are a few fragments of board, with nearly obliterated words of Latin, not sufficient to make out what was meant; the roof of the chapel was said by him to have had the Apocalypse written upon it, and I suspect these fragments to be the remains of it. The beams and wall-plates of the Chapel are still remaining, and after removing several coats of lamp-black, etc., four lines were discovered upon each, written in the old English character, which are alternately Norman French, and Latin. By removing also several coats of whitewash from a part of the chapel wall, a great deal of writing in the old English character was discovered. It was in a great state of decay, but I could make out that part was in Norman French and part in Latin; this is also thought to be in Trevisa's day; but not one certain vestige of him remains here, not even his grave in the church is known, though he is said to have been buried in the chancel.'

Cooke examined the chapel walls, and gives us an interesting description in his paper, 1876. In speaking of the inscriptions, among other things he says:[2]

'They are not mentioned in any of the county histories, and almost all local knowledge or tradition of their nature or origin seems to have passed away. They are portions of the Book of Revelation translated into Norman French by the venerable Trevisa, the first translator of Higden's *Polychronicon*. . . . They are interesting not only archaeologically, as specimens of early decorative religious art, but they possess a high historical value and significance as being one of the earliest attempts to render any part of the Holy Scriptures into the language of Englishmen: one of the first manifestations of that spirit of enquiry to which we owe our present religious and intellectual liberty.

'The Chapel dedicated to St. John is situated in the southeast angle of the inner court-yard, and is generally considered to be of the 14th century. It is 36 feet long by 18 feet wide, not including an arched passage or cloister 3 ft. 4 in. wide which extends along the southern side. The roof is nearly flat and covered with lead. It is supported by heavy tile beams, the spaces between which are divided by the purlius and ridge-pieces into nearly square panels. On the flat part of the sides of all roof-timbers the inscriptions may be traced. The writing, of which there are generally one or two, but sometimes three or four lines on each beam, is in black on a white ground, the initials in red; the lettering is of the kind most in use in the

---

[1] Op. cit., vol. i, p. 142.   [2] Op. cit., vol. i, p. 138.

14th and 15th centuries. The beams and timbers seem to have been originally painted white, the spandrels being picked out with red, but the whole has been at some subsequent period painted over black and white. Five centuries of gradual decay and the scarcely distinctive process of ignorant or careless repair have, however, left the inscriptions legible in very few places. On the stone work inside the arched passage I have mentioned a good deal of similar block-letter writing may also be traced, but having been repeatedly white-washed over, it has become totally illegible. Except here the walls have all been plastered, so that it is now impossible to ascertain whether the inscriptions originally extended to them, but it is very probable they did.

'The specimens here shown are taken from careful tracings of all that remains legible. Two of the lines are parts of the 12th and 13th verses of the 8th Chapter. In the authorised version in this place we read, "An angel flying", which is here rendered " un egle volant ". The Vulgate, however, from which Trevisa probably made his translation, has "aquila", and this reading, supported by many other versions, is received as genuine by most Biblical critics. Trevisa himself tells us that the Apocalypse was here written in Latin as well as French, but the Latin version, probably in another part of the chapel, has now quite disappeared.'

Lewis gives a few of Trevisa's Bible translations, particularly from his translation of *De Proprietatibus Rerum*, which were communicated to him by Dr. Waterland. These are:

Matt. xviii. 32. I forgave the al thy det bycause thou praydest me, wicked seruant.

Matt. xxv. 18. The slowe seruant hidde his lordis talent in the erthe.

Matt. xxvii. 19. Moche have I suffred by syghte bycause of him.

Luke xii. 45. My lord taryeth to come.

Luke xii. 46. If a seruant begynneth to drink and is dronken, and smiteth and beateth the meyny his lord shall come.

Luke xix. 13. The nobleman called his seruauntes and bytoke hem ten minas, and he said to these seruauntes marchaundise with it tylle I come.

Luke xix. 16, 17. Lo, Lord, the mina hath made ten minas, and his lorde sayde to him, and be thou hauynge power ouer ten cities.

II. ORIGINAL WRITINGS.

(1) Dialogue between the Lord and Clerk on Translation, and (2) Epistle to Lord Berkeley on Translation.

These two short original writings of Trevisa are mentioned by Pits, Bale, Tanner, and subsequent writers, but sometimes spoken of under the *Dialogue* only. They were written as an introduction to the translation of the *Polychronicon*, and are found in the various MSS. usually preceding the *Polychronicon*. They are preserved for us in MSS. Cotton Tib. D. VII, Harl. 1900, Burghley House, Add. 24194, and Stowe 65 (where they follow the *Polychronicon*, ff. 217, 218).

They were first printed by Caxton as prefaces to his edition of the *Polychronicon*,[1] also by W. de Worde and P. Treveris. Both are printed in *Fifteenth Century Prose and Verse* (English Garner Collection),[2] but modernized in spelling. Smyth[3] prints about half of the *Dialogue*, beginning with the words of the Lord: 'And yet for to make a sermon of holy writ all in Latin to men that can English and no Latin' (see *Fifteenth Century Prose and Verse*, p. 206), and ends with the words of the clerk: 'Then God grant us grace grathly to gin, wit and wisdom wisely to work, might and mind of right meaning to make translation tresty and true, pleasing to the Trinity, three persons and one God, in majesty that euer was and euer shall be' (*Fifteenth Century Prose and Verse*, p. 207). The Epistle is printed by Smyth.[4]

The Rev. Jas. Townley printed part of the *Dialogue*, beginning 'The Clerk. The Latin is both good and fair' (*Fifteenth Century Prose and Verse*, p. 205), and ending, 'and Jerome translated thrice the Psalter' (*Fifteenth Century Prose and Verse*, p. 207).

---

[1] Petrie in *Mon. Hist. Brit.*, vol. i, p. 4, note 5, says: 'He (Caxton) has omitted the dialogue between the translator and Thomas Lord Berkeley on the utility of translation, as well as the first thirty-eight chapters of the first book.' This is a strange mistake of Petrie, especially when he was so careful in clearing up the mistake in dates 1357 and 1387, a few lines before.

[2] *Fifteenth Century Prose and Verse*, Introd. A. W. Pollard. Constable, 1903, pp. 203–10.

[3] *Lives of the Berkeleys*, vol. i, p. 141. Miss Greenwood writes as if the whole were printed, op. cit., p. 504.

[4] Ibid., vol. i, p. 343.

cxxviii   *Introduction*

(3) Latin Pedigree Roll.

This is Roll 102 of Abbot Newlands Rolls (Nos. 97–102) among the muniments of Berkeley Castle. It was written by John Newland, Abbot of St. Augustine from 1481 to 1515, and contains the history of the Berkeley family from Harding. In his Preface he says that he compiled and translated it 'out of Latyn into Englishe'. Mr. Jeayes,[1] who was for years Superintendent of the Department of Manuscripts in the British Museum, and who catalogued the Charters and Muniments of Berkeley Castle, says that Roll 102 'was the original production, if not in the very handwriting of John Trevisa'. Roll 101 is described thus:

'Copy made by W. F. Shrapnell, F.S.A., on Jan. 18th, 1808, of the "Ancient Vellum Roll written by Abbott Newland" in 1489, "part of which he translated from a more ancient roll written in latin by John Trevysa, Vicar of Berkeley" in 1398. Mr. S. adds that both these Rolls are at Berkeley Castle, Abbot Newland's in good preservation, but Trevysa's much injured by time.'

Under No. 102:

'Pedigree (this is the only remaining portion of Trevisa's Latin Pedigree Roll, which formed the foundation of Abbot Newland's Roll (Roll 87) and which as the latter states in his introduction he "translated out of latyn into Anglische") of Berkeley from Thomas, Lord Berkeley (1281–1321) who married Joan Ferres down to 1351. Lat. Vellum, Imperfect at the beginning, mutilated by damp, etc., and the ink much faded ; stated to be in the handwriting of John Trevisa (ob. 1412) Vicar of Berkeley, and Chaplain to Thomas, Lord Berkeley ; the translator of Higden's Polychronicon and other works.'

(4) Poetry.

Trevisa has placed a poem of twenty-four lines, six stanzas, at the head of his translation of Bartholomaeus, *De Proprietatibus Rerum*. Prof. MacCracken published this poem, taken from the MS. Harl. 614, fol. 46, in *The Nation*[2] as an illustration of

---

[1] Isaac Herbert Jeayes, *Desc. Cat. of the Charters and Muniments in Possession of the Rt. Hon. Lord Fitz-hardinge at Berkeley Castle*, 1892, Introd. xxxv, p. 293.

[2] July 30, 1908, vol. lxxxvii, No. 2248, p. 92.

Introduction cxxix

the writer's 'childlike naïveté'. He entitles it 'God me Speed'. The poem stands thus:

> A Croys was maked[1] al of reed
> In the bigynnyng of my book
> That is clepid god me speed,
> In the first lessoun that I took.
>
> Thanne I lernede A and B.
> And other lettris by her names:
> But alwey god spede me
> Thoughte me needful in alle games
>
> If I pleyede in feeld or medis
> In stillnesse either with noys,
> I praiede helpe in alle my deedis
> Of him that dyede on the croys.
>
> Now dyuerse pleyes in his name
> I shal lete passe forth, and fare
> And auenture to pleye o, long game:
> But yit also I schal spare.
>
> Bothe wodis, medis, and feeldis,
> Places that I haue pleyed inne:
> And in his name, that al thing weldis,
> This game I schal bigynne.
>
> And pray help, counseil and reed,
> To me that he now wil sende,
> And this game wel rule and leed,
> And bring it to a good ende.

Prof. MacCracken prints a number of poems in *Herrig's Archiv*,[2] under the heading 'Lydgatiana', from MS. Trinity College, Cambridge, R. 3. 21. This MS. is of Edward IV's time. Prof. MacCracken thinks that John Stow, the Elizabethan antiquary, wrongly ascribed the poem to Lydgate. He shows that the Trinity MS. was in the possession of Roger Thorney, a citizen of London, and the patron who furthered the printing by Wynkyn de Worde of Trevisa's version of the *De Proprietatibus Rerum*. The ownership of the MS. by Thorney raises

---

[1] 'maad' in MS.
[2] *Herrig's Archiv*, Bd. 130, 1913, pp. 286–311.

i

an interesting question as to the authorship of the two little childlike ' Prayers at bed and at uprising ' which are given below. They markedly resemble in metrical form and in tone the little ' God me Speed ', which Trevisa inserted at the beginning of his translation from Bartholomew. Thorney's interest in this work by Trevisa makes it possible that he had access to some other MS. by that author, from which he had the prayers copied.

The poems printed are:

1. Vita Beate Anne matris Beate Marie Virginis (fols. 221–30), 658 lines.
2. Psalmi Passionis domini (fols. 174ᵛ–7ᵛ), 167 lines.[1]
3. A deuout prayere toward thy bedde at nyght (fol. 276), 24 lines.
4. A deuout prayere at thy vprysyng (fol. 276ᵛ), 32 lines.
5. A Lament of our Lady at The Passion (fols. 276ᵛ–7ᵛ), 120 lines.
6. An Exortacion to auoyde and to put away the seuyn synnes (fols. 275ᵛ–6), 70 lines.[2]
7. A song on the Battle of Barnet (fol. 244ᵛ), 35 lines.
8. The Birds' Matins (fols. 196ᵛ–7), 70 lines.

Nos. 3 and 4, assigned by MacCracken to Trevisa, are printed from the *Archiv*.

A deuout prayere toward thy bedde at nyght.

NOW Ihesu lord, Welle of all goodnes,
For þy gret pyte I the pray
Foryeue me all my wykkydnes,
Wherewith I have greuyd the to day.

Honoure & praysyng to the be,
And þankyng for þy yeftys all,
That I thys day receuyd of the
Now, curteyse Cryst, to þe I call.

Thys nyght from parell thow me kepe
My bodyly reste whyle that I take,
And as long as myn eyen slepe
Late my hert in þy seruyce wake.

---

[1] Prof. MacCracken suggests these two poems seem to be the work of the author of *Magnificentia Ecclesia*, printed by him from MS. in Publications of the Modern Language Association of America, Dec. 1909.

[2] This appears more like Lydgate than others (MacCracken).

For feryng of þe fende oure fo
Foule dremes, and fro fantasies,
Kepe me this nyght fro syn also
In clennes þat I may vpryse.

Saue my good doers fro greuaunce,
And quyte hem þat þey on me spende,
Kepe myne enemyes from noyaunce,
And yeue hem grace to amende.

Mercy, Ihesu, and gramercy,
My body and soule I the beken,
In nomine patris & filii
Et spiritus Sancti, Amen.
 Explicit.

 A deuout prayere at thy vprysyng.

(I)N nomine patris & filii,
Et Spiritus Sancti, Amen,
Mercy, Iesu, and gramercy,
My body and soule I the beken.

Now Iesu lord blessyd þou be
For all þys nyght þou hast me kept,
From the fende and hys postee,
Whether I wakyd or slept.

In grete dissese, in dedly syn,
Many on thys nyght fallen hase,
That mysylf shuld haue fall in,
Had þou not kept me of thy grace.

Lord yeue me grace to þy worshyp
Thys day to spende in þy plesaunce,
And kepe me fro wyked felyschyp
And from þe fendes encombraunce.

Iesu, my tong þou rewle also
That I nat speke but hit be nede,
Hertyly to pray for frend or fo
And harme no man in worde ne dede.

Cryste yeue me grace of mete and drynke
Thys day to take mesurably,
In dedely syn þat I nat synke
Thorough outrage of foule glotony.

Iesu, my lord, Iesu, my love,
On all þat I am boundyn to
Thy blessyng sende from heuyn aboue,
And yeue hem grace þy wyll to do.

My good Angell, þat art to me sende
From god to be my gouernoure,
From euyl spyrytes thow me defende,
And in my desease be my socoure.
                                        Amen.
Explicit.

Trevisa also appears as a poet in his translation of the poetical parts of the *Polychronicon*. Here he breaks away from his Latin original, and we get in his additions examples of his own poetry. The following occur as taken from the Rolls Series:

Vol. i, Book I, chap. xxxvi, p. 415.

Treuisa. In bookes ȝe may rede,
þat kynde failleþ not at nede:
Whanne no man hadde craft in minde,
Þan of craft halp God and kynde;
Whan no techere was in londe,
Men hadde craft by Goddes sonde;
Þey þat hadde craft so þenne
Tauȝte forþ craft to oþere menne;
Som craft, þat ȝit come nouȝt in place,
Somme men schal haue by Goddis grace.

Vol. i, Book I, chap. xxxvi, p. 419.

Treuisa. What wight wolde wene
Þat a fend myȝt now gete a childe?
Some men wolde mene,
Þat he may no werk soche wilde
That fend þat gooþ a nyȝt.
Wommen wel ofte to begile,
Incubus hatte he ryȝt;
And gileþ men oþer while
Succubus is þat wight;
God graunte vs non suche vile.
Who þat in hir myȝt
Comeþ wonder hap schal smyle.
Wiþ wonder dede
Boþe men and wommen sede

>   Fendes wyl kepe
>   Wiþ craft, and brynge in on hepe.
>   So fendes wilde
>   May make wommen bere childe;
>   ȝit neuere in mynde
>   Was childe of fendes kynde.
>   For wiþ oute eye
>   There myȝte childe non such deye.
>   Clergie makeþ mynde
>   Deep sleep nouȝt fendes kynde;
>   But deth slowe Merlyn,
>   Merlyn was ergo no gobelyn.
>
>   Vol. i, Book I, chap. xxxvi, p. 421.
>
> *Treuisa.*   Siluestris is wood,
>   Other wilde of mood;
>   Other elles,
>   Þat at þe wode he dwelles.

PART III

LANGUAGE OF THE MANUSCRIPTS.

INTRODUCTION.

Trevisa did most of his work as a translator while Vicar of Berkeley, Gloucestershire, during the last half of the fourteenth century. His language is therefore West Southern. Thus have concluded Morris and Skeat, and Emerson, in whose works selections have been given from a pure Southern MS., viz. Cotton Tiberius D. VII. The former, referring to it, says: 'The Cotton MS. (here chiefly followed) has been preferred as preserving the author's own (Southern) dialect.'[1] The selection is taken from the *Polychronicon*, Lib. I, parts of caps. 41 and 59, and Lib. VI, cap. 29 (*Specimens*, Part II, pp. 235–47). Emerson says:

'Our selection is from Cotton Tiberius D. VII, a contemporary MS. in pure Southern. The translator, John Trevisa, was vicar at Berkeley, then Canon at Westbury, Gloucestershire. He

---

[1] Morris and Skeat, *Specimens of Early English*, Part II, 1889, p. 340. Morris, *Specimens of Early English*, Oxford, 1867, pp. 333–44, contains Book I, chaps. 41, 42, and 59.

finished his translation in April, 1387, as he tells us. The language is therefore Southern of Gloucestershire in the last half of the fourteenth century. As to language, Trevisa's Southern shows no voicing of initial *f*, *þ*, and *s*, so far as orthography is concerned, but otherwise well represents the dialect. The selection shows *ā* for *hā* (*ha*), besides *hi* (*hy*) in the plural of the third personal pronoun: cf. "Juliana", p. 191.'[1]

His selection is from the *Polychronicon*, Book I, chaps. 58 and 59 (pp. 220-5).

Mr. Babington uses the Southern MS. in his Rolls Series of the *Polychronicon*, beginning its use in vol. ii, designating it in his notes as γ. In his Introduction he gives some description of it:[2]

'In the last printed catalogue (of the Br. Mus.) it is said to be wanting, "Desideratur"; but a note in the copy in the Museum says, "Restored, J. Holmes." It had been seen by T. Smith, who wrote the Catalogue of the Cotton MSS. printed at Oxford in 1696, and afterwards by the Hon. W. Burton in the following century, who annotated the copy in the British Museum. It is likewise mentioned in the Report on the Cotton MSS. after the fire, printed in 1732. The MS. is in quarto, on vellum of 296 leaves, each page containing about 37 lines, and is rubricated and slightly illuminated. It contains, moreover, the Dialogue of Dominus and Clericus, and Trevisa's Epistle to Lord Berkeley. It is injured by fire, though not very considerably; a few leaves, however, at the beginning and end are only partially legible. It would seem to be written towards the close of the fourteenth century, or rather a little later. Some extracts from it have been lately printed in Mr. Morris's "Specimens of Early English", whose book first made me acquainted with its existence. It differs much from the standard MS. and δ (i.e. Cambridge H. 1 and Add. 24194) in the form of pronouns, and preserves in some cases the true text, where they have corrupted it.'

Mr. Lumby, in his study and use of this MS., has this remark:

'Some of the forms in this MS. are extremely strange, and worthy of special notice. In the personal pronouns the favourite forms for the first person singular are *ych*, *ich*, and *y*, and for all genders of the third person singular, as well as for

---

[1] O. F. Emerson, *A Middle English Reader*, p. 311.

[2] Trevisa's translation of the *Polychronicon*, Rolls Series, ed. Churchill Babington, vol. ii, 1869, Introd., p. xxxviii.

the third person plural, the not unusual form is *a*. This is most common for the masculine, and least common for the neuter of the singular. The feminine likewise appears as *heo*, also the neuter *hyt*, and the plural *hy*. The orthography is also peculiar: *v* is very frequently used instead of *f*, indicating the southern character of the MS., but there occur an equal number of instances of the contrary interchange. There is marked preference also shown for forms with the vowel combinations *eo, eu, uy, aa, ee, oo*. The mark of the feminine form in nouns is *as* (as *wolvas*, a she-wolf, *godas*, a goddess), and a frequent form of the plural is *on* (as *roþeron*, oxen). In the words *live* and *have*, the *v* is always represented by *bb* as *lybbe, habbe*, and *y* by *gg* in *ligge* for *lay*, and *sigge* for *say*. Preterites and perfect particles have unusual forms, as *leop*, leapt, *ful*, fell (Sth. forms). Now and then we find a word entirely differing from the reading in the text (St. John's MS.) and of a more antiquated character, as *teer*, clean, *fulled*, baptized, *eldede*. lived.'[1]

Mr. Lumby then gives a list of words illustrating the characteristics mentioned.

A complete study of the language of the Cottonian MS. of Trevisa's translation of the *Polychronicon* has been made recently by Bernhard Pfeffer at the University of Bonn.[2] He uses the selection from Morris and Skeat, also the collections of Babington and Lumby, vols. ii-viii, designated in their notes as γ, and furthermore prints folios 240-60 b of the Cotton MS., occupying pp. 99-144 of his volume. This work has been so excellently and minutely done that I have thought it advisable to study only briefly the vowels and diphthongs in my basic MS., viz. Harl. 1900, and then compare my various MSS. with this, and also with Pfeffer. In doing this I have also listed some of the forms as found in Chaucer's prose,[3] in the London documents,[4] also those by Wiclif,[5] Peacock,[5] and Caxton,[5] and a

[1] J. R. Lumby, *Trevisa's Polychronicon*, Rolls Series, vol. iii, 1871, pp. xxv-xxvii. This passage is quoted by Skeat, *Specimens*, Part II, p. 340, and by Pfeffer in *Die Sprache*, p. iii.

[2] Bernard Pfeffer, *Die Sprache des 'Polychronicons' John Trevisa's in der Hs. Cotton Tiberius* D. VII, Diss., Bonn, 1912.

[3] Johann Frieshammer, *Die Sprachliche Form der Chaucerschen Prosa* (*Morsbach's Studien zur engl.* . . . *Phil.*, xlii), Halle, 1900.

[4] Julius Lekebusch, *Die Londoner Urkundensprache von* (1430-1500), Diss., 1906.

[5] I take these forms in the main as given by Lekebusch.

few as used by Capgrave.[1] Mr. Pfeffer has been most careful to compare the language of the Cotton Trevisa MS. with that of other Southern works, viz. the Katherine Group, as worked out by H. Stodte, *Ueber die Sprache und Heimat der Katherine-Gruppe*, Diss., 1887 ; Robert of Gloucester's *Chronicle*, F. Pabst, *Die Sprache der Reimchronik des Robert of Gloucester*, Diss., Berlin, 1889 ; and the Gloucester Legends, E. Mohr, *Sprachliche Untersuchungen zu den Mittel-engl. Legenden aus Gloucestershire*, Diss., Bonn, 1888.

In the course of this study it will be seen that the Chetham's MS. is distinctly Southern. Stowe 65 has also many Southern characteristics.

The following abbreviations are used in these notes : D = Dialogue, S = Sermon, M = Methodius Tract ; in references to MSS., as in my collation notes, viz. H = Harleian, A = Additional, C = Cambridge, S·= Stowe 65, Ch = Chetham.

Pf. = Pfeffer's *Die Sprache*, &c. Fr. = Frieshammer's *Chaucer's Prose*. Lek. = Lekebusch, London Deeds, &c. Dib. = Dibelius's *John Capgrave*.

I. Vowels and Diphthongs.

A. Short Vowels.

I. OE. i and ī shortened. (Cf. Morsbach, *ME. Gram.* §§ 112-15.)

Written i and y.

(a) i in closed syllables appears as follows : ȝif D 2/2, miche D 2/1, myche M 110 1, myche D 23/5, over myche M 95/12, wille D 10/14, writ D 5/5, knyȝt D 1/1, þrid M 97/11, pricke D 23/14, whiche D 17/15, schrifte D 11/6. Other examples are : schip, bischops, riht, riȝtful, riȝt, ynne, in, hit, ich, ȝiftes, chirche, bygynneþ, drynke, drynkeþ, fisches.

(b) OE. i before consonant groups :

(1) Before -nd : fynde D 31/3, blynde D 6/11, M 96/10, M 110/4, wynde D 6/12, whirlewynde S 89/21.

(2) Before -ng : þing D 2/2, þynges D 2/14, noþinge S 68/27.

---

[1] Wilhelm Dibelius, *John Capgrave and Die Englische Schriftsprache* (*Anglia*, xxiii, pp. 153, 323, 427 ; xxiv, pp. 211, 269).

(3) Before -ld: mylde D 6/23, D 29/2, wild M 105/6, wylde 105/6.

(c) OE. i in open syllables: wite M 96/9, witeþ S 74/2, lyme D 28/9, lordschipe D 8/9, lordschips D 9/8 ; also lyuyng, kikeþ, kike, sikernesse, siker, bynymeþ.

Shortened OE. i, in fifty M 97/16, fifþe S 40/3.

Manuscripts.

OE. ȝif always appears as ȝef in Ch ; in other MSS. as above. Quite regularly miche or myche appears in H. In S nearly always as myche, in C and Ch as moche. We find it occasionally in A as meche.

Ch has whoche quite regularly for whiche in other MSS. Ch has byschops. In appears as ynne, yn, and in. Hit, hyt, it appear in all MSS. although S prefers it, and Ch hyt.

Iche is found a few times in A and C. I is found once or twice in all the five MSS. in the same place.

ȝeftes is found in Ch, cherche always in Ch, lordschepe in S Ch.

In Cot. MS. y is the prevailing form. There we find wheche, in addition to whiche and whoche. Church occurs near cherch. Fynde is found near veynde (Pf., pp. 6, 7). This last form is not found in the MSS.

In Chaucer OE. i or y is found usually as i (Fr., p. 14), e. g. shrift, briddes, midde, wikked, siker, wyngis, bringith, blynde, etc.

In London documents (Lek., p. 11) third, bryng, middell, child, blynde, also i to e in therd, wete, hedirto, wedowes.

Wycliffe has usually i or y, rarely e or u, Pecock as a rule i (Lek., p. 16).

OE. swilc appears in H as follows: siche D 4/1, D 9/3, D 14/11, M 108/15, soche D 16/12 (S such), seche D 29/3, suche S 42/21. The (1) of above is written such in all the other MSS., (2) such Ch S, (3) soche Ch, seche A, suche C S, (4) soche A Ch. Thus Ch prefers soche, C S suche, while A H have ciche or seche.

Fr. (p. 15) points out that the best Chaucer MSS. have swich ; such is not found in Ellesmere MSS., but it occurs in some of the other MSS. ; also swiche and syche are found.

cxxxviii   *Introduction*

II. OE. y and ȳ shortened. (Morsbach, *ME. Gram.* §§ 127–33.)

This vowel in Midland dialect remains an i or y (Morsbach, *Gram.*, § 7, 2), while in Sth. it becomes u (Morsbach, 9, 2 (a), 2). The only MS. which shows Sth. regularly is Ch. We often find u in other MSS.

(a) y in closed syllables: first D 9/12, M 95/14, firste S 39/20, myrþe D 26/8, synne D 8/13, S 48/17, knytting D 15/14, y-knitt D 15/3, hilles M 108/13, þilke M 102/5, fliȝt M 103/16, brigges S 48/6, fille D 17/16, Ch vulle, S fulle.

(b) Before consonant groups:
(1) -nd: kynde D 16/10, kynde M 105/7, S 41/1.
(2) -ld: buylde M 97/12, buyylde M 98/4, bildyngis S 48/3.

(c) In open syllables: bysynesse D 9/2, busy S 47/19, bisy S 47/28, bisiliche S 50/1, euel 22/6, 24/3, S 45/3, buriyng S 42/12, buryeyng S 42/27.

Shortened OE. ȳ, filþe M 96/8.

Manuscripts.

The Chetham MS. is the most consistently Sth. Even it has bildyngis, S 48/3, where the other MSS. (except H) have buldings; S 47/31, all the MSS. (except H) have ybulde. D 9/12 furste A, vurste Ch. D 26/8 murþe Ch S, merþe A C. Brigges in S 48/7 is written brugges in all the MSS. Kynde S 41/1 appears in MSS. as kunde, while the same word in D 16/10 appears as kunde only in Ch. Synne is written in all the MSS. as i or y. The y in busy varied, e, y, or u. Even Ch is not regular in its usage, e.g. S 47/9, H has regular Sth u, while A C have besy, Ch bysy. In S 47/28, H has bisy, while A Ch S have busy. S 48/10 we find S busy, A besy, and Ch bysy. Dude is found in Ch S, while A C have dede, H has almost always dide. Euel is the regular form, but yuel is found C S, D 24/3.

In the Cot. MS. the form is u, hull, sulle, þulke (Pf., pp. 11 ff.). Chaucer has usually y, also i. OE. wyrcan appears as werken, also as wirkynge, etc.; first and furste, knytting and knettynge, bisy, bisily, bisynesse, etc. Regularly yvel, although evil occurs; filthe and felthe (Fr., pp. 16–21). Wycliffe has usually y, yfel, bysig, byldan. Pecock as a rule i, bisie, stirid; Caxton has e, in mery, besy, euyl (Lek., p. 16).

III. OE. ŭ. (Morsbach, *ME. Gram.* §§ 121–6.)

Usually written u, sometimes o.

(a) In closed syllables: vppon D 3/1, 6/17, sunne M 98/9, somme, some D 6/21, S 52/9, þurʒ M 105/4 (OE. þurh), fulle S 50/30, þus, also ful, fulfilled. This appears regularly as fol in Ch. This is also the form in Cot. although vulle is found (Pf., p. 10).

(b) Before consonant groups:

(1) Before nd: wonder D 1/1, S 50/20, vnder D 1/3, ybounde D 14/12, ybounde S 44/12, hound D 19/12. Also hundrid, founden, yfounde, fonded, fonden, fonde.

(2) Before -ng: tonge S 39/16.

(3) Before -rn: ouertorned D 1/2, turne S 39/18.

(c) In open syllables: sones M 96/7, sone S 91/5, foules M 97/6, comeþ D 6/23, cupes D 6/14, loue S 52/18, dore (AS. duru) S 89/35.

Manuscripts.

In Ch we find always apon for upon; ful appears as fol in Ch; tonge also written as tunge; turne and torne. Pfeffer (p. 11) points out such forms as teurne and teorneþ in Cotton MS.

In Chaucer OE. ŭ appears as som, sonne, tonne, somme, loove, above (shortened OE. ū), thurgh, thurst, shulder, hound, tonge and tunge, hunger and honger, etc. (Fr., pp. 23 ff.).

In London documents it appears as cup, full, utter, ground, wondre, tonne, hundrid, come, love, sone, cursed. Caxton has tunge and tonge, gunnes and gonnes, further and ferther (Lek., pp. 74 ff.).

IV. OE. ŏ. (Morsbach, *ME. Gram.* §§ 116–20.)

(a) ŏ in closed syllables: flok M 105/7, horsis M 105/15, folkis M 101/2, for D 3/3, god D 24/6, goddes D 22/9 (gen. sg.), gospel D 15/16, norþe M 98/13, storm S 89/21, forþe (OE. forþ) D 15/7, D 29/8 (Ch vorþ).

(b) Before consonants:
(1) Before -ld: wolde, nolde.
(2) Before -rn: corn S 60/19.
(3) Before -rd: wordes D 5/2, S 41/25, borde S 89/34.

(c) In open syllables: openlich D 8/2, openliche S 50/3, y-tore D 13/3, oxes D 17/9, oxen D 17/10, tohaleþ (OE. hŏlian) D 24/11, bodies M 101/8, bodilich S 46/33, foleweþ D 14/16, D 22/7 (Ch volweþ).

In Chaucer's prose very often the o was long before consonant groups, e. g., soonges, woordes, hoord, foordes, etc. (Fr., p. 21).

In London deeds, the o appears as in our MSS. except u in place of o, in murdre, murdres, murtheres, murthers; also wuld and would appear occasionally, but wolde is the usual form (Lek., p. 64).

Pfeffer points out a form þurste, prt. for OE. dorste; also the form þorste. He also finds the writing before -ld to be o, oo as foold (Pf., p. 8).

V. OE. ĕ. (Morsbach, *ME. Gram.* §§ 106-11.)

(a) ĕ in closed syllables: telle D 10/13, wedlock D 14/16, weddinge M 25/1, þraschiþ (OE. þerscan) D 17/15, wrecched D 24/11, reste, nesche D 26/9, beddes D 26/9, elles M 105/3, S 46/1, stren3þe D 2/3, M 106/14, streeche M 109/15, drenchid M 109/10, berne D 17/16, helle M 109/10, wiþsigginge D 13/3, fecche D 6/18, sillers D 6/25, clerk D 7/5, clerkes D 15/9.

(b) e before consonants:
(1) Before -ld: felde D 10/8, selde S 52/8.
(2) Before -nd: ende S 89/15, ende D 21/7, yspend p. past. D 22/11.
(3) Before -ng: Englond, strenger, Engelond.

(c) In open syllables: mete, weder, forbedyng, aforbeding, speke, bedemen, bedes, whether.

The only peculiarity to be noted here is the i or y forms in only a few words of our MSS., although Pfeffer points out a number found in the Cotton MS. For a full discussion of this change with numerous examples refer to Morsbach's *ME. Gram.* § 109. The only examples we have are wiþsigginge, sigge,

Introduction cxli

and sillers. Sigge or sygge is found usually in Ch, while S has segge; the others usually show seye or saye. Sillers appears in H A and C. C has selleres, Ch has sullers. Pfeffer (p. 5) gives the following with the i or y formes: strynᵹþe, stringþe, strynger, stringer, drynch, stynch, blynche. Some of these are to be found in the MSS., and have the regular e form. Morsbach (p. 144) puts togidre, togider, among the examples in this list.

Chaucer's prose usually has e: lente, webbe, drencheth, strenges, kembde (OE. cemban), feldes, selde, feeldes; in open syllables: spere, bere, whether. Forms in i occur as dirk and derke (Fr., pp. 8 ff.). The London documents have sette, best, wedde, feld, heuy, weder, beddes, swere, seller, sell (three times sille). Wycliffe has i and e forms.

VI. OE. ă. (Morsbach, *ME. Gram.* §§ 87 ff.)

I. Not before nasals.

(a) Closed syllables: asse D 6/18, D 6/24, S 90/19, habbeþ, found only in S and Ch.

(b) Open syllables: haue D 1/7, haueþ D 2/12, made D 2/1, D 3/7, make D 3/9, same D 5/16, face M 98/7, tale D 15/6, naked D 26/5, raþer S 43/29.

II. Before nasals:

(a) Not consonant groups: man D 1/4, S 89/19, mannes S 91/6, þan S 40/26, þanne S 41/18, from S 51/15 (always vram in Ch, and fro in S), whanne D 5/12 (whan A C S), name, lame, answerde, þankeþ, many (meny A C Ch).

(b) Before consonant groups:

(1) Before -nd: lond, londes, hond, hondes, understonde, stonde, wiþstondyng.

(2) Before -ng: stronge, strounge, longe.

(3) Before -mb: wombe S 91/10.

Pfeffer points out (p. 2) that OE. ă before nasals, not consonant groups, is always a in Robert of Gloucester, and in Gloucester Legends, but o in the Katherine group. This vowel behaves in our group of MSS. as it does in the Cotton MS. (Pf., pp. 1, 2). In Chaucer we find the forms þenne and whenne, when. These are not found in our MSS. Neither do

we find þonne or whonne. Before consonant groups the forms in the Chaucer MSS. vary a or o. In London documents o and a forms are found before consonant groups (Lek., pp. 51 ff.; note his table, p. 53; also Morsbach's *ME. Gram.* § 88).
Fro as found in S is Scand. (Björkman, p. 100).

VII. OE. ǽ. (Morsbach, *ME. Gram.* §§ 95–105.)

(a) Closed syllables: þat D 1/7, hadde D 1/8, D 6/12, S 89/6, fadres D 2/11, fader D 7/4, S 51/20, faste, after, spradde, almes. OE. mǽsse appears always, masses D 21/2; in Cot. MS. this appears as mas and messe, Pf., p. 3; Morsbach's *ME. Gram.* §§ 130, 131; crafte, gladnesse, small, togidres D 14/12, D 15/14, togidre M 1/10, M 100/3, togidres S 89/20.

(b) Open syllables: water, fader D 7/4, S 51/20, bare. Togedres is found always in Ch, also in S, and occasionally in A. Both forms occur in London documents and Chaucer (Morsbach, *ME. Gram.* § 131; *Schriftsprache*, p. 30). The form in Cot. MS. is togedders (Pf., p. 4).

B. Long Vowels.
I. OE. ī.

This is written ɪ or ȳ: tymes D 1/2, D 6/2, tyme D 6/3, S 91/5, wise, wyn, fyue, lif, side, sides, stryue, wyues, wif, wifes, alyue, styȝeuþ, abide, wide, OE. wīfman, wymmen, S 73/9.

The London dialect has womman (sg.), wõmmen, women (plu.), also wȳmen. Chaucer has womman (sg.), wŏmmen (plu.); Caxton both forms (Morsbach, *ME. Gram.* § 112). The form wĕmmen does not occur in our MSS.

OE. hī appears as hy in Ch, as hey in S, but does not occur in A C and H. There the form þei is always used. The form huy does not occur, but is found in Cot. MS. (Pf., p. 18).

OE. ɪ is shortened in fifty M 97/16.

II. OE. ȳ.

hyde M 108/12, mynde S 50/30, litel (OE. lȳtel), S 68/22, S 78/12; fyre (OE. fȳr) S 45/2 (fuyre S), fier S 91/10, fuyre S 81/70; huyre S 89/32 (OE. hȳr), hyred D 17/10 (hyre A C, huyre Ch S).

Introduction cxliii

In Cot. MS. the usual form is uy, although u is very common. Ruþeren S 41/18 (reþeren A, roþeren C S), OE. hrūðeru (sg. hrūðer), also hrȳðeru (sg. hrȳðer). Morsbach, *ME. Gram.*, p. 169. *N.E.D.* has only roþeren from OE. hrȳðeren.

III. OE. ū.

It is written ou or ow. These forms are found side by side in the various MSS. souþe M 101/5, foule M 103/6, defouliþ M, mouþe D 17/9, S 90/12, hous D 10/7, down, doun, þousand, aboute, now, how.

But (OE. būtan) appears quite regularly in H A C as but, often in A C as bot or bote, while in Ch it appears almost without exception as bote. In H it occurs as bote. The London speech has the same two forms, ow being the more common (Lekebusch, p. 78; Morsbach, *Schriftsprache*, p. 48).

IV. OE. ō.

Written o and oo. The scribes appeared to have no regular way of writing, as we find the same man using o, with a final e, alongside of oo without the final e. Sometimes the same writer will have both oo and final e. Ch has very often simply o, and no final e.

The form ou for OE. ō does not appear in the MSS. It was quite common in Cotton (Pfeffer, p. 19).

good. sb. D 2/3, anoþer D 6/3, blode D 6/4 (all MSS.), book D 4/12 (all MSS.), soþe D 11/1, soþness D 28/6 (sooþnes A, soþenes C, soþnes Ch), doom D 13/2 (dome C, dom Ch), doome D 15/10 (dome A C, doom S, dom Ch), hook D 31/2 (hoke A, hooc S).

Shortened forms: moneþe S 49/2 in H (monþe other MS.).

In the London documents are found such forms as goodes, footes, blood, doon, also godes, blode. Chaucer's prose has the two forms, occasionally oe, as mone written moene.

In Cot. MS. Pfeffer (p. 19) points out a number of forms in ou, e. g. vorsouk, houk (OE. hōc), hourdom, toules (OE. tōl).

V. OE. ē.

(a) Appears as e or ee: feet D 1/3 (all MSS.), hede D 7/7, D 10/15 (heede S), heede D 22/1 (hede A C Ch), hede D 22/1

cxliv   *Introduction*

(heede S), demeþ D 10/16, deme D 11/8, mede D 17/6, in all MSS. but C med, byhiȝte (OE. hēt) M 101/2. Pfeffer points out (p. 17) a great many examples of this form in Cot. It appears as het, heet, byheet, hyȝte, byhyȝt, hyt, hiȝte, &c., here (OE. hēr), herto, here, herof, hereby. OE. þēs, þese S 51/22 (þues Ch); þues is a common form in Cot. (Pf., p. 29).

(*b*) Shortened ē: kepte, recchiþ, fedde, blessid; OE. hē appears as a in S Ch, otherwise as he.

The writing y in our MSS. does not appear for OE. ē, as it does sometimes in Cot. (Pf., p. 17), neither do such forms as eo, ue in weoþe, wueþe appear (Pf., p. 18).

In the London documents the form is usually e (Lek., p. 30). Chaucer has both forms (Fr., p. 26).

VI. OE. ā. (Morsbach, *ME. Gram.* §§ 134–7.)

The writing in Sth. and Mid. appears as o, oo, in Nth. as a (Morsbach, § 134). Pfeffer, quoting Pabst and Mohr, shows that o, oo is the writing in Robert of Gloucester and the Gloc. Legends; but the Katherine-Gruppe have nearly always a. The London documents have always o, oo (Lekebusch, p. 68). The Chaucer Prose has o, oo (Fr., p. 33).

lore D 6/25, loore S 87/17, stoones D 28/10, stoon D 29/2, stones M 104/8, hooly D 1/8, holy D 2/1, cloþes D 6/21 (all MSS.), cloþ D 23/2 (clooþ AS.), cloþed, cloþinge, loues D 6/14, oon, anoon, aloon, noon, wroþe M 96/17, wrooþe S 58/11, gostlich S 47/26, goostliche S 89/27, oþ S 46/20 (all MSS.). Also smote, abrode, so, lord, liflode, knyȝthode

Pfeffer (p. 14) shows that Cot. MS. has shortened OE. ā written a: halwynge, halwon, haly, hamward.

Pecock has o, oo, e.g. go, goostli, oonli, noon, holy, mo, moost, oon, tho, &c. (Schmidt, p. 4).

The various MSS. seem to have no special rule for o or oo. In D 28/10, stoones H, but stones in other MSS. In D 29/2, stoon H S, but stone A C Ch. D 29/5 stoon in all MSS. but Ch, which has stone.

ON. ā is found in the word fro. This is found frequently in some of the MSS. as D 9/13 (fro A C S, vram Ch).

OE. þās nom. plu. appears as þese, but in S and Ch as þues. Þues is one of the forms found in Cot. MS. (Pfeffer, p. 14).

VII. OE. ǣ. (Morsbach, *ME. Gram.* § 95.)
It is written e, ee, and gives in ME. open ẹ̄ (ę̄).
ǣ¹ = Goth ai, Angl. āē.
ǣ² = WG. ā, Goth ē, Angl. ē.

(a) The length kept : delere, menyng, neuere, euerche (OE. ǣfre, ǣlc.) ; found in S always as ech, in A and C very often as euery, but otherwise as euereche or eueriche.
OE. lǣs, lasse (all MSS.), leche (all MSS.), dedes D 6/26, D 11/9.

(b) Shortened forms:
(1) Sh. ǣ¹: wreþþe S 45/20 (OE. wrǣðo), wraþþe S, wreþ D 29/12 (wreþþe MSS.), heestes D 6/13, hestes D 13/11 (heestes S). OE. ǣr, er S 48/2 (H S Ch) or (A C). This appears in Cot. MS. as ar (Pf., p. 15).
(2) Sh. ǣ²: drede S 45/7, S 88/25.
Very often in Cot. MS. appears as a (Pf., p. 16).
OE. þǣr, þerfore (always in Ch þarvore ; cf. Cot. MS., Pf., p. 16).
OE. hwǣr, where, wherof. This appears very frequently in S as whar. This is not constant. Pfeffer (p. 16) shows that both forms are found for the compounds of þer, in Cot. MS., e.g. þer-inne, þar-inne ; þer-fore, þar-fore ; þer-fram, þar-vram. In Ch þar is always found alone and in compounds.
OE. ǣnig appears in other MSS. written in the three ways any, eny, ony. In London Charters the proportion is: any 78 per cent., eny 20 per cent., ony 2 per cent. (Lek., p. 35 ; *Schriftsprache*, p. 44).
OE. ǣ>e, ee, appears in Pecock (Sch., p. 5). In London Charters (Lek., p. 35). For OE. þǣr, hwǣr, wǣron, Wycliffe and Pecock have only e (Lek., p. 37).
OE. ǣ shortened appears in Pecock as a or e, e. g. neuerthelasse, also neuertheles, sprad (past part.) and spred, radde and red, past part. (Schmidt, p. 6). London Charters have e (*Schriftsprache*, p. 44 ; Morsbach, *ME. Gram.*, § 96, 2 b).
Chaucer has generally a, but always slepte, mente, lente, and occasionally dredde, y-spred for usual dradde, spradde (Sch., p. 6). Lesse occurs oftener than lasse (ten Brink, §§ 50, 106).

k

C. The Short Diphthongs.

I. Breaking and i-umlaut.

(a) OE. ea before r+cons. : harme D 23/14, hardere S 51/10, mask S 91/27, armes S 89/21, afterward M 94/11.

(b) i-umlaut of ea in WS. = ie, y, i, in Ang. e (Bülbring, 179 a 1) vynʒerde D 10/8. Pecock, London Charters, Chaucer have ʒerd (*Schrift.*, p. 50, ten Brink, Par. 48).

(c) OE. ea before l+cons. : also, alle, al, holdeþ, olde.

(d) OE. ea before h, h+cons. : eiʒte S 39/15, liʒt M 95/11.

(e) i-umlaut of ea before h, h+cons. = in WS. ie, early WS. i or y (Bülbring, 179): myʒt D 5/3, D 6/26, nyʒt 52/28, S 89/1.

(f) OE. eo from e before r+cons.: werk D 17/6 (work in all other MSS.), werkes D 20/9 (workes only in S). The London Charters have werk; Pecock has werk (Sch., p. 12). Herte M 96/17, S 47/11. This is the regular writing in all the MSS. Pecock has herte, also London Charters, although Lekebusch points out the modern form hearts (Lek., p. 28).

Derk D 1/5, in all MSS.

Worschip D 1/8 (always written werschip in S); D 10/6, written o in all MSS. except S, which is werschip. The regular form in Cot. MS. is o (Pfeffer, p. 32) influenced by the preceding w.

Erþe D 5/14, 6/6 (eorþe Ch), D 7/12 (eorþe Ch), D 10/5 (eorþe Ch); also berke, berkyng, swerde; sweord is found in Cot. MS. (Pf., p. 22), lerned D 18/13 (lurned Ch, leurned S); Pf., p. 22, points out a number of these forms with u and eu in Cot.; worthi S 43/24. This is the regular form. (See also Pfeffer, p. 32.)

The form in Chaucer is e, although workes, workmen is found (Fr., p. 12).

(g) OE. eo before l+cons. : OE. seolf, sielf, sylf (Siever's *Cook Gram.*, p. 52); hymsilf D 3/7 (self A C), hymsilf D 5/10 (self A C, sulf Ch); mylk M 101/10. The three forms are found throughout the MSS. Ch favours the u. Pecock has silf, London Charters and Chaucer self.

Introduction cxlvii

II. The u- and o/a-umlaut.

(a) OE. eo, u-umlaut of e : heuene D 8/6, D 10/5, world D 3/2, D 4 14.

(b) OE. eo, u-umlaut of i : siluer D 27/5 ; M 104/8. London Charters has forms as selver (*Schrift.*, p. 54). In D 27/5 the reading in Ch S is selver. Björkman (p. 112) thinks the form silver (OE. silfor) in Midland dialects may be influenced by OW. Scand. silfr, while selver, the regular form (OE. siolfor, siolufr, seolfor) depends on u-mutation. The form in Cot. MS. is selver (Pf., p. 26).

III. Effect of Palatals in Short Diphthongs.

(a) OE. ea (WG. a) : schal D 6/1, S 41/23 (Pf., p. 23, finds shal in Cot.), schalt D 4/11, schal S 14/17, ʒaf D 7/13 (all MSS.).

(b) OE. ie : ʒeue D 2/2, D 4/13, ʒeueþ D 2/2, yʒeue, forʒeue, ʒeldiþ D 21/16. OE. ʒiet, ʒit appears as ʒitt, ʒit, or ʒut, also rarely as ʒet. S 48/33, ʒitt in H A C, but ʒut in S Ch ; ʒett S 50/34 in H, but ʒit A C, ʒut S, ʒet Ch ; ʒit S 51/21, ʒut S Ch. Pecock has ʒit always (Schmidt, p. 13), Chaucer yet in Ellesmere, but other MSS. write yit or yitte (Fr., p. 11). The London Charters have ʒeve, I-yeuen, yeten, geten, yet (*Schrift.*, p. 56). Some writers place ʒif in this list, e. g. Frieshammer (p. 11) has OE. ʒief, ʒif appears as yif and if in Chaucer's prose ; always if in Pecock (Schmidt, p. 13), as yyf (yf) in London Charters (*Schrift.*, p. 56).

D. *The Long Diphthongs.*
I. OE. ēa (Gothic au).

Grete D 1/8, D 6/26, D 11/1, S 45/31. This is written in some of the MSS. greet, and quite often in Ch as gret. Breed D 6/14, brede S 45/29, deþ D 6/15, deþliche D 7/14, dede, deed, ʒere, heiʒþe (WS. hēahðo), neiʒ (see under ēa+g, h), deef, vnneþe, heyʒ (hiʒe A C S, hys Ch) (see under ēa+g. h).

Shortened ēa : chaffre (OE. cēap) S 45/28, grettest S 46/2. This diphthong appears in Cot. MS. as above (Pfeffer, p. 27). Pecock writes it as e, ee (Schmidt, p. 14).

II. i-umlaut of ēā.

Herde (p. part.) S 48/4 (I-herd A C, y-hurd S Ch); here inf. S 47/31 (huyre A S Ch), here inf. S 49/28 (huyre S, hyre Ch), here inf. S. 51/8 (hire A C, huyre S, hiyre Ch). In Cot. MS. the following forms appear: hiere inf., hurde, yhurd, huyreþ, hyre, hyryng (Pfeffer, p. 25).

III. OE. ēō.

Fredom D 2/3; this is written freodom in Cot. MS. (Pfeffer, p. 28). Beþ D 2/4 (buþ Ch), beþ S 51/3 (buþ Ch); this always occurs as buþ in Ch, rarely so in S, otherwise as beþ or beeþ; once in H we find be, once in H buþ D 33/8. The usual form in Cot. MS. is buþ, although beþ is found also (Pf., p. 30). Nediþ D 3/9, needip D 14/12 (neodeþ Ch); nedes, nedeful D 16/13 (nedful A S, nedfol Ch), nede D 29/7 (neode Ch). This is written in both forms in Cot. MS., nedeþ and neodeþ (Pf., p. 30); nedfol and neodfol, nedy and neody are also found; fendes D 6/12, deueles D 6/16, prest D 10/2 (preost A C Ch), D 32/1, prestes (preostes Ch, pruestes S), pruest is found in Cot. (Pf., p. 28); lese D 21/7 (luese Ch S). Pfeffer, p. 28, lists a number of forms in u and ue, e. g. luse, luseþ, luf, luver, luesyng; leese D 32/16 (lese A C luese, Ch S). Þeeues D 11/13 (þueues Ch); the form þueues is common in Cot. MS. (Pf., p. 28), þeeues D 30/6 (þefes A C S, þueues Ch), þeefþe D 14/2 (þefte A C, þuyfthe Ch, þefþe S); frendschip S 49/19, frendes S 90/27, teþinge S 45/28 (tiþynge A C, also tiþinges and tueþinges A), chesiþ, fendes, ferþe (fourþe A C, veurþe Ch), frelich. OE. sēoc, sīoc appears as seke (sike, syke in A C Ch), sekenesse (siknes MSS.). This appears in Cot. MS. as syyk and syk (Pf., p. 29). OE. hēōm appears in all the MSS. except Ch as hem. In that MS. always as ham.

E. Short Vowels and Spirants.

(1) OE. a+ʒ: lawes D 1/2, lawe, 2/8, wiþdrawing D 5/13.

(2) OE. æ+ʒ: dayes, sey, seyn (seiþ A C, syggeþ Sh). Forms as sey are usually written thus or seie in all MSS. except Ch (sygge), and S (usually segge); also forms such as seiþ, iseye (ysegge S), seide are found.

(3) OE. e+ȝ: wey, weyes (weyȝes Ch).
(4) OE. i+ht: almyȝty.
(5) OE. o+h: þouȝt, douȝtres, wrouȝt, brouȝt. Both forms nouȝt, noȝt are found in MSS. S is fond of noȝt. Not is found frequently in A C.
(6) OE. o+g: bowes.

F. Long Vowels and Spirants.

(1) OE. ā+ȝ: owne, always oune in Ch.
(2) ǣ+ht, ǣ+g: tauȝt, eiþer, eþer, keyes (OE. cǣg).
(3) ō+h, ȝ: ynowȝ (inow in MSS.).
(4) ē+ȝ: twey, tweyne.

G. Diphthongs and Spirants.

(1) OE. ea+h, ht: seyȝ (OE. seah, seigh A, sigh C, syȝ Ch S). (Bülbring, *Abl.*, pp. 67 ff.)

(2) i-umlaut of ea+ht (see above under C, short diphthongs).

(3) ēa+ȝ, h: neiȝbores (neyȝhebors A Ch), heyȝ (hiȝe A C S, hyȝ Ch), heiȝeste, heiȝlich, neiȝ.

OE. þēah: þouȝ (þeigh A C, þey S, þeyȝ Ch). This appears in Cot. as þey, þeyȝ (Pf., p. 36). These latter are Sth. forms, while þouȝ is Nth. (O. Icel. þō). For full discussion of this word see Björkman, pp. 72–3.

(4) ēo+h, ht: liȝtliche, aliȝt.

H. Vowels and Diphthongs+w.

(1) ā+w: noþer (or nāwþer), soules, knowleche, knowiþ, soweþ, ouȝt, slowe (OE. slāw).
(2) OE. ō+w: yblowe (past part.).
(3) ēa+w: fewe, schewe, schewide, schewid.
(4) OE. ēo+w: ytrowe, trewe, trowe, truliche, trewemen, truþe (trewþe S), trowynge, trowiþ, newe.
(5) OE. ǣ+w: lewed.

II. CONSONANTS.

(1) OE. c appears generally as ch and k.
(a) Initially: chirche, chaffare, chese.
(b) Medially and finally: þecchiþ, leche, rychesses, þenke, myche, berke, knowleche, -liche; ech found in S; also such, siche.

In the Norse words take and siker, k is kept.

(2) OE. sc: schal, schulde, schueleþ, worschippe, flesche, schame, schewe, bischop (in some of the MSS. bisshop), fische; sk is found in aske (often written axe).

(3) OE. ȝ initially: ȝeue, ȝiftes, ȝou, ȝoure, ȝeldiþ, ȝit, ȝet, ȝut, ȝif, ȝaf, ȝere, vynȝerde, aȝenes; g in bygynnyng, bygynne. OE. cȝ: brigges.

(4) OE. f initial, always appears as f in four of the MSS. H A C S, but as v in Ch. Compare this with Cot. MS. (Pf., p. 72).

(5) OE. þ, ð. þ is written for initial d in dewe S 44/19, S 45/26, in S. In S 51/1, for dewe in H A C, we find þewe in S Ch. Also in S 50/20, for dar H, durre A C, we find þere S and þurre Ch.

III. Loan Words.
French.

Distruyed, distruye, distrie, distried, rule (reule Ch, rewle A S), despised, noble, gouerne, money, cosyns, forme, scornes, denye (denyue Ch), sotil, princes, vicarie, preue, preues, douteþ, crowned, expowne, cuntrey, huge (OF. ahuge or ahoge, hoyge S), huge, foly, pore (poure A Ch), socour, toure, soudeyn, grucchying, grucchiþ (OF. groucier), chaungide, statutes, maner, chalengide, catel, ordinaunces, passion, sauter, naciouns, sacrifice, praye (preyre S in D 2/1), counseil (counsail A C Ch S), ordeyneþ, yordeyned, eyr (heire C S), (OF. heir, eir), dewe, choys, feeste, palys, wasters, pale, state, dampned, chastee, causes, matrimonye, wages, ensaumple, sclaundre, secunde, felony, reson, preche, beestis, Empyre, Emperour, mageste, maieste, heritage, rehersed, relef, medleþ, secular, noyse, seynt, plede, pleyn, fayled, pees (AN. pes, OF. pais), apaide, paye, suffriþ, suget, ducherye, peple, auctorite, caucioun, cause, bobans (OF. bobance, boub-, beub-, bueb-, bub-, -anche, Godefroy, also *N.E.D.*), D 21/3, bobaunce A C S.

Spouses S 71/6 (OF. espūse), spouse-bruch S 57/19.

Old Norse.

Boþe (ON. Scand. baðir—Skeat, *N.E.D.*, Sweet), Björkman says 'may perhaps—at least in part—quite as well

Introduction cli

be derived from OE. ba þa' (p. 108), cf. Einenkel, *Anglia*, 27/43. Cros, OIr. cros from ON. kroos (*N.E.D.*); dye, ON. deyja, Björkman, p. 66, 'may be English as well as Scand., but is probably Scand.' (See Dial. Prov., pp. 12 ff.). Wyndes (ON. vengr); þouȝ, see above, p. cxlix; prout, from AS. prut, according to Skeat and *N.E.D.*; Skeat thinks Icel. pruðr borrowed from AS.; ytake, wrong, cast; skyn (ON. skinn); þralles (Icel. þraell); skyle (ON. skil); same (ON. samr); meke (ON. miuk-r) —*N.E.D.*; birþe; fro—see above, also Björkman, p. 100.

IV. INFLECTIONS.
Nouns.

OE. endings have disappeared, except e. The use of final e is not regular. Very often, however, we find the vowel indicated long by a doubling or by use of final e, e.g. dome in A C Ch, but in S doom. The scribe in S is very fond of doubling the vowel, where the other MSS. have a single vowel with a final e. In mouþe, ac. case, mas., we find a final e in H C, but no final e in A Ch S.

There are a few OE. fem. noun-stems, where the e is kept: synne, myrþe, lore, loore, strengþe, helle, mede, filþe, dede, teþinge (near teþing).

In the following fem. stems the e is absent: nyȝt, world, also worlde, book. The e is found in the masc. and neut. nouns: wiche, wynde, felde, kynge, ȝere, name, lame, weye, also way.

Genitive sing. ends in es, is, his, hys; is is very common in H and sometimes in A; hys is the usual form in Ch; kyngis H, kynges C, kyng hys Ch, Cristis H, Cristes A C, Crist hys Ch, Crist is S. Near by we find Cristes in all MSS. except Ch, which is as above.

These examples are from H: Alisaundres bille, eny freres persone, goddes lawe, almes dede, John de Palliaco hys, Pope Martyns maundment, Seynt Austyns bokes, a manes soule, curatours oxe, bischops bischopriche, Zebedeus sones, þe apostels decre, Sathanas hys angel.

We find a few cases of gen. sing. without ending: in her fader hous, under fader & moder keping, children frendes, in þe fader riȝt side. We find þe oxes mouþe (oxe hys Ch, oxe is S).

The plural ends in s, is, es. Is is very common in H; s is found in Fr. nouns. Þingis, foules, þeeues, bedes, teþingis, weþeres, fadres & modres, ladyes, resouns, parischons, curatours, statutes, medycyns, persons, also persones, studies, frere prechours.

Weak plurals: children, ruþeren, oxen.

Umlaut plurals: feet, teeþ, wymmen.

Adjectives.

In the weak inflection, in H the final e is often retained, in Ch it is usually lost; his owne coste, þe olde testament (oolde S), by gode entent (final e should not be retained), near by is þe good entent (lost where it should be kept), goode Ch S, þe fader riȝt side.

In the strong declension, H is more careful to hold the final e: grete (gret Ch), siche, seche ȝiftes (such Ch), alle his dedes (all C, al Ch), alle gentil men (al Ch), alle (al Ch), alle (al A C, all C), oþer mysdoers.

The adjectives before noun: parisch chirche, bodiliche leche, verreiliche suspecioun, hardere conclusioun, esyere way, raþer lif, þe raþer lawe, schrifte fader, mo damages, in þe whiche bokes, verey begger, eerþe tilyers, on alle halwen day, forme fader & moder, priuy riches.

The adjective after the noun: desauauntage greuous & huge, in all þe worlde wide, lawe ciuil, a noble librarie and a grete, lawe canoun, wiþ smale ȝiftes and gileful, mynystre general.

Predicative adj.: þei beþ vnobedient & vnbuxom, he is vnclene.

Comparison of adj.: esyere way, hardere conclusion, þe lasse siker, heiȝeste, grettest.

Numerals and ordinals: þre, oon, ferþe, twey, tweyne, þre quarters, þritty þousand, þe þre ferþe deles of profits, secunde, nynþe.

Adverbs and Prepositions.

Adverbs in e: vnneþe, ful selde.

Adverbs in liche: wilfulliche, onlich, scharplich, slyliche, wilyliche.

Introduction

Adverbs in es: ones a ȝere, went þennes, togidres.
Prepositions: wiþouten ende, wiþoute end, tofore, wiþoute.

Pronouns.

Personal Pronouns.

First Person Sing. Nom.: ich (iche A), y or I frequently found in all five MSS, also ich.
Gen. Sg.: myn, my.
Acc. and Dat. Sg.: me.
Nom. Plu.: we.
Gen. Plu.: oure.
Dat. Acc. Plu.: us.
Second Pers. Sing. Nom.: þou.
,, ,, ,, Gen.: þi, þyn.
,, ,, ,, Dat., Acc.: þee.
,, ,, ,, Plu., Nom.: ȝe.
,, ,, ,, ,, Gen.: ȝoure, (ȝowre A).
Third Pers. Sing. Masc. Nom.: he (a in S).
,, ,, ,, ,, Gen.: his.
,, ,, ,, ,, Dat., Acc.: hym.
Third Pers. Sing. Fem. Nom.: heo (sche A C, hue S).
,, ,, ,, ,, Gen.: her (here MSS., hire C).
Third Pers. Sing. Neut. Nom.: hit (it C S).
Third Pers. Plu. all Gend. Nom.: þei (a Ch S), þei (hy Ch, hey D), usual form.
Third Pers. Plu. all Gend. Dat., Acc.: hem (ham Ch).

Demonstrative Pronouns: Sing. þis, Plu. þese, þose.
Relative Pronouns: þat, what, who, whos, to þe whiche.
Interrogative Pronouns: who, what.

Verbs.

Strong Verbs.

Class I: ywrite (p.p.), he droof (past), writen (Iwrite MSS.).
Class II: he flyȝ (past), lese (luese Ch S) (inf.).
Class III: ybounde (p.p.), fynde (inf.), bynde (inf.), yholpe (p.p.), ye ȝeldiþ.
Class IV: comeþ (3rd sg. pr.), bynome (p.p.).
Class V: yseye (p.p.), we ȝeueþ (pres.), ȝeuen (p.p.), (iȝeue

MSS.), ȝaf (3rd sg. past), seyȝ (3rd sg. past) bade (3rd sg. past), bade (3rd plu.), siȝ (3rd sing. pret.).

Class VI: louȝ (past) (lowȝ A, lowȝe C), stonde (pr. inf.), vnderstonden (p.p.), take (pr. inf.), ytake (pr. part).

Reduplicated Verbs.

yholde (p.p.), hoote (pr. inf.), holdeþ (3rd pres.), he feng, yblowe (p.p.), yhote (p.p.), we soweþ, het (A C Ch, heet S) (past 3rd plu.), ye fang.

Weak Verbs.

Past in d, de: ich herde, turned (turnde Ch, ede S), he rered, answerede (3rd sg.), kynges ordeynede, likide (ede MSS) (3rd plu.), correctide (3rd plu.), blamede, erride, he helde, beggide, iseide, yschewide, hit oblegide, þei hadden, þei procuride, procurede, synnede (3rd plu.).

Past in t, te: lefte (3rd past), sente (3rd plu.), Ich sent.

Past participle in d: chalengide, scorned (yscorned Ch), seide (iseide A C S), schewide (yschewed MSS.), chambred, ordeyned, longide, apassed, praysed, apaide.

Past participle in t: torent (torend A Ch S), yknytt.

Present Tense.

1st sg.: trowe, clepe.

2nd sg.: knowest, þou herest.

3rd sg. in eth and ith: takiþ, nediþ, douteþ, haþ, þe kniȝt spekiþ, schewiþ.

Plural: þei denyeth, we takiþ, ȝe speakiþ, ȝe knowiþ, we suffriþ, þei ordeyneþ, ȝe accounteþ, þei spekiþ, we repe (ripeþ S).

Imperative: deme, war, clepe, denye.

Infinitive: to afferme, destruye, ordeyne, fele.

Present participle: begginge, on kunnyng.

Preteritives and Anomalous.

OE. sculan: yschal (pret. plu.),, schulde, ȝe schal, þei schul, þou schalt, we schal, þei schulleþ, þei schul, alle þinges schulle.

OE. willan: ich wole, þei wole, no suche wolde, he wole, þat wole (3rd sg.), ich nolde, þei wolde, we wolde, ȝif þou wolt, ȝe wolleþ.

OE. bēon: beþ (3rd plu.), þou art, ich am, ffor þe wordes beþ.

Introduction

OE. magan: þei mowe, þei myʒt.

OE. dōn: ydo (past part.), he dide (dude, dede), Christ doþ, þei þat doþ, þou dost (past part.), may be do (pres. inf.), doo (past part.), haþ do.

OE. durran: freres dar, no man dar telle.

V. Remarks on the Manuscripts.

In Ch, OE. f appears initially as v. Examples are: vurst, veyr, vale (fale), vul (full), vewe (few), vorme, vuyr, vysch, vede (feede), voure, vedeþ, vor, veet, vendes (fiends), vyf (fyue), vader, volwe (follow), vram, veng, valleþ, vorþ, vreodone, vechche (fetch), vleysch, vort (forto). The origin of v is the Southern (east) dialéct. This v occurs a few times in the London dialect, and Morsbach finds it once in the London documents.[1] S has v only once in vluys (fleece). H S Ch write values, while A C have falues.

C writes th for þ in a few words: dooth, sooth, seith, the, deth (also in A once), thynke, worth, month, also þuyfthe (Ch), þuefthe (Ch), seþthe (Ch).

Peculiar Spellings.

Cwypes (S), ʒuede (S), ʒede and ʒude in other MSS., neode (always in Ch), hue (for her in S). In S and Ch a doubling of ch: þraychcheþ, rechcheþ, gruchcheþ, rychchest, luese (always in S and Ch), oerþe (once in S).

Verbal endings—ith, eth, ist, est, ide, ede, in H.

Schmidt in his study of Pecock (p. 34) found the following rules obeyed:

(1) The terminations est, eth, ed are added to verbal stems ending in i, u, m, n.

(2) If the stem ends in l, r, ʒ, g, d, this orthographical rule is not so strict.

(3) If the stem ends in another consonant, i alone is found in the termination.

---

[1] Royster, J. F., *A Middle English Treatise on the Ten Commandments*, p. xix, where he refers to Sweet, *Short Historical Grammar*, p. 189, and Morsbach, *Schriftsprache*, pp. 103, 158.

The scribe of H does not adhere closely to these rules, except in case of No. 1, as the following examination of the *Dialogue* shows:

(1) ouertorned, ordeyneþ, haueþ, weneþ, ordeyned, comeþ, serued, occupied, crowned, ȝe striueþ, demeþ, begynneþ, semeþ, likneþ, gouerneþ.

(2) chaungide, chalengide, suffriþ, nediþ, holdeþ, heled, fulfilled, traueiliþ, medliþ, longeþ, wolleþ, falleþ, nedeþ, nediþ, longide, trauailiþ, ruleþ, erride, stireþ.

(3) þow knowest, spekiþ, ȝe knowiþ, douteþ, schewide, rehersed, spekiþ, knowiþ, likeþ, touchiþ, foleweþ, axeþ, schewiþ, worschipeþ, soweþ, þraschiþ, schewide, likide, correctide, wakiþ, makiþ.

This is a Wycliffe characteristic, and places this MS. H farther North than the others.

CORRIGENDA

p. 2, l. 28.	*Read* What euer	p. 49, l. 7.	*Read* freres, is y-holde ones a ȝere
p. 3, l. 21.	*Read* resceiued		
p. 11, l. 7.	*Read* synne	p. 54, l. 29.	*Read* bitake
,, l. 31.	*Read* ouerthrowen	p. 55, l. 8.	*Read* mysuse
p. 13, l. 14.	*Read* Euereche	p. 56, l. 26.	*Read* biheestes
,, l. 29.	*Read* Euerye	p. 57, l. 16.	*Read* oure
p. 15, l. 13.	*Read* dispreues	p. 62, l. 4, p. 63, ll. 12, 32. *Read* Mathei
p. 18, l. 17.	*For* it *read* is		
,, l. 30.	*For* the (1) *read* this	p. 70, l. 30.	*For* spouese *read* spouse
,, l. 31.	*Read* euerye		
p. 19, l. 28.	*Read* awake	p. 72, l. 22.	*Read* fyue
p. 21, l. 20.	F. 14 b *begins with* peude	p. 77, l. 27.	anslauȝt. *Note:* AC *read* manslauȝter
p. 22, l. 25.	F. 15 b *begins with* to	p. 85, l. 30.	*Omit* so
		p. 86, l. 20.	*Read* ȝaf
p. 24, l. 18.	*Read* sklaunder	p. 87, l. 7.	*For* his (2) *read* þis
p. 25, l. 30.	*Read* manyfestlye	p. 95, l. 5.	*Read* in
p. 31, l. 31.	*Read* lewde	p. 96, l. 24.	*Read* warld
p. 34, l. 25.	*Read* beryue	p. 99, l. 3.	*For* gaftis, men *read* craftis men
p. 46, l. 24.	*Read* probable		
p. 47, l. 14.	*Read* Prouerbiorum	p. 101, l. 19.	*Read* tabernakyls
,, l. 20.	*Read* clereliche	,, l. 26.	*Read* to þaim of þaim-selfe
p. 48, l. 32.	*Read* hym-silf		
p. 49, l. 1.	*Read* principle	p. 108, l. 2.	*For* þei *read* & þei

PART I

DIALOGUS INTER MILITEM ET CLERICUM

Harl. 1900

Clericus. Ich wondre Syr Noble Kny3t þat in fewe dayes, tymes beþ chaungide, ri3t is y-buryed, lawes beþ ouertorned, & statutes beþ y-trode vnder feet.

Miles. Ich am a lewed man & may nou3t vnderstonde sotil
5 & derk speche; perfore þou most take more pleyn maner of spekyng.

Clericus. In my tyme ich haue y-seye þat kynges & princes hadde hooly chirche in grete worschip, & now y se þe contrary

---

A DIALOGVE BETWENE A KNYGHT AND A CLERKE CONCERNYNGE THE POWER SPIRITUAL AND TEMPORALL

Printed by Thos. Berthelet.

CLERICUS. The clerke begynneth to speke on this wyse
10 sayenge:

CLERICUS. I wounder syr noble knyghte that in fewe dayes, tymes be changed, right is buryed, lawes be ouerturned, and statutes be trodde vnder foote.

MILES. Those wordes passe my capacite, I am a lewde man;
15 and thoughe I wente to schoole in my chyldehode, yet gotte I not so profounde lernynge that those youre wordes can of me be vnderstande. And therfore worshypfull clerke, if ye desyre to haue communication with me, ye must vse a more homely & playner fascion of spekyng.

20 CLE. I haue sene in my time that, Kinges princis and all other nobles, haue had the churche in right great worshyp; and nowe I se the contrary, the churche is made a pray to you

þat holy chirche is made praye to ȝou alle, miche¹ is chalengide² of vs & no þing is ȝeve us. Ȝif we ȝeueþ nouȝt, hit is y-take of vs wiþ strenȝþe, oure good &³ catel is distruyed, lawes & fredom⁴ beþ nouȝt y-holde but dispised & wiþseide.

Miles. In þe Kyngis⁵ counseil beþ bischops.⁶ Y trowe nouȝt liȝtliche þat þe Kyng & his counseil wole do ȝow wrong, noþer distruye ȝoure lawe.

Clericus. Aȝenus al maner lawe we suffriþ wrong.

Miles. What clepe ye lawe?

Clericus. Ich clepe lawe þe statutes &⁷ ordinaunces of bischops of Rome & decrees of holy fadres.

Miles. What þei ordeyneþ or haueþ y-ordeyned tofore þis of temporalte, may wel be lawe to ȝou but nouȝt to us. No man haþ power to ordeyne statutes of þynges ouer þe whiche he haþ no lordschip. As þe kyng of Fraunce may ordeyne no statutes

Marginalia: The clerk tells the knight that the Church is not worshipped by kings and princes as of old. / In the King's Council are bishops. / Law is decrees of Holy Fathers. Bishops have no power to make laws over things over which they have no control.

¹ Money C.
² chaunged S.
³ & our S.
⁴ blotted Ch: fredoms S.
⁵ Kyng hys Ch.
⁶ byschs Ch: bischopes & prelates S.
⁷ and þe C Ch.

---

all,* and many thynges are challenged of vs, and nothynge is gyuen vs. If we gyue not oure goodes, they be taken frome vs by stronge hande, our good and catalle is distroyde, our lawes and fredome be not holden, but dispysed and withsayde.

MILES. I can not lyghtly beleue, that the Kynge (of whose counsayle they of the clergie be) wyl deale vniustly with you, nother distroye your lawe.

CLERI. Yea trewely agaynst all lawe, we suffre innumerable wronges.

MILES. I wolde fayne knowe what ye calle lawe.

CLERI. I calle lawe the statutes and ordinances of bysshops of Rome, & decrees of holy fathers.

MILES. Whatever they ordeyn, or other have ordeyned in tyme past of temporaltie, may well be lawe to you, but not to vs. For no man hath power to ordeyne statutes of thynges ouer the whiche he hathe no lordeshyp.* As the kyng of Fraunce may ordeyne no statutes vppon the empyre, nother the emperour vpon the Kynge of Englande. And lykewyse as

Dialogus inter Militem et Clericum

vppon¹ þe Empyre noþer þe² Emperour vppon þe Kyngdom³ of Englond. And also princes of þe world may ordeyne no⁴ statutes of ȝoure spiritualte, for þei⁵ haueþ no power ouer⁶ ȝoure spiritualte. Also ȝe mowe ordeyne no statutes of tempor-
5 alte, ouer þe whiche ȝe haueþ no power noþer auctorite; þerfore ich louȝ wel faste, whanne ich herde telle þat Pope Bonefas hadde made⁷ a newe statute, þat he hym-silf schuld be aboue alle secular lordes, princes, kyngis, & emperors, & aboue alle kyngdoms & make lawe vppon alle þinges, & þat him nediþ
10 nouȝt but write, for alle þinges schulle⁸ be his whanne he haþ y-write. For to make a statute⁹ is nouȝt elles but wilne þat þe decre be y-holde & ordeyne & hoote þat hit be y-holde. ȝif he wole have my castel, my toun, my feelde, my money, & alle siche þingis, hym nediþ nouȝt but wilne hit, & write,¹⁰ & make
15 a decree, & hote þat hit be y-holde, & whanne þat is y-do he

Kings cannot make laws for the spiritual power.

Also ȝe mowe ordeyne no statutes of temporal power.

The decree of Pope Boniface making himself above all secular bodies is a jape to be scorned.

¹ *blotted* Ch.
² our S.
³ Kyng C.
⁴ non C.
⁵ þei þei C.
⁶ of S.
⁷ I-made A C Ch S.
⁸ om. Ch.
⁹ a statute hys statute C.
¹⁰ write hit A C.

---

princis of the worlde maye ordeyne no statutes of youre spiritualtie, ouer the whiche they haue no power; no more ye maye
ordeyne no statutes of theyr temporalties, ouer the which ye
haue nother power nor auctoritie. Wherfore it is a thynge in
20 vayne, what euer ye ordeyne of temporal thynges, ouer whiche
ye haue of God resceived no power. And therfore but late I
lough well faste, whan I harde that Pope Boniface the VIII. had
made a newe statute, that he hym selfe shulde be aboue all
seculer lordes, princis, kinges and emperours, and aboue all
25 kyngedomes, & make lawe vppon all thynges; and that hym
nedeth nought but wryte, for all thynges shall be his, whan he * 3 b
hath wryten; and so all thyng shall be yours. For to make a
statute, his statute is nought elles, but to wyll that the decree
be holden and kepte, and ordeyne and whote that it be holden.
30 If he woll haue my castell, my towne, my felde, my money, or
any other suche thynges; hym nedeth nought, but wyll it, and
write it, and make a decree, and whote that it be holden, and
whan that is done, he hath ryght to al such thynges. Now

haþ ri3t to alle siche þingis. Now goode clerk, þou knowest
wel how worþi þis iape is to be scorned.
 Clericus. Syre kny3t 3e spekiþ scharplich, slyliche, & wilyliche y-now3. Al 3oure talkynge & menyng is þat þe pope haþ
no power to ordeyne & make statutes of youre temporalte; for
3e knowiþ nou3t þat he haþ lordschipe, power, & auctorite vppon
youre temporalte. Þou3¹ we wolde preue hit by oure lawe & by²
decrees y-write, 3e acounteþ hem for nou3t; for 3e weneþ þat³
Petre had no lordschip & power³ ouer temporalte but by siche
lawe y-write. But 3if þou wolt be a trewe Cristen man & of
ri3t bileue, þou schalt nou3t denye þat Crist⁴ was Lord of alle
þinges. To hym hit⁵ was seide in þe⁵ Sauter book: 'Axe of
me, & y schal 3eue naciouns to þee to þyn heritage, & al þe
⁵world aboute⁵ to þi possessioun.' Also of hym hit is y-write
þat 'he is kyng of kynges & lord of lordes.' Þese beþ Goddes⁶

Marginalia: The Pope hath power over your temporality. / Christ was Lord of all things.

¹ þei A C S: þey3 Ch.
² be C.
³⁻³ Petir no lordschippe hadde ne power C.
⁴ om. C.
⁵⁻⁵ blotted Ch.
⁶ God hys Ch.

---

good clerke, thou wottest well, howe worthy this iape is to be
scorned.
 Cle. Syr Knight ye speke sharpely, slyly, and wysely
ynough; all your talkyng and meanynge is (as fer as I perceyue) that the pope hath no power to ordeyne and make
statutes of your temporalties; for ye knowe not, that he hath
lordeshyp, power, and auctoritie vppon your temporalties.
Though we wolde proue it by our * lawe, and by decrees wryten
ye accompte them for nought. For ye wene that Peter had no
lordeshyp ne power ouer temporalte, but by suche lawe wryten·
But if thou wilt be a trewe Christen man, and of ryght beleue,
thou shalte not deny, but that Christ is lord of al thinges. To
hym it was sayde in the Sauter boke: Aske of me, & I shall
giue nations to thyn heritage, and all the world about to thy
possession. Psal. 2. And also of hym it is wrytten, the fyrst
pistill to Timothe the VI. Chapiter, that he is kynge of kynges,
and lorde of lordes. I Tim. 2. Apoc. 17 & 19. These be not
ours, but Goddes owne wordes; nor we wrote them not, but
God sente them, and the holy gooste spake them; and who

Dialogus inter Militem et Clericum 5

owne wordes; but what Cristen man douteþ wheþer[1] God be trewe of his wordes.

Myles. I wiþsigge nouȝt þe mageste, lordschip, & myȝt of oure Lord God, for he may[2] be wiþseide in[3] no maner wise. But ȝif
5 hit may be schewide by Holy Writ, þat þe pope is lord of al temporalte, kynges & princes mot nedes be suget to þe pope as wel in * temporalte as in spiritualte.

Christ is Lord of temporal things, but not the Pope. Fol. 1 b

Clericus. Þat may be schewide liȝtlich by auctoritees, þat beþ raþer rehersed. Þe feiþ[4] of holy chirche holdeþ þat Petre þe
10 apostle was ordeyned Cristis[5] vicarie for hym-silf & for[6] his successours; & he þat is ful vicarie may do þe same þat his lord may whanne he is made vicarie wiþ full power wiþ-oute eny wiþdrawing of power. Þanne ȝif ȝe[7] may nouȝt denye þat Crist, þat is Lord of heuene & of erþe, may ordeyne & make statutes
15 of ȝoure temporalte, ȝe may nouȝt denye wiþoute schame þat Cristes[5] vicarie haþ þe same power.

Peter was made the Vicar of Christ with full power, for himself and all his successors.

[1] wher C: war Ch: whare S. [5] Crist hys Ch.
[2] may not S.   [6] om. S.
[3] on C.   [7] he C.
[4] fey A C Ch S.

---

douteth, whether he may ordeyne and make statutes, whome he knoweth to be Lorde of all thynges?

Miles. I withsay not the maiestie, Lordeshyp, and myght
20 of * our Lorde God; for he maye not be withsayde on no 4 b maner wyse. But if it may be shewed by holy writte, that the pope is lorde of all temporalties; than Kynges & princes muste nedes be subiecte to the poope, as well in temporaltie as spiritualtie.

25 Cle. That may be shewed lyghtly, by the auctoritees that be a lytell rather rehersed. The fayth of holy churche holdeth, that Peter the apostell was ordeined Christis ful vicare for hym selfe and for his successours. And he that is fulle vicare, may do the same that his lord may, whan he is made vicar with ful
30 power, withoute any withdrawynge of power. Than if ye can not deny, but that Christe, that is lorde of heuen and of erthe, may ordeyne and make statutes of your temporalties; how can ye for shame deny Christis vicare to haue the same power?

Christ has two times, one of his manhood, the other of his power and majesty.

Myles. Ich haue herde¹ of wise doctors þat we schal distingue twey diuerse tymes of Crist: oon of his manhed and anoþer of his power & mageste. Þe tyme of his manhed was from² þat he toke flesch & blode anoon to his passioun. Þe tyme of his power & maieste was & is after þe resureccioun, whanne he seide: 'Al power is ȝeuen³ to me in heuene & in erþe.' 5

(*Treuisa.* Here takiþ⁴ hede of þe knyȝtes⁵ menyng & of þe clerkes⁶ menyng also. For þe wordes beþ nouȝt fulle chambred.

The time of Christ's manhood was when he was on earth doing his wonders and miracles.

For al þe tyme of Cristes⁷ manhed, þat was tofore his passioun, was tyme of his myȝt, power, & maieste. For bifore⁸ his passioun 10 he turned water into wyn; & heled blynde, & lame, & many maner seke men; & hadde þe see, &⁹ wynde, & weder, & fendes attendaunt to his heestes; &¹⁰ fedde fyue þousand of men wiþ fyue loues of breed & lefte twelue cupes¹¹ of relef; & rered men from¹² deþ to lif; & ȝaf his disciplis myȝt & power ouer alle þe 15 deueles & fendes; and schewide of his blis to Petre, James, & Ioon; & ȝede vppon þe see in grete tempest of weder & of þe see. Also whanne he sent his disciplis to fecche hym þe asse to ride on¹³ into Jerusalem, he seide: 'ȝif eny man seiþ ouȝt to ȝow, seiþ þat þe lord haþ to do þerwiþ'; & in his ridyng he 20 was worschiped as a Kyng, & somme spradde cloþes in his wey & somme bowes; & þanne¹⁴ was þe prophecie fulfilled, seiþ: 'Douȝtres of Syon, lo! þi kyng comeþ to þee, meke & mylde,

The time of his might and power was before his passion.

sittyng vppon¹⁵ an asse.' Also in a tyme he drof biggers & sillers out of þe temple as lord & kyng. Also his lore was in¹⁶ 25 myȝt & power, & he dide al þis & many oþer grete dedes bifore¹⁷

¹ y herd A C Ch S.
² fro S.
³ Iȝeue A C Ch S.
⁴ tak S.
⁵ *blotted* Ch.
⁶ clerk hys Ch.
⁷ Crist hys Ch.
⁸ tofore A C Ch S.
⁹ *om.* A C Ch S.
¹⁰ & he A C Ch.
¹¹ cupes ful A C.
¹² fro S.
¹³ *om.* C Ch.
¹⁴ þo A C Ch S.
¹⁵ on C S.
¹⁶ *om.* C.
¹⁷ tofore A C Ch S.

---

5 a   MILES. I haue hard of holy and * deuout men, that we shuld distingue two dyuers tymes of Christe: one of his humilite, and an other of his power and maiestie. The tyme of his humilytie was from the tyme that he toke flesshe and blode, vnto his 30 passion: the tyme of his power and maiestie, was and is after his Resurrection, whan he said: All power is yeue to me in heuen and in erthe. Mat. Vlt.

his passioun; þanne before¹ his passioun was tyme of his power
& of his my3t & after his passioun was & is tyme of his manhed.
For after his passioun Seynt Steuene sey3 hym in his manhed
stonde in þe fader ri3t side. But how hit euer be of þe distinc-
5 cioun þat is made bitwene þe clerk & þe kny3t, of þe tyme of
Cristes² manhed & of þe tyme of his my3t, power, and maieste,
take hede how þei spekiþ eiþer to oþer. For þe kny3t spekiþ
in þis manere.)

Peter was ordeyned Cristes² vicarie, for þe state of his man-
10 hed & nou3t for þe state of his blisse & maieste. He was nou3t Peter was made
made Cristes² vicarie in doyng þat Crist doþ now in blisse; Christ's vicar, to
but for to folowe hym in his doyng þat he dide here on³ erþe. follow him in his doing
þanne he 3af his vicarie þat power⁴ þat he vsed⁴ here in erþe, here on earth.
depliche. & forto preue þis by Holy Writt, y take witnesse of
15 Crist & of Holy Writt as þou dost. Lo! Crist seide to Pylat:
'My kyngdom is nou3t of þis world.' Also he seiþ þat 'he Holy Writ shows
come nou3t to be serued,⁶ but to serue oþer men.' Luce 12º. that Christ was not
And oon seide to Crist: 'Maister say to my broþer þat he judge over temporal
departe heritage wiþ me.' Crist answerde & seide: 'Man who things.

¹ tofore A C Ch S.   ⁴⁻⁴ om. A C.
² Crist hys Ch.   ⁵ om. S.
³ in S.   ⁶ I serued A C Ch S.

---

20 Peter was ordeyned Christis vicare for the state of his humilite, and not for the state of his blysse and maiestie; but to
folowe hym in doynge those thynges, which Christe in humilite
dydde here in erth; for those thynges are necessary for vs.
Ergo Christ commytted thylke power to his vicare, whiche he
25 as a man mortall exercysed, and not that power, whiche after
his glorification he resceyued. And for to proue this by Holy
Wrytte, I take wytnes of Christe and Holy Writte,* as thou 5 b
doste. Lo Christe sayde to Pilate: My Kyngedome is not of
this worlde, Jo. 18. Also he saith, he came not to be serued,
30 but to serue other men, Matt. 20. This wytnes is so manifeste,
that it maye confounde a man, resiste he neuer so moche, and
all to frusshe his necke, be it neuer so styffe. And it is wrytten
Luc. 12. howe one said to Christ: Mayster say to my brother,
that he departe herytage with me. To whom Christ answered
35 and sayde: Manne, who hathe ordeyned me iudge or departer

Dialogus inter Militem et Clericum

<small>Fol. 2 a</small>

<small>He gave Peter the keys of the kingdom of heaven not of earth.</small>

haþ made me juge to departe bitwene ȝou ? ' Luce 12º. Lo! þou herest openlich þat Crist was nouȝt juge & * deler ouer temporalte.¹ But whanne þe peple þat he had fedde ² wolde have made ³ hym kyng, he flyȝ from ⁴ hem. Also in Petres ⁵ commissioun he ȝaf hym nouȝt þe keyes of þe kyngdom of erþe, but þe keyes of þe kyngdom of heuene. Also þe bischops of Hebrewes were suget to kyngis, & kynges sett doun bischops.⁶ But forto knowe þat Petre was Cristes ⁷ vicarie in goostliche kyngdom of soules & nouȝt in temporal lordschipe of castels &

<small>This is proved by Paul, writing to the Hebrews, and also to Timothy.</small>

of londes, take hede what Poul þe apostle seiþ : ' Euereche bischop,' he seiþ ' is y-take of men & y-ordeyned for men in þingis þat longeþ to God, nouȝt to gouerne erþliche kyngdom, but to offre ȝiftes & sacrifice ⁸ for synne.' Also to ⁹ Thi. : ¹⁰ ' No

---

¹ *Inserted in* S 'y ordeyned for þe staat of þis deþlich lif þat hauynge no Kyngdom of þis world noþer gouernaunce of temporalte'.
² y fed A C Ch S.
³ y made A C Ch S.
⁴ fro S.
⁵ patre hys Ch S.
⁶ but God forbode þat it were so now A C S : but God for buede hyt þat were so now Ch.
⁷ Crist hys Ch.
⁸ Sacrafices A C S.
⁹ *om.* S.
¹⁰ þise A C.

---

betwene you ? Lo thou hereste openly, that Christ was not iudge nor dealer ouer temporaltees. Ergo in that state of dispensation taken on hym, he neyther had nor desyred temporalle kyngedome. But whan the people, that he hadde fedde, wolde haue made hym kynge, he fledde from them Jon. 6. Also in Peters commission * he yafe hym not the keys of the kyngdome of erth, but the keyes of the kyngedome of heuen. Also it is euydent and playne, that the bysshoppes of the Hebrewes were subiectes to kynges, and the kynges deposed the bysshoppes : but god forbydde, that they shulde so nowe. And for to knowe, that Peter was Christis vycar in godly kyngedome of soules, and not in temporalle lordeshyppe of castelles and of landes ; take hede what Paule the appostelle saythe wrytynge to the Hebrewes. Heb. 5. Euerye bysshoppe (saythe he) is take of men, and ordeyned for men in thynges that belonge to god, not to gouerne erthely thynges, but to offre gyftes and sacrifices for synne. (That the bysshoppe is made ruler in those thinges that long to god, thou maist perceyue by the wordes of saynte Paule wrytynge to Timothe, the. 2 * pistel, & 2. chap. where he

Dialogus inter Militem et Clericum

man,' he seiþ, 'þat traueiliþ in knyȝthode to godward medliþ
hym to¹ secular nedes² & bysynesse.'³ Þanne it is soþe þat
Crist vsed nouȝt worldliche kyngdom, ⁴noþer ȝaf Peter siche
a maner kyngdom.⁴ Also in Actibus Apostolorum, Petre seiþ:
5 'Hit is nouȝt riȝtful þat we leue þe lawe of God & serue mete-
bordes, & gouerne temporalte.' ⁵& þouȝ somme temporalte⁵ may   Peter also
be gouerned by bischops, noþeles bischops schulde nouȝt be   says that we should
occupied in gouernance of myȝt & lordschips of þis world. Þer- not leave the law of
fore sire Clerk þe auctoritees þat þou hast leyde ⁶ for þi party: God te serve temporal
10 'Axe of me & y schel ȝeue þee peple & naciouns, & al þe world things.
aboute to þyn heritage'; þis is nouȝt vnderstonden for þe first
state but for þe secunde; for in þe first state Crist vsed no
siche power, but put hit awey ⁷ from ⁸ hym & vsed onlich þat
longeþ to þe gouernaunce of oure sauacioun; & in þat maner of

¹ in A C Ch S.   ⁵⁻⁵ om. C.
² charges A: chirches C Ch: ⁶ aleide A C Ch S.
cherres S.   ⁷ alwey C.
³ besynessess.   ⁸ fro A C S.
⁴⁻⁴ om. A C.

15 saith), No man that trauayleth in knyghthode to godward,
medleth him in secular busynesses. Than hit is sothe, that
Christe neyther exercised worldely kyngedome, nor commytted
hit to Peter. And in the actes of the apostels the 6. Chaptre
Peter saythe: It is not ryghtfull that we leue the worde of god,
20 & serue meate, bourdes, (that is to saye, to dispose temporall
thynges). And all though some temporall thinges may be dis-
posed bi bishops; yet, neuertheles it is playne and euident, that
bysshoppes shulde not be occupied in gouernaunce of myghte
and lordshyppes of this world. Therfore syr clerke, the auctori-
25 ties that thou haste layde for thy partie, Aske of me, and I shall Psalm 2.
gyue to the, nations to thyn heritage, and all the world about,   I Tim. 2.
to thy possession. And that he is kynge of kynges, etc. Apoc.
17 & 19. This* is not vnderstond for the fyrst estate but for   7 a
the seconde. In the whiche fyrste estate it is playne, that
30 Christe exercised no temporall power, but put it clene away
from him, & vsed only that, that longed to the gouernance of
our Saluation. And in that maner of doynge he made Peter his
vicar, whom he nother made knyght, nor crowned kynge; but

Christ made Peter a priest and bishop and not a king. doyng, he made Petre¹ his vicarie & made hym no knyȝt noþer crowned hym² kyng, but made hym ³prest & bischop.³ And ȝif ȝe wolleþ ȝett stryue þat Cristes⁴ vicarie schuld haue þat power in temporalte, þat Crist hadde after his resureccioun in heuene & vsed nouȝt here in erþe, ȝoure strif schal not turne 5 ȝow to worschip atte laste. Euerech Cristen man knowiþ wel, þat ȝif God bade⁵ hym ȝeue to anoþer man his money, his hous, his felde, hys vynȝerde wiþout eny⁶ caucioun, wiþoute eny ple, wiþout eny axing why & for what cause, anoon he most be obedient. Þanne ȝif ȝe striueþ þat þe pope haþ þe same power, 10 þanne ȝe mot stryue also þat þe pope may take of ȝow & of vs, al þat ȝe & we haueþ & ȝeue al to his cosyns oþer whom him likeþ, & telle no cause why. Also þat he may take of princes & of kynges principates and kyngdoms at his owne wille, & ȝeue where hym likeþ. But take hede how wrongfullich þat were 15 y-do & demeþ how hit wolde myslike ȝow, & he dide so to ȝow.

¹ 'Christ' *written in line*, 'Petre' *above line* S.
² *om.* C.
³⁻³ bisshop & preost C.
⁴ Crist hys Ch.
⁵ heet A C Ch S.
⁶ *om.* S.

---

ordeyned hym to be a preest and bysshoppe. And if ye woll yet stryue, that Christis vycare shulde haue that power in temporaltie, that Christe had after his resurrection in heuen, and used not here in erthe, your stryfe shall not turne you to 20 worship at length. For it is euident to euery faythfull man, that if God shuld commande hym to gyue his money, his felde, or his vineyarde to any other man, without any prouision or reasonable request, and without any expresse studieng, he ought 7 b forth with to obey.* Wherfore if ye wyll contende, that the pope 25 hath the same power, than of necessite ye must graunt also, that the pope maye take from you, and from vs, all the goodes that ye and we haue, and gyue them all to whiche of his neuewes or cousyns, that he wyll, and tell no cause why; and also he may take away from princis and kynges, principalitees and kynge- 30 domes at his own wylle, and gyue them there as hym lykethe. But take hede how wrongfully that were done, and demeth your owne selfe, howe that wolde myslike you, if he dydde so to you. If that very reason constrayne you to forsake your folysshe

Þanne it is soþe þat he feng nouȝt so grete power as Crist in temporalte, but onlich þat power þat Crist vsed & tauȝt in his deþlich lyuyng. *Therefore he has not temporal power, but only that*

Clericus. Denyest þou,[1] þat holy chirche schal knowe[2] cor-
5 rectt men of synnes?
Miles.[3] Wrongfuliche penaunce & schrifte. *power that Christ used and taught in his deathly living.*

Clericus. Þanne ȝif a wrongful dede is synne, þe pope þat schal knowe & deme[4] of synne, schal knowe & deme[4] of riȝtful & vnriȝtful. [4]But in temporalte & in dedes þat touchiþ temporalte
10 is riȝtful & vnriȝtful.[4] Þanne þe pope schal [5]deme & rule[5] þe temporalte. *The Pope must rule the temporal.*

Miles. Þis argument is riȝt nouȝt. For here ich argue in þe same maner, in honging of þeeues & of oþer mysdoers þat beþ dampned[6] to þe deþ, is riȝtful & vnriȝtful. Þerfore bycause of
15 synne þat siche men doþ, þe pope schal deme &·be domesman?

[1] om. A C Ch S.
[2] knowe and A C Ch S.
[3] God hit forbude for who þat denyeþ þat denyeþ. A C Ch S.
[4-4] om. C.
[5-5] rule & deme C.
[6] I dampned A C Ch S.

---

argumente the poope also shall be constrayned to gyue backe. For it is sothe, that he, Christis vicare, resceyued not so great power in temporaltees, but he resceyued onely that power, that Christe in his humilite dayly vsed * and taughte. 8 a
20 CLERICUS. Wyll ye denye syre knyghte, that holy churche shall not knowe and correcte menne for synnes?
MILES. Godde forbydde, For he that wolde denye that, shall denye penaunce and confession.
CLERI. If ought be done vnryghtfully, it is synne; and he that
25 hath to do in knowledge of synne, must knowe and also deeme of ryghtefulle and vnrightfull. Therefore syns there is ryghtful and vnrightfull in businesses of temporall matters, of verye consequens the pope ought to rule and deme in temporall causes.
30 MILES. This is a forked argument, whose vanite and sklendernes must be by a like argument, overthrowen. In hangyng vp of theues and other misdoers, that be dampned to the dethe, is ryghtfull and vnryghtfull, and also synne. Therefore bycause of synne, that suche menne * doo, shall the Poope deme and be 8 b

In cause of felony & of mannes¹ deþ, þe argument is nouȝt, & þerfore hit is y-blowe awey wiþ a liȝt resoun. Now sire clerk, * ȝe most schewe how ȝe schal knowe & deme riȝtful & vnriȝtful. For hit is no doute þat riȝtful & vnriȝtful in temporalte schal be demed by lawes, þat men haueþ made of temporalte. But me mot take hede al aboute what longeþ to þe cause þat schal be demed. Þanne hit is soþe þat he þat makiþ þe lawe, haþ power to knowe & to deme riȝtful & vnriȝtful, & to expowne & declare, & telle þe menyng of lawe, & to kepe þe lawe, & to gouerne² resonabliche ³þee by lawe.³ Þanne ȝif ȝe wolleþ be as grete maistres as he, in knowleche & demynge of ⁴temporalte, & striue wiþ hym in knowleche & demyng of⁴ riȝtful & vnriȝtful, in what longeþ to temporalte, þanne ȝe ereþ wiþ an oxe and an asse aȝenus ȝoure⁵ Holy Writ. & whanne þe prince seiþ, þis is riȝtful,

Who shall deem the right and the wrong.
He who makes the law for temporal things must judge right and wrong, and govern according to law.

¹ man hys Ch.
² gouerne þe A.
³⁻³ om. A.
⁴⁻⁴ om. S.
⁵ ȝoure owne S.

domes man in cause of felonye and of mans dethe? This is a lyght argument, and therefore hit is blowen away with a lyght reason. Nowe syr clerke ye muste shewe, howe ye shulde knowe and deme ryghtfulle and vnrightefulle. For there is no doubte, but that ryghtful & vnrightfull in temporalties shal be demed by lawes, that men haue made of temporaltie. But ye mote take hede all aboute, what longeth to the cause, that shal be demed. Than it is soth, that he that maketh the lawe, hath power to knowe and to deme rightfull and vnrightful, and to expowne and declare, and to tell the meanyng of the lawe, and to kepe the lawe, and to gouerne reasonnably by the lawe. Nowe if ye wyll be as great maysters as he, in knowlege and demynge of temporaltie, and stryue with hym in knowlege and demyng* of rightfull and vnrightful, in what that longeth to temporaltie, thanne eare ye with an oxe and asse agaynst your holy wrytte. And whan the prince saythe, this is ryghtfull, the bysshop sayth, this is vnryghtfull: than is fulfylled the prophecy of Abacuc: Abac. 1. Ryghtfuldome is made, and withsayenge is stronger, throughe the whiche the lawe is torne and rent, & the rightful dome cometh not to ende. For

Dialogus inter Militem et Clericum

þe bischop seiþ, þis is vnriȝtful. Þanne is fulfild þe pro- *If the Pope striveth for*
phecie of Abacuc. In þe bygynnyng was made riȝtful doom, *temporal power then*
& wiþsigginge of þe prophete is stronge; þe lawe is y-tore & *is fulfilled the pro-*
to-rent; þe dome com nouȝt to þe ende, for þat schal nouȝt be *phecy of Habakkuk*
5 to-rent riȝtwisnesse in erþe. Now y schal schewe ȝou by þe *1.4.*
apostle whare ȝoure knowleche & doom schal bygynne. Þe
princes by her lawes schal knowe & deme riȝtful & vnriȝtful,
& þe ende þerof, euereche man schal take hede as he is y-holde &
be obedient to hym, as hit is yhote Deuteronomy 17º: 'Si quis
10 autem tumens, ȝif eny man is prout & wole nouȝt be obedient
to þe princes¹ hestes, & þe princes office haþ no power to deme *If a man is*
& to chastee siche mysdoers,' þanne bigynneþ ȝoure knowleche *disobedient of the*
& ȝoure dome. For ȝoure monicioun schal refreyne & chastee.² *King's law, then the*
For þe apostle Poule ad Titum³ seiþ: 'Evereche soule schal be *bishop may admonish*
15 suget to þe ouer power.' Whanne he seiþ euereche soule, hit *him.*

¹ prince hys Ch.   ³ ad titum 3º S.
² chastise C.

---

truely that is not to do ryghtfull dome and iustyce in erthe.
Nowe I shall shewe you, after the apostelle Paule where your
knowlege and dome shall begynne. The prince by his lawes
shal deme right and wronge, and euery man shall be redy at
20 his commandement, as he is bounde: and shall be obediente to
hym. Nowe if any man waxe stubborne, and wyll not be
obedient to the pryncis hestes, nor the prynce (Whose office is
deme and iudge)* is not able to resyste and compell hym : 9 b
than begynneth your knowlege and your dome. For youre
25 monitions shal refraine and chastice hym, accordynge as Saynte *Tit. 3.*
Paule saythe to Titus the 3. Chap. Admonyshe and warne them,
that they be subiectes to princis and high powers. And also
wrytynge vnto the Romayns the thyrtene chapiter he sayth on
this wyse: Everye soule shall be subiecte to the hyghe powers. *Rom. 13.*
30 Whan he sayth euery soule, it semeth than, none is excepted.
Also where as misdoynges and synfull dedes are manifest and
open, as robbery, thefte, and suche lyke, norther is none that
can or wyl redresse these offences: I deny not, but that ye
shall and may vse your power in suche cases, but not of ryght-
35 full or vnrightfull: for it falleth not for you to knowe and

When the sin is openly known as in robbery, and there is none to amend the trespass, then the priest may use his power.

semeþ þat noon is outtake. Also þere þe mysdoyng & synne is openliche y-knowe as hit is in takinge of robberie & of þeefþe, and whanne þere is noon þat wole and may amende þe trespas, y denye nouȝt þat ȝe schal & may in siche caases vse youre power; but nouȝt aboute riȝtful and vnriȝtful, for hit falleþ nouȝt to [1] ȝou to knowe & deme þerof, noþer to putt ȝoure hond þerto. But whanne hit is openliche y-knowe by sentence & dome of lawe oþer by open euydence & knowleche of þe trespas þat nedeþ noon oþer witnesse & preues, [2] þanne hit may longe to ȝou [2] in mater & forme as hit is seide toforhond. & ȝif ȝe 10 wolleþ needes knowe & deme in siche caases,[3] bycause þat vnriȝt & synne beþ y-bounde to-gidres, þanne hit nediþ nouȝt but close þe ȝates of princes & speke nouȝt of her lawes, but speke of þe lawes of bischops aloone. Hit longeþ to ȝou to knowe & to deme in cause of matrimonye 15 & of wedlok, y praye ȝou wole ȝe þerfore sey þat hit foleweþ þat ȝe schal knowe & deme of al þat longeþ þerto, for þe knyt-

[1] *om.* S.   [3] *causes* C.
[2] *þan may it longe to ȝou* C.

---

10 a deme thereof; nor to entermeddle therewith. But when * it is openly knowen by sentence and dome of the lawe, or els by playne euidence and knowlege of the trespace, that nedeth none 20 other wytnesse nor proues: than may it longe to you in maner and forme, as hit is sayde before.

And if ye woll nedes knowe and deme in suche causes, bycause that wronge and synne be lynked to gether; than there nedeth nought els, but shutte vp the gates of princis, and 25 speke naughte of theyr lawes and statutes, but speke of the lawes of bysshops all onely. It dothe belonge to you to knowe and to deme   cause of matrimony and of wedlocke, I pray you, wyll ye therfore say, that it foloweth, that ye shall knowe and deme as al that longeth therto for the knyttyng of the 30 dede? Lo! I go into your countreye for to aske heritage in my 10 b wyfes name; for she is heyre therof, ye see, that by * reason of matrimonye it longeth to me to requyre this heritage; shall I therfore plede before you for my wyfes heritage, and telle my tale in this manner: I Roberte at Stile aske for my wyfe a 35

Dialogus inter Militem et Clericum

tinge of þe dede? Lo! ich go into ȝoure cuntraye forto axe heritage in my¹ wyues² name, for heo is eyr þerof; hit longeþ ³to me to axe þat heritage, for hit is y-knytt to þe matrimonye & hit longeþ³ to ȝou to deme & to knowe of þe matrimonye.
5 Schal ich þerfore plede tofore ȝow for my wyues heritage & telle þe tale in þis manere: 'Robart atte Style axeþ for his wif a ducherye in⁴ name of⁵ dower, & so forþe?' Wheþer⁶ schal ich plede tofore þe kyng oþer tofore þe bischop? Ich saye þlaynlich to ȝou alle clerkes, forbedying ȝou þat ȝe entremete
10 ȝou nouȝt of doome & knowleche of dower, aȝenus God & riȝt- wisnesse. For þe byheeste of dower is verrey couenaunt of temporalte, & schal* be preued oþer dispreued, by preues oþer dispreues, of þe kynges⁷ lawe. Þanne hit is a iape of sich a manere onyng of þinges, to feyne a knyttyng to-gidres in dome
15 & in knowleche of causes, þouȝ oon auctorite be ynouȝ to ȝou for al þis doyng. For Crist in þe gosþel seiþ: 'Man who haþ made me domesman oþer deler bitwene ȝou?' Luce 12°. Here

An illustration of the function of the priest, as seen in matrimony and wedlock.
He should know of the matrimony, but has no power to judge in regard to the wife's dowry.
Fol. 3 a
The dowry comes under the King's law.

¹ myn C.
² wyf hys Ch.
³⁻³ om. C.
⁴ in þe A C.
⁵ of a A C.
⁶ where C Ch.
⁷ kyng hys Ch.

---

duchery, in the name of dowerye, and so forthe? Whiche ought to be pleded before the kyng, and not before the bysshoppe.
20 Yea I saye vnto you all clerkes forbyddynge you, that you entermeddell you not of dome and knowlege of dowere, agaynst God and ryghtousness. For the beheste of dowery, is very couenant of temporaltie, and shall be proued or disproued, by proues or disproues, of the kynges lawes. And for so moch as
25 ye vsurp and take vpon you that, that belongeth vnto other, it is ryghte mete, that ye suffre as ye do.

Now thus it appéreth, that it is but a iape and a vanite of suche maner of onynge of thynges to feyne a* knyttynge to gethers in dome and in knowlege of causes. For to the con-
30 foundynge of all those reasons (that ye make) the only wordes are suffycient, that I afore recyted to you oute of the gospelle of Luke, where our Lorde Jesu sayth: O man who hath ordeyned me domesman or dealer betwene you? Here Christ sheweth vs

11 a
Luc. 12.

Christ did not deem and deal heritage. Crist schewiþ vs openlich, þat hit longide nou3t to hym to deme & dele heritage by þe power þat he vsed in þat þat he was man y-schape forto dye.

The spiritual must rule the temporal. Clericus. Þe temporalte schal serue þe spiritualte, & 3if hit is so, temporalte schal be suget to [1] spiritualte, & spiritual power schal gouerne & rule þe temporal power.

Miles.[2] Soþlich þe temporalte schal serue þe spiritualte, so þat þei þat [3] haueþ temporalte schal fynde what is necessarie to hem þat worschipeþ & serueþ God. For alle naciouns doþ so **The temporal shall serve the spiritual in the case of those who administer sacraments. This is given in Moses' law, and by Paul to the Corinthians.** as hit were by wey of kynde, [4] & kynde 3af dome by lawe [5] of kynde,[4] þat to hem þat worschipiþ God & mynistres sacramentes & soche as longeþ to God, me schal mynistre necessaries & dewe [6] worschipe & what is nedeful to liflode, so hit is yknowe, 47o of Pharao; & þe lawe þat God 3af, Moyses ordeyned largelich for prestes. But þat lawe ordeyned hem no temporal

---

[1] to þe S.
[2] Miles, *written in right margin,* H.
[3] *om.* C.
[4–4] *om.* C.
[5] wey *written and crossed out in text, and* lawe *in right margin,* H.
[6] þow A C: þuwe Ch: þew S.

---

openly, that it longed not to hym to deme and deale herytage, by the power that he vsed in that that he was man shapen for to dye.

CLERI. Can ye denay but that the temporalties ought to obey and be seruiseable to the spiritualtie? If ye can not, ye must nedes graunt that the temporaltie must nedes be subiect to the spiritualtie; & that the spirituall power oughte to rule the temporall.

MILES. Sothely the temporaltie shall serue the spiritualtie in this case; they are bounde to fynde them, that worshyp and serue * god, all that is necessary for them. For so do all nations (as it were by way of kynde) honour and ministre vnto the liuelod & other necessaries, that worshyp God, & ministre sacramentes and such as longeth to God. For in the lawes that our Lord gaue to Moyses, the Phariseis and pristes were largely prouided fore: but yet that law did not ordein for them ani temporall kyngedome or lordeschyp. And the apostell to Cor. 9. the Corinthees saythe: If we have sowen thynges spirituall amonge you, it is no great thing if we repe carnall? But if

Dialogus inter Militem et Clericum

kyngdom & lordschipe. And þe apostle to Corinth: '3if we soweþ to 3ou spiritualte, hit is nou3t þe moste 3if we repe 3oure temporalte.' But 3if þou wolt wite what maner lordschip Crist ordeyned[1] his seruauntes þat sowiþ spiritualte, take in ordre þe
5 wordes of Crist & of þe apostle Paul. Crist sende his disciplis to preche & seyde: 'Þe werk-man is worþi his mede,' & Poul seiþ: 'Who[2] trauailiþ in kny3thode vppon his owne coste, as who seiþ no man.' And in Moyses[3] lawe hit is writen: 'Þou schalt not bynde þe oxes[4] mouþe þat praschiþ.' Lo! how
10 Crist likneþ 3ow to werk-men, to hyred[5] men, to oxen & nou3t to kynges. Hit is knowen[6] þat werkmen & her men beþ nou3t lordes of þinges. Þanne hit semeþ þat temporalte is grauuted 3ow to helpe of 3oure lyuynge & nou3t to lordschipe. And of þe spiritualte[7] hit is writen[8] in Moyses lawe[9]: 'Þere 3e beþ
15 likned to an oxe þat praschiþ, to þe whiche hit is y-now3 to take his mete þou3 he fille al þe berne wiþ his trauail.' And

Christ told his disciples: the work-man is worthy his mede.

[1] ordeyned for A C Ch S.
[2] who so S.
[3] Moyses hys Ch.
[4] oxe hys Ch.
[5] hyre A C Ch S.
[6] I knowe A C Ch S.
[7] spiritual A C.
[8] I write A C Ch S.
[9] lawes A C Ch.

---

thou wylte witte, what maner lordshyp Christe ordeyned for his seruauntes, that sowe spiritualle sedes: take of the wordes of Christe and of the apostelle Paule, as they folowe in order.
20 For Christe to his disciples, sente forthe to preache, sayde: The worke man is worthye his meate: and, The worke man is worthy his * mede. And Paule of hym selfe and other apostles sayth, I. Cor. 9. Who trauaylleth in knyghtehoode vpon his owne coste? As who sayth: no man. I. Cor. 9. And in Moyses lawe
25 it is written. Deut. 25. Thou shalte not bynde the oxe mouthe that thressheth. Lo to whom doth Christe & his apostell Paule lyken you? To workmen, to hyredmen & oxen, and not to kinges. I pray you, be worke men and hyred men, lordes of thynges? Than it semeth, that temporaltyes are graunted you
30 to helpe of your lyuynge, and for charge of spirituall administration, and not to lordeshyp. And of the spirituall it is wrytten in Moyses lawe, there Deut. 15. Ye be lykened to an oxe, that thressheth, to the whiche it is ynough to take his meate,

Mat. 10.
Luc. 10.
Tim. 5.
12 a

The bishop is taken of men, and ordained for men, in that which belongs to God, not in that which belongs to the world.

for ȝe seyn þat spiritual power ruleþ & gouerneþ þe temporalte hit is schewide toforhond by þe apostle, þat euerech bischop is y-take of men & ordeyned for men in þat þat longeþ to God, & in þat spiritual power schal rule & gouerne us & nouȝt in þat þat longeþ to þe world. For hit longeþ nouȝt to holy chirche to deme in þat, þat is outward. And ȝif ȝe ȝit stryueþ þat þe pope is aboue alle oþer also in temporalte, ȝe falleþ into wel grete scornes. ȝif þe pope whanne he is made pope ¹ is made lorde of alle ¹, þanne by þe same skyle a bischop whanne he is made bischop, is ² made lord of al þe cuntray of his bischopriche ; & þe kynges ³ preste is þe kynges ³ lord, & lord of þe kyngdom ⁴ & of al þat is in þe kyngdom,⁴ & specialiche þe primat. Also we haueþ lerned þat kynges ordeynede who schulde be prestes ; and prestes ordeynede nouȝt who schulde be kynges, & prestes were

In the former days kings ruled the priests.

5

10

¹⁻¹ he is lorde ; lorde of alle þe contrey C. ³ kyng hys Ch.
² he is C.   ⁴⁻⁴ om. C.

---

though he fyll al the berne with his trauayle. And for that ye saye, that spirituall power ruleth and gouerneth the temporaltie, * that it answered you afore by the apostell Paule, where he sayth : Euery bysshop is taken of men, and ordeyned for men in that that longeth to God, and in that the spirituall power shall rule and gouerne vs and not in that that longeth to the worlde ; for it longeth nat to holye churche to deeme in that that is outwarde.

And if ye yet striue, that the pope is aboue all other also in temporaltie, ye falle into well great skornes. For if the poope (whan he is made pope) shuld be made lorde ouer all : than by the same skylle a bysshoppe (whan he is made bysshop) is made lorde of all the countrey of his bysshoprike, and my priest shall be lorde ouer my castelle, and be my lorde. For as the power of the pope is in all, so is the power of these in that party, where they rule. Wherfore leaue the folysshenes the which is * laughed and mocked atte of euery man, and that is, with so many reasones and auctorityes of Scripture confounded. Also we haue lerned in the Olde Testament, that kynges ordeyned who shulde be priestes ; but priests dyd not ordeyne, who shuld be

12 b

Heb. 5.

13 a

15

20

25

30

Dialogus inter Militem et Clericum

nouȝt worschiped ¹ of princes & of kyngis, but princes & kynges were worschiped ¹ of prestes & of prophetes; & ² kynges sente for prestes & prophetes, & bade ³ hem do what ⁴ kynges likide.

Also in þe Olde Testament kynges correctide prestis and 5 vndertoke hem and blamede hem, whanne þei erride in gouernaunce of temporalte, as hit * is written, 3º Regum pº 4º & 12º ca.

Evidence of this in the Old Testament. Fol. 3 b

Clericus. Me wondreþ þat ȝe seyn þat þe kyng vndertoke þe bischop in gouernaunce of ⁵ temporalte.

10 Miles. ȝe stireþ me & wakiþ me as hit were of my sleep, & makiþ me speke oþer wise þan y þouȝt.

Clericus. Lete þe hound wake & berke.

Miles. For ȝe kunne nouȝt vse manhed suffraunce & pacience of princes, y trowe ⁶ ȝe schal fele berkyng & bityng.

15 Clericus. What haueþ princes and kynges to do wiþ gouernaunce of oure temporalte? Þei haueþ her owne compray ⁷ þat þei lete vs haue fre.

¹⁻¹ *om.* C.
² & of C.
³ heet A C Ch S.
⁴ what þe C.
⁵ of A C Ch S: oþer H.
⁶ trowe þat S.
⁷ compray contrarie C.

---

kynges. And priestes were not worshypped of kynges; but kynges and pryncis were worshypped of priestes and prophetes, 20 and myghte calle them and commaunde them to do what pleased the kynges. And in the same Olde Testamente the kynges dyd correcte the priestes, and vndertoke, and blamed them, whan they erred in gouernaunce of temporaltie.

Cle. I maruayle that ye say, that kynges vndertoke and 25 blamed the byshop in gouernance of temporaltie.

Miles. Ye awake the slepynge dogge, and dryue me to speake otherwyse than I thoughte before to do.

Cleri. Lette the * hounde wake and barke. 13 b

Miles. For as moche as ye can not be contente, and pacyently 30 (to your profit) suffre the princis, I fere me, that after due and iuste barkynge, ye shall fele bytynge.

Cleri. What have princis and kynges to do with gouernance of our temporaltie, lette them take theyrs, and suffre vs in peace with oures?

Priests should pray for those who die, and not waste their time in sins and vanity.

Miles. Kynges & princes haueþ myche ado wiþ ȝoure temporalte. Haue ich nouȝt to do to þenke on þe sauacioun of myn owne soule wiþ al þat y may? Falleþ hit nouȝt for ȝow to pray for fadris þat beþ apassed out of þis lif? ȝaf nouȝt oure forfadres¹ ȝou temporalte in grete wone & plente for ȝe schulde pray for hem, & spende in Goddes² worschip? But ȝe doþ noþinge herof, but ȝe spendiþ ȝoure temporalte in youre synnes & ȝoure vanite, þe whiche temporalte ȝe schuld spende in werkes of charite, in almes dedes in³ pore men & nedy. Were hit nouȝt nedeful þat þei þat beþ dede were y-holpe, & þei þat beþ⁴ alyue⁵ y-saued by dedes of mercy, for þe whiche oure forfadres haueþ y-ȝeue ȝow grete lordschipes & huge? Spende ȝe nouȝt siche lordschipes amysse & so wrongfullich, þat ȝe greueþ boþe quycke & dede & doþ hem wrong aȝenus þe wille of hem þat ȝaf ȝow so grete lordschipes & rychesses? While⁶ ȝe recchiþ

¹ forme fadres A C.
² God hys Ch.
³ to A C.
⁴ beþ dede were I holpe & pey þat beeþ C.
⁵ alyue be C. : alyue were S.
⁶ whiche C.

MILES. Syr the princis muste in any wyse haue to do therwith. I praye you, oughte nat we aboue all thynges, to mynde the helthe of our soules? oughte not we to see, that the wylles of our fore fathers be fulfylled? Falleth it not to you to pray for our fore fathers, that be passed out of this lyfe? And dydde not our fore fathers gyue you oure temporalties ryghte plentyfullye to the entente, that ye shulde praye for them, and spende it all to gether to the pleasure and honour of god? * and ye do nothyng so: but ye spende away your temporaltie in synfulle dedes and vanite, the which temporaltie ye shulde dispende in workes of charite, and in almes dedes to poore men and nedy. Were it not nedefulle, that they that be deed shulde be holpe, and they that be alyue saued by dedes of mercye? For the whiche oure fore fathers haue gyuen you great and huge dominions. And whan ye apply them to your owne vse and superfluously consume them, and contrary to their intente, that were the gyuers, and also of the resceyuers, lasshe them out to an yll vse: do ye not damnably hurte and hynderaunce bothe to them that be alyue, and also to them that be deed? ye recke

Dialogus inter Militem et Clericum

nouȝt of honeste of ȝoure owne law, & of dedes of mercy & of
charite, masses ȝe siggeþ nouȝt noþer syngiþ in chirche; but in
foly, in bobans, and in likyng of þis world, ȝe spendiþ al þat
was y-ȝeue ȝou wiþ holy entent. Schal nouȝt his wages be
5 bynome hym þat wole nouȝt do þe dedes of knyȝthode? He
þat holdiþ of anoþer & doþ nouȝt his due¹ office & seruise, he
schal lese his fee. And forto make an ende in þis questioun,
y schal schewe ȝow þat ȝe auȝt be sory & fonge remedye, wiþ
ioye & wiþ gode wille, & rediþ þe chapitre of Holy Writt,
10 2º Paralipomenon 24º. Þere it is writen in þis maner of kyng
Joas: 'He dide what was² good & plesyng al þe tyme of Joab þe
prest.' Also 4º Regum 12º cº hit is³ writen: 'Kyng Joas
cleped Joiada þe bischop & prestes also, & seide to hem, Why
restore ȝe ⁴ nouȝt þe holy helyng of þe temple? Þanne fang ȝe ⁴
15 no more money of þe peple by ȝoure owne ordinaunce, but
ȝeldiþ hit to restoring of þe temple & of Goddes⁵ hous.' Þanne
þe prestes were forbode to fonge more money of þe peple. Take

Margin: Because you spend your time in evil and folly, and do not perform your proper office and service, you should lose your fee as would a knight who neglected his duty. Joas a good priest and was praised by God.

¹ dewe A C: þew Ch S. ⁴⁻⁴ om. C.
² om. C. ³ om A. ⁵ God hys Ch.

---

not for honestye, no nor for your owne lawe, nor for dedes of
mercye and charite, but in foly and bobance and in lykynge of
20 this worlde, ye * dispende al that was gyuen you for an holy
entent. Shal not his wages be stopped, that wyll not doo dedes
of knyghthode? He that holdeth of an other, and dothe not his
due office and seruice he shall lose and forgoo his fee. And for
to make an ende of this question, and to put you to sylence,
25 I shall shewe you that, that shall make you sorye, and gladde
to fynde the mene to set a remedy. Redeth in Holy wrytte.
2. Parali. Ca. 14. There it is wrytten of kynge Joas, that
he dydde that that good was and pleasynge to oure Lorde
alle the dayes of Joidas the preeste. And of the same kynge
30 we rede iiij. Regum 12. Kynge Joas called Joida the bysshoppe,
and also the prestes, and to them he sayd: Why repayre ye not
the couerynge of the temple? Loke therefore that ye take no
more money of the people by your owne ordynaunce, but
applye it to the * instauration of the temple, and of Goddes
35 house. And thus the preestes were forbydden to take any more
money of the people. Wherefore thou seest, that kynge Joas

hede how Kyng Joas was praysed of God, for he toke heede for
þe offrynges schuld be spende in worschipe of God, by þe holy
entent of hem þat ȝaf hem. God praisiþ kyng Joas forto schewe
& leue vs ensample, þat Joas dide þat by myldnesse & by gode
entent & nouȝt by couertise. And for þe kyng wolde put of 5
euel suspeciou*n*, he wold haue þe bischop wiþ hym to witnesse.
Þane hit folewiþ, whan*n*e he siȝ to myche money in þe tresory,
þe kynges[1] writ*er* & þe bischop wente vp into þe tresory, and
helde out & tolde þe money þat was founden[2] in Goddes hous.
Lo! þe good entent of þe kyng is y-praised þat toke hede,[3] þat[4] 10
gode of þis olde chirche schuld be bisiliche y-saued & y-spend
in gode vse & holy. I knowe hit well hit likeþ ȝou nouȝt to
here þese wordes, & noþeles y speke nouȝt but wordes of Holy
Writ. It is seide ȝou, þat ȝe haueþ y-fonge alle siche lord-

[1] kyng hys Ch.   [3] hede of C.
[2] I founde A C Ch S.   [4] þat þe A C Ch S.

---

was preysed of our Lord, for that he toke hede, that the 15
offrynges shulde be spended to Goddes worshyppe, that is to
saye, to the instauration of the temple, accordynge to the holy
entente of them that gaue suche thynges. God preysethe this
Kynge Joas, for to shewe and leaue vnto vs ensaumple, that
the sayde kynge, in his soo doynge, dydde not offende, for so 20
moche as he dydde hit not for any couetousnesse, but of Goddelye
zeale, not of ambition, but of deuoute relygyon. And the
kynge, to the entente to eschewe yuelle suspeccion, he wolde
haue the bysshoppe with hym to beare wytnesse, as foloweth.
15 b And whanne he sawe to moche moneye in the Treasaurye,* the 25
kynges wryter and the bysshoppe wente vppe in to the Treasaurye, and poured oute and tolde the money, that was founde
in goddes house; and they gaue hit after the noumbre and
weyghte in to theyr handes, that were sourueyours of the
masonrye of Goddes house. Lo the good intention of the kynge 30
is preysed, that tooke hede, that the goodes of this olde churche
shulde be besyle saued, and spente to a good and a holye vse.
I knowe well it lyketh not you to here these wordes, and yet
neuerthelesse I speke not but wordes of Holy Writte. It is
sayde to you before, that ye haue resceyued all suche lorde- 35

Dialogus inter Militem et Clericum 23

schipes & riches to help of youre lif to wages * of holy chyualrie, Fol. 4 a
to haue mete & drynke & cloþ; þerwiþ þe apostle seiþ þat he
helde hym apaide; and al þat is ouer þat nediþ to mete & Priests
drynke & helyng, 3e schulde spende in pore men & in dedes of should use
5 mercy. And 3if 3e do nou3t so, [1] þanne we haueþ myche [1] to do plus on poor
þerwiþ. For þanne hit falliþ to vs to take hede of 3oure tem- deeds of
poralte, þat 3e bigile [2] þe quyk & þe dede.
 Clericus. Þis kyng toke nou3t þe godes & catel to his owne vse, This good
but he spende hit al [3] in holy chirche vse. 3e takiþ oure catel his goods
10 & spendiþ hit in chiualrie & nou3t in vse of holy chirche. & for the use
þerfore þe ensaumple þat 3e bringiþ forþ is nou3t a3enus vs noþer church and
a3enus oure werkes and dedes; but 3e coloure oþer wise 3oure chivalry as
violence & 3oure wrong.
 Miles. Alwey to 3oure owne harme 3e kikeþ a3enus þe pricke
15 of kynges. Is it nou3t greuous to 3ou þat 3oure cosyns & 3oure
kynnesmen takiþ to hem of holy chirche goodes & catel, & som-

[1-1] þanne moche haue we C.   [3] om. C.
[2] bigile not C.

---

shyppes and riches to the helpe of youre lyfe and as the wages
of holy chiualry, and to the intent to haue cloth and foode; with Tim. 6.
whiche two the apostell saythe, he * helde hym payde; and all 16 a
20 the ouer plus besyde clothe and foode, ye ought to spende in
dedes of mercye & pitie, as on poore people, that haue nede and
on suche as be sycke and diseased, and opressed with misery.
And if ye do not so, than muste we haue to do therwith: for
than it falleth to vs to take hede of your temporaltie, that ye
25 begyle not and deceyue the quycke and the deed.
 Cle. This kynge Joas toke not the goodes and cattell to his
owne vse, but he bestowed them on holye churches vse. But
nowe a dayes ye toke our goodes, whiche ye spende not to the
vse of holy churche, but on your busy and vnruly souldiors,
30 and on shippes and ingins of warre. And therfore the
ensaumple that ye brynge forthe, is not agaynst vs, nor agaynst
our warkes and dedes; but ye wold therby colour your violence
and wronge.
 Mi. Alway to your * owne harme ye kycke agaynste the 16 b
35 pricke of kynges. It is not greuous to you, that your cousins
and kynsmen take to them of holy churches goodes and cattelles,

24 *Dialogus inter Militem et Clericum*

<small>Your cousins and your kinsmen take the property of holy church. You are thus working against God Almighty.</small>

tyme oþer persoones þat beþ nouȝt honeste in grete sclaundre to ȝou & to al þe peple þat is vnder ȝow, & beþ ful venymous by ȝoure owne euel ensaumple in lyuyng? Þis ȝe suffriþ þat may be cause of Goddes [1] wreþþe vppon þe kyng & vppon [2] al þe rewme, þat rechelesliche suffriþ ȝou so frowardliche worche 5 aȝenus God Almyȝty. But ȝow semeþ þat hit is a greuous wronge, þat þe kyng axeþ myldliche [3] of ȝou & fangeþ & þankeþ ȝou, as for þinge þat is graciouslich y-graunted; and spendiþ hit nouȝt in his owne vse, but in ȝoure owne sauacioun & in defence of holy chirche, & of youre owne godes and catel. 10

Clericus. Allas! wo is me wrecched man, ȝe to-tereþ & to-haleþ & takiþ awey my flesche & my skyn, & þat ȝe clepiþ sauacioun.

Miles. Y pray ȝou leteþ be ȝoure noyse & ȝoure grucchying, & herkneþ pacientlich. Takeþ hede of ȝoure neiȝbores & of 15 ȝoure pore sugetis, þat beþ ful many in lond, & takeþ hede of oþere þat fangeþ of ȝoure catel also. ȝif þe kynges [4] power

[1] God hys C.
[2] om. S.
[3] mekeliche A.
[4] kyng hys Ch.

---

and somtyme other persons, that be not honest, to the sklaunden of you, and of all the people that be vnder you : and ye be full venomous through your owne yuell ensample of lyuynge. This 20 ye suffre, the whiche may be cause of Goddes wrath vpon the kynge, and vpon all the realme, the whiche recklesly suffreth you so frowardly to worke agaynst Almyghty God. But to you it semeth a greuous wronge, and in no wyse to be suffered, that the kyng asketh mekely of you, and thanketh you for it, as for 25 a thynge graciously granted; and yet he doth not spende hit to his owne vse, but for your saufegarde, and in the defence of holy churche, and of your goodes and cattell.

17 a   Clericvs. * Alas WO is me wretched man, ye tere & hale away my flesshe and my skynne, and that ye calle saufgarde.   30

Miles. I praye you lettethe be your noyse and your grutch-ynge, and harkeneth paciently. Consyder your neyghbours about you, that be many in londe, whiche wantyng, wherwith to lyue, gape stylle after your goodes. If the kynges power

Dialogus inter Militem et Clericum 25

fayled, what reste schulde ʒe have ? Wolde nouʒt alle gentel men & oþere nedy & wasters, ʒif þei hadde wasted her owne, turne to ʒoure¹ & distrie al þat ʒe haueþ? Þanne þe kynges strengþe is to ʒow in stede of a wal; & it is knowen² þat þe
5 kynges pees ³is ʒoure pees,³ his sauacioun is ʒoure sauacioun. For & þe kynges power were awey oþer wiþdrawe, þanne as ʒoure synnes axiþ now, þei þat comyneþ⁴ wiþ ʒou now, þei þat werreþ vppon ʒou, wolde destruye & waste ʒoure gode, and compelle ʒou to be þralles. And ʒif ʒe wolde nouʒt, al þat ʒe
10 haueþ were loste. How myche þanne wolde ʒe paye for to⁵ haue þe kynges⁶ socour & his helpe, as ʒe hadde raþer ? Þanne ʒe seeþ⁷ þat whanne ʒe ʒeueþ a lytel what⁸ to þe kyng, ʒe biggeþ ʒoure owne sauacioun & saueþ ʒoure owne⁹ goodes & catel, þat schulde be distried wiþ ʒoure owne neiʒbores & wiþ
15 men of straunge londes, nere þe kynges ¹⁰help & his socoure.¹⁰

In time of distress and trouble, the king's strength is to you instead of a wall. If the king's power were withdrawn you would become thralls, or lose all your goods.

¹ ʒoure owne C.   ⁶ kyng hys Ch.
² I knowe A C Ch S.   ⁷ sueþ S.
³⁻³ *om.* & C.   ⁸ *om.* C.
⁴ comuneþ A C S : comneþ Ch.   ⁹ *om.* S.
⁵ *om.* S.   ¹⁰⁻¹⁰ socour & his help S.

---

faylled, what reste shulde ye haue ? Wolde not the gentyll men, suche as be nedy, and suche as prodigallye haue spende away theyr substance, whanne they haue consumed theyr owne, wol not they turne to yours, and waste and distroye all that ye
20 haue ? Therfore the kynges strength is to you in stede of a stronge walle. And ye wotte very welle, that the knyges peace is youre peace; and the kynges saufegarde is your saufegarde. For if the kynges power wanted, or elles were withdrawn * 17 b from you: than (as your synnes asketh) they that commune with
25 you now, and they that wayte vpon you nowe, wold dystroy, waste, and consume your goodes, and compell you to be theyr thralles. And if ye wold not, all that ye have were vtterlye loste. Howe moche than wolde ye paye for to haue the kynges succour his helpe and defence, as ye had before ? Than thus ye
30 se and perceyue many festlye, that whan ye gyue a lyttell portion to the kynge, you bye therwith your owne safegarde, and therby ye saue to youre selfe, youre goodes and your cattals, that shuld be distroyde by your ennemies, and by men of

If the king failed you, would not your enemies make war npon you and put you out of your place?

But alwey ȝe haueþ be vnkynde to þe goodnesse þat me haþ y-do¹ ȝou; and so now ȝe playneþ & grucchiþ in ȝoure owne profit. ȝif þe kyng failed wolde nouȝt ȝoure enemyes werre vppon ȝou, & put ȝou out of ȝoure place² &³ of ȝoure lond,⁴ & take of ȝou al þat ȝe haueþ, & leue ȝou pore, naked, & bare? 5 But ȝif⁵ kynges & princes schal put hem to peryle of deþ for ȝou, & defende ȝou vppon her owne coste,⁶ & ȝe reste vnder her wynges, &⁷ ete & drynke wiþ grete solace & myrþe, & lye in nesche beddes & sikerliche slepe, & do hem no socour wiþ ȝoure riches in help of her coste, þanne it semeþ þat ȝe wolde 10

Fol. 4 b   mene þat onliche ȝe * beþ verrey lordes, and kynges & princes of bonde condicioun, & so made þralles. Þouȝ men of holy chirche haue reste y-graunted hit is nouȝt grete, but þe riches mot serue for men of holy chirche. ȝe seyn þat þis is harde, & ȝe resteþ nouȝt but gruccheþ alwey, er ȝe be ouercome & 15

¹ y do to S.
² places S.
³ & out C.
⁴ londes S.
⁵ ȝif þe C.
⁶ costes C.
⁷ om. A C Ch S.

---

straunge londes, ne were the kynges helpe and his succour. But as ye haue alway ben vnkynd, for the goodnes that he hathe done to you; euen so now ye playne and grutche, agaynste that that is

18 a   youre owne profyte. If the kynge fayled * you wolde not youre ennemyes waire vppon you, and putte you oute of your place, 20 and out of your lande, and take frome you all that ye haue, and leue you poore, naked, and bare? and so stryken with terrible drede, wolde ye not put your selfe to flyghte, and wander ye forced not whyther? But and kynges and princis at theyr owne costes, and to theyr great peryll and daunger of 25 theyr lyfes, be holden to defende you; and you to reste vnder theyr wynges, and to eate & drynke with great solace and myrthe, and to lye in softe and delicate beddes, and sikerly to slepe, than it semethe, that ye wolde meane, that onely ye be verye lordes, and kynges and princis be of bonde condicion, and 30 vnto you seruantes and thralles.

If reste be graunted to men of the churche, it is no great

18 b   thynge if the ryches be reserued for vs of the lay * fee. This is an harde thynge, saye ye, but ye wyll not reste, tylle ye be

y-schend as ȝe beþ wont by Holy Writ, þat ȝe¹ mowe nouȝt *Holy Writ tells how*
wiþstonde. For of kyng Joas þat we spake of raþer, hit is *Joas king of Juda took*
writen,² 4º Regum 2º cº: 'Joas kyng of Juda toke al þat was *the hallowed silver from*
halwed þat Josophath, Aaron & his fader Ocosias kyng of Juda *the temple and sent it*
5 had halwed, & þat he had y-offred, & al þe siluer þat he myȝt *to the king of Assyria*
fynde in þe tresory of þe temple & in þe kynges³ palys, & sent⁴ *to pay the*
to Asael kyng of Siria, & þo he went from⁵ Jerusalem.' Lo!⁶ *ransom of the people.*
openlich þou myȝt se þat he toke þat þat was halewide in
Goddes⁷ hous, forto paye raunsoum for⁸ þe peple, & noþeles he
10 spared nouȝt þe kynges⁹ palys whanne he toke al þat out of þe
temple. Also 3º Regum 18º cº, Ezechias brake þe values of *Ezechias did likewise.*
þe temple of oure Lord & toke þe plates of golde þat he hym
silf had do¹⁰ þere, & ȝaf hem to þe kyng of Assiria. And ȝif

¹ *om.* S.   ⁶ lo hou S.
² I write A C Ch S.   ⁷ God hys Ch.
³ kyng hys Ch.   ⁸ to C.
⁴ sent hym C.   ⁹ kyng hys Ch.
⁵ *left margin* H; to *deleted in text.*   ¹⁰ I doo A C Ch S.

(as ye are wont) conuicted and also confounded by holy scrip-
15 ture; ageinst the whiche ye can not resiste. For of Joas the
kynge, (of whome we spake before) hit is wrytten in the 4. boke
of Kynges, the 12. chaptre, and in the seconde booke of Parali,
the 24. chapyter thus: wherfore Joas the kynge of Juda tooke
all that was halowed the which thinges Joram & Ochozias his
20 fathers, kynges of Juda had halowed, and whiche thynges he
hym selfe hadde offered vppe, and all the syluer that he coude
fynde in the treasaurye of the lorde, and Palaice of the kynge,
and sente it to Azael, the kynge of Syrie, and he departed
from Jerusalem. Lo, here thou mayst plainly see, that for to
25 paye the peoples raunsomme, he toke those thynges oute of the
temple not withstan*dynge he spared not the kynges palayce, 19 a
whan he toke those thynges out of the temple.

Also in the 4. boke of Kynges, Cap. 18, it is thus redde of
the holy Kynge Ezechias. The same season Ezechias braake
30 the gates of the temple of the lorde, and toke the plates of
golde, that he hym selfe had there stycked vppe, and gaue them
to the Kynge of Assiriens.

And if thou woldest saye, that Ezechias did amysse, I

Dialogus inter Militem et Clericum

                Þou seist þat Ezechias dide amys, ich answere for [1] Paralipo-
menon 32º cº, it is writen þat Ezechias was blamed [2] for
noon of alle his werkis [3] & dedes, but onliche for þe message of

Holy Writ praises these men, whom you condemn.
þe princes of Babilon. Who schal dampne hym þat Holy
Writ praiseþ in alle his dedes? But 3e erreþ & knoweþ nou3t 5
þe soþnesse & þe vertue of Holy Writ. But what is þat a3enus

God chooses not the people for the places, but the places for the people.
kynges & princes? 2º Machabeorum 6º cº, hit is writen
þat 'God chesiþ nou3t þe peple for þe places, [4] but þe places [4]
for þe peple.' Þanne me schal not spare þe chirche of lyme &
of stoones whanne Cristen men beþ in peryle. & Ezechias [4] & 10
Josephath vnderstode wel þat, & Ezechias [4] fulfilled hit wel

Your good is the good of Holy Church, and therefore of the people who make the church.
truliche. 3if 3oure [5] gode is holy chirche gode, & þe peple is
a grete partye of holy chirche, schal nou3t þanne holy chirche
gode skilfullich be spend in helpe & sauacioun of þe peple?
And so hit folewiþ, þat hit longeþ to þe goostlich [6] holy chirche. 15
And oure Lord, by [7] Math. in [7] 12º cº seiþ: 'Y telle 3ow þis is
more þanne þe temple.' For hit is no doute þe gostliche temple,

[1] to C.   [5] oure A C.
[2] not I blamed A C.   [6] goostlich of A C.
[3] werk C.   [4-4] om. C.   [7-7] om. A C Ch S.

---

    aunswere as it is sayde Secundo Paralipo, cap. 32. Ezechias is
not blamed for any of all his workes, that he dyd, but onely for
the message of the princis of Babylon. Thanne who shall 20
dampne hym, the whiche Holye Wrytte preysethe in all his
dedes? If he erre, not vnderstandynge the sothenesse and the
veritie of Holye Wrytte, wherfore than stryue you agaynste
19 b kynges and princis? * It is red Secundo Machab. quinto.
Godde chose not the people for the place, but the place for the 25
people. Therfor the churche of lyme and stone shuld not
be spared, whan the Chrysten people be in perylle. The which
thynge the holy kynge Ezechiel and Joseph vnderstode and
truly dyd fulfyll.

    If your goodes be holy churches goodes, and the people is a 30
great parte of holy church; shal not than holy churches goodes
skylfully be spended for the succour and saufegarde of the
people? And so it foloweth, that it longethe to the ghostlyche
of holy churche. And our Lorde saythe, Matthei duodesimo.
I tell you, this is more than the temple. For it is no doubt 35

Dialogus inter Militem et Clericum

þat is mankynde, is more worþe þan þe temple þat is made of lyme & of¹ stoon. Þanne a kyng þat is mylde & wys most knowe ² Goddes wille Almyȝty²; & hym nediþ nouȝt to seche ³ auctorite of oþer men. & me schal nouȝt spare þe temple of
5 lyme & of⁴ stoon forto wynne pees and sauaciou*n* to þe peple þat is in p*er*yle. And me schal flatrie wiþ þe chirche þat haþ y-nowȝ & somwhat more, but me schal socour þe grete nede of Cristen men. But for þe kyng as forþe as he may wole do what is lawful to hym by þe lawe of God Almyȝty by ȝoure assent &
10 ȝoure gode wille, ȝow schameþ nouȝt to aȝensaye⁵ þe kyng þat doþ *gra*ciouslich wiþ ȝou, & gou*er*neþ ȝow godelich alwey. But beþ war for⁶ Salomon seiþ⁷: 'Þe kynges⁸ wreþ is deþes messag*er*.'

*Cl*ericus.⁹ May what is ones yȝeue be wiþcleped & wiþdrawe?
15 Þanne may eu*er*eche avowe be dest*r*ied & fordo.

The spiritual temple of mankind is more worthy than the temple made of lime and stone.

The duty of the king to his people in need as by the law of God, which you oppose.

¹ *om*. C.
²⁻² God Almyȝties wil A C Ch S.
³ such S.
⁴ *om*. A C.
⁵ wiþseie A C Ch S.
⁶ of C.
⁷ *om*. A C Ch.
⁸ kyng hys C.
⁹ *above line in red ink, and in left margin*, H.

---

the ghostly temple, that is mankynde, is more worth than the temple that is made of lyme and stone.

Therfore a mylde and a prudente kynge mote by these wordes knowe * the wylle of Allmyghty God; and hym nedeth
20 not to seke auctorite of other. Nor the temple of lyme and stone, nor the thynges dedicated therin, shulde not be spared to wyn peace and saufegarde to the people, that is in perill. Nor we shuld not smyle (after a flaterynge facion) at the superfluite of the churche, but se that the great multitude of
25 Christen people be holpe and succoured in theyr nede. And though the kynge dealeth gratiously with you, and goodly gouerneth you alway, yet ye be not ashamed to withsay hym in that that he may lawfully do by the lawe of God Almyghty, and wyll not with your good wyll therto assent. But take hede and
30 beware by the wordes of Solomon: The kynges wrathe is the messanger of deathe.

CLE. If those thynges that are ones gyuen to God, may be withdrawen & taken away agayne * than all vowes may be made voyde & fordone.

Myles.[1] Þat ich haue yseide is nouȝt wiþclepyng of ȝiftes þat beþ yȝeue to God Almyȝty; but hit is þe puttinge & turnyng of siche ȝiftes to þe[2] vse to þe whiche vse þei were first y-ȝeue. What is y-ȝeue to God is halwed to holy vse & mylde. What is more holy þan þe sauacioun of Cristen men? What is licher to þe doom of God þan[3] wiþstonde & put of enemyes, þeeues, mansleers, * from Cristen men, & bigge pees to trewe men þat beþ suget[4] to ȝow? Þanne whanne þei beþ trulich y-spend in siche vse,[5] þei beþ verreilich y-spend in þe vse[5] for þe whiche þei were halewed & y-ȝeue to.[6] Ȝif ȝe takiþ ȝow to Holy Writ, why wiþsigge ȝe oure priuyleges & oure fredom þat we haueþ by Holy Writ? Math. 17º, Oure Lord spekiþ to Petre & axeþ of hym in þis maner: 'Þe kynges of erþe, of whom fangeþ þei tribute, of þe sones oþer of straungers?'. [5]& Petre answerde & seide 'of straungers'.[5] And þanne Crist seide: 'Þanne þe sones

Marginalia: What is given to God is hallowed to holy use. What is more holy than the salvation of Christian men? Fol. 5 a

[1] *in margin* H.
[2] *om.* A C.
[3] þan to C.
[4] sogettis C.
[5-5] *om.* C.
[6] Clericus *after* to A C Ch S.

MI. That that I haue sayd is not to withdrawe and take away gyftes, that are gyuen to Allmyghty God; but to tourne and apply those gyftes to suche vse, for the whiche they were fyrste gyuen. For those gyftes that are gyuen to God, the very same gyftes are dedicated to holy and charitable vses. And what thynge can be more holy thanne the sauation of Christen people? And what is more precious vnto oure Lorde, thanne to defende and sauely kepe the Christen people from the ⁱnuasion of theyr ennemies, theues & murtherers, & to bye peace to the true and faythfull subiectes? Therfore whan the goodes of the churche be spent on this wyse, than are they bestowed to suche vse, for the whiche they were fyrst dedicate and gyuen.

21 a CLERI. If ye take you to Holy Wryt, why do ye with * saye and breake our priuileges and fredomes; whiche lyberties we haue by Holy Wrytte? For our Lorde Mat. 17, sayde vnto Peter: Howe semeth hit vnto the Symon, The Kynges of the erthe, of whome take they tribute, of theyr owne sonnes or els of other? of other sayde Peter. Jesus sayde to hym: Than are the sonnes free. But leste we offende them, go vnto the

beþ fre. Þat we sclaundre hem nouȝt, go þou to þe see & cast yn a fische hook, & þe first fische þat comeþ[1] vp opene his mouþe & þou schalt fynde a stater; take þat & ȝeue hem for [2]me & for þee[2]'. Knyȝtes, ȝe seeþ þat clerkes þat beþ occupied *Clerks that are occupied*
5 in Cristes[3] seruise, beþ fre in alle poyntes. *in the service of*

Miles. ȝif þe gospel is take ariȝt, þe tribute was axed onlich of *Christ are* Crist, & onlich for hym þat[4] ȝaf,[5] answere was y-ȝeue; for he is *free in all points.* Goddes[6] sone & þe grete kynges[7] sone. &[8] as þe kynges[7] sone is gretter þan þe bischop, so is Goddes[6] sone gretter þan[9] Emper-
10 our, & so þat answere was y-ȝeue for Crist & nouȝt for ȝow.
Noþeles þei þat[4] serueþ þe kyng in his presence schal nouȝt be *We grant that clerks* put to comyn & greuouse charges; so we graunteþ þat clerkes in *in their own* her owne persoone beþ fre, but nouȝt þei þat lede her lif as lewide *persons are free, but not* men & nouȝt as clerkes to þe worschipe, but to[10] gyle & fraude *those who live lewd*
15 of oure Lord, as hit is y-seye alday. But clerkes þat folewiþ *lives.*

[1] come S.
[2-2] þe & for me A C.
[3] Crist hys Ch.
[4] þat þat C.
[5] om. S.
[6] God hys Ch.
[7] kyng hys Ch.
[8] om. A C.
[9] þan þe A C Ch S.
[10] om. A C: to þe Ch S.

---

see, and caste in a fysshe hooke, and the fyrste fysshe that commethe vppe, open his mouthe, and thou shalte fynde a stater, take that, and gyue it for me and for the. Ye se Sir Knyght that the clergie, bonde to the seruice of God is free in
20 all poyntes.

Mi. If ye wyll consider, and vnderstonde the gospelle aryght (ye may se) that the tribute or dragme was demaunded onely of Christe: And onely for Christe this aunswere semeth to be gyuen: for he is the verye sonne* of God, the sonne of the
25 greatte myghty kynge. And as the kynges sonne is greatter than the bysshop; So is Goddes sonne greatter than the emperour. And so that aunswere was gyuen for Christe, and not for you. Neuer the lesse bycause they, that chieffely serue the kynge in his presence, shulde not be put to common and
30 greuous charges, so we grant that clerkes in theyr owne persones be free, but not they, that leade theyr lyfes as leude men, and not as clerkes to the worshyppe, but to the gyle, and fraude of oure Lorde, as hit is all daye sene. But clerkes that

Dialogus inter Militem et Clericum

The clerks who follow Christ are free, not by the gospel, but by the privileges of kings and princes.

Crist, as prestes þat serueþ þe auter, & beþ occupied in holy seruise of God, we graunteþ atte fulle þat þei beþ fre; but y say nouȝt playnlich by þe gospel, but hit semiþ acordyng to þe gospel, hit is graunted hem by pryuyleges of princes & of kynges. For siþþe þe bygynnyng of holy chirche, Poul seide 5 ad Romanos 13º cº: 'Euerech soule be suget to þe heiȝeste lordes nouȝt onliche for wreþþe, but for good conscience'; & afterward in þe same chapitre:[1] 'Ȝeldeþ & payeþ to alle men what is dewe,[2] to hem to whom tribute is dewe,[2] payeþ tribute.

Paul says: 'to whom tribute is due pay tribute', but ye are now free in your own person by privilege of princes.

And to whom[3] oþer rente and seruise [4]is dewe payeþ hem 10 oþer rent & seruise.' Lo! take hede þat euereche is y-holde to be suget to tribute oþer rent & seruise.[4] But ȝe beþ now fre in ȝoure owne persoone by priuylege of princes. But schal ȝoure feldes haue now þe same fredom, ȝif holy chirche biggeþ a felde þat is able to be y-telied? Schal he þat haþ þerof euerech ȝere 15 rente & tribute leese his rent & his tribute?

Clericus. We spekiþ nouȝt of rente & tribute, but of doyng & dedes.

[1] manere C.
[2] þewe Ch S.
[3] wam Ch.
[4-4] om. C.

---

folowe Criste, as pristes that serue at the aulter, and that are fully gyuen and occupied in the seruyce of God, we graunt that those be free, I saye not clerely by the gospelle: but bycause in 20 theyr so doynge hit discordethe not from the gospelle, that fredome is gyuen * them by priuileges of princis. For sith the begynnynge of the churche Paule ad Ro. 13. saith: Euery soule be subiect to the higher powers, not onely (saythe he after) for wrathe, but also for conscience. And after folowynge he sayth: 25 Yelde and paye to all men that is due to them: to whom tribute is due, paye tribute: to whom custome is due, paye custome. Than ye se, that euery soule must be subiecte, beare tribute, and pay custome. But as I haue sayde, ye be nowe free in your owne persone, by priuileges of princis: but shal your 30 feldes haue now the same freedome? If holye churche bye a felde that is able to be tylled: shall he that hath therof euery yere rent and tribute, lose his rente and trybute?

Cle. Our communication nowe is not of rent and tribute, but of exactions.

Dialogus inter Militem et Clericum 33

Miles. As ich haue of somme feldes certayn siluer oþer gold, so haþ þe Emperour of his empire, & þe kyng of his kyngdom may at his owne will arere skilful tribute for defens of þe comyn profit. Hit is graunted by clere resoun, þat þe comyn profit
5 schal be defended vppon þe cost of þe comynte; & what partie hit euer be þat is defended by þis defens, hit is riȝtful þat he put wiþ oþere men his schulder vnder þe charge. Þanne ȝif possessiouns buþ as riȝtfullich suget to þe comyn charge as to þe ȝeres¹ rente, þei² schul be vnder charge who þat hem³ euer
10 owe specialich, ȝif hit nediþ for defens of þe comynte; for hem nediþ þe comyn defens as alle oþer nediþ. Ȝif ȝe⁴ seyn nay, by cause of prescripcioun and custom, þat ȝe haueþ y-vsed in þe contrarie⁵ in longe fredome, we answereþ ȝou in as myche as ȝoure fredom is þe⁶ lenger by goodness & myldnesse of princes* Fol. 5 b
15 & of kynges, in so myche ȝe schulde be þe more redy & wilful

The king must have tribute to defend the common people.

¹ ȝeres ende A : (but ende crossed out) : ȝer hys Ch.   ⁴ he C.
² he A C : a Ch S.   ⁵ cuntreye S.
³ þei A : þen C : ham Ch : evere   ⁶ om. S.

Mɪ. Lyke as I haue of some felde certayne rente; so the * 22 b Emperour of his empire, and the kynge of his kyngdome, may at his owne wyll reyse skylfull tribute for the defence of the common welthe. It is graunted by clere reason, that the
20 common welthe shall be defended at the costes of the commontie; and what so euer part therof enioyeth this defence, it is moste agreinge with ryght, that he set to his shulder, and helpe to beare the burthen. Than if possessions be as ryghtfully subiecte to the common charge, as to the yeres rente, he shall
25 be vnder charge, who so euer oweth them, specially if it nedeth for the defence of the common welth; for they nede the comon defence, as al other nede. If ye say nay bycause of prescription and custome, that ye haue of so longe tyme vsed that lybertie: We answere you, In as moche longer, and of olde continuance
30 that your fredome & libertie, by the good*nes and liberall 23 a benignite of kynges and princis, so moche the sooner ye shulde be prompte and redye with haste and mynde to pay your part. and helpe forwarde, where nede required. For Holy Wrytte fordoth this prescription, that ye alledge. For from Salomon

D

Dialogus inter Militem et Clericum

The Church should do its share in a time of need, as certain cities which were freed by custom, paid with good will.

forto paye in tyme of nede.¹ Also many citees þat were fre of paiyngis by prıuyleges & customs, payde wiþ gode wille, & ȝitt doþ atte prınces wille for defens & sauacioun of þe kyngdom, of þe² persones & of þe comynte. Ȝif God for vnkyndenesse³ wiþ-clepiþ forȝeuenesse of synne, beþ ȝe⁴ war þat ȝe be nouȝt worþi to bere more charge bycause of ȝoure vnkyndnesse³ & rebelnesse, & to lese atte laste youre catel & ȝoure power.

Can the king take from us grace that was granted to us by his predecessors?

Clericus. Schal þe kyng take from us grace þat is graunted us by kynges þat were his predecessours & by oþere noble prınces? & may he⁵ vndo prıuyleges þat beþ graunted to⁶ hym of olde tyme by noble prınces?

Kings of old granted you certain

Miles. Forsoþe y graunte þat grete prıuyleges beþ graunted to ȝou by noble prınces & kynges. Þerfore ȝe schulde knowe þat al þat⁷ gouernours of þe comynte doþ, þei doþ hit al for

---

¹ Written after 'nede': 'Vor holy writ vordoþ þis prescrıpcyon þat ȝe aleggeþ. Vor vram Salomon to Joas & vram Joas to Ezechias, hyt ys yrad of no suche doyng, as Ezechias dude yn tyme of neode.' A C Ch S.

² om. C.
³⁻³ repeated C.
⁴ þe A: om. C Ch.
⁵ be A C Ch.
⁶ to ȝow A.
⁷ þat þe A C Ch: þat þat S.

---

to Joas, and from Joas to Ezechiell it is redde of no suche doynge, as Ezechiell dydde in tyme of nede. Also many cytyes, that were by prıuileges and custome free from payenge of exactions; haue both paciently payde, and also do pay with good wyll at this day, at their princis pleasure, for the defence of the realme, of the commonaltie, or of persons. If God for vnkyndenes, calleth agayne forgyuenes of synne; beware lest for your rebellyon, that ye deserue no lesse, but also to be further charged, and at the laste to be strypped from al your goodes and power.

23 b CLE. Shall * the kynge beryne and take awaye from vs, the gracis granted vs by kynges, that were his predecessours and by other noble princis? And may he fordo the prıuileges of blessed fathers granted to holy church?

MI. I deny not it is trouthe, great and large prıuileges be to you granted by kynges and princis. Therfore ye oughte to vnderstande and knowe that what so euer the gouernours of the

*p*rofit of þe comynte [1] tofore her owne sauacioun; and þat doyng is blisful in *pr*inces & in kynges by ensau*m*ple of Holy Writ. 2º Regu*m* 6º cº. Þ*er*fore it is knowen by witnesse cleer and trewe & by c*er*teyn resou*n*, þat þei grauntep nouȝt by her wityng [2] þat schuld after*ward* be harme & damage to þe comy*n*te. But ȝif eny *pr*iuylege þat is gra*u*nted, is y-founde & y-knowe harmful & greuous to þe comynte, hit schuld be wiþcleped i*n* tyme of nede [3] in help of þe rewme. *Pr*inces & kynges may bynyme [4] ȝow grace þat is to ȝou [5] y-gra*u*nted. & as tyme axeþ we fyndeþ þat Salomon þe wise i*n* peynyng of þeefþe, chaungide

priviloges for the profit of the people, and not for harm and damage.

[1] in so muche þat hey putteþ þe sauacion of þe comynte S.
[2] writynge A C.
[3] for profiȝt of þe comynte;
[4] Doute ȝou nouȝt þat in tyme of nede S.
[5] bemene C.
[5] *om.* C.

---

comon welth do, they intended it all together for the profite of the comon weale, hauynge regarde speciallye thervnto accordynge to this rule. They dispose all thynges in suche wyse, that they preferre the common welthe before theyr owne; whiche in a prince is a thynge moste gloryous, wherof Dauid is example. II. Regum. Therfore it is knowe*n* by witnes clere and true and eke by very reason, that they graunte nothyng by theyr writinge,* that shulde afterwarde be harme and domage to the common weale. But if any priuilege that is graunted, be founde and knowen hurtefull and greuous to the common weale, it maye be repelled and fordone in tyme of nede. Therfore it is not to be doubted, but that the hygh princis for the necessary busynes of the realme, maye alter and chaunge (as reason and tyme requireth) the gracis and priuileges to you granted, and by the lawes establysshed. As we rede of the mooste wyse kynge Salomon, in the peyne of thefte, chaunged some what of goddes lawe.

CLERI. The emperours and not the kynges haue establisshed tho thynges. Therfore, nowe Syr Knyghte the emperours must gyde the raynes of the lawes.

MI. This answer is blasphemous. And eyther (as it semeth) ye are ignoraunte of the begynnynge of a * kyngedome, or else (whiche is moste lykely) ye enuie the hygh estate of the realme. If ye well beholde the actes of greatte Charlemayne, or lysted

36   *Dialogus inter Militem et Clericum*

<small>Because the king is above all others in the land, he is above customs, privileges and freedom while he is a rightful king with full power.</small>   somwhat of Goddes¹ lawe. For as þe Emperour may make lawe in þe empire & put oþer law þer-to, oþer wiþdrawe somme of his owne lawe, so may þe kyng of Fraunce put of² al þe emperours lawe, & change euereche partie þer-of at his owne likyng, oþer exile hem & put hem out of his lond & make newe lawes at his owne wille. For ȝif any happe falliþ wherfore hit nediþ to make eny³ maner statute, ȝif þe kyng may nouȝt do hit in his owne lond, þanne noon oþer may; for aboue hym is no man in his lond. & þerfore sire clerk chastiþ ȝoure tonge & knowlechiþ þat þe kyng may be aboue⁴ customs, priuyleges, & fredoms while he is riȝtful kyng wiþ ful power, & þat he may putt to priuyleges & lawes, & wiþdrawe &

¹ God hys Ch.   ³ euery C.
² *om.* C.   ⁴ aboue ȝoure S.

---

to rede the auncient approued hystories; ye shall fynde, that the realme of Fraunce is but a portion of the empire by a iust diuision seperated from it, and was by the space of 500 yeres egall therto bothe in dignitee and auctoritie. Therfore what so euer priuilege of dignite the empire holdeth in one part the same holdeth the realme of Fraunce in another. For whan by brotherne the realme of Fraunce was deuyded from the other parte of the empire: What so euer lawes power, or dignite the empire opteined and exercysed ouer and vppon the sayde parte thus diuided, the verye selfe power fell to the frenche kynge. And therfore lyke as all thynges conteyned within the boundes of the empire,* is well knowen to be subiecte to the empyre; so lykewyse all thynges within the boundes of the realme, be subiecte to the realme! And lyke as the emperour may make lawes ouer al his empire, and to them adde more or diminisshe, as he thinketh good; so maye the Kynge of Fraunce, eyther vtterly repelle the emperours lawes, or change which of them hym lyste: or els cleane exilynge and fordoynge these lawes, maye at his pleasyre ordeyne and make newe. For whan nede shuld requyre (as it ofte chaunceth) to enact and ordeyne a statute, if the kynge that is the chiefe, coude not do it; than there is none other that canne; for there is none aboue hym. And therfore syr clerke refrayne your tongue, and aknowlege the kynge by his royall power to be aboue your lawes, customes

Dialogus inter Militem et Clericum 37

chaunge & redresse euereche þat erreþ by[1] consail of resoun & assent of lordes as hit semeþ þat resoun axiþ. & perfore ȝif ȝe haueþ y-seye[2] ouȝt redressed oþer chaungide in help of þe kyngdom, suffre ȝe hit pacientliche. For Poul þe apostle ad
5 Romanos 13º cº seiþ: 'Who þat wiþstondiþ [3]power wiþstondiþ[3] Goddes[4] ordinaunce.' Þanne no man kike[5] vnriȝtfullich aȝenus þe pricke & þat ȝe busche[6] nouȝt ȝoure self aȝenus þe pricke of synne. 'Beþ suget to ȝoure souereynes & beþ vnder hem', so seiþ Paul ad Thimotheum 19º cº. In Abiathars tyme
10 prince of prestes, David eet & ȝaf hem þat were wiþ hym to ete in tyme of nede, loues þat were cleped panes proposicionis, þat were ordeyned onliche for prestes, & noon oþer had leue þerof forto ete. Also in þe gospel hit is writen: 'Þe holy day is made for man & nouȝt man for þe holy day.'

Be subject to your sovereign and be under him.

The holy day is made for man, and not man for the holy day.

15   Explicit dialogus inter clericum & militem.

¹ be C.
² y saye at þis tyme A C Ch S.
³⁻³ *wr. in margin* Ch.
⁴ God hys Ch.
⁵ like A : *crossed out and* kike *in margin* S.
⁶ busshe   A C :   boysche   Ch :   booche S.

---

priuileges, and liberties; and that he may by the aduise * of 25 b
his nobuls adde or diminyssche what so euer he thynke
accordynge with equite and reson : and therfore what so euer
he changeth in those dayes for the welthe of the realme, take it
20 well in worthe and paciently suffre it. For so Paule teachethe
you writynge to the Romaynes the XIII. Chapter, where he
sayth : who that resisteth the hygh power, resysteth the
ordynaunce of god. And agayne in the ende of the pistell to the
Hebrewes he saythe : Obeye ye to your soueraynes, and humble
25 your selfe to them.

Also Kyng Dauid, I. Regum 21, vnder Abiathor the prince
of the pristis, in tyme of nede dyd not alonelye eate the breade
called panes propositionis, (Wherof to eate it was not lefull for
any man except the priestes) but also gaue the same breade to
30 eate to them that were with hym. And it is written Marke
the II. Chap. The * holy day is made for man and not man 26 a
for the holy day. And so the Lorde is the sonne of man, and
also is Lorde of the holy day. It is written in the fyrst boke

of Parali, the 39. Chap. In thy hande is the greatnes and
empire of all. It sayth farther there: They honored God, and
than the kynge. And it sayth there. They secondely anointed
Salomon the sonne of Kynge Dauid, they anoynted him in our
Lorde to be their prince, and Sadoch to be theyr bysshop. And,
2. Parali, 23, it saythe: Nor none other shulde entre in to the
house of our lord but priestes, and suche of the deacons as
ministred, they all onely shulde entre in, bycause they be
halowed: and all the residue of the common people shulde kepe
the watche of our Lorde. The deacons inuironned the kynge
aboute euery man hauynge his armour. And if any other
entred into * the temple of the Lord he was slayn. They shulde
attende vpon the kynge bothe whan he entred in, and whan he
wente out. Also Joada the bysshoppe anoynted hym, and his
children prayde for hym and sayd,
God saue the Kynge.

CLE. It draweth faste towarde nyght: to morowe mornyng
I wyll answere you to euery thynge. FINIS.

Imprinted at London in Flete-strete, in the house of Thomas
Berthelet nere to the cundite at the sygne of
Lucrece.

CVM PRIVILEGIO.

PART II

RICHARD FITZRALPH'S SERMON:
'DEFENSIO CURATORUM'

Harl. 1900.

'Demeþ nouȝt by þe face but riȝtful doom ȝe deme,' John 8º cº. John 8. 15?
Holy fader, in þe bygynnyng of my sermoun, ich make a protestacioun, þat it is nouȝt myn entent to affirme to say, noþer
to holde eny þinge, þat is contrarie to Cristen feiþ, oþer to
5 Cristen lore.   Also, þat it is nouȝt myn entent to counsaile,
noþer¹ axe destruccioun & vndoyng of þe ordres of beggers,
þat beþ² appreued by holy chirche, & confermed of popes; but I shall make
y schal make euidence,³ & consaile þat þese⁴ ordres schulde be counsel that
brouȝt to þe clennesse of her first ordenaunce; & ich am alwey should be
10 redy to þe correccioun of ȝoure holynesse. And forto descende the clear-
anoon to my mater; Lo! holy fader, ich came in a tyme to first ordin-
Londoun for certeyn nedes of my chirche of Armachan, & fonde ance.
þere wise doctors stryue vppon þe beggerie, & beggyng of þe London
Lord oure Saueoure.   & ofte ich was preyed to preche to þe and preache
15 peple, and ich preched seuen sermouns oþer eiȝte to þe peple in eight ser-
her owne tonge, wiþ þe⁵ protestacioun þat ich haue seide & people.
tolde, ⁶þere nyne⁶ conclusiouns.   For þese⁷ conclusiouns, & oþer Friars have
þingis, þat ich þere seide, freres þouȝ⁸ hit turne hem to a iape, nine con-
appelide to þis⁹ court. a jape.
20   Þe firste conclusioun was þis: Oure Lord Ihesus, in his con- The nine
uersacioun of manhed, alwey was pore, nouȝt for he wolde & 1. Jesus was
loued pouert by-cause of hitsilf.   Þe secunde conclusioun is ¹⁰ 2. He never
þis: Oure Lord Ihesus neuer beggide wilfulliche.   Þe þridde begged.

---

¹ noþer to C.
² buþ Ch.
³ euydences S.
⁴ þues Ch.
⁵ *om.* C.
⁶⁻⁶ þerynne C.
⁷ þe A C: þe whiche S.
⁸ þei (y) A C: þeiȝ S.
⁹ þis holy S.
¹⁰ was A C Ch S.

conclusioun: Crist neuer tauȝt wilfulliche to[1] begge. Þe ferþe
conclusioun was þis: Oure Lord Ihesus tauȝte þat no man
schuld wilfulliche begge. Þe fifþe[2] conclusioun was þis: no
man may redilich & holiliche wilful beggyng vppon hym take,
euermore to holde. Þe sixte conclusioun was þis: hit is nouȝt 5
of þe reule of frere menours, wilful begginge to kepe & holde.
Þe vii[3] conclusioun in þat mater was þis: þe ferþe pope
Alisaundre's bille,[4] þat dampneþ þe libel of maistres, wiþseiþ
noon of þe forseide conclusiouns. Þe viii[5] conclusioun, & þe
first, in mater of priuyleges was þis: for parischons of eny 10
chirch to schryue hem wiþ exclusioun of oþer places,[6] þe parische
chirche is more worþi to be chosen[7] þan oratory oþer chirche
of freres. Þe ix[8] conclusioun, [9] & þe secunde[9] in þis[10] mater is
þis: for parischons of eny chirche to schryue hem onlich to
oon persone, þe ordenarye persone is more worþi to be chosen 15
þan eny freres persone.

Þese conclusiouns, holy fader, in myn open sermouns, wiþ
Holy Writ, & resouns, ich preued, as ich myȝt & schal also
declare hem at þis time as God graunteþ[11] grace, & somwhat
harder y schal put herto now in þis place as ich bihet freres at 20
þat tyme. And y pray ȝowre holynesse mekelich & deuoutlich,
þat ȝe take hede to þe forseide conclusiouns & to þe resons þat
ich haue made þerfore, and schal make at þis time; and also
þat ȝe take hede to þe resouns þat[12] freres makiþ for þe contrarie. & ȝif her resouns beþ strenger þan myn, y pray[13] þat 25
ich be punysched; & ȝif my[14] resouns[15] be strenger þan her
resouns, be þei[16] punysched for þat þei[16] haueþ sclaundred me,
dispised & diffamed priuylich & openlich. But touchyng[17] þat,
me is leuer suffre þan folowe þe lawe to her punyschyng. To
holde alwey as y seide first: 'Demeþ nouȝt by þe face but 30
riȝtful dome ȝe deme.'

[1] om. A C Ch S.
[2] fifte A C.
[3] seuenþe A C Ch S.
[4] bulle A S.
[5] eightþe A C: eiȝteþe S.
[6] place S.
[7] chose A C Ch S.
[8] nynthe A C Ch S.
[9-9] om. A: & þe firste C.
[10] þe C.
[11] graunteþ me C S.
[12] þat þe C.
[13] preye ȝow C.
[14] myne S.
[15] resoun A C.
[16] hey S.
[17] techinge S.

But for by lawe of God & of kynde, þe comyn nedes schal be sett tofore singuler nedes, ich wole bigynne atte mater of priuyleges þat touchiþ al þe clergie, & alle Cristen men. Y say, as me semeþ, ȝif* me axe what place is moste worþi to be chose for parischons of eny chirche syngulerliche to schryue hem ynne, hit semeþ me þat þe parische chirche is a place more worþi to be chose þan oratorie oþer[1] chirche of freres; for þe parische chirche is for schrifte of þe parischons þat is schryuen, more siker, more profitable, & voydeþ mo damages; þat þe parische chirche wiþ excluding of alle oþer places is most siker place to be schryue & buried ynne. Y preue hit is a place y-hote of God & his lawe[2]; Deuteronomii xiiº cº, hit is writen: 'Þese beþ heestes & domes þat ȝe schal do & holde. Ȝe schal come to þe place þat ȝoure Lord God chesiþ of alle ȝowre lynages to sette þere his name & to wonye þere. In þat place ȝe schal offre ȝowre offryngis, and sacrificis; ȝoure teþingis & þe[3] firste fruyt of ȝoure hondes; ȝoure avowes and ȝiftes; þe first birþe[4] of ruþeren[5] & of foules[6].' Þanne hit foleweþ in a forbeding wise: 'War þat þou offre nouȝt þyn offrynges in euereche[7] place þat þou seest[8] wiþ [9]ynne þee;[9] but onliche in [10]þat place, þat[10] God chesiþ in oon of ȝoure lynages; þere offre þou þyn offrynges & al þat ich hote þee.' & so it is soþe þat God hoteþ þat euerech man schal do offringis, & schrifte, & al þat[11] þe lawe hotiþ of sacramentis, in a place þat God chesiþ, þat is, þe parische chirche, as þe wordes meneþ. Þerfore hit is written, Leuitici 4º cº: 'Euerech[7] man þat synneþ by vnkunnyng, schewe hymsilf to þe prest, & hit schal be forȝeue hym.' And also alle oþere places beþ forbode by þe lawe. And hit semeþ certeyn þat þe place of freres is nouȝt of God y-chose by þe lawe to do siche deuociouns, but onlich y-graunted by popes, & as it is seide toforhand, forbode by þe lawe. But þe place þat God hotiþ is more certeyn & more[12] siker[13] for schrifte of

Fol. 6 b
8th Conclusion:
The parish church is the more worthy to be chosen for shrift, as it is more profitable and avoideth more damages.
It is the place commanded by God and his law, as shewn in Deut. 12: 5, 6,
and also in Deut. 12: 13, 14,
also in Leviticus 4.
All other places are forbidden by the law.

---

[1] or A C.
[2] lawe for S.
[3] ȝoure S.
[4] burþe A S.
[5] reþeren A : roþeren C S.
[6] scheps *written above* foules C.
[7] euery A C : ech S.
[8] sixte A C Ch S.
[9-9] þyn eyȝe A C Ch S : *after* eyȝe *is written* þat þou sixte wiþ þyn eyȝe C.
[10-10] *om.* C.
[11] þat þat C.
[12] *om.* A C Ch S.
[13] siker þan þe place þat god forbedeþ by his lawe and is boþe

parischons þan eny oratorie eþer¹ chirche of freres. Also, comynliche, a parischon² schal nouȝt haue suspecioun þat his parische chirche³ is entredited, but he may verreylich haue suspecioun þat þe chirche of⁴ freres is entredited. Þerfore⁵ it semeþ þat þe parische chirche is þe⁶ more siker place. And þat hit myȝt seme þat þe chirche of freres is entredited, hit is preued by þe decretal *de sepulturis* in 6º cº 'animarum periculis'. Þerein, a certeyn manere, alle religious men beþ forbode vppon peyne of entredityng of her chirche, & chirche heye,⁷ þat þei⁸ schul nouȝt counseil no man to swere neþer to make avowe; noþer to pliȝt his truþe, noþer to behote in oþer manere wise to chese buriyng place at her chirche; so þat ȝif þei counseileþ þerto eny maner wise, her chirche is entredited, & her chirche heye⁹. Oþer ȝif þei counseileþ hym, þat haþ y-chose his buriels among hem, nouȝt to chaunge his wille; & comynliche it is seide þat freres counseiliþ so men; þanne a parischon may verreilich haue suspecioun þat her place is entredited. Þis may be confermed in oþer manere: a parischon knowiþ, as he is y-holde to knowe, þat his parisch chirche is a place for vsyng of sacramentis, y-chose & y-hote of God; and þe place of freres forbode by Goddes lawe, & no suche wolde chese his burielis among hem but by informacioun, & consail of freres; for hit semeþ siker ynouȝ þat no seculer man conforteþ, noþer counseiliþ so for to do. Here-of hit semeþ, þat hit may be concluded as me may in moral mater: þat for schrifte of parischons her owne parische chirche is more siker place þan eny place of freres.*

I seide, & efte y seye, þat for schrifte & buriyng of parischons, her owne parische chirche is more profitable place þan eny place of freres. First for hit is a place y-chose of God, & þer¹⁰ by¹¹ more alowed of God þan eny chirche of freres, þat is nouȝt so expresslich y-chose of God, noþer of holy chirche, but y-grauntud

suffred & graunted. Þanne hit semeþ þat þe parische chirche is mor certayn and more siker A C Ch S: place S.

¹ oþer A S: or C.
² aparischon comynliche S.
³ *om.* A.
⁴ of þe A.
⁵ þat for A.
⁶ *om.* S.
⁷ þey A: ȝerde C: hey S.
⁸ hey S.
⁹ hawe A: ȝerde C: hey S.
¹⁰ þei A C.
¹¹ be A C.

by[1] procurynge of freres. Þerfore hit semeþ þe more profitable place, & more alowed & leef[2] to God; for hit is y-chose of God. Also þe parischon, þat is lawfullich y-schryue in his parische chirche, haþ mede of double obedience. For he haþ mede, in
5 þat he[3] is obedient to Goddes heest, & schryueþ him. [4] Also he haþ, in þat he[3] is obedient to Goddes heeste, & schryueþ[4] in[5] þe place þat God haþ y-chose þerto. He,[6] þat þe freres schryueþ, leesiþ his[7] secunde mede, as hit semeþ; for God hoteþ no parischon, noþer counsailiþ to be y-schryue, noþer y-
10 buried atte freres. Þanne for schrifte, & buryyng of parischons, her owne parische chirche is more profitable place þan eny place of freres. Also, in þe parische chirche, ouer alle, oþere neiȝ[8] ouer al, by lawe of God, & of holy chirche, is oþer schuld be mo bedemen þan in eny chirche of freres, ȝhe[9] siche ten.
15 Þanne, euereche parischon may trowe þat he[10] is more y-holpe by prayers of mo bedemen, þan in eny chirches of freres. Y seide, & seye efte, þat[11] schrifte & buryng in þe parisch chirche, voydeþ mo damages & desauauntages þan schrifte oþer buriyng in eny chirche of freres. For in þe parische chirche is more
20 profit & more surete; and ȝif[12] it were y-do in eny chirche of freres as I haue seide, þis[13] profit & surete were lost, & þat were damage & desauauntage, greuous, & huge.[14]

Y seide, & efte y seye, ȝif me axeþ what persoon is most worthi to be chose for singuler[15] of parischons, a frere or þe
25 ordynarie,[16] y say, þat[16] þe ordynarie is more worþi to be chose for schrifte þan eny frere. For he[17] is more profitable, & schrifte þat is schewide singulerliche to hym, voydeþ mo desauauntes & damages. [18] First y saye þat þe ordinarie is þe more siker persone[18]; for as y schewide in þe raþer article, he[17] is y-fonge
30 a persoon of God, & of holy chirche, and of þe comyn lawe; & þe frere is forbode by þe lawe. Þanne þe ordynarie is þe[19]

The man who is lawfully shriven in his parish church has a reward of double obedience, (1) he obeys God's command in being shriven, and (2) he obeys God's command in being shriven at the parish church.

In the parish church there is more profit and surety to those who are shriven.

9th Conclusion: The ordinary is more worthy to be chosen for shrift than any friar. He is the more proper, as he is chosen a parson by God and

---

[1] be C.
[2] luf A : loued C : luef S.
[3] a S.
[4-4] om. C.
[5] him in A.
[6] hem S.
[7] þis S.
[8] nyȝe A : nyh C.
[9] ȝe A C Ch S.
[10] a S.
[11] þat þat A C.
[12] om. C.
[13] þues S.
[14] hoyge S.
[15] singulerte C : singuler schrift S.
[16-16] om. C.
[17] a S.
[18-18] om. C.
[19] om. C.

holy church, and of the common law.
The parishioner has a greater trust in the ordinary.

more siker persone. Also þe ordinarie is more y-bounde to his parischons þan is a frere. Þanne þe parischon may, [1] verreilich & more sikerliche [1], triste [2] þat þe ordynarie wole more bisiliche ordeyne for his sauacioun þan wole eny frere, þat is a straunge persoone, as a bodiliche leche þat is preuy & y-knowe is more 5 y-holde to þe seke man þan a straunge leche. Also by þe [3] comyn cours, þe parischon douteþ nouʒt noþer schal doute of

He may have suspicion of the Friar, as his power is bound because he is cursed,

his ordinarie, weþer [4] his power to assoile his sugetis be y-bounde oþer no ; but of freres he may haue verreiliche [5] suspecioun, and trowe þat her power is y-bounde for diuerse cursyngis ; & wiþ 10 oute eny doute hit is more siker to be schryue to hym þat haþ fre power, þan to hym þat his power is y-bounde. Þanne þe ordinarie is þe more siker persone, & þe more certeyn. & þat me may trowe þat freres beþ acursed, hit is preued, first, by þe

as is shown in the decretal.

decretal in Cle. Decimis [6]. Þere it is seide þat 'alle men of 15 religioun þat haueþ no benefice [7], beþ a-cursed, ʒif þei [8] wiþ-holdeþ, oþer wiþdraweþ, oþer fondeþ to appropre to hem wiþout a lawful cause, by [9] any maner, colour, oþer sleiʒþe [10], riʒtes oþer teþinges, þat beþ dewe [11] to holy chirche.' & it semeþ no dowte, by Goddes owne lawe, þat teþinges of byqueestes & of fre ʒjftes 20

Fol. 7 b is detty, & * dewe [11] to parische chirches, & to curatours þerof.

Friars are cursed because they take tithings that belong to the church.

& so seyn [12] þe doctors Innocencius & Hostiensis. Þanne alle freres þat bynymeþ parische chirches þe teþinge [13] of þat [14] is y-ʒeue hem oþer biqueþe, beþ acursed. For þei payeþ neuere teþinge of siche biquystes & ʒiftes, as it is comynliche seide. 25

They are also cursed because they absolve men who have been condemned by the law of the country or the church.

Þe same is preued also by þe chapitre 'religiosi priuilegiis' in Cle. Þere alle religious men beþ acursed [15] in dede, þat assoyleþ eny men þat beþ acursed by statutes of prouynces oþer of synodes, þe whiche prelates of holy chirche and her penitaun-sers schulde assoyle. & freres beþ acursed þat assoileþ freres 30 þat hereþ [16] schriftes while her power is y-bounde. In my

---

[1-1] more sykerliche & vreryliche S.
[2] truste A C.
[3] om. C.
[4] where C.
[5] verraily haue C.
[6] Lat. Clementinis de decimis.
[7] benefices S.
[8] hey S.
[9] be C.
[10] sleiʒte A C : scleiʒþe S.
[11] þewe S.
[12] seiþ A C : seggeþ S.
[13] tueþinges A.
[14] om. C S.
[15] acorsed of S.
[16] huyreþ S.

diocesy Armacan, y trowe y haue two þousand sugettes, man- *Out of 2,000 men who*
sleers, comyn þeeues, incendiaries þat settiþ houses afyre¹, & *were condemned in*
oþer euel doeres, þat beþ acursed by sentence euereche ȝere, *Armacan for various*
of þe whiche vnneþe comeþ to me & to my penitaunsers, fourty *crimes, only 40 were*
5 a ȝere; & siche fongeþ² þe sacramentis as oþer men doþ; & *shriven by*
me³ trowiþ, þat þei⁴ beþ assoyled, & by noon oþer þan by *the parish priest. The*
freres, wiþ-oute drede, for noon oþer men assoileþ hem. & me³ *others had been shriven*
trowiþ þat þei⁴ beþ assoiled. & so parischons may verreiliche *by friars.*
trowe þat þese confessours beþ wrapped & snarled in þe same
10 curs, so þat her power is y-bounde. And so it is þe lasse siker *Friars may*
to be schryue to hem, while þei⁵ mowe nouȝt assoile wiþout *not absolve without*
dedly synne. & ȝif þei⁵ þat⁶ beþ schryue trowiþ hit, þei⁵ beþ *deadly sin, and those*
assentinge to þe synnes of freres, ȝif þei⁷ faugeþ absoluciou*n*. Þe *who are absolved*
apostle seiþ ad Romanos 2°: 'Þei⁵ þat doþ siche dedes, ⁸ beþ *also sin. See*
15 worþi þe deþ, & nouȝt onliche þei þat doþ siche dedes, but also *Romans 2.*
þei þat assentiþ to hem þat doþ siche dedes⁸'. Also 2° Para- *Also*
lipomenon c° 19° hit is writen þat John⁹ þe prophete seide *IIChronicles 19 : 2.*
to Josophath kyng of Juda: 'þou helpest¹⁰ þe wicked ma*n*
& dost frendschip to hem þat hateþ Oure Lord; þerfore þou
20 schalt disserue Goddes wreþþe.' And so hit sweþ,¹¹ þat þe *Then the*
ordynarie is more siker þan eny frere. *ordinary is more siker than the*
Also þe same is preued ' per cupientes de penis ' in Cle. Þere *friar.*
is denounsed þre maner sentence ¹² of cursinge. By þe firste *Three curses*
sentence,¹² alle men of religiou*n* beþ acursed, þat spekiþ in *by the decretal:*
25 sermou*n*s oþer elles-where aȝenus paiyng of teþinges, þat is *(1) Those who in their*
dewe¹³ to holy chirche. ¹²& so doþ, as one seiþ, comynliche,¹² *preaching speak*
confessours of freres, & telleþ openlich, þat ȝeuers of almes in *against paying of*
teþinge, of wynnyng of chaffare, beþ nouȝt y-holde to paye *tithes, as do friars.*
teþingis of brede,¹⁴ of wyn, of ale, & of oþer¹⁵ smal þingis. Y tolde
30 þe contrarie, & seide, þat þei¹⁶ beþ y-holde to make mencio*n*
among her wynny*n*g of smale ȝiftes, as wel as of þe¹⁶ grete.

---

¹ on fyre A C : afuyre S.
² om. C.
³ þei A C.
⁴ a S.
⁵ hey S.
⁶ om. S.
⁷ he A C : a S.
⁸⁻⁸ om. C.
⁹ ion S.
¹⁰ kepest S.
¹¹ seweþ A C Ch S.
¹²⁻¹² om. C.
¹³ þewe S.
¹⁴ of almesse of bread S.
¹⁵ om. S.
¹⁶ a S.

For¹ elles, marchauntes myȝt, by siche smale ȝiftes, ȝeue & dele al þe wynnyng of þe ȝere, & so, of þe grettest wynnyng, no teþing paie, & dele to pore men al by smale ȝiftes, & so were holy chirche y-scorned. Þanne siche freres beþ y-wralled², & y-snarled in sentence of þe grete curs. Also by þe same decretal, alle freres beþ suspended of þe offyce of prechyng, & so acursed³ wiþ-ynne a certeyn terme, ⁴ȝif þei⁴ wole nouȝt enforme & charge hem þat beþ yschryue to hem, & make hem charge her conscience & paye wel her teþingis. As it is verreilich seide, alle confessours of freres, oþer neiȝ alle, beþ wrapped in þis sentence of cursyng; for as it is comynliche seide, & hit may be preued by hem þat beþ y-schryue to freres, þat al þat þei⁵ spekiþ in þat mater is but wordes wiþoute eny effect, & þat is scornyng and nouȝt * makyng of conscience. For ȝif þei⁵ made conscience to þe menyng of þe lawe, þei⁵ schulde enforme hem þat beþ y-schryue to hem, wher of þei⁶ schulde teþe,⁷ & of þe maner & tyme. And for þei⁸ doþ nouȝt, y can nouȝt se but þei⁸ beþ acursed. Also by þe same chapitre alle men of religioun beþ acursed þat counseiliþ oþere counfortiþ oþere men to bihote, by a vowe oþer by oþ, oþer by truþe-pliȝtyng for to chese sepulture at her chirches, oþer comforteþ hem þat haueþ y-chose, nouȝt for to chaunge her choys & her wille; but þe comyn opinioun of lewed men & of clerkes telliþ þat freres doþ so, and herto helpiþ þe probeble euydens þat was made for þe confirmacioun of þe secounde resone of⁹ þe firste conclusioun of þe raþer article.

Also þat þe ordynarie is more siker to þe¹⁰ paryschon, hit is preued oþer wise in þis maner: for þe parischon may skilfulliche deme þat his ordynarie is a Juge lasse suspect & more skilful for to enioye¹¹ hym skilful penaunce & profitable for his synnes. For he schal nouȝt suppose noþer haue suspecioun, þat his ordynarie hereþ¹² his schrifte for couetise of getyng & of wynnyng of bodilich help & socour; for þe ordynaries liflode longeþ

---

¹ or S.
² I-warled A C.
³ acursed þat A C S.
⁴⁻⁴ om. A C S.
⁵ hey S.
⁶ he A C: a S.
⁷ tiþe A C: tueþe S.
⁸ a S.
⁹ om. A.
¹⁰ om. C.
¹¹ eniune A: enioyne C S.
¹² hireþ C: hoyreþ S.

Richard FitzRalph's Sermon: 'Defensio Curatorum' 47

to his offys by lawe of God¹ and of holy chirche. Of freres *he heareth his shrift* þei² may suppose & wene, þat þei³ doþ hit for to haue socour *for the desire of* & help of⁴ her liflode; for in here appele þat þei⁵ made aȝenes *getting money and* me in Engelond hit is conteyned þat by⁵ her fundacioun, þei *goods, as do*
5 beþ⁶ y-bounde to beggerie & to þe heiȝest pouerte, nouȝt wiþ- *friars. In their* stondyng þat þei telliþ þat þei haueþ powere to here⁷ þe *foundation they profess* schriftes of alle men þat wole be schryue to hem. Þerfore þe *beggary, but they* parischen may skilfulliche suppose & haue suspecioun þat, by- *create suspicion by* cause of⁸ getyng somme releue of her beggerie, þei beþ so busy *being so busy to hear*
10 to here schriftes. Þanne may þe parischon skilfulliche argue *shrifts.* in his herte, why wolde þis begger sitte & here my schrifte & *The parishioner* leue his beggyng & getyng of his liflode, but he hope to haue of *argues that the friar* me siche maner help, and nede⁹ drieuþ to synne, by þe which *leaves his begging and* synne þe nede myȝt be releued, as Proverbiorum 30° c°, *shrives him in order to*
15 Salomon seiþ & prayeþ: 'ȝeue me noþer beggerie noþer riches, *get money,* but ȝeue me onliche what¹⁰ is nedeful to my liflode lest y be *and thus sin—as* excited to denye & saye who is oure Lorde, & conpelled by nede *Solomon says:* for to stele & forswere þe name of my God.' Þanne hit foleswiþ, *Proverbs 30: 8, 9.* þat for all maner synnes, he wole ioyne¹¹ me almes dede for to *So it follows that for all*
20 releue his owne beggerie, & so y schal nouȝt be cleneliche by- *manner of sins, he will* quyt of my¹² synnes; þerfore¹³ whanne hise disciples axide of *require alms to relieve his* oure Lord: 'Why myȝt we nouȝt cast hym out?' & spake of a *beggary, and I shall not* fende, oure Lord answerde & seide: 'Þese¹⁴ manere fendes beþ¹⁵ *be truly forgiven of my* nouȝt cast out but wiþ bedes & fastyng,' Math 16° c°. Of þis *sins, as per*
25 worde hit is y-take, þat as for euereche diuerse sekenesse of *Matt. 17: 19, 20, 21.* body dyuerse medicyns helpiþ; so for euereche gostlich seknese most be ordeyned his propre medicyn. And þis begger þat is bisy about his beggerye wole nouȝt with-out suspecioun ordeyne me siche medicyns for my synnes. Þis resoun is confermed, for *Friars have through*
30 hit semeþ in dede in al þe worlde wide, after þat freres hadde *hearing of shrifts built* gete priuelege for to here schriftes, þei¹⁶ haueþ y-bilde¹⁷ fayre *huge buildings.*

---

¹ Chetham MS. begins with God and of holy chirche.
² he C A S Ch.
³ hey S: hy C.
⁴ to A C Ch S.
⁵ om. S.
⁶ hey were S.
⁷ huyre A Ch: hoyre S.
⁸ of here S.
⁹ nedeþ C: neode Ch.
¹⁰ þat C.
¹¹ ioyerne C: June Ch.
¹² myn C.
¹³ wherfore C.
¹⁴ in þis C Ch S.
¹⁵ buþ Ch.
¹⁶ hey S: hy Ch.
¹⁷ I-bulde A C Ch S.

mynstres¹ & rial palyces þou3² hit were for kynges, & þe cause þere of semeþ þe power of heryng of schriftes. For er³ þei hadde þat⁴ power þei⁵ my3t noon siche bildyngis make. Also hit is neuere herde þat freres enioyneþ hem þat þei⁵ schryueþ to 3eue syche almes⁶ to amendment of parische chirches,* noþer 5 of hey3⁷ weyes, noþer of broken brigges; noþer þe menoures chargeþ nou3t noþer ordeyneþ to 3eue siche almes to⁸ þe prechours, but al to hem-silf oþer to her owne ordre. Þerfore me may skilfulliche deme þat his owne getyng is cause why siche a begger is so bisy aboute a straunge man, & forgendriþ his 10 beggynge tyme & takeþ al his hede to þe straunge man. Also ich made & here now y make þe fifþe resoun. Þe conclusioun of þis resoun ich wolde nou3t afferme; but y seide openliche & 3itt⁹ y seye þat y couþe nou3t assoyle þe resoun. Þe conclusioun of þat resoun is þis: euereche parischone þat is 15 y-schryue to freres & leueþ þe ordenaries by þe power þat þei⁵ haueþ, after sich a schrifte, lyueþ in dedliche synne & of no dedliche synne is assoyled. To preue þis conclusioun in oþer maner ich fonded for to preue oon principal.

But for þe constitucioun *Johannina vas eleccionis*, y graunted 20 nou3t þat conclusioun. For þerof maister John de Polliaco hys sawes beþ þre articles y-dampned. Þe firste is, þat þei þat beþ y-schryue to freres þat haueþ general leue to here schriftes, beþ y-holde to schryue hem efte of þe same synnes to her owne preste; þe secunde article is þis, þat stondyng þe statute þat 25 was made in þe general consail, *Omnis vtriusque Sexus*, þe pope may nou3t make þat parischons beþ nou3t y-holde to schryue hem of alle her synnes ones a 3ere to her owne preste, þat þei¹⁰ clepiþ þe curatour of þe parische, ¹¹noþer God my3t do þat, as he seide, for hit closiþ contradiccioun & wiþsaiyng 30 wiþ-ynne hit silf; þe þridde article is þis, þe pope may nou3t 3eue leue to here schriftes noþer God him-silf. But he þat is y-schryue to hym þat haþ general leue to here schriftes is 3itt y-holde to schryue hym of þe synnes to his owne prest, þat is þe curatour of þe parische,¹¹ as it is seide toforehond. Þe 35

---

¹ monasters A Ch S : monasteries C.
² þei A C S : þey3 Ch.
³ or A C.   ⁴ suche C.
⁵ hey S : hy Ch.
⁶ almes dede Ch.
⁷ hi3e A C S : hy3 Ch.
⁸ *om.* C.   ⁹ 3ut S Ch.
¹⁰ he A C : a S Ch.
¹¹⁻¹¹ *om.* C.

principle is þis: hit may stonde to-gidres wiþout eny wiþsaiyng   The princi-
þat what parischon hit be þat is yschryue to freres, ¹ þe same   ple is this:
parischon is y-holde by heste of holy chirche to schryue hym of   by a friar,
alle his synnes ¹ ones a ȝere ² to his owne prest, þat is his   is held by
5 curatour & his ordinarie.   First y preued hit in þis maner: to shrive
for hit semeþ nomore wiþseyyng þat he, þat is y-schryue to   once a year
freres ³ ones a ȝere, is y-holde ³ to be schryue to his owne preste
of alle his ⁴ dedliche synnes in þat, þat schrifte may be rehersed   It is a good
in þe same, þanne hit doþ for to offre ones, twies, oþer þryes   man to
10 in ⁵ parische chirche, þouȝ ⁶ he offre elles where; for eiþer dede   rehearse his
is medeful & may be ofte y-do.   Þese laste tweyne wiþsiggeþ nouȝt   as it is good
eiþer oþer. ⁷ Þanne noþer þe firste tweyne wiþsiggeþ eiþer oþer ⁷.   other help-
No man douteþ her-of þat euerech dede þat may ofte be do, of ⁸
dyuerse persons oþer of þe same for dyuerse places & tyme, may   just as the
15 stonde wiþ-out wiþsigginge, as þus hit may wel stonde þat   mass often
a man hereþ oon masse oþer meny atte freres, & also atte   thing.
parische, namelich ones in a moneþe, & nameliche while eiþer
dede is medeful and plesyng to God, and so is schrifte wiþ-out ⁹
eny drede.   Alle doctors acordeþ þat þe dede of schrifte may   The doing
20 be do medefullich ofte touchyng þe schewyng of synne &   may take
fongyng of penaunce.   And we alle ofte doþ so & trowiþ to   place often.
plese God ofte in þat doyng, and hit is as ¹⁰ certeyn þat siche
medeful dedes may falle vnder comaundement and heeste, ¹¹ as
y schewide toforhond in þe bygynnyng of þe raþer article.
25 Þanne it may be vnder comaundment & heste ¹¹, þat he þat is
y-schryue ¹¹ to a frere be efte y-schryue ¹¹ of þe same synnes to
his owne prest and * his ordinarie.   Also þe ferþe Pope Martyn   Fol. 9 a
graunted frere menours leue for ¹² to here schriftes; & in þe
ende of þat priuylege he seiþ in þis maner: 'We wolleþ þat þei   Pope Martin
30 þat beþ y-schryue to freres be y-holde to be schryue of þe same   friars leave
synnes to her ¹³ parische preste, namelich, ones a ȝere as it is   shrifts, but
ordeyned by þe general counseil; & ¹⁴ þat þe same freres as

¹⁻¹ om. C.
² aȝere is I holde to be schreue C.
³⁻³ ys yholde ones a ȝer Ch.
⁴ om. C.
⁵ in a A C: in his S.
⁶ þeigh A C: þey S: þeyȝ Ch.
⁷⁻⁷ om. C.

⁸ by C.
⁹ wiþ A.
¹⁰ a A C.
¹¹⁻¹¹ om. C.
¹² om. S.
¹³ his owne preost A C.
¹⁴ and *written twice in* C.

those who are thus shriven must go to their parish priest once a year.

God ȝeueþ hem *grace* schal bisiliche cou*n*seile and charge hem þat þei schryueþ, to schryue hem efte of þe same synnes to her owne *prest*'. & so þis pope comau*n*deþ & hoteþ[1] openliche þat nouȝtwiþstondi*n*g þe schrifte þat is schewed to freres, he þat is y-schryue to freres is y-holde efte to schryue hi*m* of þe same synnes to his parische prest by þe statute of þe ge*n*eral co*n*sayl.

But friars read the opposite meaning in the decree and so do damage to themselves and to other men.

But hit semeþ þat þis constitucio*u*n *Johannina vas eleccionis* is co*n*t*r*arie[2] hereto, by þe meny*n*g[2] þat[3] freres takiþ of þat constitucio*u*n, and so þei enforme*þ* þe peple openlich, & so doþ damage to hem-silf and to o*þ*ere men also.

This constitution should be at once declared.

Ȝif pope Martyns maundment be ferme & stable, as hit semeþ by þe forseide reso*n*s, *þ*erfore holy fader þat no sich damage be among C*r*iste*n* men, ordeyneþ for C*r*istes loue þat þis constitucio*u*n be swiftlich declared. Me semeþ þat hit myȝt be þus vnd*er*stonden, and so ich vnd*er*stonde hit þat no man þat is y-schryue to freres [4] for defaute of power to assoile in freres[4], is y-holde to schryue hy*m* of þe same synnes to his owne *prest*; & hit semeþ þat mayst*er* Joon de Polliaco menede þe co*n*t*r*arie herof. Also hit semeþ grete wonder wit*h* what face freres dar[5] telle þat hit may nouȝt stonde, þat a man is y-schryue to freres & is y-holde to schryue hym of þe same synnes to his owne *prest*, while þei haueþ in here owne rule, as it is co*m*ynliche seide, þat euerech man þat takiþ her ordre in his entri*n*ge oþ*er* in his professio*u*n, he schal schryue hym to oon of hem of alle his synnes, nouȝt-wiþstondinge þat he is y-schryue to-forhond of þe same synnes. Þanne hit is wond*er* why þei denyeþ þat we mowe so do[6], while

Pope Benedict XI commands friars that they shall charge them whom they shrive, to be shriven again to their priest.

þei hem-silf doþ so. Also þe XI pope Benet in co*n*stituci*one sua re notoria* co*n*stit*ut*us bono*n*s*us*[7] *sup*er *cathedram*. Þat constituci*oun* bigy*n*neþ, ȝif ich haue þerof fulle mynde *in* þis man*er*, *ad perpetua*m. Þere he comau*n*deþ freres, þat þei schulleþ charge hem þat þei schryueþ, to schryue hem efte of þe same synnes to her[8] *prest* & her ordinarie. Þanne hit semeþ þat he meneþ þat, nouȝtwiþstondinge þe oon schrifte, ȝett þe oþ*er*

---

[1] hoteþ & comau*n*deþ S.
[2-2] by þe menyng hereto A C.
[3] þat þe C.
[4-4] om. C.
[5] durre A C: þere S: þurre Ch.
[6] doo soo C.
[7] Lat. Bonifacii.
[8] her owne A C Ch S.

schrifte is dewe¹. For ʒif þei mowe stonde togidres, þe² oon may be fonge & þe² oþer frelich abide as me semeþ, by³ resouns þat beþ made. Also Seynt Austyn *de vera & falsa penitencia*, & Seint Thomas Bonauenture, & holy doctors, & expositors affermeþ ofte þat it is spedeful to be ofte y-schryue of þe same synnes. Y can nouʒt se þanne why hit myʒt nouʒt be y-hote by þe lawe, forto make þe peple haue þe more mede, as a *prelate* myʒt holilich hote þat euerech Cristen man schulde here twey masses euereche Sonday. Now þis *principle* is þus skilfullich y-preued, hit semeþ þat me myʒt *conclude* a ful hardere⁴ *conclusioun*, þat is þis : euerech parischon þat leueþ⁵ al þe⁵ ʒere his *ordynarie*, þat is his parisch *curatour*, & schryueþ hym to a frere, trespaseþ aʒenes þe heeste of holy chirche, in þat⁶ *decretal Omnis vtriusque Sexus*. & þanne it folewiþ þat þei comeþ from þe frere wiþ dedlich synne, & God forʒeueþ nouʒt oon⁷ dedlich synne * but he⁸ forʒeue alle dedlich synnes. Þanne folewiþ a more meschef þat he þat is so y-schryue to a frere, comeþ from þe frere wiþ alle þe⁹ dedlich synnes þat he had wiþ hym whanne he wente to þe frere ; & what doyng is¹⁰ wors þan þis myʒt be suffred in holy chirche. Trulich, holy fader, y coupe neuer, noþer ʒit can assoile þis resoune.

Þerfore at Londoun y *prayed* þese freres openlich, þat þei wolde wiþ worde oþer¹¹ wrytynge enforme me how y myʒt assoile þis resoun, but þat myʒt ich nouʒt gete of hem ʒit to þis day. Þanne me semeþ, by þese forseide resons, þat þe ordynarie is more siker for his parischon to schryue hym syngulerliche to oon *per*soon þan is eny frere; and here vppon, holy fader, 'demeþ nouʒt by þe face but riʒtful dome ʒe deme'. Y seide and efte y seye, þat þe ordinarie is more ¹² profitable for þe schrift of his parischon þan is eny frere¹². For þe ordinarie is ordeyned by þe¹³ lawe of God & holy chirche & by heste for to

It is affirmed by others that it is spedeful to be shriven often of the same sins.

From this I will state a harder conclusion, that he who leaves all the year his priest trespasses

against the command of holy church, which is a deadly sin. Then it follows that he who comes from a friar, comes with all the deadly sins that he had with him when he went to the friar.

The ordinary is the more profitable for the shrift of a parishioner than is a friar,

¹ þewe S Ch.
² þat A C.
³ by þe A C Ch S.
⁴ hard C Ch S.
⁵⁻⁵ ech S.
⁶ þe A C.
⁷ in S: o Ch.
⁸ om. S: a Ch.

⁹ om. C.
¹⁰ om. S.
¹¹ oþer wiþ C Ch.
¹²⁻¹² siker for his parischon þan is eny frere A : siker for his parischoun to schryue hym singulerliche þan any frere C.
¹³ om. Ch S.

do þat dede; þe frere haþ no leue þerto but by graunt & leue of þe pope, & hit is no doute as hit semeþ þat no man haþ mede to do þat þinge þat he may nouȝt do but onlich by leue, & euerech þat holdeþ þe heeste of God & of holy Chirche haþ mede. Þanne it sueþ¹ by þe comyn cours, þat euereche parischon 5 may more sikerliche schryue hym to his owne curatour þan to ony frere; but y graunt þat þe contrarie myȝt happe, yn caas & þat but ful selde, as ȝif þe ordinarie were suspect to his parischon for somme certeyn cause. Also as hit is seide in þe raþer article: he þat schryueþ hym to his ordinarie haþ mede 10 of double obedience, for he² is obedient in þat he² schryueþ hym, & also in³ þat he² schryueþ hym to his ordynarie, þat is his curatour; and he² leseþ oon of þese medes whanne he² schryueþ hym to a frere, for hit is nouȝt⁴ y-hote noþer y-counceiled þat he² schulde schryue hym to a frere; þanne hit 15 is more profitabil to schryue hym to his curatour. Also þe ordinarie is more y-bounde to his parischon þan a frere; & as me schal suppose by þe comyn cours, he² schal for loue be þe more bisye to ordeyne hym profitable medicyn for his soule þan wolde eny frere, þat is a straunge persone; ⁵ þanne hereby hit 20 semeþ þat þe schrifte is more profitable. Also by þe laste conclusioun þe ordinarie is þe more siker persone; þanne he is þe more profitable persone.⁵ Also Innocencius c⁰ & si animarum⁶, assigneþ oon cause for þis conclusioun, þat hit is better be⁷ schryue to þe curatour þanne to a straunge man, & concludeþ 25 þat hit is more profitable be⁸ y-schryue to þe curatour þan to a straunger⁹; & þis cause holdeþ manliche¹⁰ in tyme of sekenesse by¹¹ nyȝt, whan þe seke man may nouȝt come to þe frere noþer þe frere to þe seke man by¹¹ nyȝt. For þanne, nouȝtwiþstondinge þe schrifte þat is made toforhond, þe parischon most schryue 30 hym to his ordinarie; þanne hit were wel spedeful þat þe ordynarie knew his raþer lif; for þanne he myȝt enioyne¹² hym

¹ seweþ A C S: syweþ Ch.
² a Ch S.
³ om. A C.
⁴ noþer S.
⁵⁻⁵ om. C.
⁶ Lat. Item Innocentius in cap. illo et si animarum.
⁷ to be S.
⁸ to be C.
⁹ straunge man A C S.
¹⁰ nameliche S.
¹¹ be C.
¹² eniune Ch.

þe more conuenable penaunce. For hit is knowen¹ þe ofter a man haþ forȝeuenesse of his synne, & þe gretter þe synnes beþ þat he haþ forȝeuenesse of², þe gretter is þe synne þat he doþ afterward. Þanne how may þe ordinarie þat is curatour sette
5 his parischon couenable penaunce, ȝif he knowiþ nouȝt his olde synnes, oþer namlich so couenable as he schulde ȝif he knewe his olde lif. ³ Y se nouȝt how he schuld do so couenablich * as he schuld ȝif he knewe his olde lif³. Þanne for siche poyntes hit were more profit be y-schryue to þe curatour þan to eny
10 frere. Also Innocencius telliþ anoþer cause, for a man is more schamfast to schryue hym to his ordinarie þan to eny frere, for a man is more schamfast to schewe his synnes to hym þat he seeþ⁴ al day þan to hym þat he seeþ⁴ but ones a ȝere. Also hit is spedeful to a wedded man þat oon man here his schrifte
15 & his wyfes also ; so her schrifte fader as a singuler leche of twey lymes⁵ of oon body may more profitablich ordeyne salue to hem þat beeþ gostlich seke. As in bodilich sekenes oon leche may better heele twey lymes, þan oon leche hele oon lyme & anoþer leche anoþer lyme of þe same body ; for þe husbond & þe wyf
20 beeþ tweyne in oon flesche.⁶ Mathei 19º cº. Here-by hit semeþ clere y-nowȝ þat þe ordinarie is more profitable for þe schrifte of his parischons þan is eny frere. Here-vppon holy fader, 'demeþ nouȝt by þe face but riȝtful dome ȝe deme'.

Þe þridde þat y seide & seye is, þat schrifte y-schewide to þe
25 ordinarie syngulerliche as y seide, voideþ mo damages þan doþ schrifte þat is schewide to eny frere. Þere y began to sprede þe mater & to schewe þat þe priuyleges, þat semeþ y-graunted to freres in þe chapitre dudum, beþ causes⁷ of many grete damages ; þanne þe kepyng of þe comyn lawe in þe mater of
30 priuyleges schulde voide many damages. Þanne y seye þat nouȝt onliche þe mysuse of þese⁸ priuyleges, but also þe holding of þese⁸ priuyleges by freres, doþ many damages to hem þat beþ y-schryue, & also to þe clergie, to⁹ Cristen peple, & to þe freres. Y say þat, for freres mysuseþ þese⁸ priuyleges, hit doþ

---

¹ y-knowe þat S.
² om. A C Ch.
³⁻³ om. A C.
⁴ sykþ Ch.
⁵ lemes C.
⁶ vleysch Ch.
⁷ cause A C Ch S.
⁸ þues S.
⁹ of C.

many damages to hem þat beþ y-schryue; þerfore he schulde be y-holde vnsuffrable. Also by¹ þe ferþe² Innocentius wordes, oþere damages comeþ of þese priuyleges, & seiþ we takiþ hede þat of þe mystakinge of þese priuyleges comeþ nouȝt onlich dispisingis & slakinge of deuocioun in þe peple aȝenes her owne 5 prestes, but also schamfastnesse is bynome, þat is þe grettest partye of penaunce, while a man schewiþ nouȝt his synnes³ to his synnes³, to his owne preste þat is⁴ present wiþ hym al wey,⁵ but to⁶ a straunge man, oþer a lond leper to whom hit is harde for to come, oþer impossible. Lo! twey damages, oþer þre, þat 10 men haueþ, dispisynge of her owne prest, slakinge of deuocioun, & bynymyng of schamfastnesse, þat is þe grettest party of penaunce, as he seiþ. Þese damages comeþ of schrifte y-schewide to þe freres. And anon hit folewiþ in þis maner: hit is harmful damage of wiþ-holdyng of offryng & perylous of wiþdrawyng of 15 teþingis⁷ þat passeþ nouȝt as cerymonyes of Jewes, as lyers telliþ⁸; but teþingis beþ reserued and dewe⁹ to hym¹⁰ of whom we fongeþ al þat we haueþ; & so teþingis beþ dewe¹¹ to him in token of his lordschip & schal be payed to parysche chirches; þis is y-write þer. He reherseþ twey oþer damages: wiþhold- 20 inge of offryngis þat men þat beþ y-schryue vseþ for to paye hem þat heriþ her schrifte; and freres appropreþ siche offryngis to her owne vse; & by¹² þe¹³ lawe siche offryngis beþ dewe¹¹ to parische chirches; & hit is damage to freres & worþi to be dampned wiþholdinge of teþingis þat parischons telliþ of freres 25 & is double damage to curatours; for teþingis beþ ordeyned * to hem for her liflode, & by cause of þese priuyleges, þei beþ wiþdrawe by freres. Numeri 18º cº hit is writen: 'What is halewide of þe children of Israel ich haue betake hit to þe & to þi sones for þe office of prest, lawful wiþouten ende.' Also þere 30 hit is writen: 'Al offring and sacrifice & al þat is y-ȝolde to¹⁴ me for trespace & for synne &¹⁵ þat longeþ to þe holy place, þou schalt haue hit & þi sones.'

¹ om. C.
² veurþe Ch.
³⁻³ om. A C Ch S.
⁴ is alwey S.
⁵ om. S.
⁶ om. C.
⁷ tweþinges S.
⁸ tellen C.
⁹ þuwe Ch: þewe S.
¹⁰ hym in tokene of his lordschippe C.
¹¹ þewe Ch S.
¹² be C.
¹³ om. C.
¹⁴ om. C.
¹⁵ om. S.

Also by vse of þese priuyleges, curatours haueþ anoþer vnkynde damage, þat þei knowiþ nouȝt þe face of her owne bestes
and þei haueþ y-fonge of her bischop cure of þe same bestes, *Another damage to curates is that they do not know the face of their own beasts.*
& þat were grete damage [1] in oon þat hadde bodilich cure of
5 bestes. Also hit is grete damage to curatours to be dispised of
her parischons, and as Innoce*n*cius seiþ toforhond : such dispisyng
is in þe peple for parischons beþ schryue to freres. Curatours *Another damage to curates is the misuse that friars make of the three-quarters of all the profits that falleth to them either of bequest or of gifts.*
haueþ anoþer grete damage by cause of mysvse of priuyleges,
þat freres haueþ touchyng þe þre quarters of alle profites, þat
10 falliþ to [2] hem oþer wise of biquyst oþer of ȝifte, distinctliche,
oþer indistinctliche, & al maner mysvse þat þei vseþ of þat, is
conteyned in þe chapitre *dudum*; and touchyng þe ferþe part
þat is I-graunted to curatours & y-taxed þere, þe whiche ferþe
part of many biquystes, offryngis, & ȝiftes, freres payeþ nouȝt to
15 curatours, but freres appropreþ hit to hem-silf wiþ many cautels
and wyles as curatours telliþ; so þat bitwene hem & freres as it
were in eue*r*eche place among Cristen men is ple & strif wiþ-
oute ende. So þat in many placis charite is fer, & after wordes
comeþ strokes.
20 Also curatours haueþ damage of mysuse of anoþer priuylege *Another damage, Friars have two con-servators, and summon men before the more distant.*
þat freres haueþ, for freres haueþ twey conseruatours & wolleþ
nouȝt plede wiþ curatours noþer wiþ oþer þat haueþ catel tofore þe next conseruatours,[3] & makeþ hem so somned in-to fer
cuntreys. So þat for drede of trauail & cost, he appeleþ from
25 þe sentence of þe cause, and in my [4] prouynce haueþ ful ofte, as [5]
somme telliþ þat beþ myȝty in þis court, and þerof is comyn
fame. Curatours haueþ þese damages & many oþere by cause
of mys-vsynge of priuyleges þat beþ graunted to freres [6].
Y preue hit, for by occasioun of priuyleges þat beþ graunted
30 to freres for to here schriftes, children in general studyes & *Friars be-come privy in homes because they hear shrifts, and so they beguile the children with small*
in her fader hous beþ homliche & priuy wiþ freres; for in þe
fader hous freres beþ priuy by cause of heryng of [7] schriftes, &
children beþ y-schryue to freres, & freres begileþ hem wiþ
smale ȝiftes & gileful, & makeþ hem come in-to her ordre, for

---

[1] damage to curatoures C.
[2] to freres bycause of sepulture & of alle profiȝtes þat falleþ to S.
[3] conseruatour but to ferreste conseruatour S.
[4] myn C.
[5] and C.
[6] freres for to here schriftes C.
[7] om. C.

freres mowe nouȝt so begyle olde men. And as þe comyn fame telliþ, after þat children ben[1] bigiled in-to her ordre, þe children haueþ no fredome for to wende out, but beþ holden wiþ hem aȝenus her owne wille forto þei be professed in þe ordre[2]. & ȝett more me seiþ, þat in þe mene tyme, þe children beþ nouȝt suffred to speke wiþ fader noþer wiþ modir, but [3]vnder keping[3] and drede of freres. In euydence herof, þis day as ich come out of myn Inne, come[4] to me a good man of Englond þat is comen to þis court for socour and remedye; and he tolde me þat anoon after Ester,[5] þat last was at Oxenford, freres by-name hym his sone þat was nouȝt xiii ȝere olde, & he came þider to speke wiþ his sone &[6] moste nouȝt speke wiþ his sone, but vnder warde & keping of freres. & Holy Writt biddiþ, þat[7] who þat[8] steliþ a man & silliþ him, & is I-*preued vppon hym þat trespas, he[9] schal dye. Exodi 21º cº. Why haueþ þei not þis peyne oþer anoþer lawful peyne? Hit semeþ me nouȝt riȝtful þat þei beþ vnpunysched. By þe lawe a man schal be punysched for þe stelyng of an oxe oþer of[10] a scheep. For more greuous þeſþe[11] & greuyng of his emcristen by a more greuous trespas, euerech þat so doþ schulde be more greuouslich punysched; & siche þeſþe[11] and trespace is siche stelyng of children wiþinne þe[12] ȝeres of discreciouo while þei beþ vnder fader & moder keping; & freres mowe nouȝt soþliche saye þat children beþ brouȝt þere to serue God wiþ þe more deuociouo, & þerfore it is lawful to bygile hem wiþ fraude & lesyngis & wiþ fals byheestes. Þis may nouȝt stonde, for hit is contrarie to þe[13] apostles decre: 'Do we nouȝt, as we beþ dispised & yscorned & as som men telleþ þat we seyn, do we euel þat good may bifalle; her dampnacioun is riȝtful,' ad Romanos 3º cº. & wolde God þat þei syȝe inwardlych Seynt Austyns bokes of lesyng & aȝenes lesynge, in þe whiche bokes he declareþ clerelich, þat me schuld make no lesyng noþer for to avoyde & ascape[14] harme, what harm hit euere were, noþer for to wynne

---

[1] beeþ A C S: buþ Ch.
[2] here owne ordere S.
[3-3] vnkeynge C.
[4] þere come A C.
[5] Esterne A C.
[6] & he C.
[7] om. S.
[8] so A C.
[9] a Ch.
[10] om. S.
[11] þefte A C S: þuyfthe Ch.
[12] om. S.
[13] om. Ch.
[14] skape A C Ch S.

gode oþer¹ profiȝt, noþer for to saue a manes soule noþer his life; and so hit semeþ of² alle oþer synnes. &³ among oþer, Seynt Austyn schewiþ oon feire reson & seiþ in þis maner : ' ȝif *He condemns lying even though good may come.*
me myȝt somtyme lawfulliche lye & make a lesyng for somme
5 manere cause, þanne al þe loore of hooly⁴ chirche were loost;
for þanne he þat prechiþ openliche þe feiþ of holy chirche, myȝt
lawfulliche lye, while he prechiþ þe feiþ for sich a maner cause,
while he techiþ þe feiþ and prechiþ þe peple.' Þanne men þat
hereþ hym preche myȝt argue in her⁵ herte in þis maner: by *No such thing as lawful lying, so says St. Austin.*
10 his owne loore þis⁶ may lawfulliche lye & make lesyngis lawfulliche in many maner⁷ caas⁸; y noot noþer may wite wheþer
he haue sich a cause now oþer no; þanne y schal noȝt trowe
hym while he precheþ & techiþ. Þanne Seynt Austyn concludiþ
& seiþ: 'To þe riȝtful manes office in noon wise⁹ to telle will-
15 fulliche a lesyng.' Also þat is þe¹⁰ comaundement & heeste of *Also the commandment of the new law.*
þe newe lawe as it is writen, Mathei 10º cº : ' Me axide of youre
Lord, what schal y do for to haue lif wiþouten ende ? ', & oure *Mark 10 :17-19.*
Lord answerde and seide : ' Þou knowest þe heestes, þou schalt *Matt 19 :16-19.*
do no spouse-bruch, noþer sle, noþer stele, noþer bere fals
20 witnesse, noþer do fraude noþer gile, worschip þi fader & þi
moder, & so forþ.' A man may nouȝt lawfullich breke Goodes *A man may not break God's command.*
heeste for eny cause þat he hym-silf wole fynde, as hit soþlich
semeþ. For by cause þerof Saul was cast out of þe kyngdom, *This is seen in the case of Saul, who*
for God had y-hote hym þat he schulde distruye al þe catel &
25 riches of þe Amalachites, & he dide þe contrarie & kepte þe *disobeyed God.*
best¹¹ beestes for he wolde offre hem to God. & Samuel þe
prophete answerde hym & seide : ' Obediens is better þan *I Samuel 15 :22.*
sacrifice & do as God hoteþ is better þan offre fatnesse of
weþeres.' For hit is as hit were þe synne of sorcery & of *It is a sin of sorcery and*
30 wicchecrafte to wiþstonde, as hit were þe synne of mawmetre¹² *witchcraft.*
to be nouȝt buxom to Goddes heste. pº¹³ regum 19º cº. Also *I Samuel 15.*
Osa put his hond to Goddes schryne¹⁴ so þat he was in poynt

¹ ne A C.
² om. A.
³ om. C.
⁴ al holy S.
⁵ om. C.
⁶ þese A C Ch S.
⁷ maneres C.
⁸ om. C.
⁹ it longeþ in no wise S.
¹⁰ om. A.
¹¹ om. S.
¹² mametrie A C Ch S.
¹³ primo C.
¹⁴ & hueld it vp for þe oxene hadde ystarteled & ouer cast þe schryne S.

to falle; and God was wrooþe wiþ Osa & smote hym for his foly & so Osa was ded. 2⁰ regum 6⁰ c⁰. Also oure Lordes prophete þat was sent out of Juda into Bethel & was y-hote þat he schulde noþer ete ne drynke in þat place, but anoþer prophete þat was þere counseiled & prayed hym þat he schulde ete & drynke, & he seide how God had y-hote. '& ich am a prophete' quoþ þat oþer, 'as þou art', & he eet & dranke & was slayn of a lyoun as he went* þennes, as it is writen. 4⁰ regum 13⁰ c⁰. Þese & oþer siche preueþ þat freres doþ dedlich synne in sich stelyng of children from her fadres & modres. And it semeþ þat þei synneþ dedliche nouȝt onlich in þefþe, but also in fraude & gyle; for þe forseide auctorite seiþ, þat hit is y-hote: 'Þou schalt do noþer fraude ne gile, noþer sle noþer stele, noþer bere fals witnesse.' & aȝenus þe whiche heestes freres doþ as hit semeþ, whanne þei tolleþ to hem children wiþ fraude & wiþ gile; & Paul þe apostle hoteþ, þat no man schuld ouer passe noþer begile his broþer, for oure Lord is wrecheful in alle siche dedès, ad Thessalonicences 4⁰ c⁰. Here of comeþ grete damage boþe to þe peple & to þe clergie; also to þe peple, for many men what þei loueþ best in þis worlde, þat is her owne children.

Also hit is grete damage to þe clergie; for now in þe Vniuersitees of þe rewme of Englonde, for children beþ so y-stole from her fadres & modres, lewed men in euereche place wiþholdeþ her children & sendeþ hem nouȝt to þe Vniuersite, for hem is leuer make hem eerþe tilyers & haue hem þan sende hem to þe Vniuersite & lese hem. So þat ȝet in my tyme in þe Vniuersite of Oxenford were þritty þousand scolers at ones, & now ben vnneþe sixe þousand. And me trowiþ þat þe grettest occasioun & cause why scolers beþ so wiþdrawe, hit is for children beþ so bigiled & y-stole; & y se noon gretter damage to al þe clergie, þan is þis damage.

---

[1] for to A C Ch S.
[2] 8⁰ S.
[3] seyde S.
[4] þis A C: þe Ch S.
[5] om. C.
[6] suche oþere A C.
[7] & C.
[8] þan A C.
[9] om. A C Ch S.
[10] synweþ Ch.
[11] no C.
[12-12] noþer stele ne slee C.
[13-13] yn best yn þis Ch.
[14] to make C.
[15] leuse Ch : luese S.
[16-16] and vnneþe now beþ S.
[17-17] om. C.
[18] No A C S.

Richard FitzRalph's Sermon: 'Defensio Curatorum'

Also þere is more [1] grete damage þat vndoþ & distruyeþ þe [2] seculers of al maner faculte. For þese ordres of beggers for endeles wynnynges [3] þat þei geteþ by beggyng of þe forseide priueleges of schriftes and sepultures & oþer, þei beþ now so multiplyed in couentes and in persons, þat many men telliþ þat in general studies vnneþe is y-founde to sillyng a profitable book of þe faculte of art or of dyuynyte, of lawe canoun, of phisik, oþer of lawe ciuil, but alle bookes beþ y-bouȝt of freres. So þat in euerech couent of freres is a noble librarie and a grete; and so þat euerech frere þat haþ state in scole siche as þei beþ now, haþ an huge [4] librarye. And also y sent of my sugettes to scole þre oþer foure persones; & hit is seide me þat somme of hem beþ come home aȝen for þei myȝt nouȝt fynde [5] to selle [5] oon good Bible noþer oþer couenable bookes. ȝif þis be nouȝt grete damage in þe clergie, [6] no damage,[6] no damage may be þerinne. For hit semeþ þat [7] herof schulde come siche an ende þat no clergie schulde leue in holy chirche, but oonlich in freres; & so þe feiþ of holy chirche were loste but oonlich in þe [8] freres. & so hit semeþ þat hit were myche bettre þat prelates lefte al to hem þan þat þei distruye al holy chirche þat þei [9] beþ now so about [9] for to wynne.

Ich wondre & nouȝt onlich wondre, but ich am astonyed also why & by what maner hardynesse siche men praiseþ hem-silf in kunnyng aboue alle men, & aȝenus þe [10] resoun of philosophie & loore of Holy Writ,[11] in siche a maner wiþ-oute [12] ende. Þe philosofer in his secunde book de anima seiþ þat þe worst þat is in kynde is passyng resoun of gretenesse & of encresinge. Þanne it foleweþ þat þei holdiþ nouȝt þe lawe of kynde but forsakiþ hit, for þei wexiþ grete & encresiþ wiþ-oute eny ende. Also Holy Writ techiþ vs, Sapiencie xi c°, þat God made & ordeyned al in mesure, noumbre, & wiȝt. But sich multiplicacioun y-founded vppon beggyng & beggerye, as freres telleþ, may nouȝt * ordeyne a certeyn noumbre of persones þat þei

^{margin:} Another damage is that the friars buy up all the useful books for their libraries, and also the Bibles. Thus it may come to pass that no learning remains in the church except among the friars. These men against Philosophy praise themselves in cunning. Also against Holy Writ which says God ordained all in measure, number and wit. Proverbs 11:1. Fol. 12 a

---

[1] anoþer A C Ch S.
[2] þe lore of S.
[3] wynnynge A C.
[4] hoyge.
[5-5] om. C.
[6-6] om. C S.
[7] om. C.
[8] om. C Ch S.
[9-9] beeþ so aboute now A C: beþ so now aboute S.
[10] om. S.
[11] chirche C.
[12] oute an C.

schulde fynde, noþer þei mowe¹ of certein oon person fynde.
And beggers haueþ no wiȝt, þat² is a stidefast place, noþer
mowe ordeyne for hem-silf a stidefast place, for verrey beggers
euereche day ³oþer as hit were euerech day,³ beþ compelled to
wende out of her place for nede. Also siche mowe nouȝt ordeyne 5
mesure in persones, ³& in Goddes seruise most be certeyn
noumbre of persons,³ but beggers compelled by nede most leue
þe seruise & go abegged ofte tyme.

Þanne hit folewiþ þat þese⁴ of þe ordres of beggers multepliéþ
hem in þis maner aȝenus þe⁵ ordenaunce of God Almyȝtyes 10
³witt & his³ wisdom, and bynymeþ þerby þe fleece⁶ of þe peple
& of þe clergie, & chargiþ hem in euerech place. For now
vnneþe may any grete men oþer smaal, lewed or lered, take a
morsel⁷ of mete, but siche beggers come vnbede, & begge nouȝt
as pore men schuld atte ȝate oþer atte dore, axing almes mekelich 15
as Fraunces tauȝt and hoteþ in his testament, but þei comeþ
into houses⁸ & courtes & beþ y-harberwide & etiþ & drynkeþ
what þei þer fyndeþ vnbede and vnprayed. & noþeles þei bereþ
wiþ hem corn, oþer⁹ mele, brede,⁹ flesche oþer chese. Þouȝ¹⁰ þere
be but tweyne in þe hous þei bereþ ¹¹wiþ hem¹¹ þat oon. & 20
no man may hem werne but þei put of al kyndeliche schame.

And it is wonder þat þei drediþ nouȝt þe sentence of Pope
Gregorye þat writeþ in a comyn priuelege to prelates of holy
chirche in þis maner: 'For ofte vices of priuy riches entreþ, &
Sathanas his angel degiseþ hym in þe liknesse of an angel of 25
liȝt. By þis present auctorite we comaundeþ & hoteþ þat ȝif
eny þat telliþ þat þei beþ of þe ordre of frere prechours, precheþ
in ȝowre contrayes & turneþ hem to begging of money, wharby
þe ordre of hem þat haueþ made professioun to pouert myȝt be
diffamed, take ȝe hem as fals faytours & dampneþ hem.' Þei 30
beþ now so sotyl in þis crafte of beggerie þat pore vikers &
persons & al þe peple pleyneþ þerof, neiȝ in euerech place. Þis
semeth a wonder maner lyuyng in hem þat seyn, þat þei mot
holde þe gospel by her professioun & doþ aȝenus Cristes owne

---

¹ om. C.
² þat þat C.
³⁻³ om. C.
⁴ þues Ch S.
ᴸ manner of þe C.
⁶ vluys Ch S.
⁷ mossel A Ch.
⁸ hous.
⁹ & C.
¹⁰ þei A C S: þeyz Ch.
¹¹⁻¹¹ away C.

sentence þat sente his disciples to preche þe gospel, & seide: They do contrary to
'Passe ȝe nouȝt from hous to hous.' Luce 10º cº. Also þei doþ Christ's gospel.
aȝenus anoþer scripture þat seiþ: 'Voide & war þat þou be noȝt Luke 10:6.
herberwed from hous to hous.' Ecclesiastici 29º cº. Bot þei goþ Ecclesiasti-
5 so about from court to court & from hous to hous, for her cus 29:24.
cloystre schulde nouȝt be her prison. Ys nouȝt þis¹ grete They go from court
damage to þe clergie & to þe peple also? Soþlich hit semeþ to court and
so² to many men; & al hit haþ occasioun of þe¹ mysvse of to house, which is a
pryuyleges, for þei telliþ þat þei vseþ so þe priuyleges of great
10 prechyng & of heryng of schriftes, neiȝ euerech man schameþ to the clergy
werne hem oþer to put hem of. and the people.
And also þese priuyleges and oþer þingis þat schal be touched This comes from the
wiþynne doþ freres many damages.. For hit semeþ þat þese misuse of privileges by
priuyleges infecteþ hem with many maner synnes: wiþ þe synne the church.
15 of iniurie & of wrong, wiþ þe synne of vnbuxomnesse, wiþ which arise therefrom,
þe synne of couetise, & wiþ þe synne of pride. Hit semeþ þat i.e. injury, wrong, un-
boþe þe procurynge & þe holdynge of þese priuyleges, alle þat buxomness, covetous-
beþ conteyned in þe chapitre dudum de sepulture in Clementinis, ness and pride,
& of þe oþere þat beþ rehersed toforhonde infecteþ freres wiþ
20 ³synnes. Hit semeþ þat þe procuring of þese priuyleges
infecteþ freres wiþ³ þe synne of iniurie and wrong, touchyng
curatours, for þat procuryng is agenus Goddes heeste⁴ þat seiþ: which sins are against
'Þou schalt nouȝt coueite, noþer desire þi neiȝbores hous, noþer God's com-
his wif, noþer his seruaunt, noþer his oxe noþer his asse, noþer Exodus 20:17.
25 any þinge þat is his.' Exodi xxº * cº. Hit is soþe þat þese riȝtes, Fol. 12 b
þat freres haueþ y-procured⁵, were þe riȝtes of curatours; þanne These were the rights
hit was aȝenus Goddes heeste⁴ so to coueite þese riȝtes. Coue- of curates, which friars
tise longeþ to procuryng & is tofore procuryng in euereche man have taken.
þat procuriþ. Also hit is nouȝt lawful to coueite þe curatours curing of
30 oxe noþer his asse, ffor hit is aȝenus Goddes heeste. Þanne the rights of curates is
hit is more wrongful to coueite þingis þat beþ more profitable against God's law.
to þe curatours, & siche beþ þese riȝtes. Also þat procuryng
was y-do aȝenus þe⁶ heeste of loue of þe⁷ neiȝbore þat seiþ: 'Þou
schalt loue þi neiȝbore as þi-silf.' &⁸ euerech man loueþ so
hymsilf⁸ þat he wolde nouȝt þat oþer men schulde coueite his

¹ om. C.
² om. A C.
³⁻³ om. S.
⁴ ⁴ om. C.
⁵ procred Ch.
⁶ om. S.
⁷ þi A C S.
⁸⁻⁸ om. C.

catel wrongfulliche. Hit is soþe þat riȝtes of curatours þo were nouȝt due¹ to freres; þanne þei were wrongfulliche y-procured of hem & so aȝenus þat heest of God. Also hit may be preued by Cristes lore, Mathi 7º cº, þat seiþ: 'Al þat ȝe woleþ þat men do to ȝou, doþ ȝe² to hem, þat is þe lawe & þe prophetes.' Þere³ doyng mot be take for dede & for sparyng of⁴ dede, so þat we schal spare & nouȝt do to oþere men þat we wolde nouȝt þat oþere men⁵ dide to vs,⁶ ⁷ þat we schulde nouȝt wilne þat oþere men dide to vs⁷. But what frere wolde oþer by hem wilne schulde, þat monkes oþer chanons reulere⁸ oþer⁹ freres of oþer ordre, schulde bynyme hem þe priuyleges þat þei now haueþ? Y trowe þat no frere so wolde. Þanne schulde þei nouȝt do¹⁰ siche wronges to curatours of hooly chirche.

Also procuryng of siche priuyleges infecteþ hem wiþ þe synne of vnbuxomnesse, for¹¹ priuyleges beþ contrarie to þe reules of her professioun. Y preue hit, for in her appele þei supposeþ & makeþ suggestioun & telleþ, þat þese foure ordres beþ ordeyned of holy chirche, & y-founded vppon beggerie & vppon heiȝest¹² pouert. Hit semeþ þat hauyng riȝt to preche and to cristen men may nouȝt stonde wiþ sich a foundment of beggerie, ȝif power of¹³ axing & of¹³ chalenging of liflode longeþ to þis priuylege, as hit doþ to riȝtful lawe, so þat freres myȝt chalange her liflode of hem þat þei prechiþ to þe gospel; as Cristes disciples hadde whanne Crist hem sent to preche þe gospel & seide: 'In what hous ȝe goþ yn¹⁴ þere abideþ, þe werkman is worþi his mede.' Luce 10º¹⁵ cº. Hit semeþ þat siche schulde nouȝt be clepede¹⁶ beggers. How schulde he be¹⁷ cleped verrey begger? Y saye nouȝt begging þat haþ fre riȝt to chalange his liflode. Y se nouȝt how hit schuld stonde. Noþer inquisitours noþer freres of her ordre þat haueþ office, by þe whiche þei mowe certeynlich chalange her liflode schuld be cleped beggers for

---

¹ dewe A C : þewe Ch S.
² ȝe þe same A C.
³ here A.
⁴ for A C.   ⁵ om. S.
⁶ þat oþere men dide to vs repeated in H.
⁷⁻⁷ om. A C S.
⁸ reguler A C.
⁹ oþer of S, and of crossed out.
¹⁰ vse C.
¹¹ for þes S.
¹² þe hiȝeste C.
¹³ om. C Ch S.
¹⁴ om. S.
¹⁵ 18 C S.
¹⁶ kept in A but crossed out, with cleped written.
¹⁷ by C S.

schame of þe name, whanne þei schulde knowe in cause of heresie & of þe laste riȝtful dome. Me seiþ þat þei vseþ siche office ful ofte & takeþ maisterfullich grete summes of money.¹ Noþer a penytaunser noþer a lystere þat haþ his liflode by
5 certeyn couenaunt schuld be cleped verrey begger, as hit semeþ. And so þei brekiþ her professioun in procuryng & vsyng of þese offices ; & so hit semeþ þat boþe in willyng & in procuring of siche priuyleges þei wolde put of & doo away her rule of beggerie; y saye nouȝt of begging þat bitokeneþ² þe dede.
10 And so in her herte þei haueþ y-put of & y-do awey her rule as Crist seiþ in siche a doyng: 'Who þat seeþ³ a woman for to desire hir⁴ now he haþ do lecherie⁵ in his herte.' Mathi 9º cº. But ȝif freres telleþ, & soþlich, as me semeþ, as y schal schewe ynnermore þat to þe offys of prechyng longeþ power to chalange
15 nedeful liflode of hem þat me precheþ to.* But freres beþ nouȝt cleped noþer committed to vse þat office, but haueþ a baar leue & beþ nouȝt y-hote noþer chargide to vse þat office.

By⁶ anoþer hed followiþ þe same of priuyleges of sepultures, of leue to here schriftes, ⁷ of fonginge of offrynges þat beþ þanne
20 offred to God & of þe priuylege of heryng of schriftes⁷ of alle þat wole be schryue to hem. For God hoteþ: 'Þou⁸ schalt nouȝt schewe þi-silf to-fore þe Lord God voyde wiþ-out offryng, whanne þou gost into chirche for to haue þe sacramentis', as it is writen Exodi 23º cº. Þei falleþ into þe synne of vnbuxom-
25 nesse aȝenus obedience, for þei vseþ þat office aȝenus þe lore of þe apostle, ⁹ ad Romanos 10º¹⁰ cº, þere þe apostle⁹ seiþ: 'How schul þei preche but þei be sent?' As it is writen: 'How faire beþ þe feet of þe prechours þat prechiþ pees, þat prechiþ good!' Ad Hebreos 9º cº: 'No man to hym-silf takiþ worschip, but he
30 þat is cleped of God.' Also þei doþ aȝenus Cristes lore þat seiþ: 'Ȝe schal haue no wille to be cleped maister;¹¹ oon is ȝour¹¹ maister, þat is Crist.' Mathi 20º cº. Þanne þei beþ vnobedient & vnbuxom, þat bihoteþ¹² in her professioun¹² to holde & kepe

---

¹ symonye S.
² tokeneþ A C Ch S.
³ seweþ A C S: suweþ Ch.
⁴ om. C.
⁵ spouse breche A C Ch S.
⁶ but C.
⁷⁻⁷ om. A.
⁸ þat þou A C Ch S.
⁹⁻⁹ om. C.
¹⁰ 18 S.
¹¹⁻¹¹ and beeþ nouȝt ycleped A C Ch S.
¹²⁻¹² *Repeated in* A Ch.

Cristes gospel.¹ Also of frere menours hit may specialich folewe, for no man douteþ but hit is y-knowe þat þei haueþ more worldliche & more esy lif & lasse medeful lif wiþ þese priuyleges, ² þan wiþ-out þese pryuyleges,² of prechyng, of heryng of schriftes, of hauyng sepultures, &³ appropreþ to hem þe þre ferþe deles of profites þat comeþ. Hit is lasse medeful to⁴ lyue wiþ þese priuyleges þanne wiþ-out þese priuyleges, as Seint Fraunceys had ordeyned hem for to lyue. Þanne in procuryng of þese priuyleges þei by-heelde bacward, after þat þei hadde⁵ y-put her hond to þe plowe, aȝenus þe heest of God & aȝenus Seynt Fraunceys reule. In his rule in þe secunde chapitre hit is writen in þis maner : ' Whanne þe ȝere of assaye is y-do þei schul be⁵ fonge to behote obedience '; for as þe gospel seiþ: 'No man þat putteþ his hond to þe plowe & by-holdeþ bacward is worþi þe kyngdom of God'; so it is write þere.⁶ Þanne þei þat procured siche priuyleges felle into þe synne of vnobedience & vnbuxomnesse, for þei by-helde bacward wiþ-oute any doute.

Also in þe bygynnyng of þe same chapitre, hit is writen : ' Ȝif eny men⁷ wolleþ fonge þis lif & comeþ to oure freres, þe freres schal sende hem to her mynistres prouyncial ; for þei & noon oþer haueþ leue to⁸ fonge freres. Þanne þe mynistres schal examyne hem bisiliche of þe riȝt feiþ & of þe sacramentis of holy chirche, & ȝif þei trowiþ al þis & knowlechiþ & wole truliche holde & kepe hem to her lyues ende,' & so forþe. But freres procureþ a priuylege þat boþe þe mynistres prouyn-cial & lasse men in þe ordre þan þe mynistres prouyncial, mowe fonge men to her ordre. And freres doþ so indifferentlich, & in procurynge of þat priuylege, þei wolde distruye & slake a partie of þe rule; þanne it folewiþ þat þei dide⁹ þe synne¹⁰ of vnobedience & of vnbuxomnesse. And ȝif þei doþ¹¹ wiþoute priuylege, þei doþ⁹ neuerþelas vnobedientliche aȝenus her pro-fessioun. Also aȝenus þis clause of þe rule, þe mynistres schal

---

¹ *After* gospel *is written* & pro-cureþ such priueyleges aȝenste the lawe of þe gospel S.
²⁻² *om.* C.
³ & to S.
⁴ for to S.
⁵ *om.* C.
⁶ þe C.
⁷ man C S.
⁸ *om.* A C Ch S.
⁹⁻⁹ *om.* C Ch S.
¹⁰ synnes A.
¹¹ doþ by & Ch.

examyne hem bisilich,[1] freres doþ al day. For neiȝ no man
comeþ to hem but þe child þat is bigiled, þat knowiþ[2] what
noþer how many sacramentes beþ of holy chirche, noþer can
knowe bitwene riȝt feye & heresie. & ȝitt vnneþe is y-founde
5 eny notable place of freres wiþout a couent oþer half of children
wiþ-ynne ten ȝere olde. & who may doute þat* þat is nouȝt Fol. 13 b
in freres þe synne of vnobedience, & comeþ by þe forseide The power of friars over children.
priuyleges, by þe whiche þei beþ so made riche & y-worschiped
þat children assenteþ liȝtlich for to do her wille, & namelich
10 her wille þat hereþ schriftes in her owne hous,[3] oþer in þe
hous[3] of children frendes. Þanne þe procuryng &[4] mysuse of
þese priuyleges infecteþ þese freres wiþ synne of vnobedience &
vnbuxomnesse, as hit semeþ.

Also in Seynt[5] Frounceys rule, & in þe chapitre *Exiit, de* St. Francis declares that friars shall not preach in the bishop's district without his consent.
15 *Verborum Significatione, libro* 6to, hit is seide & declared þat
freres schal kepe & holde þat þei preche in no bischops
bischopriche ȝif þe bischop wiþ-seiþ hem. Also Seynt Frounceis
in his testament seiþ: 'Þouȝ[6] ich had as grete kunnyng as euer
had Salomon, & ich fynde pore prestes of þis world in parische
20 þere[7] þei woneþ, y wole nouȝt preche aȝenus her wille, & hem
alle ich wole drede & louye & worschipe as my Lordes, & þei
beþ my Lordes'; þis is writen þere. But what worschip freres
doþ now to pore prestes hit may nouȝt be hidde while hit is
newe[8]; but vnreuerence in euerech place may be founde y-do Friars do not show reverence to priests.
25 in stede of reuerence. And þei procureþ[9] þe priuylege þat is
conteyned in þe chapitre, & in þat procurynge þei hadde in her
wille þe synne of vnbuxomnesse, for þei wolde vndo þat lawe
þat þei hadde toforhonde & were wiþ y-chargide. Vppon þis vers
of þe Psauter, '*legem pone mihi domine viam iustificacionum*
30 *tuarum*,' & so forþ, Seint Austin seiþ[10] in þis maner: 'He þat St. Augustine says of a man who holds the law for fear and not for love that he is its enemy.
holdeþ the lawe for drede of peyne & nouȝt for loue of riȝtwisnesse,
he holdeþ þe lawe maugre[11] his teeþ; for ȝif he myȝt leue he wolde
nouȝt holde þe lawe but he wolde þat hit were no lawe & so he
is no frende of þe lawe but enemy þerof, while he wolde þat[12]

---

[1] bisiliche as C.
[2] knoweþ noȝt S.
[3] houses C.
[4] of C.
[5] seyn Ch.
[6] þeiȝ A C Ch S.
[7] of þere C.
[8] noon S.
[9] procreþ A Ch.
[10] *om.* C.
[11] maugreþ S.
[12] *om* S.

hit were nouȝt, & no man is clensed by þe dede, ȝif he is vnclene in his wille.' Þus¹ seiþ Seint Austyn. Hit is soþe þat he þat procureþ as freres dooþ, may nouȝt wiþ-out leue of þe bischop ²preche in his bischopriche, noþer² here schriftes. Þanne þei wolde þat þe rule þat is contrarie were nouȝt; & so þei holdeþ 5 hit nouȝt for loue of riȝtwisnesse bote for drede of peyne; & so þei wolde þat þei hadde noon heeste to holde þe reule; & so þei were no frendes but enemyes to þe raþer lawe & vnclene of wille

Those who procure privileges may not say 'Thy will be done'. as Austyn seiþ. Also þese þat procureþ priuyleges contrarie to here reule & to her professioun & to her parfitnesse also, 10 mowe nouȝt truliche seye þis clause of þe paternoster in þat caas: 'Fiat voluntas tua sicut in celo & in terra', þat is, 'Þi wille be do in erþe as hit is in heuene'. And ȝett þei be y-holde þerto by þe professioun þat þei makiþ of þe gospel.

St. Francis's rule in regard to friars. Seynt Fraunceys bygynneþ his rule in þis maner: 'Þis is þe 15 reule & þe lif of³ frere menours to holde & kepe þe gospel of oure Lord Ihesu; and it is Goddes wille þat his heeste & his counseil be y-holde as euereche knoweþ'. Þanne it is Goddes wille þat freres holde her rule atte fulle, þat þei haueþ y-made in⁴ her professioun to holde;· also þat is y-hote in þe secunde 20 chapitre of þe rule. And þese freres in her herte procureþ þe contrarie, & procureþ þat þe keping of þe reule be y-slaked & wiþdrawe. And so hit sueþ⁵ þat freres, þat so procureþ, beþ infect wiþ þe synne of vnobedience & vnbuxumnesse aȝenus God & aȝenes her owne rule. Hit semeþ þat þis folewiþ also of 25

Friars may not do thus without being obedient. anoþer bed. For þese freres noþer oþer freres mowe here schriftes, noþer use⁶ þe⁷ office of prechyng, noþer fonge holy ordres, þe whiche þei fongeþ wiþ þe synne of vnbuxomnesse as

Fol. 14 a hit* semeþ. For it is comyn lawe of holy cherche þat no man schulde fonge holy ordre, but he haue suffisaunt tytel⁸ to haue 30

Friars should have meat and drink before they take on holy orders. mete & drynke and cloþe; and siche a tytel haueþ nouȝt freres while þei beþ verrey beggers as þei telliþ hem-silf. Þanne it semeþ þat aȝenes þis lawe alle freres fongeþ holy ordres; & so in procuryng of so heiȝ a⁹ state þei falleþ nouȝt onlich into þe

---

¹ þis A C Ch S.
²⁻² om. C.
³ of þe C.
⁴ om. A C Ch S.
⁵ seweþ A C S: syweþ Ch.
⁶ use of C Ch S.
⁷ om. C Ch S.
⁸ tyme C.
⁹ om. A C Ch S.

synne of vnobedience & vnbuxumnesse, but also into þe synne of coueitise. Also in¹ Seint Fraunceys reule in þe same chapitre of prechyng, hit is y-hote þat no frere schuld be hardy in eny² maner wise to preche to þe peple, but he be examyned &
5 appreued of þe mynistre general, & haue leue³ of hym, & graunt³ to vse þe office of prechyng. But now is a priuylege y-procured for.þe contrarie þat þe mynistres prouyncial schuld do þe same, & þei þat procureþ hit doþ hit⁴ aȝenus her owne rule. Þanne þei doþ þe synne of vnobedience & vnbuxomnesse.

[margin: Thus they are coueitous. St. Francis says that a friar should not preach until he is examined and approved by the minister general.]

10 Also Seint Fraunceis in his testament hoteþ & seiþ in þis manere: 'Ich hote alle freres heiȝliche by⁵ obedience where þei euer be, þat þei be nouȝt hardy to axe eny lettre in þe court of Rome by hem-silf, noþer by mene persone, noþer for chirche, noþer for eny place, noþer for hope of preching, noþer for
15 persecucioun of heres'; þis is I-seide þere. & freres haueþ y-do þe contrarie in her owne persone & y-procured þese⁶ priuyleges, ⁷& also by lettres. For in þe priuyleges⁷ hit is conteyned in þis maner, we beþ y-bowed to ȝoure prayers; & so it semeþ þat þis procuryng infecteþ þe procuratours wiþ þe synne of vnobedi-
20 ence & vnbuxomnesse; but on caas here þei wole seye as it is seide in þe decretal⁸ of þe ferþe pope Nichol, Exiit, þat þe nynþe⁹ pope Gregorie declared, þat freres beþ nouȝt y-holde to þe heste of Seynt Fraunceis þat is conteyned in þat testament. And me answereþ hem þat pope Nichol seiþ nouȝt þat þe nynþe⁹
25 pope Gregorie declared so, but he seiþ as me seiþe; & so hit semeþ þat freres had no declaracioun per vppon. For it is seme- lich þat¹⁰ ȝif þei hadde eny lettre þei wolde haue schewed hit to- fore pope Nichol, & þanne it semeþ þat þei wolde nouȝt saye as me seiþ, but as me haueþ y-seye conteyned in his lettres. Also
30 be hit þat pope Gregorie so declared, ȝet his entent was noon oþer þan his resouns concludiþ. Pope Nichol in þe same decretal Exiit, spekiþ of þe nynþe⁹ pope Gregorie & seiþ in þis maner: He, as me seiþ, syȝ¹¹ þe peryl of soules & difficulte þat þei myȝt falle ynne þerby, & meuede þe doute out of her hertes,

[margin: Friars should not ask letters in the court of Rome by themselves. They have done so. The ninth Pope Gregory's declaration in regard to St. Francis's rule. This has been misinterpreted. Pope Nichol's interpretation of Pope Gregory's decretal.]

¹ om. C Ch.
² meny Ch.
³⁻³ and graunt of hym S.
⁴ om. S.
⁵ be C.
⁶ þe C.
⁷⁻⁷ om. C.
⁸ decretales A C.
⁹ nyþe Ch S.
¹⁰ om. S.
¹¹ sei A C.

& seide þat freres beþ nouȝt y-holde to kepe þat heeste þat may nouȝt oblege wiþ-out assent of freres, & namelich wiþ-oute assent of mynystres, for hit touchiþ alle freres; & hit oblegide[1] his successour in noon[2] maner wise, for of twey peres noþer haþ power & heeste ouer oþer. Aȝenes þis present article we beþ nouȝt avised eny þinge to renewe; þis is y-write þere. Þerfore pope Gregorie seiþ: 'ȝif he ouȝt dide in þat he made nouȝt a decre oþer[3] a[4] declaracioun, þat freres were nouȝt y-bounde to þat heeste of Seint Fraunceys to vnderstonde in þat þat hit was his heeste; for his resouns preueþ nouȝt elles, þat þei were[5] alle y-cleped þat hadde to doyng þerwiþ. For of twey peres neiþer[6] haþ power & heeste ouer oþer'. By[7] þis declaracioun hit semeþ þat hit may stonde þat freres be neuerþelasse y-holde[8] and holde[8] þat testament, ȝif Fraunceys bitoke hem þat by[9] auctorite of God; for hit neded nouȝt to clepe þe mynystres noþer Fraunceys successours to examyne Goddes* heeste. So þat nouȝtwiþstondinge þese[10] resouns freres were þo y-holde,[11] & ȝet be[11] to kepe & holde þat testament by auctorite & heeste of God, by Fraunceys y-schewide to[12] freres. And þat it was so, hit semeþ by þe same testament[13] atte ende[13], þer it is seide in þis maner: 'And seye nouȝt freres þis is anoþer reule, for hit is[14] mynde and warnyng & chargyng & my testament, þat ich litel & symple frere Fraunceys make to ȝow my[15] blessed freres. Þerfore to kepe & holde þe better & more holiliche þe rule, þat we haueþ byhote to oure Lord, þe mynystre general & oþer mynistres & custodes, be þei y-holde by[16] obedience in þese noþinge to putt to, noþer wiþ-drawe'. Also haue þei þis wiþ hem y-write riȝt fast by þe reule & yn euereche chapitre, þat þei makeþ whanne þei rediþ þe reule: 'Rede þei þese wordes to alle my freres lered & lewed, ich hote by obedience þat þei sette no glose in þe reule noþer seye þese wordes so þei wolde mene & vnderstonde, but as oure Lord ȝaf me to saye & write

---

[1] oblege A C.
[2] no S.
[3] oþer of C.
[4] om. C S.
[5] were noȝt S.
[6] noþer A C Ch S.
[7] why A C Ch : wiþ S.
[8-8] om. C : to holde S.
[9] be C.
[10] om. C.
[11-11] om. C.
[12] to þe S.
[13-13] at þe A C S : attenende Ch.
[14] is in C.
[15] myn Ch.
[16] be C.

þe reule purelich[1] & sympeliche; & þese wordes vnderstonde ȝe wiþ-oute glose & kepe ȝe[2] & holde ȝe hem with holy entent[3] anone to þe ende'; þis is y-write þere.

 Hereby hit semeþ þat freres mowe chese oon of[4] tweyne,
5 oþer saye þat þe founder of here ordre Fraunceys in his testament [5]made a lesyng & is y-dampned, oþer soþ seide þat his testament[5] is nouȝt anoþer reule, but mencioun & mynde[6] of þe raþer rule þat was hem y-ȝeue. And so as þei beþ y-holde to kepe & holde þe reule, so þei beþ y-holde to kepe & holde
10 þat testament. Also Frauceys seide þat he made this testament to his blessed freres, for þei schuld þe better & þe more holilich kepe & holde þe[7] reule þat þei hadden bi-hote to God. Þanne oþer he made anoþer lesyng, & þei schul efte seye, þat he is dampned, oþer by kepyng & holdyng of his testament þei
15 schuld þe better & þe more holyliche kepe & holde þe reule; & so wiþ-out kepyng & holdyng of þis testament þei schulde kepe & holde[8] here þe lasse holilich, þei procured declaracioun for þe contrarie &[9] biheelde bakward in þe wey of þe kingdom of god,[10] & wente bakward & were vnable to þe kingdom of god[10];
20 and so þei were infect wiþ þe synne of vnobedience & vnbuxomnesse. Also he hoteþ his freres by obedience þat þei schulde nouȝt put to noþer wiþdrawe þerof, & þat þei schulde alwey haue wiþ hem þat testament riȝt by her rule. Þanne oþer þei schal seye þat he heet & dide wrechchidlich in þe cause of[11] so grete
25 peryl & is y-dampned for þat synne, oþer þat he ȝaf hem þat heeste riȝtfulliche & holiliche. And þanne þei most schewe why þei byheelde bakward & made hem[12] self vnable to þe kyngdom of God, whanne þei put of & forsoke so grete holynesse.

 Also in þese wordes Frauceys seiþ þat oure Lord ȝaf hym,
30 purelich[13] & symplelich wiþ-out condicioun, þis reule & þese wordes to say and to write. Þanne oþer,[14] for a[15] grete lesyng[16] at his lyues ende, freres schal saye þat he is dampned oþer þat

Marginalia: St. Francis made the testament to better his blessed friars. But the friars procured another declaration contrary to St. Francis, and so they are infected with the sin of disobedience. St. Francis commanded by the Lord to give this rule.

---

[1] poreliche S.
[2] om. C.
[3] intent Ch.
[4] or C.
[5-5] om. C.
[6] muynde Ch.
[7] here A Ch S: hire C.
[8] om. A C.
[9] and þei A.
[10-10] om. C.
[11] and A C.
[12] hym C.
[13] poreliche S.
[14] om. A.
[15] om. A C Ch: so S.
[16] alesynge A C Ch.

he soþlich seide þat oure Lord ȝaf hit to hym, so for he schulde telle hit þe¹ freres, & so ²he tolde to his freres Goddes owne heeste. And so, þouȝ³ þei be² not y-holde to holde & kepe þat testament by-cause of Seynt Frаunceys heeste, ȝet þei beþ y-holde to kepe & holde hit, for hit is Goddes owne heeste, y- tolde hem & y-schewide by her owne founder Seynt⁴ Frаunceys.

It is God's command told to them by their founder St. Francis.

Fol. 15 a   Þanne freres mowe chese wheþer party hem * likeþ of tweyne. Y trowe þat þei wolleþ chese & saye þat he seide⁵ wiþ-out siche⁶ leesyng & synne. Þanne hit semeþ⁷ þat freres, in⁸ procuryng lettres of þe pope aȝenus þe heeste of God & of her owne reule, infecteþ hem-silf wiþ þe synne of vnobedience and vnbuxom-nesse.

Y speke þe more largelich in þis mater aȝenus frere menours,⁹ for þei biguɴne þe cause at Londoun & ȝaf occasioun to oþere freres of oþere ordres ; for þei disputeþ more þan oþere of þe¹⁰ parfitnesse of þe gospel & telliþ þat hit stondiþ in skilful¹¹ beggerye. So þat oon of þat ordre prechide on¹² Alle Halwen Day, as hit was reported to me, & discreuede foure degrees of pouert, & seide þat þe ferþe degre is of¹³ most parfiȝtnesse of þe gospel & is to haue no-þynge in þis worlde in propre noþer in comyn but begge wiþ Crist. & þat sawe sclaundriþ þe staat of ȝow & of vs alle þat beþ in lowere degre. Þerfore holy fader, here vppon as vppon¹⁴ oþer poyntes þat beþ seide toforhond, 'demeþ nouȝt by þe face but riȝtful dome ȝe deme'. Hit semeþ grete wonder & more verreilich to speke, hit semeþ nouȝt soþe þat a þousand ȝere¹⁵ & neiȝ two hundred, noon ordre was in Cristes chirche here in erþe, þe whiche chirch Joon¹⁶ þe¹⁷ apostle clepeþ Jerusalem toward þe ende of þe Apocalips¹⁵ : 'And y Joon¹⁶ syȝ þe holy cite þe newe Jerusalem come doun from heuene arayed as a spousesse y-socyed to hir spouese'; & noon ordre was in Cristes chirche þat helde þe parfitnesse of þe

Friars at London dispute of the perfection of the Gospel and tell that it stands in beggary. One of them preached a sermon in which he described four degrees of poverty.

St. John the apostle calls Christ's Church the holy city of the new Jerusalem, which came down to earth.

---

¹ to C.
²⁻² om. S.
³ þeyȝ Ch.
⁴ seyn Ch.
⁵ deyde S.
⁶ om. C.
⁷ syweþ C.
⁸ & C.
⁹ minors S.
¹⁰ om. C.
¹¹ wilful S.
¹² an Ch : in an S.
¹³ om. C.
¹⁴ þan Ch.
¹⁵ om. S.
¹⁶ ion S.
¹⁷ in C.

gospel, but Fraunceys þat was ȝitt a nouys fonde vp[1] þe first ordre; for holy chirche here[2] in erþe is cleped Jerusalem in seynt[3] Joones wordes, & seynt Joon seiþ þat hit comeþ doun from heuene. Þanne it is soþe þat holy chirche here in erþe,
5 þat come doun from holy chirche þat is in heuene, had parfitnesse of hir founder, þat is Crist, & was arayed as a spouses[4] to Crist, þat was & is hir spouse, & was nouȝt so vnsemelich þo, & so many ȝere þerafter wiþ-oute þe state of[5] grattest parfitnesse. Also who myȝt suffre abliche &[6] here þat Fraunceys,
10 þat was but[7] a nouys[8] in þe fey ordeyne þe wey of parfitnesse of mankynde,[9] better & more profitabliche, þan God þat is al good & al witty. & in þe first ordynaunce of man God ordeyned hym so þat anoon as man was made, God put hym in Paradys for he schuld worche & kepe Paradys; so hit is writen in þe
15 bygynnyng of Hooly Writ. Hit semeþ me þat þere God tauȝt þat bodilich werk, possessioun and plente of riches & vnmebles,[10] & warde & keping þerof for mannes vse, schuld be sett to-fore beggerie; for god sett man in Paradys for he schuld worche. And hereto acordeþ Hooly Writ in anoþer place & seiþ: 'Man is
20 y-bore to trauail & a foul to fliȝt'. Job 5º cº. For man schuld kepe Paradys as his owne & haue [11] þere plente of good [11], & catel, meble & vnmeble; but hereof y schal speke more largelich. Þanne hit semeþ þat freres infecteþ hem-silf wiþ þe synne of vnbuxumnesse in procuryng[12] of þese priuyleges.
25 [13] Also hit semeþ þat freres infecte hem-self wiþ þe synne of couetise in procuringe of þese prieleges[13]; first for þei procured nouȝt oþere priuyleges in helpe of oþere peryls of þe office of presthode, as to folly[14] children in help of curatours, & housle paryschons on [15] Ester day and anoynt seke men at her ende[16] day.
30 And þese dedes myȝt be as medeful as þe oþere; but þese þei lefte & procuride priuyleges, to þe whiche longeþ worldlich wynnyng & profit in oon maner wise oþer oþere. And so þei

<small>Therefore the holy church that came down from heaven must be perfect.

It was ordained by God, not by St. Francis.

God taught that man should work.

Holy Writ teaches that man should work. Job 5:7.

They left the work of the church and procured priviledges which</small>

---

[1] vppon A C: ap Ch: vp S.
[2] here here C.
[3] seyn Ch.
[4] spouse A C Ch S.
[5] of þe S.
[6] om. S.
[7] hote A Ch: hoote C.
[8] noon A: non C.
[9] mankynge C: mankunde Cb.
[10] vnmeble A C Ch S.
[11]–[11] þerof good & plente C.
[12] procryng Ch.
[13]–[13] MS. omits. From A.
[14] cristene AC: volly Ch: fully S.
[15] and A.
[16] ending C.

beþ made more wondrefull þan eny chapmen oþer craftes men, for to gete profit * & wynnyng wiþ her professioun þat þei feyneþ to holde in beggerie. Y trowe nouȝt þat siþþe þe world was first made, was an esyere wey, more slyȝ & wyly to gadre riches, þan by þe forseide priuyleges wiþ þe obligacioun of beg- 5 gerie soþlich oþer y-feyned[1]. Also nouȝtwiþstondinge þat freres hadde fre[2] power to fonge dede bodyes to sepulture in her place, ȝett myȝt þe comyn riȝt & lawe abide in þe persoon so þat alle þe offrynges & riȝtes of sepulture schuld be dewe[3] to parische chirches & to[4] curatours þerof. Þanne for freres haueþ procured 10 þat oon wiþ þat oþer hit is clerelich y-knowe þat coueitise was cause of þat procuryng. *Primo posteriorum*, hit is Aristotels reule for to fynde redelich what is þe principal cause of[5] entent & of desire, and seiþ þat ȝif þat cause is had þe entent & desire is[6] had, and[7] ȝif[8] þat cause faileþ[9] þe entent and desire faileþ[9]. 15 Þis reule preueþ þat worldliche profit & wynnyng was chief cause in procuryng of þese priuyleges, for þerwiþout was nouȝt þat procuryng, & þei procurede oonlich þe priuyleges to þe whiche longeþ sich profiȝt & wynnyng. Hereof hit[10] is an open token þat þei rauyschiþ no[11] pore dede[12] mennes[13] bodyes for to 20 burie as Thobie dide; but þei smelleþ her mete & witeþ where hit is & feccheþ hit fyve hundrid myle ouer þe see as vulturs[14] doþ, as þe comentor Aueroys seiþ, 2º *de anima*, cº *de odore*, as ich haue in mynde. Þis token schewiþ cleere y-nowȝ þat freres procuride þis pryuylege of sepulture wiþ þe offrynges þat longeþ 25 þerto, principalich for fode & nouȝt for to vse medeful dedes of mercy.

Also of þe priuylege of heryng of schriftes indistinctlich of alle men,[15] hit semeþ[15] a grete euydence, for me may not skilfulliche suppose oþer wise, for oþere holy men hereþ nouȝt 30 schriftes in þat wise. Hit is y-nowȝ to euerech man to knowe his owne synne þouȝ he lerne nouȝt of oþere men[16] synnes. Þer-

---

[1] in feyned C.
[2] þe C.
[3] dede C: þewe Ch S.
[4] to þe A Ch S.
[5] of þe S.
[6] *om.* C.
[7] and I ȝeue C.
[8] *om.* C.
[9] falleþ C.
[10] *om.* C.
[11] noon A C.
[12] *om.* A.
[13] men A C Ch S.
[14] vowtreres C.
[15–15] *repeated* A.
[16] menis A C.

fore noþer white monkes, ne blak, noþer chanouns reuler, noþer oþer hooly men desireþ sich an office. And wiþ-out drede ȝif sich procuryng cume of deuocioun, hit schuld be somtyme y-knowe in oþere hooly men & nouȝt onlich in hooly freres. Þanne it may be skilfullich concluded þat coueitise enfecteþ þe soule of þe procuratour as cheef cause in siche a [1] procuryng. *Covetousness and not devotion impells friars to obtain the privilege of hearing shrifts.*

Also Seynt Frraunceys in his rule hoteþ in þis maner: 'Ich hote heiȝlich alle freres þat þei haue noon [2] suspect company as counseil of wymmen; also þat þei come nouȝt in Abbayes of monchons [3] out-take þilke freres þat haue special leue of þe court of Rome; also þat þei be nouȝt [4] gossippes [5] to men noþer to wymmen, leste sclaundre arise by occasioun þerof among freres'. And freres procureþ þe contrarie for to here þe priuyeste counseile of wymmen, of queenes, & of alle oþere, & [6] leggeþ hed to hed. Wiþ grete obedience þei folewiþ Seynt Job þat seide: 'Ich haue made couenaunt wiþ myn eiȝen þat y wolde [7] þenke of a mayde'. And so now by sich company þei disputeþ wiþ ladyes in chambre; þerfore in al þe worlde wide sclaunder springeþ of freres, þe wiche sclaundre y wole nouȝt reherse at þis tyme. Of many hit semeþ openlich þat þei infecteþ hem-silf wiþ þe synne of vnobediens & vnbuxumnesse by þe mys-vse of siche priuyleges, & of her owne reule by occasioun of siche priuyleges. *Further rules of St. Francis. Friars commit sin with women. This slander arises in connexion with friars.*

And þat þe procuryng of þese priuyleges infecteþ þe soules of þe procuratours wiþ þe synne of pruyde, y preue hit first. For in þe decretal *Exiui de paradiso, in Cle. de Verborum Significatione,* hit is seide þat Seynt Frraunceys wolde founde his ordre in þe heiȝeste pouert and * mekenesse. And procuryng of heiȝ state [8] of worschip of holy chirche inpugneþ mekenesse, and haþ by couetise, pride, & synne, longinge þerto. Þanne þe procuryng of þese priuyleges infecteþ þe soules of þe procuratours wiþ þe synne of pride [9]; & þat procuryng of heiȝ state of [10] worschip of holy [11] chirche [12] inpugneþ mekenesse, & haþ by *The sin of pride comes from this procuring. Pride instead of meekness. Fol. 16 a*

---

1 *om.* C.
2 no S.
3 mynchouns A C S.
4 none C.
5 gossibbes A C : godsybbes Ch S.
6 þat C.
7 wolde noȝt S.
8 estate C.
9 prute Ch : pruyte S.
10 & C.
11 hiȝ S.
12 statt S.

74 *Richard FitzRalph's Sermon: 'Defensio Curatorum'*

<small>This is shown in our Lord's answer to the sons of Zebedee.</small>

couetise & pride¹ longinge þerto, hit is preued by þe answere þat oure Lord ȝaf to ȝebedeus sones, & seide: 'Ȝe witeþ nouȝt what ȝe axeþ.' Þei axide by her moder þat þe oon of hem schulde sitte in² his riȝt side & þe oþer in his lifte³ side in his Kyngdom. Þere-vppon, *opere imperfecto*, Joon wiþ þe gilden moupe seiþ: 'Heelful errour þat vndide þe errour of al þe worlde. Ȝif þe apostles hadde nouȝt y-erred how myȝt we knowe, þat nouȝt al þing þat semeþ is good? But now we knoweþ for somwhat is beste & most good to þe primate of worschip. & anoon þerafter for⁴ þe desyre of primate comeþ of pryde of herte; for he⁵ þat is meke of herte desireþ neuer to seme heiȝ aboue oþere. And ynner-more he seiþ to desire seculer primate þouȝ it be noȝt riȝtful⁶ resone; ȝet þere is somme cause þouȝt it be nouȝt riȝtful⁶, ȝet it is profitable. But to⁷ desire primate of⁸ holy chirche, hit is nouȝt resoun, noþer cause, noþer riȝtful, noþer profitable'. Þis is writen þere, & he telleþ þere many siche sawes by þe whiche he wole preue þat neuer wiþ-oute couetise is desired primate of holy chirche.

<small>John with the golden mouth says:</small>

<small>The desire of supremacy comes of pride of heart.</small>

<small>The man who desires supremacy in holy church is covetous.</small>

Þis is confermed in anoþer maner; for þe apostle seiþ: 'How schul þei⁹ preche but ȝif¹⁰ þei be y-sent?' as hit is y-write, How feir beþ þe feet of hem þat precheþ pees & of hem þat precheþ good!' ad Romanos 10ᶜ c⁰. & by noþinge þat iche¹⁰ haue ȝett y-seye þei¹¹ beþ nouȝt y-sent of God to þat office. Þanne it semeþ þat by her owne presumpcioun þei stieþ vp to þat office. Þan war hem þat þei come nouȝt yn by anoþer wey þan by Crist, þat is þe dore. For þanne Crist demeþ hem robbers & þeeues¹², as Johannis 10º cº: 'For soþe y telle hit ȝow, he þat comeþ nouȝt yn by þe dore into þe folde of scheep but styeþ up by anoþer weye, he is a robbere and a þeef'; & comynlich Crist clepeþ hym-silf þe dore. And it semeþ þat þei beþ of þilke prophetes oþer siche maner prophetes as þe prophet spekiþ of, Jeremie 22º: 'Ich sent nouȝt þe¹³ prophetes & þei runne¹⁴;

<small>Romans 10:15.</small>

<small>The desire for office. Friars are thieves and robbers. John 10:1.</small>

<small>The proper method of calling to preach, not like the prophets, see Jeremiah 23:21;</small>

---

¹ pruyte synne S.
² on A C.
³ left A.
⁴ *om.* C.
⁵ *om.* S.
⁶⁻⁶ *om.* A.
⁷ *om.* C.
⁸ noȝt riȝtful S, *and crossed out between* primate *and* of.
⁹ *om.* Ch.
¹⁰ *om.* S.   ¹¹ *om.* C.
¹² þueues Ch.
¹³ *om.* C.
¹⁴ rounde A Ch : rownede C.

y spake nouȝt to hem & þei propheciede '; & anoon¹ hit folewiþ:
' Lo! ich speke² to þe prophetes, quoþ³ oure Lord, þat steleþ⁴ also 23:30.
my wordes euereche of his neiȝbore'. Ȝif þei beþ nouȝt sende of
Crist þei steleþ þe wordes of⁵ curatours & of her souereynes, þe
5 whiche & noon oþere haueþ þe office of prechyng, by þe comyn
lawe, as it is seide.

Also þat þe holdynge of þese priuyleges infecteþ þe holders,
hit is preued. For hit is nouȝt y-hote to freres noþer hit longeþ
to her professioun noþer to her reule forto· vse þe office of
10 prechyng⁶. Þanne it semeþ þat þei vseþ wilfullich to preche *Friars sin deadly in*
openlich among þe peple oþer to here schriftes, & þei wolleþ *taking over the office for*
fonge siche an offyce; þanne it semeþ þat þei synneþ dedlich. *preaching and hearing*
First, for þei knoweþ oþer schuld knowe þat þese priuyleges *shrifts.*
were procured by mene of þe dedliche synnes þat beþ rehersed
15 toforhond for þe vse of þese pryuyleges, & þei vseþ⁷ hem also.
Þanne þei assenteþ & alowiþ þe procuryng⁸, as ȝif a man eteþ
of robberie & of þefþe⁹ þat is y-gete for his vse in his etynge,
he aloweþ þe robberie & þeefþe⁹. And he þat haþ a benefice *A man who has a bene-*
to his profit y-procured by symonye, & comyneþ¹⁰ wiþ þe pro- *fice to his profit*
20 curatour in þe synne of symonie & aloweþ þat doyng, he is *is under the Apostles'*
vnder þe apostels decre, ad Romanos 3º cº: ' Þei¹¹ þat doþ siche *decree,*
dedes beþ* worþi þe deþ. & nouȝt onlich þei þat so dooþ, but Fol. 16 b
also þei þat assenteþ to hem þat doþ siche dedes', as y seide *Romans 1:32 and*
toforhand. And þei mowe nouȝt be excused by leue oþer graunt 2:3.
25 of þe pope as hit semeþ, for þe pope in his graunt setteþ nouȝt *They are not even*
þe obstaunce¹² þat he schuld semelich sett in þis maner. We *excused by the grant of*
graunteþ þis to freres nouȝtwiþstondinge her wicked conscience; *the pope.*
but it semeþ þat hit was his entent to relesche¹³ onlich þe
obstaunce of mannes lawes. As¹⁴ ȝif oon¹⁵ haþ do manslauȝter,¹⁶
30 oþer symonye, oþer haþ a wemme¹⁷ and defaute¹⁷ in his body þat
is vnknowe, þat makeþ hym¹⁸ vnable to a benefice of holy

¹ anon riȝt C.
² om. S.
³ seide S.
⁴ stele A C Ch S.
⁵ of þe S.
⁶ preching by þe comon lawe C.
⁷ vsen C.
⁸ wickede procurynge S.
⁹ þefte A C : þeufþe Ch.
¹⁰ communeþ C: comneþ Ch: comuneþ S.
¹¹ om. C.
¹² substance, sub *crossed out and* ob *in margin* A.
¹³ relese A C Ch S.
¹⁴ And C.
¹⁵ he C.
¹⁶ manslauȝt Ch S.
¹⁷⁻¹⁷ om. S.
¹⁸ hem Ch.

chirche, & haþ ¹graunt & leue¹ of þe pope to holde many benefices wiþ cure; ȝett her-fore may he² no benefice of holy chirche holde lawfulliche noþer riȝtfulliche; but þat lawe þat þe pope dispenseþ wiþ letteþ hym nouȝt, & ȝitt nouȝt wiþstondinge þat dispensacioun, he synneþ dedliche ȝif he holdiþ eny benefice of holy chirche. So it is in oure purpos as it semeþ me. For þouȝ³ þe pope dispense wiþ freres touchyng þe lawe, by þe whiche lawe siche riȝt & doyng is dewe⁴ to curatours, ȝett mowe nouȝt þe⁵ freres vse þese wiþ fulle riȝt & lawe; but þe lawe þat þe pope dispenseþ wiþ letteþ hem nouȝt, ⁶ & it semeþ þat þei mowe nouȝt⁶ vse þese priuyleges wiþ-out dedlich synnes.

Þanne it semeþ þat þei beþ alwey in dedlich synnes by alowance & holdyng of þese priuyleges, as⁷ þouȝ þei procurede hem oþer were assentinge to þe procuryng. And þese⁸ freres telliþ þat freres myȝt & mowe be repentaunt & do penaunce for þat synne, & so it may nouȝt be concluded þat somme ne⁹ beþ ȝett in synne. Þe contrarie schal be seide; for riȝt as in þefþe¹⁰ & stalþe¹¹ may no man be verrey repentaunt & do verrey penaunce, but he¹² quyte¹³ aȝen þat he haþ y-stole; noþer in oure purpos. But þei wole saye þat now touchyng þe curatours, þei haueþ riȝtfullich þese priuyleges & profites þat comeþ þerof, for hit is y-graunted¹⁴ þe¹⁵ same; & so to restore hem aȝen¹⁶ beþ þei nouȝt y-holde. Here þe contrarie schal be seide; for nouȝt-wiþstonding þe titel þat is y-gete by þe pope, þei beþ y-holde to make restitucioun in somme maner wise, for þe synne of þe allowyng & assenting¹⁷ þat is touched toforhond, in grauntyng¹⁷ of þe priuyleges, þat¹⁸ synne was nouȝt relesched¹⁹, noþer myȝt be relesched¹⁹ to þese²⁰ freres but þei were²¹ verrey repentaunt

---

¹⁻¹ leue and graunt A S.
² be Ch.
³ þei A C S: þeyz Ch.
⁴ þewe Ch S.
⁵ om. A C.
⁶⁻⁶ om. C.
⁷ And C.
⁸ þe C.
⁹ om. A C Ch S.
¹⁰ þefte A: þe fecte C: þeufþe Ch: þe fre S.
¹¹ steleþe A.
¹² be Ch: he be S.
¹³ aquyte C.
¹⁴ y-graunted hem by S.
¹⁵ pope þat haþ ful power to graunte hem þe S.
¹⁶ aȝe Ch S.
¹⁷⁻¹⁷ om. C.
¹⁸ þanne C.
¹⁹ relesed A C Ch S.
²⁰ þeus Ch.
²¹ om. C.

& contrite . & as longe tyme as þis synne leueþ & dwelliþ in freres hit semeþ þat þei mowe nouȝt be verrey repentaunt, but þei restore aȝen[1] to persoons as forþ as þei mowe, þat þei haueþ wiþdrawe . & so it semeþ þat while freres restoreþ nouȝt aȝen[1] {*margin:* The sin of friars in holding what is not theirs.}

5 þese[2] riȝtes, þei mowe nouȝt be verrey repentaunt[3], for þei beþ nouȝt dewe[4] to þe[5] freres by mannes lawe, þouȝ þei haue graunt of þe pope. Who is verrey repentaunt of wrongful [6]& euel getyng[6] of eny þinge, & is proude & glad of þe holdyng? No man as hit semeþ for to deme skilfullich. Þanne freres þat pre-
10 sumptuouslich holdeþ & kepeþ þese priuyleges beþ y-wrapped & y-snarled in þe forseide dedlich synnes. {*margin:* They are wrapped and snarled in deadly sins.}

Also þis licence & leue in a caas þat is y-liche, Seynt Bernard tretiþ in þe secunde pistle to Adam þe monk . Þe caas is þat þis monk after his professioun þat he made to dwelle þere
15 alwey to his lyues ende, as me seiþ, went with his abbot to anoþer abbay & dwellide þere by heeste & leue of his abbot, & þerto he axide[7] & hadde leue of þe pope; but Seynt Bernard repreueþ hym & fondeþ to preue by many * maner resone[8], þat wiþ-oute synne he myȝt nouȝt so do by heeste of his abbot {*margin:* Such a case is treated by St. Bernard, in Adam the monk.} {*margin:* Fol. 17 a}
20 noþer by leue of þe pope whos leue he schuld nouȝt axe. Þat forto preue, he takiþ oon principle þat Aristotle discreueþ & setteþ, 3º ethicorum, þat is þis : þat somme dedes beþ so good þat þei mowe nouȝt be euel y-do ; & somme beþ so euel[9] þat[10] þei mowe nouȝt be wel y-do[11], & somme beþ mene bitwene þese {*margin:* To prove this the principle of Aristotle is used. The three kinds of deeds.}
25 tweyne & mowe be wel y-do, & mowe also be euel y-do. Of þe first he setteþ ensaumple : charite, feiþ,[12] & hope. Of þe secunde : þeefþe, manslauȝt, incest, & siche maner dedes. Of þe þridde : redyng, fastyng, & somme maner dedes, þat may be do wel oþer euel as þe condiciouns beþ þat longeþ þerto.
30 Hit semeþ þat onlich in siche dedes obedience haþ place. He supposeþ þis & axeþ in what degre was þat dede, in þe[13] whiche dede he dide þe[14] abbotes heeste, & seiþ þat hit was in þe secunde

---

[1] aȝe Ch S.
[2] þeus Ch.
[3] repentaunt and contrite C.
[4] þewe Ch S.
[5] *om.* A C.
[6-6] *om.* C, *but* mater *is written.*
[7] axed leue C.
[8] resons A C.
[9] euel I doo C.
[10] þat þat A.
[11] *om.* C.
[12] fey A C Ch S.
[13] *om.* A.
[14] his A C Ch S.

degre of euel dedes þat myȝt nouȝt be wel y-do; & concludeþ
þerof as hym¹ semeþ þat it myȝt nouȝt be wel y-do. & þerfore
in þat dede he schulde nouȝt do his abbotes heste, but he schuld
wiþstonde him pleynliche in sich a dede þat is euel of hit-self,
& so he schuld holde his avowe & wiþstonde his abbot in sich a 5
maner dede. Also he settiþ for a reule, þat ȝif tweyne hoteþ
contrarie dedes, his heeste² schal be do þat is more worþi; &
God hoteþ þat avowe & obedience to hym schuld be y-holde.
Þanne ȝif his abbot þat is nouȝt so worþi as God, hoteþ to breke
þe avowe³, he schal be obedient to God & nouȝt to⁴ do his 10
abbotes heeste. Also Seynt Bernard aleiþ þat oure Lord seiþ.
Mathei 18º cº.: 'Who þat sclaundriþ oon of þese litel þat
trowiþ in me, hit is spedeful to him þat a grete stoon be hongide
aboute his nek, &⁵ be adreynt in þe depnesse of þe see. Wo þe
worlde wiþ sclaundre; hit is nedeful þat sclaundre come, but 15
wo þat man by whom sclaundre comeþ.' And herto Bernard
seiþ þat Adam þe monke in forsaking his abbay, nouȝt onlich
sclaundred oon of Cristes smalle children, but many & fale.
Hereby as him semeþ, he concludeþ⁶ þat þis⁷ monke⁶ fil into
þat wo þat oure Lord spake of, for he dide his abbotes heeste 20
in þat cause⁸. & wolde God þat freres wolde take hede in what
maner in al holy chirche þei sclaundreþ fewe & many, smale &
grete, by þe mysvse of þese priuyleges; & þerby þei myȝt
holilich conclude⁹ to-for God what þei beþ worþi. And þere
Seynt Bernard telleþ many oþere þingis. And touching þe pope 25
þat graunteþ leue, he seiþ: 'Who denyeþ þat hit is euel to
assente to euel? Þat wolde y nouȝt trowe þat þe pope dide but
he were begiled wiþ lesyng¹⁰ oþer ouercome wiþ gredynesse.'
Þis is Seynt Bernardes sentence. Þese freres take¹¹ þei hede,
wheþer¹² hit be nouȝt aȝenus þe licence & leue þat¹³ was I-pur- 30
chased for Adam þe monk; and conclude¹⁴ þei wiþ Seynt
Bernard þat þe synne of procuryng of leue wiþ¹⁵ vnbuxumnesse

---

¹ hit A C.
² hestes C.
³ vow C: avowȝ S.
⁴ om. A C Ch S.
⁵ & he A C Ch S.
⁶⁻⁶ om. C.
⁷ þe A.
⁸ case Ch : caas S.

⁹ miȝte conclude holyliche S.
¹⁰ lesynges S.
¹¹ takeþ C.
¹² where C S.
¹³ þat hey habbeþ y-purchased as
it is aȝenste þe sentence & leue þat S.
¹⁴ concluded C.
¹⁵ wiþ þe A C.

& breking of her owne reule, bryngeþ to hem euel quytyng¹, as Seint Bernard seiþ in þe same maner doyng of Adam þe monk. Also euerech frere whanne he prechiþ oþer hereþ schriftes myȝt leue hit, ȝif he wolde, wiþ-oute eny synne.

5 Þanne it semeþ þat he² takiþ þat office wilfullich aȝenus his owne professioun. And so as it is schewide toforhond þat in þe procuring of priuyleges, þe procuratours synnede dedlich aȝenus alle Goddes heestes³ þat þere⁴ beþ rehersed; so þis⁵ synneþ⁶ dedlich aȝenus þe same heestes of God, for he vseþ wilfulliche
10 þe leue þat is wickedlich y-procured, and is⁷ infect wiþ þe synne of iniurie & of wrong,* & vnobedience & vnbuxumnesse, of couetise, & of pride; for hit semeþ þat he vsiþ þe leue þat is y-procured for þe same cause, for þe whiche cause hit was y-procured, þat is for riches &⁸ worschip⁹. Þe þridde cause
15 is nouȝt of þe¹⁰ outrage of þis licence & leue, þouȝ¹¹ þere be þerof comyn diffamacioun among lewed & lered¹². *The deadly Fol. 17 b sins when Friars disobey God, and procure privileges for riches.*

Of þis mater of priuyleges & of þe mysvse þerof, & how þei beþ contrarie to þe professioun of freres touchyng þe twey conclusiouns þat ich haue y-schewide, þis is ynowȝ¹³, at þis tyme.
20 Many oþere þinges y schal telle herto ȝif hit nedeþ. And y drede nouȝt þouȝ¹⁴ ich wolde nomore þerof. Oþere men wole¹⁵ not leue touchyng al þis þat ich haue y-axed & y-schewide, & 'holy fader demeþ nouȝt by þe face, but riȝtful dome ȝe deeme'. By ȝoure owne holynesse, oþer by oþere þat beþ my lordes þe
25 cardynals, & hongyng þe ple suspendeþ in alle poyntes þe vse of þe priuyleges, þat touchiþ þe mater þat ich haue y-touched & declareþ¹⁶ þe forseide constitucioun, ȝif it semeþ riȝtful. *This is enough at this time touching the two conclusions.*

Þat oure Lord Ihesus in his conuersacioun of manhed, alwey was pore, nouȝt for he wolde oþer louede pouert by cause of hit
30 silf; but for touchyng þe¹⁷ pouert þat oure Lord suffred, myn¹⁸ aduersaries & ich beþ nouȝt contrarie, but touchyng þat y *The first conclusion: that Jesus did not love poverty because of itself.*

¹ coueytynge S.
² þei in H and crossed out.
³ heste C.
⁴ om. C.
⁵ þese A C Ch S.
⁶ synweþ Ch.
⁷ þis S.
⁸ & for C.
⁹ pouert C.
¹⁰ here S.
¹¹ þey S.
¹² lered & lewed C S.
¹³ I-now for me S.
¹⁴ þei A C : þeyȝ Ch S.
¹⁵ wolde C S.
¹⁶ declared C.
¹⁷ of A C.
¹⁸ mynd C : my S.

> No man loves wretchedness for itself.

seide also þat he loued noȝt pouert for hit-silf. Þis particle y preue first, for it is wrecchednesse to be pore & no man loueþ wrecchidnesse for hit-silf; þanne no man loueþ pouert for hit[1] silf. Also by Aristotles loore, *primo ethicorum*, noþinge is worþi to be loued for hit-silf, but what schuld be take & 5 y-loued, þouȝ[2] al profit were awey þat longeþ þerto. Sich is nouȝt pouert þouȝ[3] men deserue mede by þe suffraunce of pouert. Ȝit ȝif no profit schuld[4] come by suffraunce of pouert, pouert[5] schuld nouȝt be loued & y-holde of God, noþer of man, noþer of þe deuel of helle; þanne Crist loued neuer pouert for hit-silf 10

> The effect of sin is not worthy to be loved of itself. Poverty is the effect of sin. This is proved thus in the case of our forefathers.

aloon. Also noon effect of synne is worþi to be loued for hit-silf aloon þouȝ hit be loued in herte þat is infect[6]; but pouert is þe effect of synne; þanne pouert is nouȝt worþi to be loued for hit-silf aloon. Þat pouert is þe effect of synne, y preue hit, for ȝif oure forme fader & moder hadde neuer y-synned[7], schuld 15 neuer haue[8] be pore man of oure kynde. Also no priuacioun of good hauyng is worþi to be loued for hit-silf aloon. And by Aristotles reule *in topicis*[9], purpos is seide of purpos & þe con-

> No privation of good having is worthy to be loved of itself alone. Riches is good having and worthy to be loved of God for he is rich in all things. Poverty is evil.

trarie of þe contrarie. So þat ȝif þe hauyng is good þe priua-cioun is euel; and ȝif þe priuacioun is good þe hauyng is euel. 20 But riches is good hauyng & worþi to be loued[10] of God, for he is richest[11] of alle, & pouert is contrarie & ys priuacioun of riches[12]; þanne pouert is euel; þanne pouert is noȝt worþi to be loued for hit-silf aloon. For to abide longe about þe[13] preuyng[14] herof, hit semeþ me[13] to childlich a dede, for y trowe þat no 25 man seiþ þe contrarie but hit be for defaute[15] of philosophie oþer of logik.

> The second conclusion: Our Lord never begged wilfully.

Þe secunde conclucioun was þis: oure Lord Iheſus neuer beggide wilfullich. Þis conclucioun y preued first in þis maner. Ȝif he had wilfullich beggide he had y-do aȝenus Goddes heeste þat seiþ: 30 'Þou schalt nouȝt coueite þi[16] neiȝbores hous, noþer desire[17] his

---

[1] hym C.
[2] þei A C : þeiȝ Ch S.
[3] þeiȝ A Ch : þei C.
[4] schal C.
[5] om. C.
[6] in effecte C.
[7] y-synwed Ch.
[8] om. A C Ch S.
[9] thopicis A C Ch S.
[10] loved for it self C.
[11] richesse C : rychchest Ch.
[12] richesses S.
[13] om. C.
[14] reprefynge C.
[15] diffauȝte A : þe defaute C.
[16] þyn A C Ch.
[17] *after* desire *the words to* serde *are written and crossed out* C.

wif, noþer his seruaunt man, noþer womman, noþer¹ his oxe, noþer his asse, noþer any þyng þat is his.' Exodi 20º cº. But he þat beggeþ wilfulliche axeþ & he desireþ his neiȝbores þynge. Þanne he þat beggeþ wilfullich doþ aȝenus Goddes heeste, & no
5 man dar² telle þat Crist dide aȝenus Goddes heeste. Also ȝif Crist had y-beggide wilfullich, he had y-broke anoþer heeste of God þat seiþ: *'In al wise a nedy man & begger schal nouȝt be among ȝow.' Deuteronomii 19º cº. For he þat suffreþ oþere men to be vnarmed while he myȝt helpe hem of armure, brekiþ
10 þe kynges lawe³ þat hoteþ, þat in þe cite schuld be⁴ no man vnarmed; & nouȝt onliche he brekiþ þat lawe, but also he þat myȝt abide y-armed & þroweþ his armure into a depe ryuer. Also þis⁵ prest⁶ þat makiþ hym-silf wilfulliche vnmyȝty & vnable to offre ȝiftes & sacrifices for synnes, ⁷brekiþ þe lawe of
15 hooly chirche þat hoteþ þat he schuld offre ȝiftes & sacrifice⁸ for synnes⁷. I trowe þat no man dar⁹ say of oure Saueour þat he brake Goddes heeste. Þanne he neuer beggide wilfulliche noþer made hym silf wilful beggere, & no man may feyne þat the forseide heeste is cerymonial to be vsed among þe¹⁰ Jewes
20 aloone. For hit is verrey moral longynge to good þewes & harder¹¹ y-chargide¹² in þe newe¹³ þanne in þe olde lawe; for¹⁴ Luce xiº, oure Saueour hoteþ & seiþ: 'What is ouer þat nediþ ȝeue almes dede, & lo! alle þinges beþ clene.' Þere hit is y-hote, þat¹⁵ leueþ ouer þat nediþ schuld¹⁶ be y-ȝeue¹⁶; for no
25 begger schulde be amonge þe peple noþer eny man in al wise nedy schuld be amonge þe peple.

And who þat¹⁷ holdeþ nouȝt þis heeste is¹⁸ manassed with peyne withoute ende, Mathei 25º cº: 'In þis manere ich was an-hungred & ȝe ȝaf me nouȝt to ete,' & so forth: 'Goþ
30 acursed into þe fuyre wiþ-outen ende þat is ordeyned to þe deuel & to his angels.' And so it is cleere þat Cristen men

He would have discharged God's command, Exodus 20:17. He that begs wilfully desires his neighbour's Fol. 18 a things, which is against God's commands. Christ never disobeyed God's command. Another command of God. Deut. 15:11. The king's law. The law of holy Church in regard to gifts and sacrifices.

Christ's command as to alms. Luke 11:41. No beggar should be among the people, nor needy men.

Matt. 25:35, 41. Christian men are to

---

¹ om. C.
² þar Ch.
³ lawes C.
⁴ om. A C.
⁵ þes A Ch.
⁶ preostes C.
⁷⁻⁷ om. C.
⁸ sacrefices A S.
⁹ þar Ch.
¹⁰ om. A C.
¹¹ harder I-have C.
¹² y charged & y hote S.
¹³ newe lawe A : lawe newe C.
¹⁴ om. C.
¹⁵ þat þat S.
¹⁶⁻¹⁶ bey ȝeue A.
¹⁷ so C.
¹⁸ ys ys Ch.

G

suffer no beggars among them. Christ was subject to the Emperor's law, for he paid tribute. Matt. 17:24-7.

beþ harder y-bounde to suffre no beggers among hem, þan men vnder þe¹ olde lawe. Also Crist was suget to þe Emperours lawe, for he payed tribute to þe Emperour, Mathei 17º cº: 'Whanne² þei come³ to Cafarnaun⁴, þei þat feng þe tribute come to Petre & seide: "ʒoure mayster haþ nouʒt y-payed tribute": "no," quoþ⁵ Petre. And whanne þei come into þe⁶ hous Ihesus spake raþer þan he, & seide: "Symon what semeþ þee, of whom fongeþ kynges tribute, of her owne children oþer of alyens?" "Of alyens,⁷" quoþ⁵ Petre. "Þanne þe children beþ fre," quoþ Ihesus, "þat we sclaundre hem nouʒt. Go to þe see & þrowe in⁷ an hook, & þe first fisch þat comeþ vp take hym & open his mouþe, & þou schalt fynde a stater, a þinge þat weyeþ half⁸ an vnce; take þou þat & ʒeue hit hem for me & for þee".' Þis is y-write þere. Also he demed þat me schuld paye

He also commanded to pay tribute to the Emperor. Matt. 22:17-21.

tribute⁹ to þe Emperour, for men axide of hym¹⁰ & seyde: 'Ys hit lawful to ʒeue tribute to ¹¹þe emperour¹¹ oþer no?' & schewide a peny þat had þe printe of þe Emperours ymage & of his name; & Ihesus answerde hem & seide: 'Payeþ to þemperour what is his, & to God payeþ¹² what is his.' Mathei 22º cº. & it were nouʒt¹³ semeliche þat he wolde deme þat lawe to be holden as comyn lawe, ʒif he wolde nouʒt be vnder

Christ was subject to the law, as he was subject to his father Joseph. By the Emperor's law no beggar should be in the city. If Christ had begged wilfully he had broken the Fol. 18 b law of his neighbour. This he never did.

þat lawe; þanne he wolde be suget to þat lawe as he was suget to Joseph þe carpenter. Myche more as it semeþ he wolde be suget to þe Emperours lawe, þat was lawe of kynde, by þe which lawe no myʒty beggers schulde dwelle in citees; miche more noon¹⁴ wilful beggers schulde dwelle¹⁵ in citees.

Also ʒif Crist had wilfullich y-begged, he had y-broke þe lawe of þe neiʒbore wiþ his beggyng; for he þat loueþ his neiʒbore verreilich as him-silf, greueþ him nouʒt vnskilfullich, as he wolde nouʒt þat¹⁶ his neiʒbore greued hym vnskilfullich *. And he þat axeþ of his neiʒbore vnskilfullich his neiʒbores goode wiþ-out nede, greueþ his neiʒbore vnskilfullich; þanne Crist

---

¹ ye C.
² om. C.
³ comen A C Ch.
⁴ Capharnaun A C Ch S.
⁵ quod C: seyde S.
⁶ om. Ch S.
⁷ om. C.
⁸ al A C: hal Ch.
⁹ om. C.
¹⁰ hem C.
¹¹⁻¹¹ þamperour S.
¹² om. A C S.
¹³ nouþe C.
¹⁴ no A C S.
¹⁵ om. Ch.
¹⁶ om. C.

dide so neuer. Also Holy Writ seiþ þat þe pore schal be
hated of his neiȝbore. Prouerbiorum 14º cº; miche more a
begger schal be hated of his neiȝbore. Þanne ȝif Crist had
wilfullich ¹ y-begged, he had made wilfullich ¹ him-silf y-hated ²
5 of his neiȝbores; þat semeþ nouȝt skilful but ȝif þere were
anoþer skilful cause.

Also ȝif Crist had wilfullich y-begged, he had y-sclaundred ³
& diffamed ⁴ his owne gospel, þat he confermed by myraclis;
for hit semeþ þat þei þat herde þis ⁵ loore & syȝ ⁶ his myracles,
10 myȝte skilfullich seye þat þei were iapes & wicchecrafte raþer þan
verrey myraclis, for skilfullich euereche man schal raþer help
hym-silf þan anoþer. Þanne how schuld þis ⁷ feede foure
þousand men by myracle & may nouȝt fynde hym silf mete ⁸,
as somtyme whan he heng on þe cros þei scornede hym & seide:
15 'Oþere men he haþ saued, hym-silf he may nouȝt saue. ȝif he
is kyng of Israel, come he now doun of þe cros & we trowiþ
hym.' Mathei 29º cº. Al o ȝif Crist had wilfullich y-begged he
hadde y-broke his owne lawe, þat echeþ ⁹ þe lawe & þe prophetes.
'Al þat ȝe wolleþ ¹⁰ þat men do to you do ȝe to hem. Þis is þe
20 lawe and þe prophetes.' Mathei 6º cº. & no man wolde þat
oþere men greuede hym beggyng of hym wilfullich wiþout nede;
but so doþ euerech begger þat beggeþ wilfullich wiþ-out nede.
Also prima ad Thimotheum 6º cº, Paul þe apostle dampneþ her
trowyng & her opinioun þat trowiþ þat beggerie & gaderyng
25 is holy myldnesse; & al þat Poul dampneþ Crist dampneþ by
Poul, þat feng his gospel by reuelacioun of Crist, as Poul seiþ
hym-silf, ad Gal. pº cº. Þanne ȝif Crist beggide wilfullich he
dide in his owne persone þat he dampned by Poul, & so he was
contrarie to hym-silf; but it is nouȝt lawful so forto sigge.
30 Þanne Crist neuer ¹¹ beggide ¹² wilfullich. ¹³ Also ȝif Crist
beggide wilfullich ¹³ he made a lesyng in dede; for as he þat
spekiþ aȝenus þe soþe þat he knowiþ makeþ a lesyng ¹⁴ in dede;

The poor shall be hated of his neighbour. Proverbs 14:20.

If Christ begged wilfully he then slandered his own Gospel, that he confirmed by miracles. This is shown in feeding of the five thousand. Also in his death on the cross: Matt. 27:42.

Matt. 7:12.

Paul condemns begging. 1 Tim. 6:10, 11. Christ condemns the same thing through Paul. Gal. 1:1. Then Christ was contrary to himself, which is not lawful to say.

---

¹⁻¹ om. C.
² wilfulliche Ihated A C Ch S.
³ desclaunderd S.
⁴ Ifamed C.
⁵ hys Ch.
⁶ sey A : sye Ch : siȝe S.
⁷ þes Ch S.
⁸ a melis mete C.
⁹ he clepeþ S.
¹⁰ wole C.
¹¹ om. S.
¹² beggide neuer S.
¹³⁻¹³ om. C.
¹⁴ om. C : in speche so he þat doþ aȝenste þe soþe he knoweþ, makeþ a lesynge S.

[1] but he þat beggeþ wilfullich wiþ-out nede & seiþ þat he is a begger & neody he [2] makiþ a lesyng in [3] dede [1] ; þanne ȝif Crist beggide wilfullich he made a lesyng in dede, but God hit [4] forbede.

Also ȝif Crist beggide wilfullich he was a verrey ypocryte, semyng a begger, & was no [5] verrey begger, for Crist was neuer a verrey begger, for no man þat may haue y-nowȝ at his [6] wille, is a verrey begger, þouȝ [7] he begge. But he is a verrey faytour, & he þat beggeþ wilfullich may haue y-nowȝ at hys [6] wille; for elles he beggeþ nouȝt wilfullich, but he is dryue to [8] by nede, and Crist was neuer ypocrite. Þanne Crist beggide neuer wilfullich, noþer as a faytour. Also ȝif Crist beggide wilfullich, why wolde Petre þe apostle blame & repreue þe moder of his owne disciple Seynt Clement, for he found hir among beggers, & wende þat heo [9] had be strong y-nowȝ to worche with hir hondes, as hit is y-write in Seynt Clementes lif? & Petre folewide Crist in þat doyng. Þanne þei þat seyn [10] þat Crist beggide, moste assoyle þis questioun, but it semeþ þat þei mowe nouȝt; þanne Crist neuer beggide wilfullich.

Also ȝif Crist was a wilful begger, Clement [11] þat was [11] Peteres successour erred gretelich, for he trauailed wiþ al his myȝt for no * beggerie schuld be among hem þat were turned to þe feiþ of holy chirche, & is specialiche y-preysed of holy chirche for þat dede, þouȝ þese oþer seye þat beggerie schuld make hem haue þe more perfeccioun. Also ȝif Crist beggide wilfullich & ȝif beggerie perteyneþ to parfitnesse [12] of lif [12], why bade [13] Clement be obedient & buxum to þe lore [14] & ensaumples of þe apostlis, & among þe apostles & disciples was no man nedy? Þei [15] þat telliþ þat Crist so beggide, most assoile þis [16] questioun; but hit

---

[1-1] om. A.
[2] & C Ch : om. S.
[3] in speche, so he þat beggeþ wilfulliche wiþoute ony nede seiþ indede þat a is a beggere & nedy & makeþ a lesynge S.
[4] om. C S.
[5] non C.
[6] is S.
[7] þouȝ Ch : þey S.
[8] þerto C.
[9] sche A C : he Ch : hue S.
[10] seiþ A : seide C : syggeþ Ch : seggeþ S.
[11-11] om. S.
[12-12] om. C.
[13] het A C Ch S.
[14] lere S.
[15] om. C.
[16] þes Ch.

wole nouȝt be. & Clement so bade¹ in þe pistle þat was sent to James Bischop of Jerusalem. And þat pistle is sett in decrees 12º dilectissimis. Also ȝif Crist þat was & is heiȝeste preste beggide wilfulliche, holy chirche erred witynglich whanne hit² ordeyned, þat no man schuld fonge holy ordre wiþout suffisaunt titel of liflode, ȝif Crist hed of holy chirche tauȝte to begge by³ his owne ensaumple. Also ȝif Crist beggide wilfullich he sclaundred þe ordre of clergi, for holy lawes telliþ þat a bischop oþer a clerk þat beggeþ doþ dispite to þe ordre of clergie. Also ȝif Crist beggide wilfullich, he made⁴ hym-silf suspect of synne for he made for⁵ hym-silf a schame⁶; for wilful beggerie is nouȝt meedeful for⁷ oþer þing þan for schame; for⁸ þe begger haþ but schame⁹, for hit is a lowe¹⁰ dede and greuous by cause of kyndelich schame þat longeþ þerto. Also in a parfit studious man falleþ no schame as Aristotle seiþ in 4º Ethicorum in fine. Þanne in Crist was no schame, þanne Crist neuer¹¹ wilfullich beggide¹¹.

If Christ begged wilfully, then the Church erred when it ordained that no man should take holy orders without sufficient title of livelihood. He also slandered the order of clergy. He also made himself a shame.

Also ȝif Crist beggide wilfullich, wilful begginge perteyneþ to parfitnesse of lif. Þanne he ȝaf vncouenablich þe olde lawe & ordeyned þat prestes þat schulde be most parfite of lif, schulde haue possessiouns & teþingis, ȝif hit were more¹² parfit lif forto begge. Also al þe worlde vnder þe lawe of kynde erride, þat ordeynede prestes certeyn liflode of þe comyn bernes, as it is rad in þe ende of Genesis, ȝif it were more meedeful forto begge. Also ȝif Crist beggide wilfullich, beggery perteyneþ to þe parfit-nesse of þe gospel, & holy chirche erride witynglich whanne þei fenge dowyng of chirches, & so wiþ-drouȝ¹³ þe parfitnesse of pre-lates of holy chirche; and þat semeþ nouȝt lawful ¹⁴to me¹⁴ forto¹⁵ saye. But y not what þei wole seye, þat telleþ þe contrarie. Also ȝif beggerie & begginge perteyneþ so to þe parfitnesse of Cristen lif, as freres beggers telliþ, hit is grete wonder why noþer Crist, noþer þe Holy Gost wolde vs enforme¹⁶ þerof in

If Christ begged wilfully, then wilful begging pertains to perfection of life. Then the law of kind erred that ordained priests a certain livelihood. Wrong to endow certain churches. Holy Writ does not give us any information on this matter.

---

¹ hete A C Ch S.
² he A C: a Ch. S.
³ om. A C Ch.
⁴ made fore C.
⁵ om. S.
⁶ aschamed A C Ch S.
⁷ for of C.
⁸ þat S.
⁹ om. A C Ch S.
¹⁰ lewede A C S.
¹¹⁻¹¹ beggede wilfulliche S.
¹² om. C.
¹³ drow C S.
¹⁴⁻¹⁴ om. C.
¹⁵ to C.
¹⁶ informe Ch.

somme place of Holy Writ. And hit may nou3t be skilfullich y-trowide; & y trowe þat from þe bygynnyng of Holy Writ to þe ende, may nou3t be y-founde oon notable worde, þat hit nys[1] seide to anoþer menyng. Also Crist bihett his disciplis & seide: 'Whanne þe spirit of soþnesse comeþ, he schal teche 3ou al soþ- nesse.' Johannis 16º[2] cº. Þanne oþer þe Hooly Goost for3ate his office, whanne he come to þe apostles a Witsonday, for he seide nou3t to þe apostlis of þis beggerie, for þerof is nou3t y-seen in her dedes; oþer þe[3] apostles hadde enuye to hem þat schulde come after hem, & wolde nou3t teche hem þe soþnesse þat þe Holy Gost had [4]y-tau3te hem. But no wise man wole saye þat þe Holy Gost had[4] for3ete his office, noþer þat þe apostles hadde sich enuye; þanne no sich begging noþer beggerie per- teyneþ to þe soþnesse þat þe apostles tau3te. Also what schal þei seye of Melchisedech þat was þe hei3est Goddes prest & kyng of Salem? Poul praiseþ[5] hym aboue Abraham, ad Hebreos, 7º cº. How was he so grete wiþ-out wilful begginge? Why was nou3t Crist a prest by anoþer * ordre & nou3t by þe ordre of Melchisedech? For Melchisedech beggide nou3t as Crist whan he 3if his ordre. Þei þat telliþ þat Crist beggide schulde assoile þese,[6] 3if þei couþe.[7] Also þe prophete seiþ in þe Sauter: 'Y sy3e neuer þe ri3tful man forsake noþer his childe begge & seche brede.' & Crist was most ri3tful; þanne it semeþ not skilful to bere hym an hond, þat he beggide & sou3t brede a3enus[8] þe prophetes worde. Also 3if Crist beggide wilfullich, why bade[9] he nou3t hys disciplis[10] begge? But he[11] bade[9] hem þe contrarie, whanne he sent hem for to preche, and bade[9] hem ete & drynke of þe mede of her trauail, & seide in þis maner: 'In what hous 3e comeþ, dwelliþ in þe same hous, & eteþ & drynkeþ siche as is þere; þe werk man is worþi his mede.' Luce 10º cº. Also 3if Crist beggide wilfullich, he wolde neuer putte trauail before[12] beggery to gete his liflode[13], [14]he wolde haue vsed noon

[1] is C.
[2] John 6º. A C.
[3] om. A C.
[4-4] om. C.
[5] preyseþ A C Ch S.
[6] þis A C.
[7] koude C.
[8] a3enst A C S.
[9] hete A C Ch S.
[10] disciples forto A C Ch S.
[11] om. C.
[12] tofore A C Ch S.
[13] for 3if he hadde þat beggerie tofore trauayle to gete his liflode S.
[14-14] om. C.

of þe craftes þat men vseþ to gete wiþ her liflode.[14] Hit semeþ
þat Crist gat his liflode somtyme wiþ trauail and wiþ his hond
werk[1]; for he was nouȝt y-cleped oonlich[2] a carpenters sone, but
also he was openlich y-cleped a carpenter. Marci 6º cº. And
5 for he was cleped a carpenter openlich among þe peple, hit
semeþ þat for his liflode he vsede somtyme carpenters crafte wiþ
Joseph þat was cleped his fader. For his conclusioun is now[3]
at þis tyme, til[4] þe aduersaries inpugne hit wiþ strenger[5]
resouns.

10 Þe þridde[6] was þis: Crist[7] tauȝt neuer[7] wilfullich to[8] begge.
Þis conclusioun is schewide in þis maner: Crist bigan to do &
to teche. Actibus pº. cº. Þanne ȝif Crist tauȝt to[9] begge &
beggide neuer hym-silf, as hit is preued toforhond, þanne he
was contrarie to hym-silf as hit semeþ in worde & in dede, ȝif
15 he tauȝt ouȝt þat he dide[10] nouȝt in dede[10]. Þat is nouȝt[11] probable. Also Crist beggide neuer wilfullich; þanne ȝif he tauȝt
to[9] begge wilfullich[12] he made hym-silf suspect of his loore as
hit is preued toforhond in þe preuying[13] of þe next conclusioun.
Also he had sclaundred his owne gospel, as hit is y-preued þere
20 [14] also; þanne he had y-tauȝt to[15] breke his owne riȝtful lawe[16] as
hit is preued þere[14] in þe þridde argument. Also ȝif he hadde
tauȝt to[9] begge, he had tauȝt to[17] do aȝenus neiȝ alle þe lawes &
resoun, þat beþ made for þe next conclusioun, þat preueþ boþe
þis conclusioun & þat conclusioun also. Also ȝif Crist tauȝte to[17]
25 begge wilfullich, Petre þat knewe[18] his loore dide vnwiselich,
whanne he aleyde þe medeful dedes & spake nouȝt of þis beggery
þat is so medeful, & hit were as þei telleþ, for Mathei 19º cº,
Petre spekiþ to Crist & seiþ: 'Lo we haue forsake alle þinges[19]
& folewiþ þee': & seiþ nouȝt we haueþ y-beggide wilfullich for

Christ gat his own livelihood with the work of his hands, for he was a carpenter, Mark 6:4, and so he used the carpenters' craft.

The third conclusion: Christ never taught to beg wilfully. Acts 1:1. It is not probable that Christ taught to beg, when he did not himself.

He would have slandered his own gospel, and would have taught to break his own law.

Peter's statement shows that Christ did

---

[1] handework Ch.
[2] oonlich ycleped A C Ch S.
[3] inow A C Ch S.
[4] forto A S: for C: vort Ch.
[5] certeyn A C.
[6] þridde conclusion S.
[7-7] neuere tauȝt S.
[8] om. A C Ch: forto S.
[9] om. A C Ch S.
[10-10] om. C.
[11] now C.
[12] om. S.
[13] prechynge C.
[14-14] om. A.
[15] om. C Ch S.
[16] lowe S.
[17] om. A Ch S.
[18] knoweþ C.
[19] þyng A C Ch S.

þee. & Petre seiþ nouȝt so. Hit semeþ þat þe condicioun of siche beggerie perteyneþ nouȝt to þe state of parfitnesse.

Þe ferþe conclusioun was þis: oure Lord Ihesus[1] tauȝte þat no man schuld wylfullich begge. For Crist tauȝt as hit is y-write, Luce 14º cº: 'Whanne þou makest a feest clepe þou þerto pore 5 men, halt & blynde, & þou schalt be blessed, for þei haueþ noȝt wherof þei mowe quyte hit [2] to þee [2].' Þanne pore men þat beþ[3] stalworþe[4] and stronge schulde nouȝt be cleped to þe feeste of beggers, for þei mowe quyte hit wiþ her trauail. Noþer riche feble men, noþer riche halt men, noþer riche blynde men schuld 10 be cleped to þe feeste of beggers, for þei mowe quyte hit wiþ her catel[5]. & for Crist rekeneþ nouȝt deef, noþer dombe[6], noþer lame þat beþ nouȝt halt among hem þat schuld be cleped to þe feeste of beggers, y see nouȝt þat siche men schulde be cleped to siche a feeste;* for[7] ȝif þei beþ noþer feble, ne[8] blynde, 15 ne halt, þei mowe go aboute[9] &[10] begge[11] from place to place, & so may nouȝt þe feble, blynde, & halt; but freres settiþ þis exposicioun among errours. Also[12] by his[13] sentence of dome & decree, Poul seiþ: 'Who þat wole nouȝt trauaile schal nouȝt ete'; & spekiþ of men þat haueþ no[14] liflode in oþerwise, 2. Thess. 3º 20 cº; & telleþ þere what peyne þei schulleþ[15] haue þat wole nouȝt be obedient to his wordes, and hoteþ in þis manner: 'ȝif eny man is þat wole nouȝt be obedient to oure Lord[16] by þis pistle, takeþ hede what he is & deleþ nouȝt wiþ hym þat he be aschamed & y-schent.' & it is no drede þat þe apostle wolde nouȝt hote 25 þat he þat wole nouȝt trauaile schuld haue so grete a peyne, but ȝif he dide a grete trespas in þat he wole[17] nouȝt trauail. & þere he spekiþ of hym[18] silf in þis maner: 'ȝe knoweþ ȝowre silf how ȝe most folewe[19] us; for we ete noon ydel brede þat we hadde of eny man, but we trauailede bisiliche & wrouȝt day & 30

---

[1] ihesus spak & A C.
[2-2] om. A.
[3] ben C.
[4] stalword Ch S.
[5] trauaille C.
[6] dome Ch.
[7] vor Ch.
[8] nor C.
[9] om. S.
[10] a S.
[11] begged S.
[12] also as S.
[13] om. S.
[14] none C.
[15] schal Ch S.
[16] word A C Ch S.
[17] wolde A C.
[18] hem C.
[19] knowe C.

nyȝt, for we wolde greue noon of ȝou alle. Nouȝt as þouȝ we hadde no power, but we wolde ȝeue ȝou ensaumple in vs silf how ¹ ȝe schulde folowe us. For whanne we were wiþ ȝou we warnede ȝou & seide þat he þat wole nouȝt worche schal nouȝt ete.'

5 Þere it semeþ cleer y-nowȝ þat he wolde argue siþþe ², þat he þat hadde power as verrey apostle to take liflode of hem þat he tauȝte goostliche, wolde nouȝt take hit of hem, but trauailed & wrouȝt bisilich day & nyȝt for his liflode, for he wolde greue noon of hem alle. Þanne mych more, þei þat haue noon sich 10 power schulde trauayle & worche for her liflode, for þei schulde nouȝt greue oþere men wiþ begginge. *Paul worked and did not beg, and yet he had great power as an apostle.*

And wold God þat þei þat puttiþ begging tofore trauail & werk, wolde take hede of Seynt Austyns book þat he made of þe werkes of monkes. Þere he tretiþ þis conclusioun neiȝ from þe 15 bygynnyng to þe ³ ende, & fondeþ to preue þat trauail schuld be put tofore contemplacioun. His resouns ich ouerpasse at þis tyme, but y schal brynge hem forþe anoþer tyme ȝif hit nediþ. *St. Austin's advice to those who put begging before work, which I pass over at this time.*

Also Holy Writ repreueþ & blameþ þe slowe ⁴ in þis maner: 'How longe slepest þou, þou slowe man? Þou schalt but awhile 20 þriste ⁵ þyne hondes to-gidres forto reste lest þi nede come to þee as a storme of whirlewynde & beggery as a man of armes.' Prouerbiorum 6º cº; & Prouerbiorum 20º cº: 'Þe slowe man wolde nouȝt erye a wynter for cold; þanne he schal begge a ⁶ somer & me schal nouȝt ȝeue hym.' & Holy Writ preyseþ 25 a strong womman þat takeþ þe spyndel wiþ hir fyngres. Prouerbiorum 26º cº. Herby it is y-preued þat me schuld nouȝt begge, & leue trauail & werk. *Holy Writ blameth the slow thus: Proverbs 6:9-11, and Proverbs 20:4. Holy Writ praises a strong woman. Proverbs 31:19.*

And Seynt Frounceys in his testament seiþ in þis maner: '& ich trauailed wiþ myn hondes, & ich wole heiȝlich þat alle 30 myn freres trauail in werkes þat longeþ to honeste, and þei þat kunneþ nouȝt schal lerne noȝt for coueitise of mede & of huyre, but for ensaumple of good werkes & dedes, & forto put awey sleuþe ⁷ & ydelnesse. & whanne me ȝeueþ hem nouȝt for her trauail, þan þei schul go to Goddes borde & axe almes from 35 dore to dore.' Þis is ⁸ y-write þere. And in his reule he seiþ *St. Francis in his testament says on this matter: He works with his hands and desires his friars to do the same.*

---

¹ om. C.
² seþþe A C S : suthe Ch.
³ om. S.
⁴ soule C : sclowe man S.
⁵ þruste A Ch S : þurste C.
⁶ on A C.
⁷ slewþe A Ch S : slouþe C.
⁸ om. C.

90   Richard FitzRalph's Sermon: 'Defensio Curatorum'

<small>In his rule he says: It is a great wonder, therefore, that friars go contrary to the advice of their founders.</small>
in þis maner: 'Freres þat haueþ of¹ þe ȝifte of² God grace of trauail þei schulleþ trauaile trulich & deuoutliche.' Þerfore hit is grete wonder wiþ what face freres dar³ vse wilful beggery⁴ tofore trauaile & do þe contrarie of her founders loore;

<small>Also man is born to travail. Job 5:7.</small>
& it is þe more wonder for man is y-bore to trauail, as hit is y-write. Job 9º cº. & begging is contrarie to þe lawe of þe firste ordynauns. Ȝif þat lawe were holde schulde no⁵ man begge. Also here-by hit semeþ þat Crist tauȝt þat no

Fol. 20 b
man schulde begge wilfullich; for in his owne persone* he

<small>Christ would rather use miracles than beg. He sent Peter to the sea to get his tribute from a fish's mouth.</small>
wolde raþer vse miraclis þan he wolde begge. For he sente Petre to þe see, for he schulde ⁶take þe stater þat⁷ he schuld⁶ fynde in þe fisches mouþe, & paye hit to hem þat gadride tribute for hym-silf & for Petre. & ȝet in þat caas so worschipful a man as he was miȝt lyȝtlich haue⁸ y-gete a stater ȝif he wolde haue⁸ beggide.

<small>Christ did not beg but told his disciples: Luke 10:7, other examples of Christ's doings rather than beg.</small>
Also oþere dedes preueþ þe same, & hit semeþ þat he wolde raþer vse Goddes lawe þat seiþ: 'Þe werkman is worþi his mede.' Luce 10º cº. & he⁹ seide to his disciples: 'Þe¹⁰ werk man is worþi his mete'; & het brynge hym þe asse þat he sate vppon; & het Ȝacheus come doun, & seide: 'Ȝacheus hyȝe þou fast & come doun for y mot dwelle in þyn hous to day.' & þere as he þat had power he comaundide & heet hyȝe faste & come doun. Also whanne he was in þe temple & byheld alle men aboute, whanne it was eue he went out of þe temple into Bethanye wiþ þe twelue, Marci XI cº, & wolde raþer vse þat riȝt þat¹¹ he wolde begge of any men. He had toforhond preched in Bethany as þouȝ he had noȝt vsed þat power, & wente to his frendes¹² & wolde þanne¹³ raþer schewe

<small>And so he taught us with his works that no man should beg without need.</small>
hym to hys frenes¹² þan he wolde begge of any men; & so he tauȝt vs wiþ his werkes þat we schuld of no man begge wiþout nede. Also he heet his disciples whanne he sent hem forto preche & seide: 'Goþ nouȝt from hous to hous.' Luce 10º cº.

<small>Christ told his disciples, Luke 10:7,</small>
But hit is þe¹⁴ comyn cours of¹⁵ beggers forto go from hous to hous. & in anoþer place Holy Writ forbediþ & seiþ: 'Be war

---

¹ om. A C.
² of þe in margin A : of þe C.
³ þerre Ch.
⁴ beggery oþer putte beggerye A C Ch S.
⁵ om. A C Ch S.
⁶⁻⁶ om. C.
⁷ þe S—a hole in parchment of S.

⁸⁻⁸ om. A C Ch S.
⁹ om. C : hey S.
¹⁰ þat þe C.
¹¹ þan A C Ch S.
¹²⁻¹² om. C.
¹³ þo A Ch S.
¹⁴ om. C.
¹⁵ for C.

þat þou be nouȝt y-herbored from hous to hous. Ecclesiastici 29⁰ c⁰. & in anoþer place Holy Writt repreueþ siche a begger in þis maner: 'Þe foot of a nice fool is liȝtlich in his neiȝbores hous.' Ecclesiastici 21⁰ c⁰. & Ecclesiastici 40⁰ c⁰: 'Sone
5 be þou¹ nouȝt nedy in þi lif tyme; hit is better be ded þan nedy.² A¹ man þat weyteþ anoþer mannes borde, his lif is nouȝt in þou t of liflode; he fedeþ his soule wiþ oþer men mete. A wys man & wel³ tauȝt schal kepe hym-silf in þe mouþe o a wise man & redy⁴; nede is dispised & fier⁵
10 schal brenne in his wombe.' Þis⁶ is y-write þere. Also for þe ȝong man schuld be parfit, Crist counsailed hym sille al þat he had & ȝeue hit pore⁷ men & come & sewe⁸ hym. Þere wiþ-out drede, sewyng⁹ schal be take in maner of lyuyng. And þe seconde conclusioun seiþ þat Crist neuer beggide wilfullich;
15 þanne Crist tauȝt þe ȝong man to sewe⁸ hym & be parfit wiþ out wilful begging; & so he tauȝte specialiche þat parfit men schulde nouȝt begge wilfullich. Herof hit¹⁰ may be skilfullich concluded þat oure Lord Ihesus tauȝt þat no man schulde begge wilfullich.
20 Þe fifþe conclusioun of þis mater of beggerie was þis: no man may redilich & holilych wilful beggerie vppon hym take euermore to holde. Þis conclusioun folewiþ pleynlich of þe oþere conclusiouns þat beþ y-preued toforhond; for Crist & his apostlis & disciplis &¹¹ holy chirche & Holy Writ dispreueþ &
25 repreueþ sich begging & beggery. Þanne¹² hit may nouȝt be take¹³ rediliche & wislich in þat maner, þouȝ hit myȝt be take¹³ in somme wise forto folowe God, as Mark for good entent kitt¹⁴ of his owne þombe, vnredilich & vnwiselich. Also he þat takeþ vppon hym beggerie, lediþ & bryngeþ hymsilf into temptacioun
30 aȝenus þe lore of þe pater noster, Mathei 6⁰ c⁰: 'Lord lede þou us nouȝt into temptacioun.' ¹⁵ Wiþ what conscience may a man praye God þat he lede hym nouȝt into temptacioun noþer suffre him be lad into temptacioun,¹⁵ while he lediþ hym-silf wilfullich

also Eccles. 29:24.
Holy Writ reproves beggars thus:
Eccles. 21:22,
also Eccles. 40:28-30.

Christ advises the young man who would be perfect.

Christ taught that perfect men should not beg wilfully.

The fifth conclusion.

This conclusion follows plainly from the preceding.

He opposes the teachings of the Paternoster Matt. 6:13.

---

¹ om. C.
² a nedy C.
³ awel C.
⁴ aredy C.
⁵ fuyre A C Ch S.
⁶ þat C.
⁷ to pore C.
⁸ sywe Ch.
⁹ sywyng Ch.
¹⁰ om. C.
¹¹ of A C: om. S.
¹² þat C.
¹³⁻¹³ om. C.
¹⁴ kut A C Ch S.
¹⁵⁻¹⁵ noþer suffre hym be lead into temptacioun C: wiþ what conscience may man praye hym be lad into temptacioun S.

Fol. 21 a into temptacioun? What is[1]* gretter occasioun of temptacioun
To take in hand such beggary is temptation according to Solomon. þan take on honde siche beggerie? For Salomon [2]prayeþ God openlich[2] &[3] seiþ: 'ȝeue þou me noþer beggerie ne[4] riches, but onlich ȝeue þou me what nediþ to my[5] liflode, lest ich be fulfild & tempte[6] to forsake & sigge who is oure Lord, oþer be dryue for defaute & nede to stele, & forswere myn[7] [8]owne
Default and need driveth a man to do amiss. Eccles. 27. Goddes[8] name.' Defaute & nede dryueþ a man liȝtlich to do amys. Þerfore, Ecclesiastici 27º cº, hit is y-write: 'For defaute & for[9] nede many men haueþ y-do amys.' He þat
He who takes on such beggary makes himself unfit for the priesthood. takeþ vppon hym sich beggerie, makeþ hym-silf vnable to þe office of prest & to ech[10] holy ordre. For by the lawe of holy chirche, no man may haue siche a state wiþout suffisaunt title of mete, & drynke, & cloþ.

Þanne hit is nouȝt redilich but vnwiselich y-do to take on
He breaks God's laws, which are: hond sich beggery. Also hit semeþ þat he þat takeþ vppon hym siche beggerie, byndeþ hym-silf to breke þe lawes of God, þat beþ rehersed & aleggide[11] for þe secunde conclusioun of Cristes beggerie. Þese lawes: 'Þou schalt noȝt coueite þi[12] neiȝbores hous, noþer desire his wif noþer his seruaunt man noþer womman, noþer his oxe noþer his asse noþer eny good þat is his. In al wise a nedy man & begger[13] schal nouȝt be amonge ȝou. Al þat ȝe woleþ þat men do[14] to ȝou do[15] ȝe[16] to hem.' And neiȝ alle[17] resouns þat beþ made for þe raþer concluciouns preueþ also þis conclucioun. Þerfore as[18] y seide in þe sermouns of þe whiche y made of mencioun in þe bygynnyng of þis pro- posicioun, y se nouȝt how þis opinioun of kepyng & holdyng of beggerie was brouȝt yn but hit were for defaute of kunnyng of Holy Writ; oþer me feyned þat hit schuld be like to Cristes maner of[19] lyuyng, forto gadre & haue þe more catel wiþ siche beggyng.

---

[1] is is C.
[2-2] om. A: prayeþ God, om. C.
[3] om. C.
[4] noþer C.
[5] me C.
[6] tempted A C Ch S.
[7] my A.
[8-8] goddis owne A.
[9] om. S.
[10] al A C Ch S.

[11] aleide A C S: alleyd Ch.
[12] þyn S.
[13] a begger C S.
[14] doþ C.
[15] doþ Ch S.
[16] ȝe þe same A C.
[17] al þe S.
[18] is C.
[19] om. A C Ch S.

Þe sixte conclusioun of þis mater was þis: hit is nouȝt of þe rule of¹ frere menours wilful beggyng to kepe & holde. Þis conclucioun may be preued by open feiþ & truþe, for Seynt Fraunceys in his testament setteþ trauail before² beggerie & 5 chargeþ so alle his freres. Also³ resouns þat beþ made in þe bygynnyng preueþ þis conclusioun, so þat þis rule be good & holy as hit is seide & preued in þe chapitre Exiit. *The sixth conclusion. Friars should not wilfully beg. St. Francis put work before begging. This conclusion is proved by the above.*

Þe seuenþe conclusioun in þis mater was þis: þe ferþe pope Alisaundres bulle þat dampneþ þe libel of maistres wiþ-seiþ 10 noon of þese forseide conclusiouns. Þat is schewide in þis maner: for þe two & twentiþe pope Joon in his constitucioun þat⁴ bygynneþ, *Quia quorundam*, seiþ openlich þat þe þridde pope Nichol wiþcleped þe⁵ bulle of þe ferþe pope Alisaundre touchyng alle þe articles þat his declaracioun conteyneþ. Þe 15 þridde pope Nichol declared how streyt schuld be þe pouert of frere menours. Also pope Nichol made declaracioun of þe trauail of freres & of her prechyng in a bischops diocesy þere freres beþ wiþseide. Þanne pope Nichol fondede⁶ & wiþcleped þat bulle of þe ferþe pope Alisaundre touchyng alle þe articles þat beþ 20 conteyned þerynne. & ich haue no mynde of eny þynge conteyned in þat bulle þat wiþ-seiþ eny of þese conclusiouns. *The seventh conclusion. 4th Pope Alexander's bull says: Pope says in his constitution. The third Pope Nicholas declared that the friars should be poor.*

Ich wolde saye myche more & argue aȝenus me-silf & assoile þe argumentes forto conferme þat ich haue seide; but ich haue y-trauaylled ȝoure holynesse y-nowȝ & þe reuerence of my lordes 25 þe Cardynals. Þerfore ich conclude & pray mekelich & deuoutlich as y prayed in þe first þat y touched: 'Demeþ nouȝt by þe face but riȝtful doome ȝe deme.'

Explicit.

¹ of þe A C.
² tofore A C S.
³ also þe S.
⁴ þat he C.
⁵ þat S.
⁶ vndede A C S.

PART III

METHODIUS : 'þe Bygynnyng of þe World and þe Ende of Worldes.'

Harl. 1900

Fol. 21 b (1)   In þe name of Crist here bygynneþ þe book of Methodii þe bischop of þe chirche of Paterenis, & martyr of Crist, which he chargide to translate of Hebrue & Greek speche into Latyn, þat is, of þe bygynnyng of þe world & þe rewmes bitwixe, of folkis & þe ende of worldes, which þe noble man Seynt Jerom in his werkis praysed.

The creatures of the heaven and the earth, Adam and Eve.

For why it is to wite to us, moost dere breþeren, how in þe bygynnyng, God made of nouȝt heuene & erþe; & by hym alle þingis beþ made, & how he made man, & helpe like to hym, & put hem togidre in Paradise. And cleped þe names of hem Adam & Eue, whiche afterward by disseyte of þe serpent bigyled, þei beþ cast out virgyns of Paradise. In þe XXX ȝere soþly

Add. 37049

Fol. 11 a   In nomine Christi incipit liber Methodii episcopi ecclesie Paterensis martiris Christi. This tretys is drawen oute of Latyn into Ynglysche, þe whilk a holy bischop & martyr drewe oute of Hebrew & Greeke into Latyn, & it tretys of þe begynyng of þe warld & of þe endyng, & also of þinges þat has fallen & sal falle.

It is to be knawen to vs, dere breþer, how þat God in þe begynyng made heuen & erthe, & by hym al þinges ar formed, & how he made man, & a helpe lyke vn-to hym & put þaim in Paradyse. And he cald þe names of þaim Adam & Eua, þe whilk afterwarde with þe serpent gylefulnes war disceyfed, & þai beyng vergyns castyn oute of Paradys. In þe thyrty ȝere, aftyr

Harl. 1900

after þat þei were cast out of Paradise, þei gendride Caym þe first geten, & his suster Calmanam. And afterward in þe XXXII ȝere þei gendride Abel, & his suster Delboran. In þe hundrid ȝere & þritty of þe lif of Adam, Caym slow his broþer Abel, & put hond vppon him. Soþly, in þe CCC ȝere & XXX of þe lyf of Adam, a sone is born to him Seth by name, to liknesse of hym a man geaunt & grete. Afterward þei gendride sones & douȝtres. Soþly in þe sixe hundred ȝere of þe lif of Adam, þe sones of Caym bygunne to mysuse þe wyues of her breþeren in many fornicaciouns.

Cain slew Abel.

Fornications and sins arise.

Þe eiȝte[1] hundrid ȝere soþly of þe life of Adam, fornicaciouns beþ ouermyche enlargide vppon erþe, & vnclennessis of þe sones of Caym. In þe IX^c ȝere soþly & XXX Adam is deed, & is buried in Ebron in þe first þousand of þe world. Þanne þe generaciouns of Seth beþ disioyned or departed from þe generacioun of Caym. And Seth toke his cuntrey aȝenus þe eest into an hil þat was next to Paradise. And Caym dwellide & his kynrede, where he had do þe cursed slauȝter of his broþer in

Adam dies. Seth settles East of Paradise, and Cain dwells in Inde.

Add. 37049

þai war castyn oute of Paradyse þai gat Caym þe fyrst son. And in þe hondrethe & thyrty ȝere of Adam, slewe Caym his broþer Abel & put his hande vpon hym. And in þe two hundreth & thyrty ȝere of þe lyfe of Adam was borne his son Seth, lyke vnto hym. And after þai gat doghtyrs & sonnes. In þe sex hundreth ȝere of þe lyfe of Adam began þe sonnes of Caym to myshuse þe wyfes of þair breþer in gret fornycaciouns of lychery.

And in þe eght hundreth ȝere of þe lyfe of Adam war spred abrode gretly fornicaciouns & vnclennes of þe childer of Caym. In þe neyne hundreth ȝere & thyrty, Adam dyed & beryd in Ebron, in þe fyrst þowsand ȝere of þe warld. Þan was þe generaciouns, þat is þe kynredyn of Seth, * dyuyded fro þe generacioun of Caym. And Seth toke his generacioun agayns þe este in to a mownte þat is next vnto Paradyse. And Chaym dwelt þer as he slewe his broþer Abel vnlefully, þat is to say in

Fol. 11 b

---

[1] v̇iij appears in left margin.

Harl. 1900

Ynde, in þe same place of Delicis[1] where raþer þilke Caym made a cite, to which he put a name Effrem. * & þis is þe first made before þe flode.

In þe fourtiþe ȝere, soþly in þe tyme of Iareth, þe first þousand of þe world passid. In[2] þe CCC & XL⁰ ȝere of þe[3] lif of Iareth, in þe secunde þousand of þe world, þere were men wickid doeris & fynderis of worst crafte of þe sones of Caym, & of al vnclennesse & filþe, þat is Obal & Tubal, þat is to wite þe sones of Lameth þe blynde, which was þe first blynde man, þat slow Caym. Þese fonden firste þe werkes of bras & of iren, of gold & of silver, & of grindinge; and þei firste fonde alle þe artes of musik.

And after VII⁰ ȝere of þe lif of Iareth, in þe secunde þousand of þe world, myche malice bigan to wexe wors þan þe raþere vppon erþe, which of vs is to be dispised & not to be seide. Þanne þe sones of god coueitede þe douȝtris of men; and þe Lord God is wroþe, & wiþ dolour of herte touched. He seide: 'It forþinkiþ me þat y made man; my spirit schal nat dwelle in man, for þat þat he is flesch.' After þese þingis þe sones of God beþ entred to þe douȝtris of men, and gendride of hem geauntes

Marginalia:
- The sons of Cain wax wicked and unclean.
- They invent works of brass and iron, &c.
- The Lord is angered because of their great sin.

Add. 37049

Ynde, in þe same place of deliciousnes, wher he fyrst made a cyte & cald it Effrem. And þis was fyrst byggyd before Noe flodde.

In þe fourty ȝere of Jareth, in þe secunde thowsand of þe world, war wykkyd men & of ylle craft, þe fynders of þe sonnes of Chaym, & of vnclennes & filthe, þat is to say Obal, Tobal þe sonnes of Lamech, þat was blynde, þat was first blynde man, þe whilk slewe Chaym. Þir men fande þe werkes of yren & bras, & gold & syluer to be made soft. And þir men fande fyrst al þe craftes of musyk. And after seuen hundreth ȝere of þe lyfe of Jareth in þe secunde þowsand ȝere of þe warld, began wars þan þe first for to grow mykil ylle & malyce opon erth, þe whilk we lefe now on-spokyn of. Than our Lord God was

---

[1] Large 'I' written in red, three lines deep. [2] 'þe' above the line; 'his' written and crossed out.

and þe Ende of Worldes'

Harl. 1900

vppon erþe; & þei beþ made most wickid vppon alle men þat dwelliden vppon erþe. And þe Lord comaundide to Noe þat he schuld make to hym a schip & he schuld ilede his wife & iij sones wiþ þe wyues of hem, whiche he reserued (*or kepte*)[1]
5 in þe flowinge of þe flode. And þe flode is made vppon al erþe. And Noe toke of eche soule lyuynge, as wel of fowles as of beestis. And alle þingis þat were vppon erþe were kepte in þe schip. In þe VI^c ȝere & oon Noe is goon out of þe schip wiþ alle þingis þat were wiþ hym. And þan Noe offered sacrifice to
10 god, & God blessid Noe & his sones.

In[2] þe VI^c ȝere & XII of þe life of Noe, in þe þrid þousand of þe worlde Noe bigan to buylde agein newe possessioun, & his sones in þe erþe; & þei cleped þilke regiouns Tamun after þe cle*pinge of þe noumbre in which þei went out of þe schip. I. Fol. 22 a
15 viii. In þe III^c ȝere, soþly, in þe þridde þousand of þe world, (1) Noe gat a sonê & cleped him Ionitum.[3] In þe III^c ȝere & fifty after þe flode, Noe ȝaf þe lond Eocham[4], þat is þe eest, into þe

Noah is commanded to build the ark.

Noah's sons begin to re-build the earth.

His son Ionitum takes the

Add. 37049

greued & bad Noe make a schip & bryng in his wyfe & his thre sonnes & þair wyfes, and safed fro drownyng of þe flode. And
20 þer was made a flode opon þe erth. And þan Noe toke in to þe schip of al lyfyng þinges both of fewles & of bestes. & al þinges þer war oupon erth þay wer keypd in þe schip. In þe sex hundreth ȝere went Noe oute of þe schip with al þat war with hym. Þan made Noe offerand to God, & God blissed Noe
25 & his childer.

In þe sext hundreth & twelft ȝere of þe lyfe of Noe, in þe thyrd þousand of þe warld, began Noe & his childer new* pos- Fol. 12 a session in erþe. And þai cald þos regions Tamnon after þe callyng of þe nowmer of þaim þat come oute of þe schip, þat is
30 to say eght. In þe thre hundreth ȝere in þe thyrd þowsand of þe warld, gat Noe a son & cald hym Jonitum. In þe thre hundreth & fyfty after þe flode, gaf Noe þe lande of Etham, þat is

---

[1] Bracketed thus with red ink.
[2] Large 'I' written in red, five lines deep.
[3] Lat. Ionithum.
[4] Lat. etham.

Methodius: 'þe Bygynnyng of þe World

Harl. 1900

<small>land of Eotham at his death.</small> lordschip of his sone Ioniti, & Noe is deed. Whanne þe dayes of him were fulfilled þe ȝeres were IX^c & L. After þe deþ of Noe, þe sones of hym camen in þe iii¹ þousand of þe world &
<small>They build a tower, and God divides them.</small> descendede into þe lond of Senaar, & þei bygunne to buyylde a toure to hem, þe heiȝþe of which schuld neiȝ to heuen. And 5 þere God by his wraþ diuided þat þei bigunnen to make, and þei beþ disparpled vppon þe face of al erþe, & þei beþ diuided vppon al þe lond. Jonitus soþly þe sone of Noe entride into þe lond of Eocham, þat is þe eest, whennus þe sunne springiþ, & he dwelled þere, & he toke wisdom of God; & al astronomye 10
<small>Noah's sons divide the earth.</small> & sterres of heuene he fonde. Sem, þe sone of Noe, toke þe lond of Asie. Cham þe lond of Meridie², þat is þe souþe partie vnto þe west. Japhet entride aboute þe norþe, vnto þe see of Occean. And þei beþ diuided into ech lond. Jonitus þe sone of Noe gat
<small>Nemproth, son of Jonitus, builds Babylon, and the sons of Cham make</small> a man geaunt & a stronge hunter. And þilke Nemproth, after 15 þe flode, buylde a tour þat is cleped Babiloyne. In þe VII^c ȝere in þe þrid þousand þe grete Babiloyne is bilde. After þese þingis soþly, þei made to hem a kyng, þe sones of Cham, to

Add. 37049

to say þe este parte, in-to gyft of his son Ioniti. And Noe dyed when he was neyne hundreth & fyfty ȝere. After his deth 20 in þe thyrd þowsand ȝere of þe warld, his childer descendyd into þe lande of Sennaar & began þer to make a tower of whos hyghnes suld towche vn-to Heuennes. And þer dyuyded God his ire opon þaim þat began to bygge it. And þai war sparpyld opon þe face of al þe erth, & þai war dyuyded opon al erthe. 25 Jonitus þe son of Noe entyrd into þe erth of Eotham, þat is to say þe este wher þe son sprynges vp, & dwelt þer. And he toke wysdom of God, & he fande al astronomy & þe sterres of heuen. Sem þe son of Noe toke þe lande Asye. And Cham þe lande of þe sowthe vnto þe Weste. Jonitus þe son of Noe gat Nembrot 30 a gret man & a strang hunter. And þat Nembrot after þe flode byggyd a cyte þat was cald Babilonia. In þe seuent hundreth ȝere in þe thyrd þowsand of þe warld was byggyd gret Babilon. And after þis þe sones of Cham made þaim a kyng whos name

---

¹ 'þrid' written in left margin.   ² Lat. meridianā.

Harl. 1900

whom þe name was Pontibus¹ which helde Pontum, & þerof he toke þe name. Afterward þe sones of Iaphet senten to Ionitum men and gaftis, men of heliynge & buylderis, & þei camen to Ionitum in Eocham, & þei bilde to him a cite þat is cleped
5 Ionita. And þere was pees bitwixe þe kyngdom of Nebroth & þe kyngdome of Pontibus þe sones of Cham, þat hemsilf togidre bygunne to fiȝte. Whanne Ionitus herde he wrote a pistle to Nemproth þat helde Babiloyne. Þis was þe writ for þe rewme of þe sones of * Iapheth here bigynneþ to do awey þe rewme of
10 þe sones of Cham.

Þese stryues firste apperide betwixe rewmes & rewmes vppon erþe. Þe ² VIII ȝere in þe IIII þousand of þe worlde, euermore þei fauȝt, euereiþer in fiȝte, & þe rewme of Cham is ouercomen aȝenus þe rewme of Nemproth. And þe rewme of Nemproth
15 gat þe maistere vnto Hesdrem þe kyng. Hesdres soþly brent þe rewme of Cham & toke prisoneres alle þat were dwellinge,

a king called Pontibus.

There is strife between the sons of Cham and the sons of Ionitum.

Fol. 22 a (2)

The kingdom of Nemproth defeats the kingdom of Cain.

Add. 37049

was Pontubus. Aftyrward þe sonnes of Japhet sent to Jonitum men & craft-men of theker craft & byggers, & þai come in to Eotham to Jonitum. & þai byggyd þer a cyte þat was cald
20 Jonita. And þer * was pees betwyx þe kyngdom of Nembrot & þe kyngdom of Pontubi þe sonnes of Cham. And fro þan forth þai began for to make batell ilk one with oþer. And when Jonitus hard þis, he wrote a pystel to Nembrot þe whilk held Bobilon. & þat was written for why þe kyngdom of þe sonnes
25 of Japhet began fro þine to do away þe kyngdom of þe sonnes of Cham.

Her apperyd fyrst batels betwyx kyngdom & kyngdoms opon erthe. In þe eght ȝere, in þe fourte þowsand of þe warld, alway þai faght with manly power. And þe kyngdom of Cham
30 was ouercummen of þe kyngdom of Nembrot. And þe kyngdom of Nembrot opteyned þe principalite vnto Esdrem kyng. Esdres byrned þe kyngdom of Cham, & put in thraldom al þat war

Fol. 12 b

---

¹ Lat. Pontipius.
² 'Þ' a large flowered letter in red, six lines deep.

Harl. 1900

Iebuseos, Amorreos, Palestinos & Affros, þat were atte west.
Afterward Hesdres gat Cusdrom þe kyng. Þe sones soþly of
Cham gadride hem-silf to-gidre, III^c & XX þousandes of fote
men, & þei come into þe rewme þat was of Ioniti, þat þei schulde
bete him doun & fiȝte wiþ þe kynge Cusdro. Cusdro herynge, lete hem aloon til þat þei passide þe flood of Tigre. Cusdro þe Kyng sent his oost wiþ olifauntis & slouȝ hem alle, & þanne rewmes beþ armed aȝenus hem-silf togidre.

In[1] þe XXV ȝere in þe V þousand of þe world Sannlab[2] þe kyng descended of Eocham wiþ a grete oost, dispeplid many citees. & he passed into þe þrid rewme of men of Ynde. After þat he was turned aȝen from Ynde he come into Arabie, & he went into þe desert of Saba, in þe lond of Hismaelites, & he put þere castels or tentis[3], in þe lond of þe sones of Ismael. And þere Sannlab þe kyng ouercomen of þe Sarasyns, & many þousandis fillen & flowen. And þan þe sones of Hismael wente

Marginal notes: Cusdrom defeats / the children of Cain at the Tigris river. / Sannlab overcomes Inde and Arabia / and defeats the Saracens.

Add. 37049

dwellyng, Jebusecs, Amorreos, Palestinos & Affros, þe whilk was at þe weste. After Esdres gat Cusdron þe kyng. And þan þe childer of Cham gydyrd þaim to-geder, thre hundreth & twenty þowsand of fote men. And when Cusdro hard þis he left þaim to þai war past þe flode of Tygyr. And þan sent Cusdro his compeny agayn þaim with elyfantes, & slewe þaim al þat neuer one scapyd of þaim. And þan was þe warldes made byttyr.

In þe fyft ȝere in þe fyfe þowsand of þe warld descendyd Sannsab Kyng fro Eotham with a gret compeny, & destroyed þe pepyl of many cytes, þat is to say seuenty & eght regions of hym. And he went vnto þe thyrd kyngdom of Ynde. * And when he turned fro Ynde, he come in-to Araby & went in-to desert Sabia in þe lande of Ismael & put þer his hostes of pepyl in þe lande of þe childer of Ismael. And þer was Sannsab þe kyng ouercummen of þe Sarsyns. And þer fell þer many þowsandes & oþer fledde. And þan at fyrst went þe sonnes of

Marginal note: Fol. 13 a

---

[1] 'I': large letter three lines deep.
[2] Lat. Samsabus.
[3] 'or tentis' heavily underlined in MS.

Harl. 1900

out firste of wildirnesse to stryue in batail. & þei entride into
þe rewmes of folkis. After þat þe Lord byhiȝte to Ismael, þat in þe
regioun of his breþeren he schulde ficche[1] tentis or tabernaclis.
Þe castels or tentis[2] of hem was myche multitude. And þei
5 bigunne to fiȝte aȝenus þe eest lond & þe souþe. And þei bigunne to make citees desolate, & þei made to hem naueyes &
comen into þe west regiouns neiȝ Rome, & þei hadde lordschipe
of þe * toure in þat tyme. Wherfore þei eten þe bodies & þe
flesch of camels, & þei dranke þe blode of iumentis medled wiþ
10 mylk ; & þei made of hem foure princis, Oreb, ȝeb, ȝebee, &
Salmona. And whanne þei entriden vppon þe sones of Israel,
þe Lord smote hem þere & bitoke hem into þe hondes of Gedeon
Hebrei, þe sone of Jonas. Þere were soþli an CXL þousand ; &
þere fillen þe princes of hem, & Gedeon persued hem vnto her
15 cuntrey, & he delyuered alle þe sones of Israel of þe seruage of
þe sones of Ismael. Soþly þei beþ to come ones þat þei wite

marginalia: The sons of Ismael over-run the country even to Rome.
marginalia: Fol. 22 b (1)
marginalia: They are defeated by Gideon of the sons of Israel.

Add. 37049

Ysmael oute of wildernes to feght with batels. And þai entird
in-to þe kyngdoms of folk after þat God beheste vnto Ysmael,
þat in þe region of his breþer he suld fest tabernakyles; þair
20 compenys war gret multitude. And þai began to feght agayn
þe este land & þe sowth. & þai began to make cytes desolate.
And þai made paim schips, and þai come vnto þe weste
Kyngdoms nere vnto Rome, & þai had lordyschip of landes þat
tyme. And þai ete vnclene bodys þat is of camels & hors, &
25 þai dranke blode of bestes mengyd with mylk. Than made þai
to þaim-selfe foure princes, Oreb, & ȝeb, & ȝebee, & Salmana.
And when þai entyrd opon þe childer of Israel oure Lord stroke
þaim euen þer, & toke þaim in to þe handes of Gedeon Eberrie,
þe son of Joel. Þer was þer a hundreth & fourty þowsand. And
30 þe pryncis fel downe þer, and Gedeon persewed þaim to þair
awn cuntre. And God delyuerd þe childer of Israel fro þe
thraldom of þe childer of Ismael. It is to cum þat þai sal do

---

[1] Lat. figeret.   [2] 'or tentis' heavily underlined in MS.

Harl. 1900

The sons of Ismael shall arise again, but

anoþer, & make þe erþe destitute; & þei schul holde regiouns of þe world wide, from risinge of þe sunne vnto þe west, fro þe souþe vnto þe norþe, & vnto Rome; & þe ʒok of hem schal be heuy vppon þe nolles of folkis. And þere schall not be folke eþer rewme, þat may hem aʒenstonde vnto þe noumbre of þilke 5

shall be overcome of Christians, and shall be subject to the Roman Empire.

tymes. And afterward þei beþ ouercomen of Cristen men, & to þe regioun of Romayns, þe sones of Hismael schul be vndercast. And þe rewme of Romayns schul be greet vppon alle rewmes of folkis, whan þei were to-gidre beten of þe empire of Romayns. Wheþer þei regnyde not a M ʒere, vnsobre[1], & of 10 Romayns were ouercomen. Men of Babiloyne regnyde IIII

There is strife between the nations.

þousand ʒere. Men of Macedonye tormentide þe rewme of men of Parthie wiþ armes. Men of Scithia & of Inde made meke to hem men of Affrik, of Spayne, of Fraunce, of Germanye, of Sueme, & Britouns fiʒteris wiþ armes þei gaten. And now efte 15 þe sones of Hismael schule arise of þe wildernesse, & þei schule aʒenstonde þe rewme of Romayns.

The sons of Ismael in the last six

In[2] þe laste sixe þousand of þe world, soþly, þe sones of Hismael schulen go out of wildernesse. And þe comynge of hem

---

Add. 37049

swilk ane oþer lyke vn-to þis þing, & make destitute þe erthe 20 & opteyne al erthe & oþer kyngdoms fro þe rysyng of þe son vnto þe weste, & fro þe sowthe vnto þe north, & vnto Rome.

Fol. 13 b And þe ʒok * sal be greuos to al folk. And þer sal be no folk or kyngdom þat may feght with þaim, to þe nowmer of þair tymes. And after þai sal be ouercummen of Cristen men. And 25 þe sonnes of Ismael sal be subiect to þe kyngdom of Romaynes, & þe kyngdom of Rome sal be gret abowne al kyngdoms of folk, when þai er brokyn done to þe Romayne empyre. Than agayne sal ryse þe childer of Ysmael oute of wildernes, & withstande þe kyngdom of Romaynes, þe whilk scriptur makes mencion of 30 Australia brachia Danyel hoc preuidens[3], & þai sal gayne-say þe kyngdom.

In þe laste sext þowsand ʒere of þe warld, sal þe childer of Ysmael go out of wildernes. And þair chastyssyng sal

---

[1] Lat. uiri hebrei.
[2] Large 'I' written in red, seven lines deep.
[3] These five words are underlined in red ink.

Harl. 1900

schal be as chastisynge wiþout mesure & wiþout mercy. And
God haþ betaken into þe hondes of hem alle rewmes of folkes,
for synnes & * myscheues þat þei han wrou3t a3enus þe comaund-
mentis of God.¹ And þerfore he haþ betaken vs pollute to men
5 of barbarie. Cristen men soþly doþ many vnleueful þingis, for
þei defouliþ hem silf wiþ þat, þat is most foule forto saye.
Þerfore þe Lord haþ betaken hem into þe hondes of Sarsyns.
Persidia schal be in caitifte & slau3ter. Capadocia also, þe lond
of Sire schal be into wildernesse, and þe dwellers of hit schule
10 be led caytif. Cilicia also, & þe dwelleris of hit in swerde
schul perische. Grece schal be in slau3ter & caitifte. Auffrik
also, men of Egipte & of þe eest londes, schul be vnder heuy
tribute in siluer & gold of huge wi3t. Spayn schal perische
wiþ swerde & þei schule be led caytif. Fraunce, Germanie,
15 Gyan², wiþ diuerse batails deuoured; many of hem schule be
led caytif. Romayns schule be in slau3ter, & turned into fli3t.
Þe ylondes of þe see schulen be in dissoluciou. And þe sones

marginalia: thousand years of the world, shall [Fol. 22 b] (2) scourge the world because of its sins. The Lord punishes Christian people because of their sins. Saracens overcome all the nations.

Add. 37049

be withouten mesure & withouten mercy. And God sal gyf
in-to þair handes al þe kyngdoms of gentyles³ folk, for
20 synnes þat we wyrk agayns þe commanndmentes of God.
Þerfor God has taken vs into þe handes of barbarynes of
hathen men, for we hafe forgytten þe commawndmentes of God.
Cristen men dos mykel vnlefull þinges, for þai fyle þaim-selfe
with syn þat is fowlest to be spokyn. Þerfore God has taken
25 þaim in-to þe handes of Sar3yns. Persida sal be in captyuyte &
in slayng & Capadoce also, þe lande of Syrie sal be made waste
& þe dwellers of it put in thraldrom. Cicilia & þe dwellers in
it sal perysche with swerde. Grek sal be in slayng & thraldom.
Affrica also, Egypcianes & þe este, & Asia sal be vnder tribut
30 greuos in siluer & gold. Spayne sal perysche with swerde & þe
dwellers of* it put in thraldom. Frawnse, Germany, Agothaina,
with diuers batels be deuoured & put in thraldom. Þe Romaynes
sal be in slayng & turned & fle in yles of þe se in dissolucion.

[Fol. 14 a]

---

¹ In left margin a hand pointing to this.
² Lat. Aquitania.
³ Crossed out very heavily with red ink.

Harl. 1900

Even Jerusalem shall be conquered by the sons of Ismael.

Evils of all kinds shall come to the Church and the people, under the rule of the Saracens.

of Hismael schule holde entree from norþe, & eest, & souþe, & west. And Ierusalem schal be filled wiþ alle folkes þat schulen be led caitif. And þe lond of biheest schal be filled of alle men. Þe ȝok of hem schal be heuy vppon alle folkis, & alle þingis schulen be vnder þe ȝok of hem & in þe tribute of 5 hem. & alle ournamntis of riche men schule be of hem; and what þingis were in þe chirchis of halowes, eiþer gold, or siluer, or preciouse stones. And alle ournamentis of chirchis schulen be of þe riche men of hem. And þei schulen dele þe mynisteries of God. And þe prestis schule be as þe peple, whan 10 chirches schule be brent. And þere schal be myche tribulacioun. And þei schul caste þe bodies of hem in þe stretis, for þat þere beþ not þat schule burye. And þe weye schal be fro þe see vnto þe see. And regiouns schulen be wiþoute weye. And þe weye of hem schal be cleped þe wey of angwische. And þei 15 schule go to-gidre seruauntis & olde men, riche men & pore,

The way of anguish.

Fol. 23 a (1) wiþ affliccioun & weilynge, schule seye: 'Blessid be þei* þat

---

Add. 37049

And þe sonnes of Ysmael sal opteyne fro þe north, fro þe este, & fro þe sowthe, fro þe weste. And Jerusalem sal be fyld of al pepyll þat sal be led in captiuyte. And þe land of beheste 20 sal be fyld of al folkes. And þe ȝoke sal be heuy opon al folkes, & þai sal be vndyr þe ȝoke of þaim, & tribute. And al þe anowrnmentes of ryche men sal be þairs. & þa þat was in þe kyrk of sayntes, owder gold or syluer, or precious stones. & al þe anournmentes[1] of þe kyrk sal be þairs. And þai sal 25 distribut þe mynyster þinges of God. & þe prestes sal be as þe pepyll sal be, when þe kyrkes sal be byrnt. & þer sal be gret tribulacion. And þai sal cast þe bodyes of þaim in þe stretes or in þe ways, & none for to bery þaim. And þe way of þe Sarȝyns sal be fro se to se. And regions sal be þe way, & þe 30 way of þaim sal be cald sorowe. And þai sal go to-geder ȝong men, ryche men, & pore men, & old men with turmentyng & sorow & þai sal say: 'Beati sunt illi qui de hac luce nos pro-

---

[1] Poorly written.

Harl. 1900

wente before vs of þis liȝt.' Seynt Poul beforseide þese þingis: 'Whanne dissencioun comeþ first, & þe sone of perdicioun, þe man of synne were schewid.' What is elles but dissencioun & discipline þurȝ which þe dwelleris of al erþe schul be corrumped
5 of þe sones of Hismael. Þerfore God cleped Hismael, þe fader[1] of hem, a wilde asse, þe prophete seiynge, wylde asses, & geet, & desert, þat is, & ech kynde of bestis vppon þe flok is rauyschinge. Þerfore þei schule bytake al erþe into dissolucioun, & many citees schul be distried. Þilke men beþ not as oþer
10 folkis, but þei beþ þe sones of wildernesse to-comynge, to men hateful. Here þe gaderinge togidre of hem, whan þei beþ to go out of wildernesse. Wymen hauynge her birþe withynne, to-gidre þei schulen sle wiþ swerde. In þe chirchis of seyntis, þei schule ligge wiþ wymmen. And wiþ holy vestimentis of
15 chirchis, þei schulen cloþe hem & her wyues. Her horsis þei schule tyȝe to þe sepulcris of seyntis, as to rackis. And grete tribulacioun schal be vppon Cristen men.

marginalia: Dissension and corruption in the earth. They shall slay women with child and desecrate the Holy Place. In the midst of this great tribulation

---

Add. 37049

cesserunt. Blissid ar þai þat went before vs fro þis light of þis warld.' Þis Saynt Paule sayd before: 'Cum venerit
20 discessio primum, & reuelatus fuerit homo peccati & perdicionis.' What is fyrst departyng bot discipline, þorow þe whilk al þe dwellers on erth er chastyd of þe sonnes of Ismael. Þerfore Onagrum deus appelauit Ismaelem. God cald Ismael þe fader of þaim a wylde asse. Þies pepyl ar not as oþer folk,* bot þai Fol. 14 b
25 are sonnes to cum oute of wildernes, & þai ar hateful to men. Here þe folewyng of þaim þat ar to cum oute of þe wildyrnes. Þai sal sla women with childe. And prestes in holy places þai sal kylle. & in þe kyrkes of sayntes þai sal lyg with þair wyfes, and with þe holy vestymentes of kyrkes þai sal clothe þaim &
30 þair wyfes. And þe bestes þai sal bynde at þe grafes of sayntes as it wer to a mawnger. And þer sal be gret tribulacion opon Cristen folkes þat dwels opon þe erth.

---

[1] In MS. after *fader* 'a' written and crossed out. In Lat. Onagrum. The scribe evidently misunderstood the word, but wrote its meaning.

Harl. 1900

Christ shall appear,

And þanne schul appere þe trewe men, þat ben to trowe in Crist. Not þerfore, God haþ sent þese tribulaciouns, þat iustly þei be doon away, þat in Crist beþ to trowe, but þat þei be schewid, whiche in him most truly beþ to trowe. As þilk truþe itself seiþ: 'ӡe beþ blessed, whanne þei haue pursued ӡou for my name.' Þus soþly þei pursuede þe prophetis þat weren before vs. But whiche dwelleþ still vnto þe ende, he [1] schal be saf. And after tribulaciouns of dayes, þat were made of þe sones of Hismael, and al þe erþe schal be dissolute of hem. And þei schule be cloþed wiþ ournamentis, wiþ gold, & purpur, & wiþ briӡt cloþinge as of spouses, seiynge: 'Þe Cristen men mowe not delyuere hem of oure hondes.' And ioiynge & of her victoryes seiynge: 'Lo we haue ouer-*comen þe erþe in oure strengþe, & alle þat dwellen in hit.' And þan þe Lord God schal haue mynde, after his grete mercy, þat he bihiӡt to hem þat loueþ him & which beþ to trowe in Crist, & he schal delyuer

Fol. 23 a (2)

who shall deliver his people from

Add. 37049

And þan sal þai appere þe trew men þat ar to trow in Criste. God sendes not þerfore þies tribulacions opon Cristen men, þat right-wis men be done away þat ar to trowe in Criste, bot þat þai be schewed þat ar for to trowe faythfully in Criste. As Veritas ait[2]: 'Beati eritis cum persecuti vos fuerint propter nomen meum. Blissed sal ӡe be when þai persewe ӡow for my name &c.' So hafe þai persewed prophetes þat war before ӡow. Bot he þat perseuers vnto þe ende he sal be safe. And after þe tribulacions of þe dayes þat sal be done of þe sonnes of Ismael, al erth sal be made desolate of þaim. And þai sal be cled with ornamentes of gold & purpyll, & with schynyng clothes, sayng, þat Cristen men may not be delyuerd * fro oure handes. And þai sal ioy in þair victorys, & say: 'Behold we hafe ouercummen þe erth in our strenthe & al þat dwels in it.' Than sal rememmyr our Lord God after hys beheste, þe whilk he hyght to þaim þat lufs hym & ar to trow in Criste. And he sal delyuer þaim

Fol. 15 a

---

[1] MS. 'þis schal', 'he' inserted before 'þis'; 'he' left margin.   [2] Lat. Salvator noster ita niquiens.

Harl. 1900

hem of þe hond of Sarsyns. A kyng[1] forsoþe of Cristen men schal arise & schal fiȝte wiþ hem, & schal sle hem with swerde, and he schal lede þe wymmen of hem caitif. And þe children of hem schule perische. And þe sones of Hismael schul falle
5 into swerde, & into tribulacioun & afflictioun. And God schal ȝelde to hem þe eueles þat þei haue do to oþere. And as reyn þe malice of hem schal falle into hem, seuene tymes so myche as þei haue doon in oþere. And he schal betake hem into þe hondes of Cristen men. And þe rewme of Cristen men schal
10 be enhaunsed vppon alle rewmes. And Cristen men schulen put vppon hem an heuy ȝok, and þei þat remayneþ schule be seruauntis.

And þan þe lond schal be peesid, þat of hem was destruyed, and whiche were taken prisoneris of hem schule turne aȝen
15 into her lond. And men shule be multiplied vppon erþe. And þere schal be grete indignacioun to þe kyng of Romayns, vppon hem þat haue denyed Crist. And þere schal be pees & grete reste vppon erþe, which was not before neþer þere schal be like

the hands of the Saracens.
A Christian king shall deliver the people from the evils.
The kingdom of the Christians shall influence all kingdoms,
and the land shall be at peace.

Add. 37049

fro þe handes of þe Sarȝyns. The Cristen pepyl sal ryse
20 vp & fight with þaim, & sal kyll þaim with swerde, & lede þer wyfes in-to thraldom, & sla þair ȝong childer. And þe childer of Ismael sal descende in-to swerde & tribulacion & affliccion. And our Lord God sal ȝeld to þaim þe ylls þat þai dyd to oþer; & þer sal falle opon þaim seuen tymes als mykil
25 malyce als þai dyd to oþer. And God sal take þaim in-to þe handes of Cristen pepyll. And þe kyngdom of Cristen pepyll sal be exaltyd abowne al oþer kyngdoms. & Cristen men sal put a heuy ȝoke on þaim, & al þat sal be left of þaim sal be seruandes.

30 And þan sal þe erth be made pesabyl, þat was dystroyed of þaim. And þai þat wer in captiuite & thraldom of þaim sal cum agayne in to þair awne lande. And man sal be multiplyed opon erth. And gret indignacion sal be to þe kyng of Romaynes opon þaim þat denyed Crist. Egipcij & Arabes has denyed
35 Crist. And þer sal be pese & gret reste opon erth, swilk as has

---

[1] A rude drawing of hand and finger pointing to this in right margin.

Harl. 1900

Gladness and peace shall be upon the earth. Then shall they be as in the days of Noah. Then shall come Gog and Magog, and the people shall be smitten with great dread.

after hit, for þat þat hit schal be in þe laste ende of worldes. And¹ þere schal be gladnesse & pees vppon al erþe, þei schulen reste from tribulaciouns. 'Whanne þere were pees & reste & sikirnesse, þan schal be sodeyn drede.' And men schulen be in þilke dayes, as þei were in þe dayes of Noe, etynge and drink- 5 inge, gladinge &² weddinge; & in þe herte of hem schal not be drede. So schal be þe commynge of hem as Gog & Magog. & whan pees were þer, þanne þe ȝates of Caspie schule be vndoon in þe sides of þe norþe. & þilke folkis schulen come wiþ Gog & Magog. And al erþe schal be smyten to-gidre for drede of 10 hem. & þei schule bigynne to wexe pale for drede, alle men

Fol. 23 b (1)

þat dwellen vppon erþe. And *þei schule hyde hem-silf in hilles and in spelunkis, from þe siȝt of hem. Of þe progenye forsoþe of hem beþ Iapht, out goynge ouer þe tentis of þe norþe. Siche þerfore schul ete þe flesche of men, & serpentis, & 15

Terror shall last for seven years,

iumentis; wymmen wiþ lytel children þei schule ete. And þere is no man þat may aȝenstonde hem. And after VII ȝere

Add. 37049

Fol. 15 b

not bene before, ne ȝit sal be lyk it afterward, * for þat þat it is in þe ende of þe warld. & þer sal be gladnes & pes opon þe 20 erth, & þai sal hafe reste of þer tribulacions. Þis is þe pes of þe whilk þe Apostil says: 'Cum fuerit tranquillitas & securitas; tunc ueniet repentinus interitus. When it is reste & sykyrnes, þan sal cum sodan dethe.' And men sal be in þos dayes as it was in þe dayes of Noe, etyng & drynkyng & weddyng; & þer sal no drede be in þe hertes of þaim. And 25 when pes is þus, þan sal be opynd þe ȝates of Caspy in þe syde of þe northe. And þai folkes sal cum oute with Gog & Magog, & al erthe sal be strykkyn for drede of þaim. And al men on erth sal drede & hyde þaim in mowntes, & caues, & dennes, fro þe sight of þaim. Þai ar of þe kynryden of Japhet; & a 30 plage sal go oute of þe north. And þai ete þe flesche of men, & serpentes, & bestes, & women with childer þai sal ete. And þer sal be none þat may feght with þaim. And aftyr seuen ȝere

---

¹ Large capital 'A' in red.
² Not in MS., but written above, with caret in text.

and þe Ende of Worldes'

Harl. 1900

of þilke tymes þei schule take þe cite Iosephen¹. & þan þe Lord schal sende oon of his *prin*cis, & schal smyte hem wi*th* sulphur & fuyre vnd*er* a moment. And þe emp*er*o*ur* of Grece schal come, & schal sitte in Ier*u*salem VII ȝere. And þa*n*ne
5 schal appere þe sone of p*er*dicio*u*n, þat is seide Antic*r*ist. He schal be bore in Coroȝaim, he schal be norischid in Bethsaida, he schal regne in Capharnau*m*. Þerfore þe Lord seide in þe gospel: 'Woo to þee, Coroȝaim! Woo to þee, Bethsaida! Wo to þee, Capharnau*m*! Ȝif þou be enhau*n*sed vnto heuene, til into
10 helle þou schalt be dre*n*chid.'

Afterward þe kyng of Romayns & of Grekis schal styȝe up i*n* Golgatha, i*n* þat place in which þe Lord vouched saaf to suffre deþ for us in þe cros. Þe kyng of Romayns schal do awey þe crou*n* of his hede, & schal put hit vppon þe cros. And he schal
15 strecche abrode his hondes to heuene, & þe kyng of C*r*isten men schal betake his soule to God, & þa*n*ne þe signe of þe cros schal appere iu heuene. After þese þingis þe sone of p*er*dicio*u*n schal

*when the Lord shall send one of his princes to smite them with sulphur and fire. Then shall come Antic*r*ist the son of Perdition,*

when Rome and Greece shall fight, and the King of Rome shall stretch his hands to Heaven, and shall entrust his soul to God, when the sign of

---

Add. 37049

Þai sal entyr i*n*-to cyte of Iosaphen. And þa*n* sal o*ur* Lord sende one of hys p*r*incys, & he sal stryke þai*m* wi*th* leuenyng
20 & fyre i*n* a mome*n*t. And þe empro*ur* of Greke sal cu*m* & sytt i*n* Ierusalem seuen ȝere. And þan sal apere þe son of p*er*dicio*n*, þat is to say Antecrist. He sal be borne i*n* Coroȝaym, & he sal be noresched i*n* Bethsayda, & reyne i*n* Capharnau*m* as o*ur* Lord say i*n* þe gospel: 'Ve tibi Coroȝaim! vc t*i*bi Bethsayda!
25 ve t*i*bi Caphar*n*au*m*! Wo be to þe, Coroȝaym! wo be to þe, Bethsayda! wo be to þe, Chapharnau*m*! for if þou sal be exalted vnto heue*n*, in-to helle þow sal be * drowned.'   Fol. 16 a

Afterward þe kyng of Romaynes & of Greke sal ascende i*n* Golgatha i*n* þe place, wher o*ur* Lord Ih*esu*s Crist vowchedsafe
30 to sufferd deth for vs opon þe cros. And þe kyng of Romaynes sal take þe crowne of his hede & put it opon þe cros, & hold vp his handes vnto heue*n*, & ȝeld his spirit vn-to God, þe kyng of C*r*isten men, & þan sal app*e*re þe tokyn of þe holy cros i*n* heue*n*. After þis sal cu*m* þe son of p*er*dicio*u*n, Antecrist. And he sal

¹ Lat. Ioppen.

Harl. 1900

the Cross shall appear in Heaven. Then shall come the son of perdition, and shall enter into Jerusalem, and shall sit in the temple of God.

come, trowynge him-self þat he is God, & þe herte of him schal be enhaunsed myche, siþþe he is a man of mannes seed, of þe kynred of Dan. & he schal make signes & many merueilis vppon erþe, þat blynde men se, lame men go, deef men here, dede men as þouȝ þei rise. And ȝif it may be do¹ þat chosen men be led into errors, he schal entre soþly into Ierusalem, & he schal sitte in þe temple of God, trowinge hymsilf as þouȝ he be God. And he schal be disseyuable, & by disseyte he schal begyle many men. After þese þingis þe Lord schal sende his most * clere seruauntes Enoch & Elye, þat in witnessinge of him were kepte, to repreue þilke enemye. And þanne þe laste schule be firste. And þe Iewis schule be to bileue. Forsoþe Helyas & Enoch schule repreue hym before al þe peple. And þei schule schewe hym to be a liere, & disseyuable, & confused. Soþly alle folkes seynge þe leesinge hym forþberinge, & of þe holy men of god confused; & þanne þe Iewes schul bileue. Of ech kynrede of þe sones of Israel schule be sleyn for Crist an hundrid XLIIII

Fol. 23 b (2)

Then the Lord shall send his servants, Enoch and Elijah, to reprove the enemy. They will show the son of perdition to be a liar.

Add. 37049

be trowed as he war God & he sal do many tokens and wonders, dede men sal seme as þai rase vp, & blynd men as þai sawe, & halt men go. And he sal entyr into Ierusalem, & sytt in þe tempyl of God, semyng as he war God. & his hert sal be exaltyd gretly disputtyng as he war God. & he sal be fals & wyrk disceytfulnes & begyle many one. He sal be of þe kynredyn of Dan, wher of Jacob sayd: 'Fiat Dan coluber in via etc. Dan sal be a serpent in þe way,² & cerastes in semita², & a horned serpent in þe strayt way.' And after þis sal our Lord send his two seruandes Enoch & Hely, þat ar left in his witnes to reprofe þis enmy; & þai sal reprofe hym before al þe pepyl, & schew hym a lyer, & fals, & confused. And when folkes sees þus confused & made lyer of þin holy sayntes, þai sal do penance. And þan sal þe Iewes of ilk a kynryden of Israel trow in Crist. And þan sal þer be slayne for Criste a hundreth & foure & fourty þowsand in þais

---

¹ Blotted.   ²⁻² Not plainly written in MS.

and þe Ende of Worldes' 111

Harl. 1900

þousandis in þilke dayes. Þane Anticrist, in woodnesse fulfilled, schal comaunde þe holy men of God to be slayn, & whiche to hem beþ to bileue. And þanne schal come oure Lord Ihesu Crist, þe sone of quyk God in þe cloudes of heuene wiþ com-
5 panyes of angels, & wiþ heuenly joye.

 Anoon whan Anticrist is sleyn, þe beest, þe enemy, þe disseyuer, wiþ þe swerde of his mouþe, & whiche þat han consented to him, þe endinge of þe world schal be, & þe dome schal be. Where of angels schule be, þousandes of þousandes & ten tymes
10 an hundrid þousandis of archaungels, cherubyn & seraphyn. Þere þe companyes of holy men, of prophetis, of patriarchis, of apostles, of martiris, of confessours, of virgyns. Þere, soþly, synneris & iuste men schule ȝelde resoun before þe siȝte of God, as þei han doon. Þe iuste men schule be departed fro þe
15 wickid; þe iuste men schule schyne as þe sunne, folewynge þe lombe of lif, & þe kyng of heuen euermore, seynge þe clerenesse of god in heuenes. And wiþ aungels þei schul be felawschiped for euermore. Vniuste men soþly with þe beest schule descende

Christ shall appear, and slay the Antichrist, and then the end of the world shall be. In Heaven shall be a great company of angels, apostles, martyrs, just men, all following the Lamb of Life and the King of Heaven.

Add. 37049

days. And þan [sal] [1] Antecriste be f[ild] [1] with wodnes, & com-
20 mande to sla þe sayntes* of God, & al þat ar to trowe to þaim. And our Lord Jhesus Criste sal cum, þe son of God, in þe clowdes of heuen, with compenys of angels & heuenly ioy. And onone he sal sla þis beste, Antecrist enmy & disceyfer, with þe swerd of his mowthe, & al þat consentyd vnto hym. And þe endyng
25 of þe warld sal be & þe dome. Wher þowsandes of þowsandes & ten tymes hundreth þowsandes of archangels, cherubyn, & seraphyn sal be þer. And þer sal be compenys of sayntes, of patriarchs, prophetes, apostils, martyrs, confessours, vergyns, & of al sayntes. Þar sal be rightwismen, & synners sal ȝelde
30 a-cownte & reson before þe sight of God how ilk one has done. & þe right-wismen sal be departed fro þe wykidmen. And þe right-wismen sal schyne as þe son, fowlowyng þe lamme of lyfe & þe kyng of heuen, seyng alway e clern es of god in heuen. & þai sal be felischipd þer to euermore. Þe wykkyd men sal descende

Fol. 16 b

---

[1] Torn away.

Harl. 1900

<small>Just men shall be glorified, but wicked men shall suffer pain.</small> into helle. Juste men, soþly, for euermore schul lyue, and wiþ þe kyng of heuene schule be glorifyed or gladed. And wickid men wiþouten ende schule suffre peyne. Wherefore þe Lord vouche he saaf to delyuere us, *qui cum prec*ibus, &c.

Explicit liber Metodij ep*iscop*i.

Add. 37049

wit*h* þe beste Antecriste i*n*-to helle. Þe right-wis me*n* sal lyf eue*r*, & wit*h* þe kyng of heue*n* sal ioy wit*h*oute*n* ende. And wikkyd me*n* wit*h*oute*n* end sal be ponesched. Fro þe whilk o*ur* Lord vowtschesafe to delyu*er* vs, þe whilk lyfes & reynes wit*h* fad*er* & son & holy goste, God by i*n*fynyte warld*es* of warld. Amen.

GLOSSARY

A

abegged, *pp.* a-begging, 60/8.
abliche, *adv.* fitly, 71/9.
adreynt, *pp.* drowned, 78/14.
aȝensaye, *inf.* contradict, deny, 29/10.
aȝenstonde, *inf.* withstand, oppose, 108/17.
aleggide, *pp.* alleged, affirmed, 92/17.
aleiþ, *pr.* 3 *s.* adduces, 78/11; *pt.* 3 *s.* aleyde, 87/26.
alowed, *pp.* approved, commended, 42/30.
arere, *inf.* raise, 33/3.
assaye, *sb.* trial, test, 64/13.
assoyle, *inf.* explain, 48/14.

B

bedemen, *sb.* beadsmen, 43/14.
bedes, *sb.* prayers, 47/24.
beheste, *pt.* 3 *s.* promised, 101/18.
betaken, *pp.* committed, 103/2.
biggers, *sb.* buyers, 6/24.
bihet, *pt.* 1 *s.* promised, 40/20.
biqueþe, *pp.* bequeathed, 44/24.
bobans, *sb.* pomp, pride, 21/3.
buriels, *sb.* place of burial, 42/14.
busche, *pr. pl. subj.* strike, beat, 37/7.
buþ, *pr. pl.* are, 33/8.
bygge, *inf.* build, 98/24.
bynyme, *inf.* take away, 35/9; *pp.* bynome, 21/5, 54/6.
byquyt, *pp.* acquitted, 47/20.

C

catel, *sb.* property, chattels, 24/10, 88/12.
caucioun, *sb.* security, pledge, 10/8.
cautels, *sb.* artifices, 55/15.
chaffre, *sb.* merchandise, 45/28.
chalange, *inf.* claim, 62/22.
chambred, *pp.* restrained, held in control, 6/8.
chanons, *sb.* canons, 62/10.
charge, *sb.* load, 33/7.
chastee, *inf.* chastise, 13/12.

chese, *inf.* choose, 46/21.
chyualrie, *sb.* knighthood, 23/1.
clergie, *sb.* learning, 59/17.
closiþ, *pr.* 3 *s.* encloses, 48/30.
compray, *scribal error for* y pray, 19/16; *cp.* MS. Stowe 65, 'y praye þat hey lete vs habbe oure'.
comyneþ, *pr. pl.* associate, 25/7.
comynte, *sb.* community, 33/5.
conseruatours, *sb.* bishops appointed by the Pope to protect the privileges of the friars, 55/23.
conuersacioun, *sb.* manner of life, 39/21, 79/28.
corrumped, *pp.* corrupted, 105/4.
couenable, *adj.* suitable, fit, 53/1, 59/14.
cupes, *sb.* baskets, 6/14.

D

deler, *sb.* divider, 15/17.
deles, *sb.* parts, 64/6.
desauauntes, *sb.* disadvantages, 43/27.
depliche, *adv.* while mortal, 7/14.
discreuede, *pt.* 3 *s.* described, 70/18.
disparpled, *pp.* scattered, 98/7.
dissolute, *adj.* = desolate, 106/9.
done, *adv.* down, 102/28.
dowyng, *sb.* endowment, 85/27.

E

echeþ, *pr.* 3 *s.* augments, adds to, 83/18.
emcristen, *sb.* fellow-christian, 56/19.
enioye, *inf.* = enjoin, 46/30.
entredited, *pp.* interdicted, prohibited, 42/3.
erye, *inf.* plough, 89/23.
eper, *conj.* or, 42/1.
euereiþer, *pron.* both, 99/13.
eyr, *sb.* heir, 15/2.

F

fale, *adj.* many, 78/18.
fang, feng, *v.* fong.
faytour, *sb.* impostor, 84/9.

ferþe, *adj.* fourth, 64/6.
fest, *inf.* set up, 101/19.
feye, *sb.* faith, belief, 65/4.
ficche, *inf.* set up, 101/3.
fillen, *pt. pl.* fell, 100/16.
flatrie wiþ, *inf.* flatter, court, 29/6.
folly, *inf.* baptize, 71/28.
fonded, *pt.* 1 *s.* tried, 48/19.
fong, *inf.* take, receive, 21/8; *pr. pl.*
 fang, 21/14; *pt.* 3 *s.* feng, 11/1;
 pl. 82/4.
forbeding, *part. adj.* prohibitory,
 41/18.
forgendriþ, *pr.* 3 *s.* disregards, 48/
 10.
forþe, *adv.* far, 29/8.
frusshe, *inf.* crush, 7/32.
fulfild, *pp.* filled full, 92/5.
fundacioun, *sb.* establishment, rules
 and ordinances, 47/4.

G

gaftis, 99/3, *read* craftis.
goostlich, *adj.* spiritual, 28/15.
gossippes, *sb.* familiar acquaintances,
 73/11.
grucchying, *sb.* grouching, murmur-
 ing, 24/14.

ȝ

ȝede, *pt.* 3 *s.* walked, 6/17.
ȝeldiþ, *imp. pl.* yield, give, pay,
 21/16.

H

harder, *adv.* more strongly, 81/21.
heeste, *sb.* command, 57/15.
heet, *v.* hoote.
heelful, *adj.* salutary, healthful,
 74/6.
heiȝlich, *adv.* especially, 89/29.
heliynge, *sb.* roofing, slating, tiling,
 99/3; helyng, 21/14; clothing,
 23/4.
heres = here [bodie]s, Lat. *suorum
 corporum*, 67/15.
heye, *sb.* (church)yard, 42/9.
homliche, *adj.* familiar, 55/31.
honging, *part. adj.* pending, 79/25.
hoote, *inf.* command, 3/12; hote,
 3/15; *pt.* 3 *s.* heet, 69/24.
housle, *inf.* administer the eucharist
 to, 71/28.
hyȝe, *imp. s.* hie, hasten, 90/20.

I

indistinctlich, *adv.* without distinc-
 tion, 72/28.

J

ioyne, *inf.* enjoin, 47/19.
iumentis, *sb.* beasts of burden, 101/
 9; 108/16.

K

kynde, *sb.* nature, 16/10.
kyndelich, *adj.* natural, 85/14.
kynryden, *sb.* kindred, 108/30.

L

lasse, *adv.* less, 45/10.
leef, *adj.* dear, 43/2.
leese, *inf.* lose, 32/16; lese, 21/7.
lered, *part. adj.* learned, 60/13.
lesyngis, *sb.* lies, 56/25.
letteþ, *pr.* 3 *s.* hinders, 76/4.
leue, *inf.* remain, 59/17; *pr.* 3 *s.*
 leueþ, 81/24.
leuenyng, *sb.* lightning, 109/19.
lewed, *adj.* lay, 1/4, 60/13; lewide,
 31/13.
leyde, *pp.* adduced, 9/9; *aph. form
 of* OF. aleier; *cp.* aleiþ.
lond leper, *sb.* vagabond, 54/9.
louȝ, *pt.* 1 *s.* laughed, 3/6.
lynages, *sb.* tribes, 41/14.
lystere, *sb.* reader, 63/4.

M

make, *inf.* bring about, 48/27.
manhed, *sb.* humanity, 19/13.
manliche, *adv. for* nameliche,
 especially, 52/27.
mawmetre, *sb.* idolatry, 57/30.
medled, *pp.* mixed, 101/9.
medliþ, *pr.* 3 *s.* concerns, 9/1.
menoures, *sb.* Franciscans, 48/6.
monchons, *sb.* nuns, 73/10.
monicioun, *sb.* admonition, 13/13.
mynyster, *sb.* minster; m. þinges,
 church ornaments, 104/26.

N

namelich, *adv.* especially, 65/9.
nere, *pt.* 3 *s. subj.* were not, 25/15.
nesche, *adj.* soft, 26/9.
nice, *adj.* stupid, 91/3.
nolles, *sb.* heads, necks, 102/4.
noot, *pr.* 1 *s.* know not, 57/11.
nouys, *sb.* novice, 71/10.

O

oblege, *inf.* oblige, pledge, 68/2.
obstaunce, *sb.* opposition, objection,
 75/26.

Glossary 115

olifauntis, *sb.* elephants, 100/7.
onyng, *sb.* union, 15/14.
opteyned, *pt.* 3 *s.* gained, 99/31.
ouer, *adj.* higher, 13/15.
outrage, *sb.* excess, 79/15.
outtake, *pp.* excepted, 14/1 ; except, 73/10.
owe, *pr.* 3 *s. subj.* may own, 33/10.

P

parischons, *sb.* parishioners, 40/10.
penitaunsers, *sb.* priests appointed to give absolution in extraordinary cases, 44/29, 63/4.
prechours, *sb.* Dominicans, 48/7.
preuy, *adj.* intimate, 44/5.
primate, *sb.* supremacy, 74/10.
principates, *sb.* principalities, 10/14.
put of, *inf.* put aside, 36/3.
putt to, *inf.* add, 36/12.

Q

quyte, *pr.* 3 *s. subj.* give up, 76/20.

R

raþer, *adv.* earlier, 5/9, 25/11.
relef, *sb.* remains of a meal, 6/14.
relesche, *inf.* revoke, 75/28.
reulere, *adj.* regular, monastic, 62/10.
ruþeren, *sb.* oxen, cattle, 41/18.

S

sauacioun, *sb.* preservation, 24/9.
sawes, *sb.* saws, sayings, 48/22.
seculers, *sb.* secular priests, 59/2.
sewe, *inf.* follow, 91/12 ; *pr.* 3 *s.* sweþ, 45/20.
seyȝ, *pt.* 3 *s.* saw, 7/3 ; siȝ, 22/7 ; syȝ, 67/33 ; *pl.* syȝe, 56/30.
sigge, *inf.* say, 92/5 ; *pr. pl.* siggeþ, 21/2.
siker, *adj.* sure, secure, 41/32.
sillers, *sb.* sellers, 6/25.
skilful, *adj.* reasonable, 33/3 ; *a mistake for* wilful (L. *spontaneae*), 70/16.
skilfullich, *adv.* reasonably, 28/14.
skyle, *sb.* reason, 18/9.
slake, *inf.* loose, slacken, 64/29.
sleiȝþe, *sb.* sleight, contrivance, 44/18.
slow, *pt.* 3 *s.* slew, 95/4.
snarled, *pp.* entangled, ensnared, 45/9.
somned, *pp.* summoned, 55/23.
souereynes, *sb.* superiors, 75/4.

sparpyld, *pp.* scattered, 98/24.
spelunkis, *sb.* caves, 108/13.
spiritualte, *sb.* ecclesiastical authority, 3/3.
spouse-bruch, *sb.* adultery, 57/19.
stalþe, *sb.* stealing, 76/19.
stater, *sb.* an ancient coin, 31/3.
styȝe, *inf.* rise up, ascend, 109/11 ; *pr. pl.* stieþ, 74/24.
stondyng, *adj.* continuing in existence (Lat. *stante statuto*), 48/25.
suffre, *inf.* endure, 71/9.
suggettes, *sb.* those under bishop's spiritual jurisdiction, 59/11.
syȝ, *v.* seyȝ.
syngulerliche, *adv.* especially, 41/5.

T

temporalte, *sb.* temporal possessions of the clergy, 2/13.
terme, *sb.* period, 46/7.
teþingis, *sb.* tithes, 41/16.
to-haleþ, *pr. pl.* pull asunder, 24/11.
tolleþ, *pr. pl.* entice, 58/15.
twey, *adj.* two, 6/2.

Þ

þeker, *sb.* thatcher, 99/18.
þewes, *sb.* manners, virtues, 81/20.
þine, *adv. for* þene, then, 99/25.
þouȝ, *prep.*, as if, 48/1.

U

vnbuxomnesse, *sb.* disobedience, 61/15.
vncouenablich, *adv.* unsuitably, 85/19.
vndercast, *pp.* made subject, 102/8.
vndertoke, *pt. pl.* rebuked, 19/5.
vnkunnyng, *sb.* ignorance, 41/26.
vnkynde, *adj.* unnatural, 55/1.
vnmebles, *sb.* goods not moveable, 71/16.
vnneþe, *adv.* scarcely, 45/4.
vnsobre = Lat. hebrei (*taken as* ebrii), 102/10.

V

values, *sb.* doors, 27/11.
vicarie, *sb.* representative, 5/10.
voide, *imp. s.* avoid, 61/3.

W

war, *imp. s.* beware, shun, 61/3.
wemme, *sb.* spot, stain, 75/30.
werne, *inf.* refuse, 60/21.

weyteþ, *pr.* 3 *s.* watches, 91/6.
wiȝt, *sb.* weight, 59/31, 60/2.
wilne, *inf.* desire, 3/11.
wiþclepiþ, *pr.* 3 *s.* recalls, revokes, 34/4.
wiþsaiyng, *sb.* contradiction, 48/30.
wiþsigge, *pr.* 1 *s.* deny, contradict, 5/3; *pl.* **wiþsiggeþ**, 49/12.
wone, *sb.* abundance, 20/5.
wonye. *inf.* dwell, 41/15.
worschip, *sb.* honour, 10/6.

Y

y-chargide, *pp.* commanded, 81/21.
y-ȝalde, *pp.* paid, 54/31.
y-herbored, *pp.* lodged, 91/1.
y-hote, *pp.* commanded, 13/9.
y-nowȝ, *adv.* enough, 4/4.
y-schend, *pp.* disgraced, 27/1.
y-seye, *pp.* seen, 1/7.
y-snarled, *pp.* entangled, 46/5, 77/11.
y-socyed, *pp.* joined, 70/30.
y-telied, *pp.* tilled, 32/15.
y-trauaylled, *pp.* tired, troubled, 93/24.
y-wralled, *pp.* bound, 46/4; *v.* N.E.D. *sub* warling.

The manufacturer's authorised representative in the EU for product
safety is Oxford University Press España S.A. of El Parque Empresarial
San Fernando de Henares, Avenida de Castilla, 2 - 28830 Madrid
(www.oup.es/en or product.safety@oup.com). OUP España S.A. also acts
as importer into Spain of products made by the manufacturer.
Printed and bound by CPI Group (UK) Ltd, Croydon, CR0 4YY

20/03/2026

02075328-0003